Decision-making and Radioactive Waste Disposal

The International Atomic Energy Agency estimates that nuclear power generation facilities produce more than 7 million cubic feet of low and intermediate level waste each year. Vital medical procedures, industrial processes and basic science research also produce significant quantities of waste. All of this waste must be shielded from the population for extended periods of time. Finding suitable locations for disposal facilities is beset by two main problems: community responses to siting proposals are generally antagonistic and, as a result, governments have tended to be reactive in their policy-making.

Decision-making and Radioactive Waste Disposal explores these issues utilizing a linear narrative case study approach that critically examines key stakeholder interactions in order to explain how siting decisions for low level waste disposal are made. Five countries are featured: the United States, Australia, Spain, South Korea and Switzerland. This book seeks to establish an understanding of the political, economic, environmental, legal and social dimensions of siting across those countries. This valuable resource fills a gap in the literature and provides recommendations for future disposal facility siting efforts.

The book will be of interest to students and scholars of environmental law, justice, management, politics, energy and security policy as well as decision-makers in government and industry.

Andrew Newman is Senior Program Officer in the Material Security & Minimization Program at the Nuclear Threat Initiative, Washington, DC, USA.

Gerry Nagtzaam is Senior Lecturer at the Faculty of Law, Monash University, Victoria, Australia, specializing in international environmental law, ecoterrorism and biodiversity issues.

Routledge Studies in Waste Management and Policy

Waste Prevention Policy and Behaviour
New approaches to reducing waste generation and its environmental impacts
Ana Paula Bortoleto

Decision-making and Radioactive Waste Disposal
Andrew Newman and Gerry Nagtzaam

Decision-making and Radioactive Waste Disposal

Andrew Newman and Gerry Nagtzaam

First published 2016
by Routledge
2 Park Square, Milton Park, Abingdon, Oxon OX14 4RN

and by Routledge
711 Third Avenue, New York, NY 10017

First issued in paperback 2017

Routledge is an imprint of the Taylor & Francis Group, an informa business

British Library Cataloguing-in-Publication Data
A catalogue record for this book is available from the British Library

Library of Congress Cataloging-in-Publication Data
Newman, Andrew (Program officer), author.
  Decision-making and radioactive waste disposal / Andrew Newman
and Gerry Nagtzaam.
      pages cm
  Includes bibliographical references.
  1. Radioactive waste disposal—Government policy. 2. Radioactive
waste disposal—Decision making. I. Nagtzaam, Gerry, author.
II. Title.
  TD898.14.G68N49 2016
  362.17'996—dc23
  2015021804

ISBN 13: 978-1-138-30418-5 (pbk)
ISBN 13: 978-0-415-81901-5 (hbk)

Typeset in Goudy
by Apex CoVantage, LLC

Contents

Figures

Boxes

Acknowledgments

No project of this magnitude is completed in isolation. We would like to thank James Voss, Barbara Christopher and an anonymous reviewer for providing invaluable insights and sage advice on the manuscript. We would like to thank Frank Schwing, Charles McCombie, Linda McKinley, Yongsoo Hwang and Mariano Molina for sharing difficult-to-access public records as well as their unique expertise on specific case studies. We would also like to thank Diana Bridges for tracking down Nebraska legislative records, and Gayla Koerting, Andrea Faling and the Nebraska State Historical Society for providing boxes of information and access to the Nebraska state archives. Of course, any errors in the text remain our responsibility.

Gerry would like to thank his coauthor for keeping him focused on the task at hand. Further, this book could not have been completed without the hard work and support of Kim, and he offers his humble thanks and gratitude. Andrew would like to thank his fiancée Teresa for her unwavering support and patience.

Introduction

Since the dawn of the atomic age, democratic societies have enjoyed the benefits of nuclear energy but have struggled to permanently manage the concomitant waste. The International Atomic Energy Agency (IAEA) estimates that nuclear power generation facilities alone produce about 350,000 cubic feet of high level waste (including spent fuel) and 7 million cubic feet of low and intermediate level waste each year worldwide (International Atomic Energy Agency [IAEA] n.d.b.).[1]

Currently, nuclear power provides more than 11 percent of electricity globally (World Nuclear Association [WNA] updated 2014). Given projected global energy demand in the 21st century, nuclear power is a necessary source of base-load power. Further, due to the negligible greenhouse gas emissions produced by the splitting of atoms, proponents, including some very prominent environmentalists, argue that a significant expansion in nuclear energy production is one solution to anthropomorphic climate change (Raupach et al. 2007, pp. 10288–10293). In addition, radioactive sources are used in a host of essential applications, including medical diagnostic procedures and radiation therapy; silicon irradiation; neutron activation analysis; sterilization of a variety of products from medical supplies to food; carbon dating; gauges for industries such as mining that monitor material flows and densities; and basic physics and chemistry research.[2] The resultant waste must be shielded from the population for extended periods of time – as discussed later, the precise length of time differs for each element. However, finding permanent and publicly acceptable solutions has proved remarkably difficult so long-term storage is often the default strategy. But without a disposal path, the viability of the entire nuclear industry is threatened.

This book critically examines efforts to site disposal facilities for one large part of that waste stream – commercial low level radioactive waste (LLRW) – in five democratic states.[3] Much of the literature on radioactive waste to date has focused on the difficulty of siting spent nuclear fuel (SNF) repositories, particularly in the United States. This is not surprising given SNF is generally the most radioactive of all the waste categories. Far less research has been dedicated to the disposal of far more prolific LLRW. This is unfortunate because many more countries produce LLRW than SNF; and LLRW has its own rich history of technically/politically sound and staggeringly irresponsible disposal paths both considered and pursued, failed and successful disposal facility siting efforts, as well as accidents averted and not. Unlike most books on LLRW that concentrate on siting at a single location or in a single country, we seek to establish an understanding of the political, economic, environmental, legal and social dimensions of siting across multiple countries. To date, very little comparative work across states has been done on LLRW facility siting and in recent years nothing has been published on this critical issue (Vari, Reagan-Cirincione and Mumpower 1994).[4] Beyond the obvious application to future LLRW disposal, this book will provide valuable lessons for the siting of facilities that handle other sorts of hazardous material and/or utilize technologies that are not well understood by the general public.

Siting LLRW disposal facilities in democracies is beset by two main problems. First, community response to siting proposals is generally antagonistic. This is often a consequence of distrust of siting authorities based on previous mismanagement at LLRW and other hazardous waste facilities. It is also a function of perceived health and safety risks associated with radiation, which is viewed as "somehow unique, more dreadful than other industrial dangers" (Weart 1988, p. 18; Greenwood 1982, p. 1). Second, and as a direct result of the first point, democratic governments have tended to be reactive rather than proactive in their policies. There has been a tendency for democratic states to adopt a default position of deferring siting decisions for as long as possible due to a fear of public opposition. The common perception that such waste is fundamentally different from, and more dangerous than, other forms of hazardous waste makes the already difficult task of siting a disposal facility even more challenging by fostering a disconnect between what regulatory bodies deem safe for public health and the expectations of the general public.

Five countries have been selected for study, representing a broad range of siting issues – the United States, Australia, Spain, South Korea and Switzerland. First, they are all democracies with vibrant civil societies, meaning that current and future siting decisions require negotiation between the siting authority (which may be the government, a private company or some combination of the two) and the host community (the definition of which may fall anywhere on the spectrum between narrow/concise and broad/diffuse) via representative stakeholders. Second, as a group the countries are geographically and culturally diverse. Finally, these countries all currently operate, or are actively trying to site, dedicated LLRW disposal facilities that are not colocated with nuclear power plants or research reactors. This is important because colocation is a much more straightforward and less controversial proposition than siting a facility at an 'away from reactor' site, regardless of whether that location is brown field or green field.[5]

These five countries have also pursued unique LLRW disposal paths that will yield valuable insights into democratic decision-making. In the United States, Congress created a compact system to collectively meet the country's disposal needs. Over several decades, successive federal governments in Australia have failed to site a national disposal facility, despite ostensibly broad authority over both the land in question and the indigenous population. In Spain, Empresa Nacional de Residuos Radiactivos S.A. (ENRESA) has participated in a process of retroactive engagement and negotiation with its host community and neighboring provinces. Despite experiencing a level of public hostility to siting efforts that is uncommon even on a subject as controversial as radioactive waste, South Korea found a willing host in 2005. Finally, the Swiss government is still searching for a politically acceptable location after having its preferred site rejected twice by the host community.

Radiation and radioactive waste

Radiation is, quite simply, energy that travels through space. It is both naturally occurring and man-made. Natural, or background, sources of radiation are responsible for the vast majority of the average 320 millirem dose that most people receive each year – although receiving a nuclear medicine procedure (for example, a CT scan) adds 300 millirems and smoking adds another 280 millirems to this total (Princeton University updated 2011).[6] These natural sources include the sun's rays and radon in the ground.

Atoms, the basic building blocks of life, are made up of positively charged protons and neutrons with no electrical charge in the nucleus, and negatively charged electrons orbiting the nucleus.[7] Atoms crave stability, and stability is achieved by a balanced ratio of protons to neutrons. It should be noted that atoms with an imbalance of protons and electrons are electrically charged and are referred to as ions but this state does not affect their radioactivity. Most atoms are naturally stable; some are not due to an excess of protons or neutrons. Unstable, or radioactive, atoms undergo spontaneous transformations ('disintegrations') in their quest for stability. This may happen many times before stability is achieved. The process is referred to as *radioactive decay* and involves the release of energy, or radiation, in the form of alpha particles, beta particles and gamma rays (United States Environmental Protection Agency [EPA] updated 2013):

- *Alpha particles* are positively charged (consisting of two protons and two neutrons), large, relatively slow-moving and travel only a few inches before running out of energy. Human skin or a piece of paper is sufficient to stop these particles but they can be dangerous if inhaled, swallowed or absorbed into the bloodstream. Alpha particles increase the risk of cancer, particularly lung cancer.[8]
- *Beta particles* are negatively charged, small, energetic and travel several feet. Skin may stop some weaker sources, and solid materials such as wood and glass are sufficient to stop stronger sources of these particles. Direct skin exposure can burn, and inhalation or ingestion can cause molecular damage. Beta emitters can cause tissue damage and increase the risk of cancer. Some emitters accumulate in specific organs; for example, iodine-131 in the thyroid gland and strontium-90 in the bones and teeth.[9]

- *Gamma rays* are pure electromagnetic energy (they have no mass or electrical charge), are "vanishingly small in size," move at the speed of light and can cover hundreds to thousands of feet before running out of energy and ceasing to exist.[10] This energy enables most gamma rays to pass through the human body, exposing all organs to damage. Shielding from gamma rays requires dense materials such as lead, concrete or water.[11]
- *Neutrons* are high-speed particles that can travel long distances and "have an exceptional ability to penetrate other materials . . . [and] make objects radioactive." Like gamma rays, neutrons require shielding with dense materials such as concrete or water.[12]

This type of energy release is known as *ionizing radiation* because the particles and rays are sufficiently energetic to rip electrons from atoms or molecules they encounter and can break chemical bonds in living cells. This property means that such radiation can be curative (for example, calibrated radiation therapy to treat cancer) or harmful and potentially deadly at higher levels of exposure. Unfortunately, radioactive sources have been used for horribly misguided and nefarious purposes. For example, in 1972 a divorced father with limited visitation rights in Houston irradiated his 11-year-old son on at least five different occasions by placing cesium oil and gas logging sources in headphones, a pillow and a couch. The boy required 16 operations over the next 5 years as well as permanent testosterone treatment. In 1993, director of the Kartontara Packing Company in Moscow, Vladimir Kaplun, died of radiation sickness after exposure to a source placed in the headrest of his office chair. While the perpetrators were never identified, business rivalry (with a possible organized crime link) was suspected. In 2006, former Russian Federal Security Service (FSB, the successor organization to the KGB) officer Alexander Litvinenko, who had received political asylum in the UK, died 3 weeks after ingesting polonium in a cup of tea. It is generally believed that the poison was administered during a meeting with two former KGB officers (Sandström 2008; Zaitseva and Hand 2003, p. 839).

Radioactive atoms decay at rates that are constant for each element. A half-life is the unit of measurement for radioactive decay and varies greatly amongst elements, and even amongst isotopes of the same element. For example, plutonium-239 has a half-life of 24,000 years whereas plutonium-233 has a half-life of 20 minutes (United States Nuclear Regulatory Commission [NRC] updated 2011). Thus, radioactive waste – defined as "any material that contains a concentration of radionuclides [atoms with unstable nuclei] greater than those deemed safe by national authorities, and for which no use is foreseen" (IAEA n.d.a.) – must be isolated from the biosphere until such time as it is rendered harmless.

Classifying radioactive waste

While many countries use different definitions consistent with their national programs or mandates – and these definitions have evolved over time[13] – radioactive waste is generally divided into three categories: spent nuclear fuel and high level waste; intermediate level waste; and low level waste.

Spent nuclear fuel (SNF) and high level radioactive waste (HLW) – SNF is the used fuel assemblies removed from nuclear reactors. HLW constitutes the liquid wastes generated from reprocessing; that is, the chemical separation of uranium and plutonium in spent nuclear fuel discharged from a reactor to be reconfigured as reactor fuel (IAEA 2005, p. 2). SNF and HLW constitute 3 percent of the volume but 95 percent of the radioactivity of all radioactive waste produced globally (WNA updated 2015; NRC n.d.a.).[14]

Intermediate level radioactive waste (ILRW) – "ILRW is defined as waste that contains long lived radionuclides in quantities that need a greater degree of containment and isolation from the biosphere than is provided by near surface disposal" (IAEA 2009, p. 14). ILRW typically comprises resins, chemical sludges and reactor components, as well as contaminated materials from reactor decommissioning. Worldwide it makes up 7 percent of the volume and has 4 percent of the radioactivity of all waste produced. It may be solidified in concrete or bitumen for disposal – shallow burial for short-lived waste and deep underground burial for long-lived waste (WNA updated 2015).

Low level radioactive waste (LLRW) – LLRW makes up roughly 90 percent of the volume but only 1 percent of the radioactivity of all waste produced. It typically includes protective clothing, rags, filters, reactor water treatment residues, tools, swabs, syringes, laboratory animal carcasses and tissues, material utilized to make smoke detectors and luminous watch dials, and diagnostic and therapeutic treatments used in hospitals (WNA updated 2015).

The precise dividing line between LLRW and ILRW is fuzzy. This is why some countries dispose of both categories in the same facility. The IAEA has described the difficulty in differentiating between the two as follows:

> A precise boundary between LLW and intermediate level waste (ILW) cannot be provided, as limits on the acceptable level of activity concentration will differ between individual radionuclides or groups of radionuclides. Waste acceptance criteria for a particular near surface disposal facility will be dependent on the actual design of and planning for the facility (e.g. engineered barriers, duration of institutional control, site specific factors).
>
> (IAEA n.d.a., p. 13)

This nebulous classification has been the source of frequent misunderstandings that have increased public distrust of government.[15]

The United States does not have an ILRW category at all, thus "LLRW is defined not by what it is, but rather by what it is not" – that is, everything other than spent fuel, high level waste and transuranic waste (United States Department of Energy [DOE] n.d.a.; General Accounting Office [GAO] 1998, p. 49). The radioactivity can range from just above background levels to very high in certain cases, such as parts from inside a reactor vessel that require shielding, usually with lead, to prevent human exposure (NRC n.d.b.). As a result, 'low level' should not be necessarily equated with low risk. To give some idea of how 'hot' LLRW can be, disposal facility operator US Ecology calculated – and the NRC concurred – that at a maximum Class C limit of 4,600 curies, unshielded cesium-137 would yield a lethal dose to 50 percent of an exposed population 1 meter away in roughly 20 minutes (GAO 1998, pp. 51–52). As the NRC's Advisory Committee on Nuclear Waste counseled in 1995, the management of LLRW poses "broader, more direct and ubiquitous potential risks to . . . health and safety than any other activity" (NRC 1997). Neither should it be equated with low volume. In 2013, US generators disposed of more than 1,243,650 cubic feet of LLRW with a combined activity level of 17,216.82 curies. This was the second lowest volume of the preceding decade – 6 years earlier, more than twice the volume with 64 times the activity level was buried at the three disposal facilities operating at that time (DOE n.d.a.).[16]

There are five, sometimes overlapping, generators of LLRW:

- nuclear reactor operators – by far the largest producers;
- academic institutions, including university hospitals and university medical and nonmedical research facilities;
- state and federal government agencies, both military and civilian (for example, neutron research at the National Institute of Standards and Technology in the United States);
- private industries, including research and development companies and manufacturers, nondestructive testing, mining, and fuel fabrication facilities and radiopharmaceutical manufacturers;
- medical facilities, including hospitals and clinics, research facilities and private medical offices.

To reduce its volume, LLRW is often compacted or incinerated in a closed container before being buried in shallow trenches. Until such disposal sites are located and licensed, waste tends to be stored on site by each generator (DOE n.d.a.). Disposal is not the only solution: for isotopes with short half-lives, generators will often store waste until it is no longer radioactive, then dispose of it – at less cost – with nonradioactive materials (a practice referred to as 'delay and decay'), while certain low activity waste may be diluted and dispersed into the environment (such as sewers) under controlled conditions.

Public attitudes to radiation and radioactive waste

Fear

The dangers of radiation were evident, although not really understood, in the first half of the 20th century – for example, Marie Curie's demise[17] and the fate of the 'Radium Girls' in the United States.[18] But for most, views about radiation and radioactive waste are informed by their perceptions of nuclear energy, which derive in large part from the first demonstration of that power in August 1945 to end the War in the Pacific – a display Richard Rhodes described as "ferocious as minor suns" (Rhodes 1995, p. 17). The mushroom cloud has been "etched in the public's memory and awareness," and this has led to a basic association between the destructive power of nuclear weaponry and nuclear power (Carter 1987, p. 42). Kirk Smith has observed:

> Nuclear energy was conceived in secrecy, born in war and first revealed to the world in horror. No matter how much proponents try to separate the peaceful from the weapons atom, the connection is firmly embedded in the minds of the public.
>
> (Smith cited in Dunlap,
> Kraft and Rosa 1993, p. 79)

It would be as if "electricity had come in with the electric chair" (Carter 1987, p. 42). Yale professor of psychiatry Robert Jay Lifton has suggested that "the uneasiness related to both nuclear weapons and nuclear power . . . represents the most fundamental, primal fears about the integrity of the human body, as threatened by the invisible poison of irradiation" (Carter 1987, p. 42). Lifton's description "invisible poison" is important – radiation cannot be seen, smelled, tasted or touched, which only heightens its perceived insidiousness. More broadly, Spencer Weart has observed that "the hobgoblin of a global chain reaction made an indelible impression on the public. One reason was that the image could serve as a symbol, reflecting rising anxieties about the entire technological future" (Weart 1998, p. 18).[19] Yet, it is not generally appreciated that life is "immersed in a sea of radiation" – from the rocks to the atmosphere to the oceans to the human body (Garwin and Charpak 2001, pp. 80–82).

This fear is periodically reinforced by accidents and leaks at nuclear plants, as well as the legacy of past waste disposal practices and fallout (historically for most countries[20]) from nuclear weapons tests.[21] As will be discussed in the next chapter, these mistakes have resulted from genuine lack of understanding, poor siting and technology choices as well as blatantly irresponsible decision-making. Yet, with the exception of the weapons component, the history of nuclear power is not very different from oil, coal and liquid natural gas, and there is evidence to suggest that it is less detrimental to human health than any of its nonrenewable competitors *but* it is still considered the riskiest technology.[22] According to Paul Slovic, survey findings suggest that laypersons perceive nuclear power as having very high risk and perceptions "of risk associated with nuclear waste tend to be even more negative than perceptions of nuclear power" (2012, p. 68). As will be discussed further in chapter 1, the effectiveness of radioactive waste disposal over the decades has not engendered confidence. Further, films, books and television series have stoked these fears.

Scientific controversy

The magnitude of the risk posed by even the lowest levels of radiation is in dispute.[23] In 1980, an extensive study done by the Committee on the Biological Effects of Ionizing Radiation found that health risk estimates were based on incomplete data and involved a large degree of uncertainty, especially in the low-dose region (Bord 1988, p. 196). More than 30 years later, reflecting on the state of the scientific debate, a 2012 special issue of the *Bulletin of the Atomic Scientists* could do little more than summarize the competing theories:

> Some researchers believe that the dose response is higher than the LNT [linear non-threshold] at low doses, while others maintain the dose response drops rapidly below the range covered by epidemiologic data; both groups can find some support in recent epidemiologic studies demonstrating the complexity of the scientific puzzle that researchers face. There are other researchers who believe that the dose response turns around at some point as dose is decreased, actually reducing the risk of cancer; this evidence can be found in data collected from home radon measurements correlated to county lung-cancer rates – albeit in contradiction to more standard epidemiologic studies of the same association, which do show the expected dose response.[24]

Despite this controversy, humans everywhere live – and thrive – in an environment that is bathed in low level radiation, a fact that is generally ignored or forgotten by the public at large, opponents of nuclear power and some experts.[25]

Trust

Public fears are compounded by a perception that the risks associated with nuclear operations are greater than acknowledged by those that work in, or with, the nuclear sector; that the dangers are being deliberately understated by the nuclear industry, the scientific community, government and regulatory bodies.[26] This distrust may be particularly prevalent if a government or commercial entity previously operated or presently operates a nuclear facility with a poor safety record and/or has tried and failed to establish such an operation in the past. Roger Kasperson has explained that risks associated with certain events considered relatively minor by technical experts but dreaded and/or poorly understood by individuals and social groups can be amplified by the public as information about those events is processed. Distrust of those experts plays an important part in this social amplification process (Kasperson 2012, pp. 59–66).

This is not to suggest that the fear is universal. Those in the nuclear industry work with radiation every day and there is strong evidence that communities hosting nuclear facilities understand, respect and are comfortable with the risks. For example, Bisconti Research Inc., which has done a great deal of work on public attitudes toward nuclear energy in the United States, observed in 2010:

"In most U.S. communities where nuclear power plants are located, support for the local plant is wide and deep, and a large majority supports new reactor construction there" (Bisconti 2010). However, accidents such as Fukushima appear to confirm the wider public's worst fears and harden opposition to the industry as a whole and can undo much of the goodwill that exists.[27] This helps explain why the use of scientific experts may do little to allay the fears of prospective host communities. It also explains why simply throwing money at those same communities is likely to be counterproductive in the absence of other activities that build trust.

Burden-sharing

Communities understandably tend to resent hosting disposal facilities for waste generated elsewhere; even more so when the waste is *radioactive*, which carries an even greater stigma than other types of industrial waste.[28] This is somewhat less of a problem for LLRW than spent fuel, as the former is ubiquitous; any community with a hospital is a LLRW producer. Taking the United States as an example, 32 states host commercial power reactors; as of mid-2009 the NRC had issued 22,400 licenses for medical, academic, industrial and general uses of radioactive materials across all 50 states (NRC 2009). However, the perception remains that one or several host communities bear all of the risks in order to provide a public service for the rest of the region, state or country. This is not entirely true: because the subject of radioactive waste disposal tends to become emotional quickly, people tend to forget that the generators also provide a public service and often (particularly nuclear power plants) pose at least as serious a radiological risk as the waste.

Of course, it is simply not possible for every community to dispose of its wastes locally, particularly waste as potentially hazardous as LLRW; one or a few communities must necessarily bear this burden in service of the greater good. Exacerbating this tension, not all communities are even considered as potential hosts to begin with: unsuitable geography, high population density and high annual rainfall are amongst the factors that can automatically rule large swathes of a region out. This is unavoidable but often viewed as inherently unfair by the communities that fit the 'potential host' profile. The challenge is to generate confidence in the safety and efficacy of the project. To do this, the siting authority must cogently explain the risks, potential benefits and expected costs to communities with the right combination of climatic and geographic conditions to host such a facility, and hope that one or more will be convinced.[29]

NIMBY

These factors – public fear of radiation, lack of trust in experts and institutions, and campaigns waged by opponents of the nuclear industry – have led to a reflexive 'not in my backyard' (NIMBY) reaction to many proposed LLRW disposal sites.

Without public support for a project, delays are inevitable and costs increase. If a project cannot be stopped at the outset, opponents will engage in delaying tactics (particularly court cases but sometimes more violent behavior) to achieve their objectives. As discussed in chapter 3, opponents of US Ecology's plan to build and operate a LLRW disposal facility in Boyd County, Nebraska, used these tactics to full effect during the late 1980s and 1990s, finally forcing US Ecology to abandon the project and prompting Nebraska to withdraw from the Central Interstate Low-Level Radioactive Waste Compact. Bargaining and negotiation to produce a mutually satisfactory outcome were viewed as a zero-sum game. While the severity will vary from location to location, NIMBY is ubiquitous. As former EPA Administrator Douglas Costle observed: "The problem is that every place is someone's backyard" (Burns 1998, p. 293).

Even in places where public attitudes are not hostile, the perfect can be the enemy of the good. Unrealistic expectations about how a disposal site should perform makes the establishment of 'good' facilities meeting regulatory requirements that much more difficult and risks the continuation of 'bad' – or at least inefficient – storage practices. As Gershey, Klein, Party and Wilkerson have noted, often "the disposal of LLRW and the fear of radiation, which translates into demands for zero exposure, are irreconcilable" (Gershey et al. 1990, p. xi).

Antinuclear opposition

Fear, uncertainty and misunderstanding, combined with the very real dangers of exposure to radiation, have helped antinuclear activists ensure that relatively few localities seriously consider hosting LLRW disposal sites. For many opponents, the waste issue has proved an effective club to achieve its overall goal: the end of the global nuclear industry. As former chairman of the Sierra Club Michael McCloskey has observed:

> I suspect many environmentalists want to drive a final stake in the heart of the nuclear power industry before they will feel comfortable in cooperating fully in a common effort at solving the waste problem.
>
> (Bodansky 2004, p. 358)

Activists worry that a viable solution to the radioactive waste problem would further legitimize – even reinvigorate – nuclear power as a solution to problems like climate change.[30] Thus, the long-term management of LLRW will always be viewed as unacceptable by a small but vocal segment of the population opposed to any application of nuclear energy.

Methodological approach: a question of fairness

To explore this issue, the authors utilize a linear narrative case study approach that critically examines key stakeholder interactions in order to explain how siting decisions are made.[31] Key stakeholders include governments (federal, state/

regional and local); legislators; regulatory agencies; national and regional public interest groups (for example, environmental nongovernmental organizations [NGOs][32]); indigenous groups; local/regional business groups; the 'host' community and local community groups that support or oppose the facility; the nuclear industry (for example, utilities and waste management companies) and other radioactive waste generators such as hospitals, universities and the mining industry; independent scientific experts; and the court system, where many disputed cases end up being decided. These stakeholders' motivations are complex and can change over time, so particular attention is paid to the difficulties decision-makers face in balancing competing political, economic, scientific and environmental interests.

Central to all of this is the issue of fairness. Some maintain that all citizens should share the burdens imposed by living in a technological society, while others argue that they had no or little choice in how technological decisions were made, so they should not bear the cost. Questions of fairness involve issues of both allocation and process. As Gerrard points out: "It is unfair to allocate burdens unequally, and it is unfair to reach that allocation through a process that is arbitrary and closed" (Gerrard 1995, pp. 83–84). In order to dig deeper into the question of equity and fairness, the authors draw on the literature associated with the environmental justice movement in the conclusion.[33] At its core, "environmental justice seeks to make environmental protection more democratic and asks the fundamental ethical and political question of 'who gets what, why and how much' " (Rechtschaffen, Guana and O'Neill 2009, p. 8).[34] What makes an environmental justice framework particularly applicable in this case is the contention that hazardous facility siting tends to disproportionately impact ethnic minorities – particularly indigenous peoples – and lower socio-economic groups (McGurty 1997, pp. 301–323).[35] Problematically for researchers who have attempted to go beyond the aspirational qualities of environmental justice and apply it as an analytical tool, these frameworks have typically tended not to focus on critically evaluating evidence (Walker 2012, p. 39). As a result, the authors attempt to apply the framework to the case studies in order to yield greater understandings of LLRW disposal facility siting challenges and to help identify a set of best practices for successful siting in the future.

Toward a framework for successful LLRW disposal

For the foreseeable future, the global community will continue to rely on nuclear energy and radioactive sources for many vital goods and services. Thus, existing radioactive waste disposal facilities must continue to operate and new sites must be found. For most countries, and certainly the countries studied in this book, long gone are the days of top-down siting when disposal locations could be chosen and facilities built absent any input from the host communities. Bottom-up, or consent-based, siting is considered global best practice. While its focus was on US SNF, the Blue Ribbon Commission on America's Nuclear Future provided an excellent six-point description of the bottom-up approach that applies equally to LLRW and the siting of hazardous facilities in general (Blue Ribbon Commission on America's Nuclear Future 2012, pp. 47–48):

• Consent-based – affected communities have an opportunity to decide whether to accept facility siting decisions and retain significant local control;
• Transparent – all stakeholders have an opportunity to understand key decisions and engage the process in a meaningful way;
• Phased – key decisions are revisited and modified as necessary rather than being predetermined;
• Adaptive – the process is flexible and produces decisions that are responsive to new information and new technical, social and/or political developments;
• Standards- and science-based – the public can have confidence that all facilities meet rigorous, objective and consistently applied standards of safety and environmental protection;
• Governed – either by partnership arrangements or legally enforceable agreements between the implementing organization and host states, tribes and local communities.

Successful siting of LLRW disposal facilities requires a mix of the technical, social, psychological, political, economic, legal and institutional to allay fears and build trust. Thus we need to understand public attitudes toward a slew of factors, including radiation, complex hazardous industrial processes, the siting authority in particular and government in general. Further we need to understand "the nature of these cognitions, how they are formed, what forces shape them, how they change over time and how they differ among various population subgroups" (Kraft, Rosa and Dunlap 1993, p. 4).

One final note: while successfully siting LLRW disposal facilities is in many ways uniquely challenging, it is far from impossible. Many countries have done so successfully. It is important not to overstate the difficulties. For example, in a book on US LLRW that was published in 1988, Richard Bord lamented: "It has become virtually impossible to establish new toxic chemical, radioactive, and, in some cases, solid waste disposal facilities" (Bord 1988, p. 194). Yet, that same year Utah licensed a facility in the town of Clive to accept naturally occurring radioactive waste. Since then, the site's license has been amended multiple times to allow for receipt of different types of LLRW. Indeed, new disposal facilities have begun operations in Texas and Gyeongju in the last 3 years. Safe and fair solutions do exist.

Structure

The book is set out as follows:

Chapter 1 provides some insight into the history of LLRW disposal. Particular attention will be paid to the US, UK, an OECD/NEA-led program and Germany.

Chapters 2–8 constitute the country studies – the United States, Australia, Spain, South Korea and Switzerland. Because of the size of its nuclear industry and extensive experience managing LLRW, the United States case study spans three chapters. Chapter 2 begins where the US section of chapter 1 left off: the capacity crisis brought about by the temporary closure of the Beatty and Hanford disposal facilities in 1979. The US case study describes the congressionally mandated solution to this problem – a nationwide compact system designed to "more equitably distribute responsibility" for LLRW disposal – and assesses how successful the legislation has been in achieving its goals. From there, chapters 3 and 4 take an in-depth look at a siting failure and a siting success: US Ecology in Boyd County, Nebraska, for the former; Waste Control Specialists in Andrews County, Texas, for the latter. Chapter 5 examines why the Australian government's efforts to site a national disposal facility have failed to date. Spain has been burying LLRW in the southwest of the country ('El Cabril') since 1961. Chapter 6 examines how the El Cabril site has been modernized over the last 54 years, how relations between the host community and federal government evolved in the post-Franco era and the methods the siting authorities have used to secure acceptance from the local populace. Chapter 7 examines the reasons why Seoul's attempts to site nuclear waste disposal facilities were spectacularly unsuccessful for 25 years and why Gyeongju finally – and overwhelmingly – agreed to bear South Korea's LLRW and ILRW burden in 2005. Chapter 8 examines why the Swiss authorities' favored site (Wellenberg) was twice rejected by host canton (state) referenda, what was learned from those failures and how the federal government has recalibrated its site selection process as a result.

In the conclusion, the case studies are drawn together to lay out a set of findings and recommendations. Particular attention is paid to the options available to decision-makers – such as financial incentives, job creation, the inclusion of larger, more desirable projects and the provision of social services – to broaden the appeal of the disposal facilities to potential host communities and how these incentives are necessary but not sufficient. Only relationships between siting authorities/governments and host communities based on transparency and full access to information are likely to produce sustainable LLRW disposal solutions. By incorporating the concept of environmental justice, a fairer, more equitable and transparent siting framework is offered that can help to inform specific national, regional and/or local siting strategies in the future. Finally, some consideration is given to the problems that have arisen when attempting to site LLRW and SNF/HLW facilities simultaneously (which is, in part, a function of risk perception), why continuing to separate these undertakings is the likeliest way to ensure the availability of sufficient LLRW disposal space and what this might mean for more holistic approaches to radioactive waste disposal.

Notes

1 Estimating the LLRW total from all sources worldwide is far more difficult because of the uncertainties associated with radioactive waste generated by institutional – research, industry and medicine – activities. The IAEA's best estimate is expressed in terms of percentages:

For countries with large nuclear power programs, institutional waste amounts to 20% to 30% of the total, while in countries with relatively small nuclear power programs the waste from institutional activities ranges between 30% and more than 50% of the total volume. In countries without nuclear power production, institutional waste represents the great majority of a very small total generation of radioactive waste even though those countries make a small contribution to the total inventory. Until more data becomes available, it is assumed that the worldwide inventory (by volume) of institutional short lived LILW is about 50% of the inventory of LILW generated by nuclear fuel cycle activities.

(IAEA 2008, pp. 17–18)

2 More commonly, most smoke detectors are activated by a very small amount of the radioisotope americium-241.

3 We do not include LLRW generated by military programs in our analysis. In most cases, military waste production volumes are not made public and disposal takes place on military facilities with little, if any, host community input into the operation of those facilities.

4 These books have tended to be country specific.

5 For the purposes of this book: brown field sites are defined as properties that host, or have hosted, activities that involve hazardous substances and are contaminated as a result; green field sites have not hosted such activities.

6 Rem (Roentgen equivalent man) is a standard unit of measurement for the biological damage to living tissue resulting from radiation exposure. It is calculated by combining the amount of energy of the specific ionizing radiation with the medical effects of that radiation (NRC updated 2012).

7 Elements are made up of atoms with the same number of protons: carbon atoms, for example, all have 6 protons. If an element has varying numbers of neutrons, the variants are known as isotopes. Carbon has three naturally occurring isotopes: carbon-12 (12 = 6 protons plus 6 neutrons), carbon-13 (13 = 6 protons plus 7 neutrons) and carbon-14 (14 = 6 protons plus 8 neutrons).

8 Alpha emission occurs for certain unstable atoms when the ratio of neutrons to protons is too low. As a result of emission, the element changes: for example, polonium-210 decays (loses two protons) to become lead-206, a stable (nonradioactive) element.

9 Beta emission occurs when the ratio of neutrons to protons is too high. In this case, an excess neutron transforms into a proton and an electron or beta particle – the new proton remains in the nucleus (thus the element changes) and the electron is ejected. For example, beta emission transforms technetium-99 into the atom to ruthenium.

10 Gamma rays and x-rays "pose the same kind of hazard . . . [but] differ in their origin. Gamma rays originate in the nucleus. X-rays originate in the electron fields surrounding the nucleus or are machine-produced." U.S. Environmental Protection Agency, *Gamma Rays* (updated 29 June 2015), www.epa.gov/radiation/understand/gamma.html

11 When a nucleus remains in an excited state following an alpha or beta emission, a gamma emission can occur almost instantaneously to move the nucleus closer to stability.

12 Making other objects radioactive, that is, 'neutron activation,' is the process that produces many of the radioactive sources used in medical, academic and industrial applications (NRC updated 2014a).

13 For example, the US Manhattan Project considered many wastes LLRW that today would be categorized as HLW (Burns and Briner 1998, p. 29).

14 Transuranic (TRU) waste is a category used by the United States and consists of items contaminated with radioactive elements heavier than uranium, such as plutonium. The Waste Isolation Pilot Plant (WIPP), 26 miles southeast of Carlsbad, New Mexico, had been accepting defense-generated TRU waste since March 1999 (DOE n.d.b.). Following a radiation leak in February 2014, WIPP has been closed; exactly when the plant will reopen is unclear.

15 A European Commission public opinion survey found that in over 16,155 interviews, 8 out of 10 people believed that "any radioactive waste is very dangerous" (Riley 2004, p. 1).

16 The curie is a unit of measurement for radioactivity. While still a commonly used term, it has been superseded by the becquerel as the international standard. One curie is equivalent to 37 gigabecquerels.

17 Marie Curie's work with radiation won her the 1903 Nobel Prize in Physics (shared with her husband, Pierre, and Henry Becquerel) and the discovery of radium and polonium won her the 1911 Nobel Prize in Chemistry. Long-term exposure to radiation also caused her to contract aplastic anemia, which took her life in 1934. See http://nobelprize.org/nobel_prizes/chemistry/laureates/1911/marie-curie-faq.html

18 From World War I to the mid-1930s, the Radium Dial Co. hired several thousand workers, mainly women, to paint watches and clock faces with radium to make them glow in the dark. Radium Dial factories were located in Connecticut, Illinois, New Jersey and New York. To keep a fine point on the paint brushes, employees were encouraged to roll the tips on their tongues and press them between their lips before dipping them into the paint. Many workers also painted their clothes, faces and teeth for fun. In the 1920s, workers started getting sick and several died of what would later be diagnosed as radium poisoning. According to one estimate, by 1988, a total of 112 workers had died from the occupational disease (Mullner 1999; Irvine 1998).

19 Vincent Covello has made the same point: "Many people are concerned about nuclear power not because of its specific risks but because of its associations with nuclear weapons, highly centralized political and economic systems, and technological elitism" (Covello cited in Jacob 1990, p. 48).

20 With the exception of North Korea, it has been at least 15 years since any country conducted a nuclear weapons test. The United States last tested in 1992, the UK in 1991, the USSR/Russia in 1990, France and China in 1996, India and Pakistan in 1998 and North Korea in 2013 (Arms Control Association, updated 2013).

21 While exceedingly rare, transportation accidents such as occurred in Nevada in 1979 (see chapter 2) can also have the same effect.

22 A study published in the *Lancet* in 2007 attempted to measure deaths and serious illnesses attributable to various methods of generating electrical power in Europe. Coal was the most dangerous method by far; nuclear the least (Markandya and Wilkinson 2007, pp. 979–990). The bar chart comparison is reproduced in "The Human Toll of Coal vs. Nuclear" (2011).

23 Off-the-wall theories from people with advanced degrees and/or in positions of responsibility are often given far more exposure than they deserve, serving only to create greater general confusion. For example, in 1997 current Oregon Republican Party chairman Dr. Art Robinson, a California Institute of Technology–trained chemist, recommended dispersing radioactive waste from aircraft as both a disposal strategy and as a way to build up resistance to degenerative disease.

> All we need to do with nuclear waste is dilute it to a low radiation level and sprinkle it over the ocean – or even over America after hormesis is better understood and verified with respect to more diseases. . . . If we could use it to enhance our own drinking water here in Oregon, where background radiation is low, it would hormetically enhance our resistance to degenerative diseases. Alas, this would be against the law. (Robinson has since clarified that such proposals would be politically untenable.)
>
> (Murphy 2014)

24 The linear nonthreshold theory about the effects of radiation at doses below the range where epidemiologic data are conclusive, subscribed to by the US National Academy of Sciences, holds that "the risk would continue in a linear fashion at lower doses without a threshold and that the smallest dose has the potential to cause a small increase in risk to humans" (Beyea 2012, pp. 10–12).

25 The position of the NRC is as follows:

> Studies of occupational workers who are chronically exposed to low levels of radiation above normal background have shown no adverse biological effects. Even so, the radiation protection community conservatively assumes that any amount of radiation may pose some risk for causing cancer and hereditary effect, and that the risk is higher for higher radiation exposures.
>
> (NRC updated 2014b)

26 For an analysis of the deleterious effect the lack of an independent regulator can have on a commercial nuclear enterprise, see Acton and Hibbs 2012. One of the leading government-nuclear industry conspiracy theories concerns the 1974 death of Karen Silkwood, a laboratory analyst at the Kerr-McGee Fuel Fabrication Site in Cimarron, Oklahoma, en route to a meeting with a *New York Times* reporter, allegedly to deliver evidence of tampering with fuel rod quality assurance records by the company.

27 Recognition that a major nuclear accident anywhere would be devastating for the entire industry, giving all participants an overwhelming interest in helping the worst performers come up to the level of the best performers, was the driving force behind the creation of the Institute of Nuclear Power Operators in the United States in the immediate aftermath of the Three Mile Island accident and the World Association of Nuclear Operators in the immediate aftermath of the Chernobyl accident (Rees 1994, pp. 2–3).

28 One of the clearest cases of radioactive stigmatization occurred in Goiania, Brazil, in September 1987, in which two scrap metal scavengers sawed open a cesium chloride capsule while dismantling a cancer therapy device they had found in an abandoned clinic. Before anyone realized what the glowing material inside was, several hundred people had been contaminated and four eventually died. The resulting publicity caused the price of products manufactured in Goiania to drop 40% and remain depressed for more than a month, despite the fact that none of those products showed any evidence of being contaminated (Slovic 2012, p. 71). The story would make international headlines, reaching into rural northern Nebraska where, as discussed in chapter 3, an increasingly bitter dispute over LLRW disposal was being fought (Letter to Governor Kay Orr from Ivy Nielsen, 14 January 1988, which included the article "Rad Fear Creates City of 'Lepers' in Brazil" [*Sunday World-Herald*, 3 January 1988]). A similar stigmatization has occurred in Fukushima.

29 As discussed in the case studies, suitable geology and climate are not the only requirements. Transportation, land use and population, for example, are also important factors.

30 *Der Spiegel* suspected just such a dynamic has been at play in Germany. Since 1979, €1.5 billion has been spent conducting research at the Gorleben salt dome to determine its suitability to receive spent fuel and HLW waste. But in 2000, the then Social Democratic Party (SPD)/Green coalition declared a 10-year moratorium on work at the site to provide time to search for an alternative.

> However, so little happened afterwards that some observers began to suspect that then Environment Minister Trittin and the Greens were dragging their feet in order to prevent nuclear power from gaining any additional degree of legitimacy. Their motivation is clear: If a final repository were approved for use, the environmentalists would lose their key argument against nuclear power.
>
> ("Dealing with Asse" 2008)

31 For the purposes of this inquiry a stakeholder is defined, building on Freeman's work (1984), as any person or organization that is impacted by, or causes an impact to, a company, government or other type of organization. For a more comprehensive discussion of the term see Mitchell, Agle and Wood 1997.

32 Growing mistrust of the role of government in the 1970s led to the rise of NGOs, particularly as an agent to protect the environment. They can be classified into three groups: "mainstream national environmental groups, the grassroots-based organizations, and the anti-nuclear groups." Greenpeace, which was borne out of opposition

to French nuclear testing in 1971, is the most well known international ENGO (Gerrard 1995, p. 213).

33 For Walker, inequality is best understood as a descriptive term

> describing a condition of difference or unevenness of something (such as income, health, pollution exposure/creation, opportunity, influence, access to resources, consumption of resources) between different groups of people (old/young, black/white, rich/poor, north/south, this generation/future generation). Accordingly, inequality can be measured and described using data of various potential forms – although such description will never be an entirely neutral or unconstructed exercise
>
> (Walker 2012, p. 12)

34 Unfortunately for the researcher there is a multiplicity of differing definitions of 'environmental justice' offered by academics and environmental NGOs, and in many ways it is a contested term. Bryant argues that the term refers "to those cultural norms and values, rules, regulations, behaviours, policies, and decisions to support sustainable communities, where people can interact with confidence that their environment is safe, nurturing, and protective" (Rechtschaffen et al. 2009, p. 7).

35 For a fuller exploration of the term 'environmental justice' see Bullard 2000; Mohai and Bryant 1992. For more on the development of the environmental justice movement see Brulle and Pellow 2006.

References

Acton, J., and Hibbs, M., "Why Fukushima Was Preventable," *Nuclear Policy*, Carnegie Endowment for International Peace, Washington, DC (March 2012), http://carnegieendowment.org/files/fukushima.pdf

Arms Control Association, *Nuclear Testing Tally* (updated February 2013), www.armscontrol.org/factsheets/nucleartesttally

Beyea, J., "Special Issue on the Risks of Exposure to Low-Level Radiation," *Bulletin of the Atomic Scientists*, Vol. 68, No. 3 (2012): 10–12.

Bisconti, A., " 'Not' in My Back Yard! Is Really 'Yes' in My Back Yard," *Natural Gas and Electricity* (January 2010), www.nei.org/resourcesandstats/documentlibrary/newplants/reports/article-not-in-my-back-yard-is-really-yes-in-my-back-yard-ann-bisconti-january-2010

Blue Ribbon Commission on America's Nuclear Future, *Report to the Secretary of Energy*, Washington, DC (January 2012), http://cybercemetery.unt.edu/archive/brc/20120620220235/http://brc.gov/sites/default/files/documents/brc_finalreport_jan2012.pdf

Bodansky, D., *Nuclear Energy: Principles, Practices, and Prospects* (New York: Springer, 2004).

Bord, R., "The Low-Level Radioactive Waste Crisis: Is More Citizen Participation the Answer?," in M. E. Burns (ed.), *Low-Level Radioactive Waste Regulation: Science, Politics and Fear* (Chelsea, MI: Lewis, 1988).

Brulle, J., and Pellow, D., "Environmental Justice: Human Health and Environmental Inequalities," *Annual Review of Public Health*, Vol. 27 (2006): 103–124.

Bullard, R., *Dumping in Dixie: Race, Class and Environmental Quality* (Boulder, CO: Westview Press, 2000).

Burns, M. E., "Living in the Past, Facing the Future," in Michael E. Burns (ed.), *Low-Level Radioactive Waste Regulation: Science, Politics and Fear* (Chelsea, MI: Lewis, 1998).

Burns, M. E., and Briner, W. H., "Setting the Stage," in Michael E. Burns (ed.), *Low-Level Radioactive Waste Regulation: Science, Politics and Fear* (Chelsea, MI: Lewis, 1998).

Carter, L., *Nuclear Imperatives and Public Trust: Dealing with Radioactive Waste* (Washington, DC: Resources for the Future, 1987).

"Dealing with Asse: Where Should Germany Store Its Nuclear Waste?" *Der Spiegel* (8 September 2008), www.spiegel.de/international/germany/dealing-with-asse-where-should-germany-store-its-nuclear-waste-a-577018.html

Dunlap, R., Kraft, M. E., and Rosa, E. A., *Public Reactions to Nuclear Waste* (Durham, NC: Duke University Press, 1993).

Freeman, E., *Strategic Management: A Stakeholder Approach* (Boston, MA: Pitman, 1984).

Garwin, R., and Charpak, G., *Megawatts and Megatons: A Turning Point in the Nuclear Age?* (New York: Alfred A. Knopf, 2001).

General Accounting Office, *Radioactive Waste: Answers to Questions Related to the Proposed Ward Valley Low-Level Radioactive Waste Disposal Facility*, GAO/RCED-98-40R (22 May 1998), www.gao.gov/assets/90/87895.pdf

Gerrard, M. B., *Whose Backyard, Whose Risk* (Cambridge, MA: MIT Press, 1995).

Gershey, E., Klein, R., Party, E., and Wilkerson, A., *Low-Level Radioactive Waste: From Cradle to Grave* (New York: Van Nostrand Reinhold, 1990).

Greenwood, T., "Nuclear Waste Management in the United States," in E. William Colglazier (ed.), *The Politics of Nuclear Waste* (New York: Pergamon Press, 1982).

"The Human Toll of Coal vs. Nuclear," *Washington Post* (2 April 2011), www.washingtonpost.com/national/the-human-toll-of-coal-vs-nuclear/2011/04/02/AFOVHsRC_graphic.html

International Atomic Energy Agency, *Classification of Radioactive Waste*, General Safety Guide No. GSG-1 (November 2009), www-pub.iaea.org/MTCD/publications/PDF/Pub1419_web.pdf

International Atomic Energy Agency, *Estimation of Global Inventories of Radioactive Waste and Other Radioactive Materials*, IAEA-TECDOC-1591 (June 2008), www-pub.iaea.org/MTCD/publications/PDF/te_1591_web.pdf

International Atomic Energy Agency, *Managing Radioactive Waste* (n.d.a.), www.iaea.org/Publications/Factsheets/English/manradwa.html

International Atomic Energy Agency, *Managing Radioactive Wastes Factsheet* (n.d.b.), www.iaea.org/Publications/Factsheets/English/manradwa.html#note_b

International Atomic Energy Agency, *Status and Trends in Spent Fuel Reprocessing*, IAEA-TECDOC-1467 (September 2005), www-pub.iaea.org/MTCD/publications/PDF/te_1467_web.pdf

Irvine, M. "Suffering Endures for 'Radium Girls' Who Painted Watches in the '20s," *Associated Press* (4 October 1998), www.hartford-hwp.com/archives/40/046.html

Jacob, G., *Site Unseen: The Politics of Siting a Nuclear Waste Repository* (Pittsburgh, PA: Pittsburgh University Press, 1990).

Kasperson, R., "The Social Amplification of Risk and Low-Level Radiation," *Bulletin of the Atomic Scientists*, Vol. 68, No. 3 (2012): 59–66.

Kraft, M. E., Rosa, E. A., and Dunlap, R. E., "Public Opinion and Nuclear Waste Policymaking," in R. E. Dunlap, M. E. Kraft, and E. A. Rosa (eds.), *Public Reactions to Nuclear Waste: Citizen's Views of Repository Siting* (Durham, NC: Duke University Press, 1993).

Letter to Governor Kay Orr from Ivy Nielsen (14 January 1988), in Nebraska State Historical Society, Government Records, RG001, Government, SG43, Orr, Kay, S1, Correspondence, Public Opinion, LLRW, Box 42.

Markandya, A., and Wilkinson, P., "Electricity Generation and Health," *Lancet*, Vol. 370, No. 9591 (2007): 979–990.

McGurty, E., "From NIMBY to Civil Rights: The Origins of the Environmental Justice Movement," *Environmental History*, Vol. 2, No. 3 (1997): 301–323.

Mitchell, R. K., Agle, B. R., and Wood, D. J., "Toward a Theory of Stakeholder Identification and Salience: Defining the Principle of Who and What Really Counts,"
Academy of Management Review, Vol. 22, No. 4 (1997): 853–888.

Mohai, P., and Bryant, B., "Environmental Justice: Weighing Race and Class as Factors
in the Distribution of Environmental Hazards," *University of Colorado Law Review*, Vol.
63, No. 4 (1992): 921–932.

Mullner, R., *Deadly Glow: The Radium Dial Worker Tragedy* (Washington, DC: American
Public Health Association, 1999).

Murphy, T., "GOP Candidate Asks Residents to Mail Him Their Pee," *Mother Jones* (20 August
2014), www.motherjones.com/politics/2014/08/art-robinson-nuclear-waste-pete-defazio

Princeton University, *Open Source Radiation Safety Training, Module 2: Background Radiation & Other Sources of Exposure* (updated 30 March 2011), http://web.princeton.edu/
sites/ehs/osradtraining/backgroundradiation/background.htm

"Rad Fear Creates City of 'Lepers' in Brazil," *Sunday World-Herald* (3 January 1998), as
found in the Letter to Governor Kay Orr from Ivy Nielsen (14 January 1988), in
Nebraska State Historical Society, Government Records, RG001, Government, SG43,
Orr, Kay, S1, Correspondence, Public Opinion, LLRW, Box 42.

Raupach, M. R., Marland, G., Ciais, P., Le Quéré, C., Canadell, J. G., Klepper, G., and
Field, C. B., "Global and Regional Drivers of Accelerating CO_2 Emissions," *Proceedings
of the National Academy of Sciences*, Vol. 104, No. 24 (2007): 10288–10293.

Rechtschaffen, C., Guana, E., and O'Neill, C., *Environmental Justice: Law, Policy and
Regulation*, 2nd ed. (Durham, NC: Carolina Academic Press, 2009).

Rees, J., *Hostages of Each Other: The Transformation of Nuclear Safety Since Three Mile
Island* (Chicago: University of Chicago Press, 1994).

Rhodes, R., *Dark Sun: The Making of the Hydrogen Bomb* (New York: Simon and Schuster,
1995).

Riley, P., *Nuclear Waste: Law, Policy and Pragmatism* (Aldershot: Ashgate, 2004).

Sandström, B., "Radiation as a Weapon: A View from Open Source Studies," NKS-B
NordThreat Seminar (30–31 October 2008), www.nks.org/download/seminar/2008_b_
nordthreat/NKS_B_NordThreat_1–2.pdf

Slovic, P., "The Perception Gap: Radiation and Risk," *Bulletin of the Atomic Scientists*,
Vol. 68, No. 3 (2012): 67–75.

United States Department of Energy, *Manifest Information Management Systems* (n.d.),
http://mims.doe.gov/GeneratorData.aspx

United States Department of Energy, Office of Environmental Management, *Low-Level
Radioactive Waste (LLRW)* (n.d.a.), www.gtcceis.anl.gov/guide/llw/index.cfm

United States Department of Energy, *Waste Isolation Pilot Project, "Why WIPP?"* (n.d.b.),
www.wipp.energy.gov/fctshts/Why_WIPP.pdf

United States Environmental Protection Agency, *Radiation: Non-Ionizing and Ionizing*
(updated 17 May 2013), www.epa.gov/radiation/understand/radiation.html

United States Nuclear Regulatory Commission, *Fact Sheet on Plutonium* (updated 4 February 2011), www.nrc.gov/reading-rm/doc-collections/fact-sheets/plutonium.html

United States Nuclear Regulatory Commission, *Glossary: REM (Roentgen Equivalent Man)*
(updated 10 December 2012), www.nrc.gov/reading-rm/basic-ref/glossary/rem-roentgen-
equivalent-man.html

United States Nuclear Regulatory Commission, *High-Level Waste* (n.d.a.), www.nrc.gov/
waste/high-level-waste.html

United States Nuclear Regulatory Commission, *Low-Level Waste* (n.d.b.), www.nrc.gov/
waste/low-level-waste.html

United States Nuclear Regulatory Commission, *National Materials Program* (4 June 2009), http://nrc-stp.ornl.gov/materials/nmpbkgrd090604.pdf

United States Nuclear Regulatory Commission, *NRC News*, No. 97–026 (14 February 1997), www.nrc.gov/reading-rm/doc-collections/news/1997/97–026.html

United States Nuclear Regulatory Commission, *Radiation Basics: Neutrons* (updated 17 October 2014a), www.nrc.gov/about-nrc/radiation/health-effects/radiation-basics.html#neutron

United States Nuclear Regulatory Commission, *Radiation Exposure and Cancer* (updated 17 October 2014b), www.nrc.gov/about-nrc/radiation/health-effecs/rad-exposure-cancer.html

Vari, A., Reagan-Cirincione, P., and Mumpower, J., *LLRW Disposal Facility Siting: Successes and Failures in Six Countries* (Boston, MA: Kluwer Academic, 1994).

Walker, G., *Environmental Justice: Concepts, Evidence and Politics* (London: Routledge, 2012).

Weart, S., *Nuclear Fear: A History of Images* (Cambridge, MA: Harvard University Press, 1988).

World Nuclear Association, *Nuclear Power in the World Today* (updated April 2014), www.world-nuclear.org/info/inf01.html

World Nuclear Association, *Radioactive Waste Management* (updated July 2015), www.world-nuclear.org/info/Nuclear-Fuel-Cycle/Nuclear-Wastes/Radioactive-Waste-Management/

Zaitseva, L., and Hand, K. "Nuclear Smuggling Chains: Suppliers, Intermediaries, and End-Users," *American Behavioral Scientist*, Vol. 46, No. 6 (2003): 822–844, http://cisac.fsi.stanford.edu/sites/default/files/abs_zaitseva.pdf

1 A short history of 'low level' radioactive waste disposal

The history of low level radioactive waste (LLRW) disposal is a story of technically/ politically sound and staggeringly irresponsible paths both considered and pursued, successful and failed facility siting efforts, as well as accidents averted and not. Operations, particularly during the first decades of the nuclear era, were based on incomplete knowledge of the dynamics of radionuclide migration and the robustness of disposal technologies. Best practice evolved significantly during these years and many practices considered unacceptable today were based on the best available evidence at the time. That being said, a culture of secrecy, combined with serious cases of mismanagement (both accidental and deliberate) and a good dose of hubris resulted in mistakes – some became public knowledge immediately and some would emerge over time, while others are still relatively unknown. These experiences are integral to understanding why many communities would come to deeply distrust government-led disposal facility siting efforts in later years. This chapter examines the ocean and land disposal histories of two of the largest Cold War waste-producing democracies (the US and UK), details the multinational ocean disposal program conducted by OECD (Organisation for Economic Co-operation and Development) member states from 1967 to 1982 and presents a short discussion of one particularly controversial disposal site in Germany.

A "garbage disposal type of operation": the United States and LLRW, 1946–1979[1]

The first significant volumes of radioactive waste generated in the United States came from the Manhattan Project – the first commercial power reactor would not come on line until December 1957, in Pennsylvania. Solid and liquid 'low level' radioactive waste was typically burnt, buried in shallow trenches or pits, diluted then poured into the sewerage system, dumped in the ocean or stored for later disposal. The Atomic Energy Commission's (AEC) approach was to manage high level waste (HLW; for example, tank storage at the Hanford Site in Washington State[2]) while it developed permanent solutions to dispose of low-level waste in ways that would not pose a risk to the public (Mazuzan and Walker 1984, p. 345). However, it is important to note that waste classifications have changed over time: "many types of wastes that were handled as low-level wastes would today be considered high-level" and even the AEC conceded that its radiation estimates might vary by a factor of 10 (Burns 1998, pp. 29–30; Mazuzan and Walker 1984, p. 354). This, combined with recordkeeping that the US General Accounting Office (GAO) described as ranging from "poor to nonexistent," means that government figures underestimate (likely quite significantly) the amount of waste and level of radioactivity released into the environment during the first decades of the Cold War (General Accounting Office [GAO] 1981, p. 9).

Ocean disposal

The United States, primarily the Navy, disposed of radioactive waste in the oceans from 1946 to 1970 at 10 locations in the Atlantic, 13 locations in the Pacific and two locations in the Gulf of Mexico (United States Environmental Protection Agency [EPA] 1980, pp. 4–7; United States Nuclear Regulatory Commission [NRC] 2007, p. 7; GAO 1981, pp. 3, 9). More containers were dumped in the Pacific but a much higher activity total was dumped in the Atlantic.[3] According to official records, two locations in the Atlantic (140 and 220 miles southeast of Sandy Hook, New Jersey, at depths of more than 9,000 feet and almost 12,500 feet, respectively) and three in the Pacific (30 miles west of San Francisco) received approximately 90 percent of the waste volume (NRC 2007, p. 7; EPA 1980, p. 6). However, several sailors who took part in dumping operations in the Atlantic during the 1950s have said that barrels were pushed overboard much closer to shore when the weather was bad (Levesque 2013).

The AEC licensed private companies to dispose of hospital, laboratory and industrial waste in the oceans and granted licensees permission to pour small amounts of LLRW into public sewerage systems if it was "readily soluble or dispersible in water, did not exceed maximum permissible concentrations after dilution, and did not produce more than one curie per year of radioactivity." Land disposal was also allowed but limited to 12 burials per year at a minimum depth of 4 feet (Walker 2009, p. 23; Mazuzan and Walker 1984, p. 349). While precise ocean disposal figures are impossible to obtain, a 1981 GAO report (relying on EPA data) estimates that roughly 90,000 containers were sunk, a 1990 EPA report estimates that roughly 75,000 containers were sunk and a 2007 report by the NRC's Advisory Committee on Nuclear Waste estimates that more than 90,500 containers (a number that is inflated to an indeterminate extent because 'containers' includes unpackaged and liquid wastes dumped in the Atlantic) were sunk (GAO 1981, p. 9; Walden 1990, p. 1; NRC 2007, pp. 7–8). Given the large accounting uncertainties, it is safe to assume that the higher numbers are closer to the truth.

By the late 1950s, waste management was making news for the wrong reasons. In July 1957 naval aircraft were required to strafe two barrels of sodium waste in the Atlantic that had not sunk of their own accord – an incident that was reported in the *New York Times* (Mazuzan and Walker 1984, p. 355). In January

1958, Houston-based Industrial Waste Disposal Corporation's application for a 2-year license to dump solid LLRW off the Texas coast into the Gulf of Mexico caused a storm of protest north and south of the border. Opposition in Texas (including from US Senator Lyndon Johnson), the Louisiana legislature and the Mexican government (the US embassy in Mexico City warned that a "violent, adverse public reaction would result from approval of the license") prompted the AEC to rule that the company would have to dispose of the waste at Oak Ridge or Idaho National Laboratories.[4] According to Mazuzan and Walker, the AEC decision was based primarily on advice from the State Department that dumping in the Gulf would have "seriously harmful effects" on relations in the hemisphere (Mazuzan and Walker 1984, pp. 355–357). This controversy was exacerbated by the June 1959 release of a National Academy of Sciences report on LLRW disposal in coastal waters that identified 28 possible disposal locations (including 16 miles off Cape Cod, 2 miles off the Florida coast, 20 miles off Savannah, Georgia, and 19 miles off the Texas coast) and advised that water as shallow as 120 feet could be utilized in certain cases (National Academy of Sciences 1959).

Farallon Islands, Pacific Ocean: 1946–1970

From 1946 to 1970, low level waste was dumped by licensed companies in three locations on the continental shelf and slope to the south, southwest and west of the Farallon Islands, a 211-acre archipelago of 10 islets – and the site of a major commercial fishery – that lies roughly 30 miles west of San Francisco (Casey 2005, p. 3). Between 47,500 and 47,750 waste packages (steel drums and concrete containers) containing roughly 14,500 curies of radioactivity, generated primarily by Californian AEC contractors, were sunk at three designated disposal sites in water ranging from 300 to about 6,000 feet. More than 90 percent of that total ended up in the deepest site (Colombo and Kendig 1990, p. 3; EPA 1975, pp. 1–4). The waste – defense, commercial and medical – was both solid and liquid. The solid waste was predominantly contaminated paper, metals, rubber, rags, glass, ash and animal carcasses. The liquid waste was predominantly filter cartridges, aqueous solutions, evaporator concentrates and solvents (Colombo and Kendig 1990, p. 4; GAO 1981, p. 2; Jones et al. 2001, p. 1). In addition to radioactive waste, a toxic cocktail of dredge spoils, phenols, cyanides, heavy metals such as mercury and beryllium, chemical munitions, acid waste, cannery waste and disused explosives have also been dumped in the surrounding waters.

In theory, LLRW containers were dumped overboard either at one of the three sites while the vessel was stationary or in a straight line as the vessel transited one of the sites (Karl, Schwab, Drake and Chin 1992, p. 9). However, in practice, due to inclement weather and navigational uncertainties, "many of the drums were probably not disposed of at the specific sites. It is more likely that they litter a 1,400-km2 [540 mile2] area of sea floor" (Karl et al. 1992, p. 1; Jones et al. 2001, p. 1). The GAO and EPA have both reported that the waste containers were not designed to be permanent barriers to radionuclide migration. In fact, quite the reverse: "The drums served to contain the waste mixtures, to minimize dispersion during handling and transportation and to offer some radiation protection to personnel." They were "intended *only* to ensure that [the waste] descended to the ocean floor where ocean currents would dilute and disperse the radioactivity to insignificant concentrations" (Colombo and Kendig 1990, p. 4; GAO 1981, p. 2). To ensure sinking, the AEC required that containers weigh at least 550 pounds (Walden 1990, p. 1). However, this evidently did not guarantee success: sailors on the tugs hauling the waste out to sea periodically shot holes in drums that did not immediately sink (Davis 2001). As has become clear over time, waste packages behaved in very different ways once they were pushed off the transport ships. In 1990, the US Geological Survey (USGS) conducted a side scan sonar survey of sites 1 and 2, and in 1998 several US government agencies, in cooperation with the British Geological Survey, conducted a radioactivity survey of sites 1 and 2 where commercial fishing occurs. According to a 2001 Department of the Interior/USGS report, the barrels were "in all states of preservation, ranging from completely intact to completely disintegrated" (Jones et al. 2001, pp. 1, 4).

In 2001, Lisa Davis wrote a lengthy article in *SF Weekly* examining the history of LLRW disposal around the Farallons. Davis makes the common mistake of equating all LLRW with short half-lives but her larger contention is valid – quantities of waste containing plutonium, tritium, strontium and cesium were disposed along with low level waste, and fairly perfunctory recordkeeping makes determining what exactly was sunk a virtually impossible task. Davis also discussed the scuttling of the small aircraft carrier USS *Independence* in January 1951. A converted cruiser, the aircraft carrier saw major action with the Pacific Fleet from 1943 to 1945 before being used as a target to study the effects of nuclear weapons on ships, equipment and material (including, in some cases, the use of live animals) at Bikini Atoll in 1946. Following extensive decontamination work, the *Independence* was one of eight major ships towed back to the West Coast for further inspection (Department of the Navy n.d.). Citing contemporaneous Navy documents, Davis made a convincing case that the aircraft carrier's final act of service was as a very large nuclear waste container scuttled southwest of the Farallons: according to a 1949 memo from the Navy's Bureau for Research and Medical Military Specialties, the aircraft carrier was

> used as a test laboratory for radiological decontaminations studies. . . . Large quantities of fresh fission product were . . . drained into empty tanks. . . . Other contaminated materials that have been used in connection with the research program of the Naval Radiological Defense Laboratory also have been put on board the *Independence*.
>
> (Davis 2001)

In the most recent government study of the area, it was estimated that 540 terabecquerels (TBq) of radioactivity (excluding tritium) had been dumped. The authors concluded: "Both in situ measurements and laboratory analyses of sediment samples indicate only very low levels of artificial radionuclides in the surveyed areas. . . . There is no evidence for significant regional-scale contamination as a result of the dumping." However, the authors tempered their findings by noting that only 15 percent of the barrel locations and 10 percent of the radionuclide concentrations had been examined and site 3 remained "virtually unstudied" (Jones et al. 2001, pp. 1, 29–30).[5]

In 1970, the AEC ended the practice of ocean dumping based on a recommendation to President Nixon by the recently created Council on Environmental Quality. There were two principal reasons for this decision. The first was economic: ocean disposal was reported to cost as much as $48.75 per 55-gallon drum compared to $5.15 per drum for burial on land (NRC 2007, p. 8). The second was the adverse public reaction to polluting the ocean: international opinion was changing. In 1972, the Convention on the Prevention of Marine Pollution by Dumping of Wastes and Other Matter (the London Dumping Convention [LDC]) was negotiated. The Convention regulated the dumping of 'grey list' substances (including LLRW) and prohibited the dumping of 'black list' substances (including HLW). The LDC entered into force in August 1975 (Convention on the Prevention of Marine Pollution by Dumping of Wastes and Other Matter 1972, Annex 1). In 1985, the LDC parties agreed to an indefinite voluntary moratorium on LLRW dumping. A permanent ban was adopted in 1993, and in 1996 a Protocol was concluded to supersede the LDC that prohibits the dumping of materials "containing levels of radioactivity greater than *de minimis* (exempt) concentrations as defined by the IAEA and adopted by Contracting Parties." The United States has signed but not ratified the Protocol as of this writing (International Maritime Organization 2013).[6]

Technically, LLRW ocean disposal was still possible – consistent with the Marine Protection, Research, and Sanctuaries Act of 1972, which authorized the EPA to issue permits and promulgate regulations for disposing of materials into US territorial waters – but any request required a permit approved by both houses of Congress, making granting of such permits unlikely in all but the most urgent safety or national security situations (NRC 2007, p. 8). Regardless, by the mid- to late 1970s, very few of those involved in the management of radioactive waste still considered dumping at sea a realistic option; the vast majority viewed the practice as a relic of the past (James Voss, personal communication, 16 January 2015).

Land disposal

The 1946 Atomic Energy Act (AEA) established a "complete government monopoly over the development and uses of atomic energy, including the ownership of materials and the facilities for producing or using them" (Allardice and Trapnell 1974, p. 33). Less than a decade later, this arrangement was seen as impractical and unnecessarily restrictive; the AEA was being described as "an island of socialism" in the sea of free enterprise (Allardice and Trapnell

1974, p. 42). The Act was amended in 1954 to enable private companies to develop the peaceful atom. It is worth noting that although the AEC laid the foundation for a market solution, the regulator did step in on occasion to make its preferences known.[7] For example, in 1976 after New Mexico received a disposal facility application from Chem-Nuclear, the newly formed NRC advised:

> Because of the lack of adequate standards and criteria for commercial shallow land burial, the need to investigate alternate methods of disposing of low level waste, the lack of adequate criteria for the perpetual funding of post-operation site maintenance, *and the lack of need for increased capacity for commercial burial, we do not consider licensing of new burial grounds to be prudent prior to the development of a comprehensive national low-level waste management program.*
>
> (Kerr 1982, p. 81, emphasis added)

The Act was amended again in 1959, providing a mechanism for states to assume regulatory authority over radioactive material use, storage and disposal (United States Department of Energy [DOE] 2001, p. 5). To be approved by the AEC, state programs needed to be at least as rigorous as federal regulations. Thus, approved states became known as 'agreement states.' During this time, land disposal of LLRW had taken place at five AEC facilities: Hanford, Washington; Idaho Falls, Idaho; Los Alamos, New Mexico; Oak Ridge, Tennessee; and Savannah River, South Carolina. In 1960, the AEC opened all five sites to all LLRW generators but also announced "at the urging of companies in the private sector" its intention to phase out the use of these facilities (DOE 1996, p. 2). In their place, the AEC would permit agreement states to license commercially owned sites, a step encouraged by private industry "which saw a potentially lucrative market developing" (Burns 1998, p. 39). As a result, the expensive practice of ocean disposal was quickly phased out – the AEC assisted this process in June 1960 by placing a moratorium on issuing new ocean disposal licenses (EPA 1977, p. 181). By 1962, the AEC was reporting that roughly 95 percent of all LLRW was being buried on land (GAO 1981, p. 2). From 1962 to 1971, six LLRW disposal facilities were licensed:

- Barnwell, South Carolina, from 1969 to the present;
- Beatty, Nevada, from 1962 to 1992;
- Hanford, Washington, from 1965 to the present;
- Maxey Flats, Kentucky, from 1963 to 1977;
- Sheffield, Illinois, from 1967 to 1978;
- West Valley, New York, from 1963 to 1975.

While only the Hanford facility was developed on AEC land, Barnwell and Beatty were adjacent to large nuclear weapons–related enterprises – the

Savannah River Site and Nevada Test Site respectively – and the Western New York Nuclear Service Center in West Valley also hosted a spent nuclear fuel (SNF) reprocessing plant.[8]

The first generation commercial sites adopted the shallow land burial approach utilized at AEC facilities: predominantly excavated trenches with dirt piled on top. Convenience was a major factor in the simple design: trenches could be built near the point of waste generation, reducing transportation costs; and construction employed practices commonly used in sanitary landfill operations that did not require unusual equipment or techniques, making them cost-effective (*Directions in Low-Level Radioactive Waste Management*, 1990, p. 5). However, they proved to be less-than-perfect containment technologies and by 1978 Maxey Flats, Sheffield and West Valley had all been closed.[9] Problems with water accumulation and radionuclide migration were common.[10] Maxey Flats was temporarily closed in 1976 after it was discovered that radioisotopes – including plutonium, strontium and cesium – were migrating from the trenches to other parts of the site. In addition, leachate emissions contaminated local milk supplies, albeit within EPA standards. While the facility reopened, the Kentucky legislature added a large surcharge to waste disposed of at the facility, effectively killing business – 97 percent of the volume of waste going to Maxey Flats was redirected to Sheffield and Barnwell – and US Ecology's license was cancelled in 1977. Maxey Flats is now a Superfund site; that is, a location where hazardous waste is possibly affecting local eco-systems and/or people (Gershey, Klein, Party and Wilkerson 1990, p. 49; EPA 1977, p. 185; EPA updated 2012; Commonwealth of Kentucky, Department of Environmental Protection n.d.). Rising water levels at West Valley required leachate to be pumped into a series of lagoons for treatment and discharge and, in 1975, a release led to the permanent suspension of operations (EPA updated 2011). At Sheffield, the Illinois Department of Public Health observed tritium migration across the site at a rate of 5 feet per day – 600 times faster than predicted when the facility was licensed – although "in concentrations that were measureable but well below the levels thought to be a threat to public health" (GAO 1998, p. 6; Illinois Emergency Management Agency 2009, p. 10). In 1977, operator Nuclear Engineering Co. (NECO) requested a license amendment to construct a new burial trench. The NRC denied the request primarily due to the discovery of highly permeable sand and gravel beneath the proposed trench as well as other trenches (GAO 1998, pp. 43–44). The facility was closed soon after. In a postscript that left a bad taste in everyone's mouth, in 1979 NECO tried to terminate its state and federal licenses and state lease. According to state officials, NECO abandoned the site, leading to rainwater infiltration of the trenches. According to the company, the infiltration resulted from soil instability, melting snow and rain rather than neglect. A decade later, NECO's successor US Ecology was ordered to purchase a buffer zone around the site and conduct remediation and stabilization activities in preparation for closure.

Box 1.1   Beatty, Nevada: 1969–1979

NECO of California, which had experience disposing of LLRW in the Pacific Ocean, was licensed by the AEC in September 1962 to operate the first commercial shallow land disposal facility in the country, 11 miles southeast of Beatty in Nye County, Nevada (Nevada Assembly Bill 444 1961; *Hazardous Materials Management* 1985).

From 1969 to 1976 contaminated tools, pieces of hardware and even dishes were removed from the site by employees for personal use and sale – enough to require 12 pickup truck loads to return the bulk of the material; some heavier items were returned separately. As reported in the *Eugene Register-Guard*: "Among the booty from the dump were 23 steel tanks which contained the contaminated material. . . . The tanks were cut open, the contents distributed and the containers converted into water, septic and storage tanks" ("Nevadans Warned of Exposure to Items Taken from Nuclear Dump" 1976, p. 5A). In March 1976, an anonymous call alerted state officials that concrete slabs for a saloon, a municipal center and several houses were being poured with a mixer from the site. During the investigation, employees admitted to removing material from the site and pouring liquid waste directly into the ground over the previous 8 years (Hastings 1996). The site was closed by the State Health Officer from 8 March to 24 May and three workers lost their jobs (Legislative Commission of the Legislative Counsel Bureau 1980, p. 52). But three incidents in 1979 would prove more consequential.

On the morning of 14 May, a fire broke out in the trailer of a truck parked outside the facility. The cause was "spontaneous heat generated by the chemical reaction involving the absorbent laboratory waste materials packaged in cardboard boxes" (Testimony of Governor Robert List 1979). On 2 July, a truck arrived from Michigan with a leaking payload (Draft of Governor List's Executive Order Relating to Transport of Commercial Low-Level Radioactive Waste 1979). Governor List closed the facility for 2 weeks (*Hazardous Materials Management* 1985, p. 5). Then, on 24 October, List temporarily closed Beatty again after five drums of waste were discovered outside the facility fence ("Revocation Hearing Set for Beatty Dump Site" 1979).

The facility closed for good in 1992. In almost 30 years of operation, roughly 5 million cubic feet of LLRW was buried in unlined trenches. The USGS speculated that elevated tritium concentrations resulted from the direct disposal of liquid waste and the practice of keeping trenches open until filled, but generally poor record-keeping by the operator led USGS to conclude that the full story would never be known (GAO 1998, pp. 46–47, 53).

The year 1979 proved to be the watershed. Hanford and Barnwell were experiencing similar problems to Beatty – in October 1979 Hanford was closed due to "transportation-related noncompliance events" (Washington State Department Ecology Nuclear Waste Program 2010, p. 4). Thus, for a short amount of time (Hanford, like Beatty, reopened in November 1979), Barnwell was the only facility in the country receiving LLRW, triggering fears that the nation might run out of storage capacity and vital medical and industrial processes that generated LLRW would be curtailed (O'Toole 1979, p. 4). Indeed, Congress described the situation as a "national crisis" (Sherman 2011, p. 13).

Given the precarious situation, a slew of task forces were created to come up with solutions. The most important of these were formed by the National Governors Association, the DOE and President Carter's State Planning Council chaired by South Carolina Governor Richard Riley. All of this activity resulted in greater press and public awareness of waste transportation and disposal (Bob List, personal communication, 15 April 2010; Carter 1987, p. 176). It added urgency to the NRC's development of regulations to provide for comprehensive standards, technical criteria and licensing procedures for LLRW transport, storage and disposal.[11] It also led to the creation of a federally mandated, state-based mechanism designed to provide for a fair and equitable solution to LLRW disposal – described in the next chapter.

"Much too small to have any harmful effects on fish or on human life": the United Kingdom and LLRW disposal, 1946–2005[12]

In the UK, the issue of radioactive waste was first addressed through the 1954 Atomic Energy Authority Act and the 1960 Radioactive Substances Act. This legislation enabled the United Kingdom Atomic Energy Authority (UKAEA) to provide a national disposal service for low and intermediate level wastes, which were buried in near-surface facilities, discharged as liquids into rivers (including the Thames) and dumped at sea (United Kingdom Nirex Limited [Nirex] 2002, pp. 1, 3). Just as in the United States, some of the waste designated as 'low level' historically would be considered high level today.

Ocean disposal

Besides the Soviet Union,[13] the UK was the most prolific ocean dumper of radioactive waste, accounting for almost 78 percent of the radioactivity in the Atlantic Ocean resulting from such disposal ("Position Paper on the Implications of Deep Sea Disposal of Radioactive Waste" 2010, p. 5). From 1949 to 1982, an estimated 73,530 tons of radioactive waste were dumped into the northeast Atlantic (Committee on Radioactive Waste Management [CoRWM] 2004, p. 6). For two decades the US and UK marched in lockstep on ocean disposal of radioactive waste. However, as Jacob Hamblin has observed,

> Anglo-American solidarity began to disintegrate during the rise of the environmental movement, as American politicians began to condemn the

practice. . . . Britain continued to defend sea dumping vigorously. By the end of the 1960s, it turned toward continental Europe, promoting joint dumping operations within the Organization for Economic Cooperation and Development's European Nuclear Energy Agency [discussed below] . . . in order to protect practices seen as indispensible to the entire nuclear program.

(Hamblin 2009, p. 8)

Waste packages could be designed either to collapse during descent or upon reaching the sea floor or sit on the sea floor and fail over time. But just as in the United States, ocean disposal was an inexact science and it was not uncommon for waste barrels to survive their journey to the bottom intact or fail to sink at all. For example, in July 1964, the M/V *Halcience* took almost one thousand tons of radioactive waste to a disposal site in the Bay of Biscay. On the first afternoon of dumping, packages – from surgical gloves to small bottles labeled 'U-235' – began appearing on the surface. A frantic rescue mission ensued. As the crew pulled up packages with hooks and buckets, "they became acutely aware of the many Spanish boats who fished in the dumping area throughout the day" (Hamblin 2009, p. 199). Of less concern, barrels sunk at Hurd Deep – a natural trough in the English Channel roughly 560 feet down at its deepest point – were designed to implode at depth (CoRWM 2004, p. 5–6). Belgium also dumped an unspecified number of waste packages at Hurd Deep, in cooperation with the UK, between 1960 and 1962 (IAEA 1999, p. 28, 55). Yet in April 2013, German public broadcaster SWR reported that two intact radioactive waste barrels had been 'discovered' (Kuhrt 2013; "Nuclear Waste Barrels Remain Strewn across Floor of English Channel" 2013).[14] Thus the controversy centered on why the barrels had not collapsed under hydrostatic pressure and how much radioactivity remained. The States of Guernsey issued a press release to clarify disposal operations and reassure the public that the health impacts were negligible (States of Guernsey 2013):

- Authorized disposal took place at the eastern end of Hurd Deep on 14 separate occasions between 1950 and 1963.
- The waste "was packaged in order to facilitate high levels of dispersion of low levels of radiation."
- The disposal site has been monitored since the mid-1960s.
- The 2011 Radioactivity in Food and the Environment (RIFE) Report found that people who consumed "large amounts" of fish and shellfish from the area could be expected to receive 0.5 percent of the dose limit for human exposure, and the impact of French nuclear facilities was less than 1 percent of the dose limit.[15]

Disposal ceased in 1963 because the trough was shallower than the International Atomic Energy Agency's (IAEA) recommended minimum requirement of 2,000 meters (about 6,500 feet). CoRWM estimated that approximately 15,300 tonnes of radioactive waste comprising 14.4 TBq of alpha activity and 41.2 TBq of beta/gamma activity ended up at the bottom of the valley (2004, pp. 5–6).

After 1963, most of these sludges were sent to the facility near the village of Drigg for land disposal. However, CoRWM also stated that contaminated soil, rubble and sludges were dumped in coastal waters from the 1960s through the mid-1970s: "The radioactive material was assumed to be immediately released and dispersed as the waste package approached the seabed" (CoRWM 2004, p. 6).

From 1967 until 1982, the UK increasingly dumped cemented low level wastes in steel drums with other OECD countries – described later (House of Lords 1999, p. 57). In 1983, UK sea disposal was halted when the LDC adopted a voluntary moratorium on dumping radioactive waste in the sea. The moratorium was extended indefinitely in 1985 and a permanent ban was adopted in 1993.

Land disposal

While effective public opposition to the siting of nuclear facilities in any country was rare during the early postwar years, in 1954 the UKAEA was forced to abandon a plan to store waste in abandoned mines in the Forest of Dean near Wales due to local resistance (Hamblin 2009, p. 63). Siting went more smoothly further north in Cumbria several years later, where a national LLRW disposal repository has been operating at a brown field site on the coast of the Irish Sea near the village of Drigg since 1959. Originally an ordnance factory, the facility received higher activity waste from the Atomic Energy Research Establishment at Harwell and the neighboring Windscale plutonium production facility, then piped it out into the Irish Sea (Hamblin 2009, p. 43).[16]

In 1957, Millom District Council granted the UKAEA permission to dispose of low level waste at the repository near the village of Drigg.[17] Waste was buried in clay-based trenches capped off with dirt and stones. In 1988, an engineered concrete vault was opened. The upgrade was finalized in 1995 with the completion of a waste monitoring and compaction facility at Sellafield and a grouting facility at the repository near Drigg. Solid waste is compacted and placed in engineered concrete vaults infilled with a cement grout then buried in engineered trenches "with a mixture of grass and shrubs in keeping with the natural environment" (Nuclear Decommissioning Authority [NDA] 2013; Low Level Waste Repository Ltd. n.d.). Since 1959, about 35 million cubic feet of LLW has been consigned to the repository near Drigg (NDA 2013a).[18]

However, as early as the 1980s it was recognized that capacity at the facility near Drigg was limited and standard volume reduction technologies were deemed either not appropriate or not properly tested. This, coupled with remoteness from many of the nuclear establishments, led the government to begin a search for additional LLRW disposal sites (Nirex 2002, p. 3).[19]

Following the announcement of the sea disposal moratorium, the Nuclear Industry Radioactive Waste Executive (Nirex) adopted the 'announce and defend' approach that had sufficed for nuclear power plant siting, and selected a clay site at a former electricity generating depot in Elstow and a disused anhydrite mine in Billingham as potential sites for the disposal of LLRW/

short-lived intermediate level radioactive waste (ILRW) and long-lived ILRW respectively (Curd 1993, p. 277). The government halted the investigation at Billingham in early 1985 as a result of local community opposition – memorably, in December 1984 a delegation from Billingham Against Nuclear Dumping that included a local member of parliament (MP) dressed as Santa Claus travelled to Number 10 Downing Street to deliver Christmas cards to Prime Minister Thatcher and Environment Secretary Patrick Jenkin (Levett 2013). A year later, the search was expanded to include sites in Bradwell, Fulbeck and Killingholme. Then in 1986, the government determined, based on input from the House of Commons Environment Committee as well as what they were hearing from community residents, that "a near-surface site should only be used for what is broadly described as low-level wastes" (Nirex 2005, pp. 2–3).

On 1 May 1987, the Secretary of State for the Environment announced that, based largely on economics, a deep multipurpose repository for low and intermediate waste was the government's preferred solution. As Curd has observed, public concern – the strong opposition at each of the locations is sometimes referred to as 'The Four-Sites Saga' (Kemp 1992, pp. 42–47) – prompted industry to develop "higher and higher standards, more and more redundancy in systems and higher and higher costs." This, combined with the House of Commons Environmental Committee's demand for a 'Rolls-Royce' solution, "eventually made the project uneconomic" (Curd 1993, p. 277).

In order to promote public consultation, Nirex released more than 50,000 copies of *The Way Forward – A Discussion Document* in November 1987 to local authorities, county associations, parish and town councils, county and district libraries and hundreds of organizations in England, Wales and Scotland, as well as members of the European Parliament. National advertising was undertaken, briefings were held and more than 2,500 responses were received.[20]

By 1989, Nirex had selected two sites, one at Sellafield in England and one at Dounreay in Scotland, for investigation "on the basis that there was a measure of local support for nuclear activities in the local communities around those sites" (Nirex 2005, p. 4).[21] In 1992, Nirex announced its intention to construct an underground Rock Characterization Facility (RCF) at Longlands Farm near Sellafield to demonstrate the viability of the geology – volcanic rock – for the permanent disposal of radioactive waste. Preliminary geological investigations concluded that both sites were suitable but Nirex opted for Sellafield in part because of expected local support and in part because it was estimated at the time that 60 percent of the wastes to be buried at the repository would be generated on site (Nirex 2005, p. 15). However, the Cumbria County Council refused to grant planning permission for the experimental shafts to be sunk. Nirex appealed and a public inquiry was held from September 1995 to February 1996. In November 1996, the inspector of the public inquiry recommended that Nirex's appeal be dismissed, and on 17 March 1997 the Secretary of State for the Environment made the dismissal official (Inspector's Report 1996; NDA n.d.). Underlying this decision "were concerns about the process by which the

Sellafield site had been selected and about the suitability of the site itself"
(House of Lords 1999). In 2005, Nirex would confess:

> The site selection exercise initiated in 1987 implied a bottom-up process
> whereby . . . the "best sites" would be identified against a range of evalua-
> tion criteria, or attributes. However the logic changed part of the way
> through the exercise to a top-down process, so that sites were identified for
> investigation on the basis that there was a measure of local support for
> nuclear activities.
>
> (Nirex 2005, p. 20)

Indeed, prior to 2005, government policy was to not publish sites considered
for selection as disposal facility hosts (with the exception of Dounreay and
Sellafield) so as to "prevent blight affecting any of the areas." This changed
when the 2004 Environmental Information Regulations and 2005 Freedom of
Information Act came into force, emphasizing openness and transparency. "We
believe that the [former] process used was technically sound, but it was conducted
in secret and did not involve stakeholders, therefore it was not a legitimate
process" (Nirex 2005, p. ii).

"A large dilution sink": OECD/NEA collaborative ocean disposal operations, 1967–1982[22]

The US, USSR/Russia, UK, Belgium, France, Germany, Italy, Netherlands,
Sweden, Switzerland, Japan, South Korea and New Zealand have publicly
declared that they disposed of LLRW in the ocean (IAEA 1999, p. 12).[23]
A subset of these countries, under the aegis of the OECD's Nuclear Energy
Agency (NEA), took part in an experimental low and medium level radioactive waste dumping program in the eastern Atlantic Ocean from 1967 to
1982. In the summer of 1967, five countries dumped approximately 36,000
drums of solid waste totaling roughly 300 TBq of radioactivity at a depth
of 16,400 feet (Coordinated Research and Environmental Surveillance
Programme [CRESP] Related to Sea Disposal of Radioactive Waste 1996, p. 11).
Dumping took place almost every subsequent year in the same region – from
1974 to 1982 all dumping took place at a single site about 15,400 feet deep
and 340 miles off the European continental shelf (Calmet 1989, pp. 47, 49)[24] –
"with the progressive cessation of purely *national* dumping operations"
(CRESP 1996, pp. 11–12). The waste packages used for NEA disposal
operations were constructed to reach the bottom intact but they were not
designed to maintain structural integrity for "tens of years" ("Position Paper"
2010, p. 6).

In 1983, the Contracting Parties to the London Convention agreed to a
voluntary moratorium on dumping operations and a ban on sea disposal of
radioactive waste was approved by the same parties in 1993, thus terminating
the NEA program (CRESP 1996, pp. 11–15; Calmet 1989). The final report

on the program concluded that dumping operations posed "negligible human radiological risk" but cautioned that the absence of baseline data made drawing firm conclusions about environmental impacts difficult ("Position Paper" 2010, p. 6).[25] According to the IAEA, dedicated surveillance of disposal operations resulted in "a greatly improved data base, a better understanding of deep ocean dynamics and transport, and more comprehensive and site-specific models for calculation of doses to people and the marine biota" (Hagen and Ruegger 1986, p. 32).

"The biggest environmental scandal in postwar German history": Asse II

In 1965, the West German government contracted to develop a pilot waste disposal facility at Asse II (a former potash and rock salt mine close to the border of East and West Germany in Lower Saxony) and trial waste emplacement began in 1967. The words 'trial' and 'pilot' are crucial because by 1971, the facility was "no longer used as trial storage . . . but was used as [a] repository" for West Germany's low and intermediate level waste (Federal Office for Radiation Protection [Germany] 2012). Thus only 4 years after experimental operations commenced, the surrounding community was presented with the fait accompli of a permanent waste disposal site. From 1967 to 1978, Asse II received an estimated 125,787 drums and other LLRW and ILRW packages at a depth of roughly 2,500 feet (Federal Office for Radiation Protection [Germany] 2012).

Waste disposal practices were somewhat primitive: "In order to keep the radiation dose at a minimum, the drums were unloaded in a hurry. The medium-level drums were thrown through an opening on the -490m mine level into chambers on the -511m level" (Schwartz 2010). Compounding this problem, record-keeping was poor, meaning that authorities were not sure how much and what sorts of radioactivity had been buried, and no thought had been given to the eventual decommissioning of the site.

In 2007, after the chambers had started collapsing and groundwater had begun flowing into the mine (with the possibility of "uncontrolled penetration of groundwater" [Federal Office for Radiation Protection (Germany) 2012]), the operator proposed flooding the mine with a magnesium chloride solution, sparking public protests and an official investigation and ushering in what *Der Spiegel* described as "the biggest environmental scandal in postwar German history" (Frölingsdorf, Ludwig and Weinzierl 2013).

After considering several options, including backfilling the chambers and placing the waste deeper in the mine, the Federal Office for Radiation Protection decided to retrieve the waste and move everything to a location to be determined, an undertaking Nuclear Engineering International has described as "highly ambitious" and "without precedent" (Schwartz 2010). There is evidence, however, that Asse II might end up being the waste's final resting place after all (Frölingsdorf et al. 2013).

Conclusion

So how do we take stock of historical LLRW dumping practices? First, 'low level' is a loose characterization of the types of radioactive waste involved. Everything from slightly radioactive rags to weapons plutonium was buried on land or dumped at sea under the guise of LLRW. Scientific studies cannot deliver definitive proof of the consequences of disposal operations and poor record-keeping ensures that complete reconciliations by disposal authorities can never be provided – and even if they could, it is not clear that an appreciable increase in public trust would result.

Second, regardless of the findings of some important official multinational scientific investigations, the public perception and international consensus is that ocean disposal is not a good idea. For example, at the London Dumping Convention's 1986 Consultative Meeting an International Panel of Experts on Radioactive Waste Disposal (IPGRAD) was established to consider LLRW disposal at sea holistically. IPGRAD divided the task into two working groups: the first focused on political, legal, economic and social aspects, and the second on scientific and technical issues. The working groups reported back to contracting parties at the 1993 Consultative Meeting. The conclusions of the scientific and technical working groups were "ambiguous," reflecting the participants' divergent views regarding the efficacy of sea disposal. Yet,

> none of the technical evidence presented to the IPGRAD working group in the seven years of its existence indicated that any significant radiological impact has resulted or would result from properly conducted sea disposal of solid low-level radioactive wastes in accordance with IAEA recommendations.
> (Sjöblom and Linsley 1994, p. 15)

"Properly conducted" is a very important qualifier. As we have seen, particularly during the early decades of the nuclear age, countries improperly conducted disposal operations, whether due to insufficient technical knowledge of radioactivity (which does not imply nefariousness but may suggest a degree of recklessness on the part of decision-makers) or less innocent motives. Despite this, it is almost inconceivable that the London Convention will again be amended to allow ocean disposal of even LLRW. Similarly, in 1988, when the University of East Anglia analyzed responses to Nirex's *The Way Forward* questionnaire, it found little support for disposal offshore or on an island based on a general concern that radioactive contamination of the sea be avoided (Curd 1993, p. 278). While the science of dilution and dispersion might be sound, the optics are awful. It is interesting to note that a fundamental misunderstanding about ocean disposal persists today. A December 2013 story in the *Wall Street Journal* makes several references to container leakage, using phrases such as "despite some leakage" and "indications of leakage" (Emshwiller and Searcey 2013). As described previously, many containers were designed to disperse their contents either during their descent or once they reached their final resting place.

Third, land disposal is the accepted approach despite a troubled past based in large part on lack of knowledge. Scientific evidence that a disposal practice is safe, or lack of evidence that a practice has deleterious effects, is often not enough to convince a skeptical public that it is safe enough. And some regulations – for example, radionuclide migration at Maxey Flats resulting in the contamination of local milk supplies fell 'within EPA standards' – were technical distinctions understandably lost on most in the affected communities. Problems at many disposal sites persist: several former LLRW disposal locations in the United States are now Superfund sites; the structural integrity of the UK's Drigg disposal site is slowly being threatened by erosion from rising sea levels; and the chambers of Germany's Asse II facility have started collapsing and leaking. Indeed, the fact that companies constructing disposal facilities in the 1980s and 1990s (in the United States, UK and France, for example) needed to explain to potential host communities that technical advances had been made that would avoid the mistakes of the past indicated how problematic the legacy was and provided an effective weapon for opponents to wield in siting fights.

Fourth, and linking to all of the points above, the lack of scientific certainty regarding the effects of low level radiation and difficulty establishing a causal link between radionuclide releases and illnesses such as cancer all contribute to the sense of unease amongst nonexperts.

This less-than-perfect disposal history, combined with the general fear of radiation discussed in the introduction, has made finding willing host communities for LLRW disposal a challenging undertaking. We now turn to the successes and failures of five countries, focusing predominantly on the period between the 1980s and the present.

Notes

1 Colombo and Kendig 1990, p. 1.
2 For more on the troubled history of operations at Hanford see GAO 1981; DOE 2013; DOE n.d.; Cary 2013a; Cary 2013b; State of Washington, Department of Ecology n.d.
3 The Atlantic Ocean container number does not include unpackaged waste dumped south of Morehead City, North Carolina, and liquid waste dumped 36 feet off the coast of Sapelo Island, Georgia.
4 As discussed in chapter 4, the Mexican government had a long memory. Explaining his opposition to a proposed LLRW disposal facility in Sierra Blanca in 1998, Senator Mario Saucedo noted that the United States had endangered Mexican safety in the past, most notably by dumping radioactive waste into the Gulf of Mexico (Betancourt 1998, p. 15).
5 The authors would like to thank National Oceanic and Atmospheric Administration (NOAA) oceanographer Dr. Frank Schwing, who was a principal investigator on a joint EPA–US Navy survey of the Farallon dumping area, for discussing the program and bringing important source material to their attention.
6 IAEA guidance included requirements for the selection of disposal sites, the conditioning and packaging of wastes, and the ships transporting the wastes to the disposal sites (Hagen and Ruegger 1986, p. 32).
7 The AEC was responsible for both the development of nuclear power and its regulation. This conflict of interest led Congress to abolish the Commission in 1974 and create an independent regulatory agency (the NRC).

8 For more on the brief and troubled reprocessing operation see GAO 2001.

9 Some sites featured multiple disposal technologies – for example, trenches, above-ground tanks, hot wells for high-activity gamma sources and special pits for larger volumes of higher activity wastes were all used at Maxey Flats (*Directions in Low-Level Radioactive Waste Management* 1990, p. 23).

10 As described by the EPA, the average burial trench at these commercial sites was 300 feet long by 40 feet wide by 25 feet deep with a volume of about 340,000 cubic feet (GAO 1981, p. 184). Detailed descriptions of all six sites can be found in *Directions in Low-Level Radioactive Waste Management* 1990, pp. 15–60.

11 The Commission would issue this guidance in December 1982 as 10 CFR Part 61, which included the creation of the four-tiered (A, B, C and Greater-Than-Class-C) waste classification system.

12 Hamblin 2009, p. 27.

13 As late as 1989, Moscow was publicly claiming that it did not dump radioactive waste into the oceans (Hamblin 2009). In fact, dumping was an integral part of the Soviet nuclear weapons program ever since it got underway in the late 1940s. The lie was fully exposed in 1993 with the publication of Facts and Problems Related to Radioactive Waste Disposal in Seas Adjacent to the Territory of the Russian Federation, commissioned by President Yeltsin. According to the IAEA, the USSR/Russia accounted for almost 60% of the radioactivity disposed of in the Pacific Ocean and the entirety of radioactivity disposed of in the Arctic Ocean (IAEA 1999, p. 16). Solid and liquid wastes of varying radioactivity were dumped into the Arctic, Pacific and the Gulf of Finland. The USSR became a party to the LDC in 1976 but continued to dump all levels of waste into the Pacific and northwest Atlantic. Dumping operations were carried out in zones of the oceans not approved by the IAEA and at lesser depths than recommended by the Agency. After the collapse of the Soviet Union, Russia continued to dump LLRW. Infamously, in October 1993 a Russian Navy tanker was spotted by Japanese television cameras releasing 900 tons of liquid waste into the Sea of Japan (Sanger 1993). On Soviet land disposal practices see Nikipelov, Suslov and Tsarenko 1997; Bradley 1997; GlobalSecurity.org updated 2011.

14 Greenpeace had conducted a more extensive survey of the area in 2000 (Kirby 2002).

15 The French facilities are the spent fuel reprocessing plant at La Hague and the two power reactors at Flamanville. A third reactor is being built at Flamanville and is scheduled to begin operation in 2016 ("Flamanville Costs Up €2 Billion" 2012).

16 In October 1957, a fire in the core of one of the two plutonium-producing reactors at Windscale (which reverted to its original name of Sellafield in 1981) burned for several days and sent a plume of cesium, iodine and polonium across Britain and northern Europe; radiation was detected in Belgium, Germany and Norway (McKie 2007; Highfield 2007).

17 Disposal facilities are often referred to by the name of the nearest town, such as Beatty and Hanford. The local community in Drigg objected to this shorthand, which is why the repository is not mentioned colloquially as 'Drigg' by the UK government. This convention is respected by the authors.

18 Controlled burials of short half-lived waste also took place at municipal dumps throughout the UK. For example, two sites in Northern Ireland – Duncrue Street in north Belfast and Culmore Point outside Derry – received hospital, university and industrial (from fertilizer plants) waste in the late 1970s and early 1980s (Phoenix 2013; "No Threat from Radioactive Waste Dumping at Culmore" 2014).

19 According to a report by the UK Environment Agency, the structural integrity of the disposal facility is being threatened by erosion caused by rising sea levels and is "virtually certain" to leak within "a few hundred to a few thousand years from now" (Edwards 2014).

20 According to Nirex, while there was "no overall unanimity of view," some positive responses came from Sellafield, Cumbria and the Caithness area of the Highland

38   *A short history*

Region of Scotland (although the Caithness District Council would later withdraw its invitation to investigate the area) (Nirex 2005, pp. 4–5; Curd 1993, p. 278).

21 Sellafield (like the repository near Drigg, formerly a World War II ordnance factory) was the site of plutonium production for the British nuclear weapons program and it is where UK commercial reprocessing takes place. The Dounreay Nuclear Power Development Establishment included three reactors (two of which were fast breeders), fuel fabrication and reprocessing facilities. The site is in the process of being decommissioned.

22 Calmet 1989, p. 47.

23 A 2005 IAEA report estimates that the Northeast Atlantic is the most contaminated part of the world's oceans but not because of radioactive waste dumping; rather because of a combination of fallout from nuclear tests, discharges from SNF reprocessing operations and releases from the Chernobyl accident (IAEA 2005, p. 16).

24 In 1978, the Greenpeace ship *Rainbow Warrior* followed an NEA dumping operation – the same *Rainbow Warrior* that was sunk by French intelligence on 10 July 1985, while berthed in Auckland, to prevent interference in a planned series of nuclear tests on Mururoa Atoll (Hamblin 2009, p. 253).

25 In 1985, CRESP determined that from a radiological perspective, the site was suitable for dumping over the next 5 years at rates no more than 10 times the average of 1978 to 1982 (Hagen and Ruegger 1986, pp. 29, 32).

References

Abbott, H., and Davies, E., "Management and Retrieval of Historical Nuclear Waste Previously Prepared and Concrete for Sea Disposal," *Waste Management 2002 Conference*, Tucson, Arizona (24–28 February 2002), www.wmsym.org/archives/2002/Proceedings/43/291.pdf

Allardice, C., and Trapnell, E., *The Atomic Energy Commission* (New York: Praeger, 1974).

Betancourt, A., "Border Skirmish," *Bulletin of the Atomic Scientists*, Vol. 54, No. 3 (1998): 14–16.

Bradley, D., *Behind the Nuclear Curtain: Radioactive Waste Management in the Former Soviet Union*, ed. D.R. Payson (Columbus, OH: Battelle Press, 1997).

Burns, M.E., *Low-Level Radioactive Waste Regulation: Science, Politics and Fear* (Chelsea, MI: Lewis, 1998).

Calmet, D., "Ocean Disposal of Radioactive Waste: Status Report," *IAEA Bulletin*, Vol. 31, No. 4 (1989): 47–49, www.iaea.org/Publications/Magazines/Bulletin/Bull314/31404684750.pdf

Camper, L., "Low-Level Radioactive Waste Management in the United States: Where Have We Been: Where Are We Going," *Waste Management 2010 Conference*, Phoenix, Arizona (7–11 March 2010), www.wmsym.org/archives/2010/pdfs/10417.pdf

Carter, L., *Nuclear Imperatives and Public Trust: Dealing with Radioactive Waste* (Washington, DC: Resources for the Future, 1987).

Cary, A., "DOE Says Just 1, Not 6, Hanford Single-Shell Tanks Leaking," *Tri-City Herald* (6 November 2013a), www.tri-cityherald.com/2013/11/06/2661413/doe-says-just-1-not-6-handford.html

Cary, A., "Hanford Radioactive Leak May Have Been Transfer System," *Tri-City Herald* (22 August 2013b), www.tri-cityherald.com/2013/08/22/2534379/hanford-tank-farm-evacuated-for.html

Casey, S., *The Devil's Teeth* (New York: Henry Holt, 2005).

Central Interstate Low-Level Radioactive Waste Compact, Pub. L. No. 99–240, 99 Stat. 1864 (15 January 1986), www.cillrwcc.org/PL99–240-CICsection.pdf

Colombo, P., and Kendig, M. W., *Analysis and Evaluation of A Radioactive Waste Package Retrieved from the Farallon Islands 900-Meter Disposal Site*, EPA-520/1–90–014 (September 1990), www.epa.gov/nscep/index.html

Committee on Radioactive Waste Management, *Sea Disposal: A Report by NNC Limited*, CoRWM Document No. 624 (August 2004).

Commonwealth of Kentucky, Department of Environmental Protection, *Maxey Flats Project* (n.d.), http://waste.ky.gov/SFB/Pages/MaxeyFlatsProject.aspx

Convention on the Prevention of Marine Pollution by Dumping Wastes and Other Matter (29 December 1972), www.gc.noaa.gov/documents/gcil_lc.pdf

Coordinated Research and Environmental Surveillance Programme Related to Sea Disposal of Radioactive Waste, *CRESP Final Report, 1981–1995* (Paris: OECD, 1996), www.oecd-nea.org/rwm/reports/1996/CRESP-1981-1995.pdf

Curd, P. J., "The Development of the Sellafield Repository Project Communications Program," *Waste Management 1993 Conference*, Tucson, Arizona (28 February–4 March 1993).

Davis, L., "Fallout: Newly Released Documents Indicate the Navy Dumped Far More Nuclear Waste Than It's Ever Acknowledged in a Major Commercial Fishery Just 30 Miles West of San Francisco. Why Won't the Government Even Study the Farallon Islands Nuclear Waste Site?" *SF Weekly* (9 May 2001), www.sfweekly.com/2001–05–09/news/fallout/

Department of the Navy, History and Heritage Command, *Operations Crossroads: Fact Sheet* (undated), www.history.navy.mil/faqs/faq76–1.htm

Directions in Low-Level Radioactive Waste Management: A Brief History of Commercial Low-Level Radioactive Waste Disposal, prepared at the Idaho National Engineering Laboratory by the National Low-Level Waste Management Program for the Department of Energy, DOE/LLW-103 (10 January 1990), www.osti.gov/scitech/servlets/purl/6161759

Draft of Governor List's Executive Order Relating to Transport of Commercial Low-Level Radioactive Waste (10 July 1979), GOV-0820, File #33, Governor Robert List Records, Nevada State Archives.

Edwards, R., "Cumbrian Nuclear Dump 'Virtually Certain' to Be Eroded by Rising Sea Levels," *Guardian* (20 April 2014), www.theguardian.com/environment/2014/apr/20/choice-cumbria-nuclear-dump-mistake-environment-agency

Emshwiller, J., and Searcey, D., "Nuclear Waste Sits on Ocean Floor: U.S. Has Few Answers on How to Handle Atomic Waste It Dumped in the Sea," *Wall Street Journal* (31 December 2013).

Federal Office for Radiation Protection (Germany), "From Salt Dome to Nuclear Repository: The Eventful History of the Asse II Mine" (16 October 2012), www.endlager-asse.de/EN/2_WhatIs/History/_node.html

"Flamanville Costs Up €2 Billion," *World Nuclear News* (4 December 2012), www.world-nuclear-news.org/NN-Flamanville_costs_up_2_billion_Euros-0412127.html

Fröhlingsdorf, M., Ludwig, U., and Weinzierl, A., "Abyss of Uncertainty: Germany's Homemade Nuclear Waste Disaster," *Der Spiegel* (21 February 2013), www.spiegel.de/international/germany/germany-weighs-options-for-handling-nuclear-waste-in-asse-mine-a-884523.html

General Accounting Office, *Hazards of Past Low-Level Radioactive Waste Ocean Dumping Have Been Overemphasized*, EMD-82-9 (21 October 1981), www.gao.gov/assets/140/135757.pdf

General Accounting Office, *Low-Level Radioactive Waste: Disposal Availability Adequate in the Short Term, but Oversight Needed to Identify Any Future Shortfalls*, GAO-04–604 (June 2004), www.gao.gov/new.items/d04604.pdf

General Accounting Office, *Nuclear Waste: Agreement Among Agencies Responsible for the West Valley Site Is Critically Needed*, GAO-01–314 (May 2001), www.gao.gov/new.items/d01314.pdf

General Accounting Office, *Radioactive Waste: Answers to Questions Related to the Proposed Ward Valley Low-Level Radioactive Waste Disposal Facility*, GAO/RCED-98–40R (22 May 1998), www.gao.gov/assets/90/87895.pdf

Gershey, E., Klein, R., Party, E., and Wilkerson, A., *Low-Level Radioactive Waste: From Cradle to Grave* (New York: Van Nostrand Reinhold, 1990).

GlobalSecurity.org, *Weapons of Mass Destruction (WMD): Krasnoyarsk/Zheleznogorsk Mining and Chemical Combine* (updated 8 February 2011), www.globalsecurity.org/wmd/world/russia/krasnoyarsk-26_nuc.htm

Hagen, A., and Ruegger, B., "Deep-Sea Disposal: Scientific Bases to Control Pollution," *IAEA Bulletin*, Vol. 28, No. 1 (1986): 29–32, www.iaea.org/Publications/Magazines/Bulletin/Bull281/28104682932.pdf

Hamblin, J.D., *Poison in the Well: Radioactive Waste in the Oceans at the Dawn of the Nuclear Age* (New Brunswick, NJ: Rutgers University Press, 2009).

Hastings, D., "Firm's History of Safety Violations Fuels Fears in Ward Valley," *Los Angeles Times* (28 April 1996), http://articles.latimes.com/1996–04–28/local/me-63660_1_ward-valley

Hazardous Materials Management – Chemical, Toxic and Low-Level Radioactive Wastes: An Overview of the State of Nevada Program, Memorandum from Donald Bayer, Senior Research Analyst, Radioactive Waste Program (25 September 1985).

Highfield, R., "Windscale Fire: 'We Were Too Busy to Panic,' " *Telegraph* (9 October 2007), www.telegraph.co.uk/science/science-news/3309842/Windscale-fire-We-were-too-busy-to-panic.html

House of Lords, Select Committee on Science and Technology Third Report, *Management of Nuclear Waste* (10 March 1999), www.parliament.the-stationery-office.co.uk/pa/ld199899/ldselect/ldsctech/41/4103.htm

Illinois Emergency Management Agency, *Site History and Environmental Monitoring Report for Sheffield Low-Level Radioactive Waste Disposal Site* (October 2009), www.state.il.us/iema/environmental/pdfs/SheffieldReport.pdf

Inspector's Report, *Cumbria County Council, Appeal by United Kingdom Nirex Limited*, File No. APP1H09001M9412470 19 (21 November 1996), www.westcumbriamrws.org.uk/documents/Inspectors_Report.doc

International Atomic Energy Agency, *Inventory of Radioactive Waste Disposals at Sea*, IAEA TECDOC-1105 (August 1999), www-pub.iaea.org/MTCD/publications/PDF/te_1105_prn.pdf

International Atomic Energy Agency, "Radiological Assessment: Waste Disposal in the Arctic Seas," *IAEA Bulletin*, Vol. 39, No. 1 (1997): 21–28, www.iaea.org/Publications/Magazines/Bulletin/Bull391/specialreport.html

International Atomic Energy Agency, *Worldwide Marine Radioactivity Studies (WOMARS): Radionuclide Levels in Oceans and Seas*, IAEA-TECDOC-1429 (January 2005), www-pub.iaea.org/MTCD/publications/PDF/TE_1429_web.pdf

International Maritime Organization, *London Convention Protocol* (2013), www.imo.org/OurWork/Environment/SpecialProgrammesAndInitiatives/Pages/London-Convention-and-Protocol.aspx

Jones, D. G., Roberts, P. D., Limburg, J., Karl, H., Chin, J. L., Shanks, W. C., . . . Howard, D., *Measurement of Seafloor Radioactivity at the Farallon Islands Radioactive Waste Dump Site, California,* United States Department of the Interior/United States Geological Survey, Open-File Report 01–62 (2001), http://pubs.usgs.gov/of/2001/of01-062/OFR_01_062.pdf

Karl, H. A., Schwab, W. C., Drake, D. E., and Chin, J. L., *Detection of Barrels That Contain Low-Level Radioactive Waste in Farallon Island Radioactive Waste Dumpsite Using Side-Scan Sonar and Underwater-Optical Systems – Preliminary Interpretation of Barrel Distribution,* United States Department of the Interior/United States Geological Survey, Open-File Report 92–178 (January 1992), http://pubs.usgs.gov/of/1992/0178/report.pdf

Kemp, R., *The Politics of Radioactive Waste Disposal* (Manchester: Manchester University Press, 1992).

Kerr, G. W., "The Evolvement of Federal/State Relationships in the Regulation of Low-Level Radioactive Wastes," *Waste Management 1982 Conference,* Tucson, Arizona (28 February–4 March 1982), http://wmsym.org/archives/1982/V1/8.pdf

Kirby, A., "Nuclear Dumping Leak Sparks Concern," *BBC News* (17 January 2002), http://news.bbc.co.uk/2/hi/science/nature/1766365.stm

Knipe, C., *UK Nirex – 1995/96 Public Inquiry into the Proposed Construction of a "Rock Characterisation Facility" (Underground Rock Laboratory) at Longlands Farm Near Sellafield, Cumbria* (n.d.), www.jpb.co.uk/nirexinquiry/nirex.htm

Kuhrt, N., "Nuclear Waste Barrels Litter English Channel," *Spiegel Online* (12 April 2013), www.spiegel.de/international/europe/legacy-danger-old-nuclear-waste-found-in-english-channel-a-893991.html

Legislative Commission of the Legislative Counsel Bureau, *Transportation and Disposal of Radioactive Material,* Bulletin No. 81–6 (October 1980), www.leg.state.nv.us/Division/Research/Publications/InterimReports/1981/Bulletin81–06.pdf

Levesque, W. R., "USS *Calhoun County* Sailors Dumped Thousands of Tons of Radioactive Waste into Ocean," *Tampa Bay Times* (20 December 2013), www.tampabay.com/news/military/veterans/the-atomic-sailors/2157927

Levett, A., "Santa Went Ballistic over Nuclear Dump," *Hartlepool Mail* (17 December 2013), www.hartlepoolmail.co.uk/news/nostalgia/santa-went-ballistic-over-nuclear-dump-1–6306213

Low Level Waste Repository Ltd., "History" (n.d.), http://llwrsite.com/our-company/history/

Mazuzan, G. T., and Walker, J. S, *Controlling the Atom: The Beginnings of Nuclear Regulation, 1946–1962* (Berkeley: University of California Press, 1984).

McKie, R., "Windscale Radiation 'Doubly Dangerous,' " *Guardian* (7 October 2007), www.theguardian.com/science/2007/oct/07/nuclearpower

National Academy of Sciences, National Research Council, *Radioactive Waste Disposal into Atlantic and Gulf Coastal Waters,* Publication 655, Washington, DC (1959), https://ia600407.us.archive.org/33/items/radioactivewaste00nati/radioactivewaste00nati.pdf

Nevada Assembly Bill 444 (1961), www.leg.state.nv.us/Division/Research/Library/Leg History/LHs/pre1965/AB444,1961.pdf

"Nevadans Warned of Exposure to Items Taken from Nuclear Dump," *Eugene Register-Guard* (16 March 1976).

Newberry, W. F., "The Rise and Fall and Rise and Fall of American Public Policy on Disposal of Low-Level Radioactive Waste," *South Carolina Environmental Law Journal* (Winter 1993).

Nikipelov, B. V., Suslov, A. P., and Tsarenko, A. F., "Radioactive Waste Management in the USSR: Experience and Perspective," *Waste Management 1997 Conference*, Tucson, Arizona (23–27 February 1997), www.wmsym.org/archives/1990/V1/7.pdf

"No Threat From Radioactive Waste Dumping at Culmore," *Derry Daily* (4 January 2014), www.derrydaily.net/2014/01/04/no-threat-from-radioactive-waste-dumping-at-culmore/

Nuclear Decommissioning Authority, "LLW Repository Near Drigg" (2013a), www.nda. gov.uk/ukinventory/sites/LLW_Repository_near_Drigg/

Nuclear Decommissioning Authority, "Radioactive Waste Inventory" (reported 1 April 2013b), www.nda.gov.uk/ukinventory/

Nuclear Decommissioning Authority, *Sellafield Geological and Hydrogeological Investigations: A Synthesis of Data Used to Assess the Hydraulic Character of the Sherwood Sandstone Group at Sellafield*, Report No. S (n.d.), www.nda.gov.uk/documents/biblio/detail. cfm?fuseaction=search.view_doc&doc_id=2500

"Nuclear Waste Barrels Remain Strewn across Floor of English Channel," *RT.com* (12 April 2013), http://rt.com/news/nuclear-waste-english-channel-785/

Office of Technology Assessment, *Nuclear Wastes in the Arctic: An Analysis of Arctic and Other Regional Impacts from Soviet Nuclear Contamination*, OTA-ENV-632 (September 1995), http://ota.fas.org/reports/9504.pdf

O'Toole, T., "A Dump Closing Threatens to Halt Cancer Research," *Washington Post* (24 October 1979).

Petrella, M. E., "Wasting Away Again: Facing the Low-Level Radioactive Waste Debacle in the United States," *Fordham Environmental Law Review*, Vol. 5, No. 1 (2011).

Phoenix, E., "NI State Papers: Files Reveal Secret Dumping of Radioactive Waste," *BBC News* (28 December 2013), www.bbc.co.uk/news/uk-northern-ireland-25470028

"Position Paper on the Implications of Deep Sea Disposal of Radioactive Waste," RSC 10/4/3-E, OSPAR Convention for the Protection of the Marine Environment of the North-East Atlantic, Meeting of the Radioactive Substances Committee, Stockholm (20–23 April 2010), www.swr.de/report/-/id=8816210/property=download/nid=233454/ 1117ugb/ospar-position-paper.pdf

Radian Corp., *Preliminary Assessment Report: Farallon Islands FUDS*, submitted to U.S. Army Corps of Engineers (June 1996), www.corpsfuds.net/reports/OTHER/J09CA7067 finalPAJune96.pdf

"Radioactive Leakage: Berlin Takes Steps to Address Nuclear Waste Scandal," *Der Spiegel* (4 September 2008), www.spiegel.de/international/germany/radioactive-leakage-berlin-takes-steps-to-address-nuclear-waste-scandal-a-576362.html

"Revocation Hearing Set for Beatty Dump Site," *Nevada State Journal* (14 November 1979) in Governor Robert List Records, Nevada State Archives.

Sanger, D., "Nuclear Material Dumped Off Japan," *New York Times* (19 October 1993a), www.nytimes.com/1993/10/19/world/nuclear-material-dumped-off-japan.html

Schwartz, M., "Clearing out Asse 2," *Nuclear Engineering International* (24 August 2010), www.neimagazine.com/features/featureclearing-out-asse-2

Sherman, D., *Not Here, Not There, Not Anywhere: Politics, Social Movements, and the Disposal of Low-Level Radioactive Waste* (Washington, DC: Resources for the Future, 2011).

"Shocked by State Radioactive Dump, Proponent Changes Mind," *Nevada State Journal* (1 April 1976).

Sjöblom, K.-L., and Linsley, G., "Sea Disposal of Radioactive Wastes: The London Convention 1972," *IAEA Bulletin*, Vol. 36, No. 2 (1994): 12–16, www.iaea.org/Publications/ Magazines/Bulletin/Bull362/36205981216.pdf

Sobelev, I. A., Ojovan, M. I., and Karlina, O. K., "Management of Spent Radiation Sources at Regional Facilities 'RADON' in Russian Federation," *Waste Management 2001 Conference*, Tucson, Arizona (25 February–1 March 2001), www.wmsym.org/archives/2001/39/39–7.pdf

State of Washington, Department of Ecology, *Nuclear Waste – Frequently Asked Questions: Leaking Underground Tanks at Hanford* (n.d.), www.ecy.wa.gov/programs/nwp/sections/tankwaste/closure/pages/tank_leak_FAQ.html

States of Guernsey, "Radiation Levels in the Hurd Deep Are Regularly Monitored" (26 April 2013), www.gov.gg/article/107407/Radiation-levels-in-the-Hurd-Deep-are-regularly-monitored

Testimony of Governor Robert List before the United States House Interior Subcommittee on Energy and Environment (19 July 1979), GOV-0820, File #33, Governor Robert List Records, Nevada State Archives.

Tyler, P., "The U.S., Too, Has Dumped Waste at Sea," *New York Times* (4 May 1992), www.nytimes.com/1992/05/04/world/the-us-too-has-dumped-waste-at-sea.html

United Kingdom Nirex Limited, *Options for Radioactive Waste Management That Have Been Considered by Nirex*, Nirex Report No. N/049 (May 2002).

United Kingdom Nirex Limited, *Review of 1987–1991 Site Selection for an ILW/LLW Repository*, Technical Note No. 477002 (June 2005).

United States Department of Energy, *Atomic Energy Act* (July 2001), Rev. 2, http://hss.doe.gov/sesa/environment/training/envlawsregs256/aeamanual.pdf

United States Department of Energy, Hanford, *Tank Farms* (updated 24 April 2013), www.hanford.gov/page.cfm/TankFarms

United States Department of Energy, Office of Environmental Management, *Hanford Site* (n.d.), http://energy.gov/em/hanford-site

United States Department of Energy, Office of Environmental Management, *Report to Congress: 1995 Annual Report on Low-Level Radioactive Waste Management Progress*, DOE/EM-0292 (June 1996), www.nirs.org/radwaste/llw/annual95.pdf

United States Environmental Protection Agency, *Operation Report: A Survey of the Farallon Islands 500-Fathom Radioactive Waste Disposal Site*, Office of Radiation Programs and Office of Water Program Operations, ORP-75–1 (December 1975), www.epa.gov/nscep/index.html

United States Environmental Protection Agency, *Region 2: Western New York Nuclear Service Center* (updated 21 March 2011), www.epa.gov/region2/waste/fswester.htm

United States Environmental Protection Agency, *Region 4: Superfund – Maxey Flats Nuclear Disposal* (updated 3 January 2012), www.epa.gov/region4/superfund/sites/npl/kentucky/maxfltky.html

United States Environmental Protection Agency, Office of Radiation Programs, *Fact Sheet on Ocean Dumping of Radioactive Waste Materials*, prepared for the House of Representatives Subcommittee on Oceanography of the Committee on Merchant Marine and Fisheries (20 November 1980).

United States Environmental Protection Agency, Office of Radiation Programs, *Radiological Quality of the Environment in the United States, 1977*, EPA 520/1–77–009, Washington, DC (September 1977).

United States Geological Survey, *A Marine GIS Library for Massachusetts Bay: Focusing on Disposal Sites, Contaminated Sediments, and Sea Floor Mapping*, Open-File Report 99–439 (October 1999), http://pubs.usgs.gov/of/1999/of99–439/mbaygis/chapt2a.htm

United States Nuclear Regulatory Commission, *Licensing Requirements for Land Disposal of Radioactive Waste*, 10 CFR § 61.56 (1982), www.nrc.gov/reading-rm/doc-collections/cfr/part061/part061–0056.html

United States Nuclear Regulatory Commission, Advisory Committee on Nuclear Waste White Paper, *History and Framework of Commercial Low-Level Radioactive Waste Management in the United States*, NUREG-1853, Washington, DC (January 2007), www.nrc.gov/reading-rm/doc-collections/nuregs/staff/sr1853/sr1853.pdf

Walden, B., *Recovery of Low-Level Radioactive Waste Packages from Deep-Ocean Disposal Sites*, EPA 520/1–90–027 (September 1990), www.epa.gov/nscep/index.html

Walker, J.S., *The Road to Yucca Mountain: The Development of Radioactive Waste Policy in the United States* (Berkeley: University of California Press, 2009).

Washington State Bldg. and Constr. Trades Council v. Spellman, 684 F.2d 627 (9th Cir. 1982), http://openjurist.org/684/f2d/627/washington-state-building-and-construction-trades-council-v-c-spellman-united-states

Washington State Department Ecology Nuclear Waste Program, *Interim Remedial Action Plan, Commercial Low-Level Radioactive Waste Disposal Site, Richland, Washington* (April 2010), www.ecy.wa.gov/programs/nwp/llrw/llrw_iap.pdf

2 A more equitable distribution of responsibility?

The low level radioactive waste policy act and the US compact system

As described in the previous chapter, by 1979 uncertainty regarding the availability of space for generators to dispose of their low level radioactive waste (LLRW) had become acute. The host states' frustration that they were being forced to bear the national radioactive burden was best evidenced in Washington State. In November 1980, voters approved Initiative 383 by a 3 to 1 margin, which banned the importation of nonmedical LLRW generated outside the state unless permitted by interstate compact (State of Washington n.d.). While ultimately declared unconstitutional (see Box 2.1), the initiative sent a very clear message that Washington would not tolerate the status quo. According to Michael Robinson-Dorn, an assistant professor at the University of Washington School of Law, I-383 was a "blunt tool" designed to force Congress to recognize the states' rights to make their own LLRW disposal decisions. "In a very real way, 383 made a difference" (Dininny 2004).

Congress favored a comprehensive federal approach to radioactive disposal. The first version of what would become the Low-Level Radioactive Waste Policy Act (LLRWPA) nationalized all disposal sites and gave the Department of Energy (DOE) responsibility for owning and operating the facilities. Nevada, South Carolina and Washington, fearing this would result in their shouldering the entire LLRW burden indefinitely, opposed such a solution. Governors Richard Riley (South Carolina) and Robert List (Nevada) were particularly outspoken, and Riley's personal relationship with President Carter was important in ensuring the passage of substitute language.[1] A National Governors Association task force, acknowledging that unlike high level waste, the LLRW problem "is not so technologically complex that it requires the leadership of the federal government," recommended state responsibility for developing and regulating disposal facilities. The task force – made up of governors from Arizona, Arkansas, Idaho, Illinois, Nevada, Pennsylvania, South Carolina and Washington – estimated that six to eight regional disposal facilities would be sufficient (Piot 1980). Similarly, a presidentially mandated State Planning Council on Radioactive Waste Management recommended that every state should be responsible for commercially generated LLRW and that each should be authorized to enter into interstate compacts (General Accounting Office [GAO] 1995, p. 53). The findings of these groups, combined with the general sense of crisis, resulted in passage of the 1980 LLRWPA; the high level waste sections of the bill had been removed when it became clear that they would derail the bill (Newberry 1993, pp. 47–48). The LLRWPA "encouraged states to form regional compacts [subject to congressional consent] to meet their collective disposal needs, minimize the number of new disposal sites, and more equitably distribute the responsibility" for LLRW disposal (GAO 1999, p. 17). The Act defined a compact as an agreement between two or more states and provided two incentives for action:[2]

- All wastes generated by a compact would be shipped to that compact's disposal facility. The belief was that a captive market and guaranteed revenue stream would make the prospect of hosting a site more attractive and also prevent other disposal facilities from undercutting host prices.
- After 6 January 1986, compact members could refuse to accept waste shipped from non-compact states. The belief was that a deadline would encourage states to join a compact or face the prospect of siting their own disposal facilities that would be open to the rest of the country; it is unclear whether legislators considered the possibility of nonaffiliated states buying, at a premium, space in a compact to which they did not belong.

Box 2.1   Compacts, the US Constitution and LLRW disposal

Compacts are often invoked by states to manage public goods. They may be limited to specific regions (for example, the four-member Atlantic Salmon Compact) or include much broader swathes of the country (for example, the 44-member Driver License Compact). Article I, Section 10 of the US Constitution gives Congress the power of consent over these agreements. The importance of this specific type of cooperation in the LLRW context is that without the protection of congressionally consented compact membership, states that host or plan to host disposal facilities are not able to exercise any control over where the waste they receive comes from. The reason for this stems from the Supremacy and Commerce Clauses. In *Pacific Gas & Electric Co. v. State Energy Resources Conservation and Development Commission* (1983), the Supreme Court held that the Atomic Energy Act (AEA) of 1954 occupied nearly the entire field of nuclear safety concerns, thus preempting state law. As a result, a federal court of appeals invalidated a 1982 Illinois law prohibiting storage or disposal of spent fuel from power plants outside the state. Similarly, the Ninth Circuit Court of Appeals determined that Washington State's Initiative 383 violated (1) the Supremacy Clause, because permission to exclude waste is conditioned on participation in a compact, and at that time Washington had joined the proposed Northwest Compact but it had not received congressional approval; and (2) the Commerce Clause, due to uneven treatment of in-state and out-of-state parties as well as "significantly aggravat[ing] the national problem of low-level waste disposal" (Glicksman 1988, pp. 64–67; *Washington State Building & Construction Trades Council v. Spellman* [1982]).

The compact boards ('commissions') would be responsible for host designation but would leave the specifics of siting, regulation and closure to the affected states. The system envisioned rotating hosts – that is, one state would not be forced to host for its partners in perpetuity – but compact language was far from uniform on this subject.[3] For example, the Southeast Compact decided that once a state hosted it would not be required to do so again until every other member had "fulfilled its obligation, as determined by the Commission, to have a regional facility operated within its borders," and it required its host facilities to operate for 20 years or until 32 million cubic feet of waste was received, whichever came first (United States Nuclear Regulatory Commission [NRC] 2012, p. 322). As the designated successor to Barnwell – and before it was expelled from the compact – North Carolina chose a deliberately restrictive design concept. The North Carolina Low Level Radioactive Waste Management Authority anticipated that the facility would receive only 7–7.5 million cubic feet of waste during its 20-year life and thus adopted 11 million cubic feet as the design and licensing limit. The size of the facility sent "a clear message that North Carolina does not intend to accept out-of-region waste" (Walker and MacMillan 1994, p. 1305). Several compacts based hosting obligations on waste generation percentages. For the Rocky Mountain Compact (Colorado, Nevada and New Mexico) an eligible host was any member "which, according to reasonable projections made by the board, is expected to generate twenty percent or more in cubic feet except as otherwise determined by the board of the low-level waste generated within the region has an obligation to become a host state" (Rocky Mountain Low-Level Radioactive Waste Compact 1986). The language is important. According to officials from the Colorado governor's office, the 20 percent generation rate was kept "deliberately flexible" to take into account improved waste management techniques. Volume reduction combined with the NRC's 1982 waste classification system (see Box 2.2) meant that radioactivity rather than volume might become a more accurate measure of a state's generation rate in the future (Whitman and Slosky 1983, p. 91). The compact also took into account Beatty's service, assuring Nevada that it was not required to host again until every other eligible state had taken a turn; and the Silver State stood a good chance of never crossing the 20 percent threshold. For the Appalachian Compact, an eligible host was any member that generated 25 percent or more of Pennsylvania's total volume or curie content over 3 successive years (NRC 2012, p. 376).

For Kentucky, the Central Midwest Compact guaranteed that it would not have to host as long as it generated 10 percent or less of Illinois's waste volume – a not unreasonable expectation, given that the only nuclear facility in Kentucky was the uranium enrichment plant near Paducah and that Illinois relied on nuclear plants for roughly half of its power (NRC 2012, p. 333).[4] The Northwest Compact simply stated that members would cooperate "in order to maximize public health and safety while minimizing the use of any one party state as the host of such facilities on a permanent basis," and Washington agreed to host for an indefinite period provided certain assurances were met by the other compact members (NRC 2012, p. 307; *Directions in Low-Level Radioactive Waste Management* 1990, p. 44).

Box 2.2 NRC LLRW classification

On 27 December 1982, the NRC issued regulations dividing LLRW into four categories or classes – A, B, C and Greater-Than-Class C. With a combination of limited concentration and short half-life characteristics, Class A waste poses the lowest potential hazard and accounts for roughly 96 percent of the total LLRW volume. Indeed, radiation levels are generally low enough to allow for direct handling. With higher concentrations of radioactivity and longer half-lives, Class B waste generally requires shielded casks or is remotely handled. With the highest concentrations of radioactivity and longest half-lives, Class C waste requires heavy shielding. Near-surface facilities are the approved disposal method for Classes A, B and C; the radioactivity of Classes A and B will not endanger the health of an inadvertent intruder into a disposal facility after 100 years, while for Class C it is 500 years. There is currently no disposal path other than geological repository (the same method of isolation as for spent fuel and HLW) for waste classified Greater-Than-Class C (Berlin and Stanton 1989; NRC 2014).

Amending the LLRWPA

Realizing the LLRWPA's vision, however, proved elusive. With three disposal sites already operating and no restrictions on where in the United States the waste could come from, 47 states preferred the status quo and were ably supported by their elected officials. By 1985, 42 states had entered into various compact agreements but none had been ratified by Congress. The only parties with any incentive to make the Act work were Nevada, South Carolina and Washington, but they were stymied by a large congressional majority that had zero interest in consenting to compacts that would close existing disposal paths in such a short amount of time (by 1986) and potentially mandate the construction of new disposal sites in their own backyards. This lack of progress prompted a fierce backlash from the disposal site states, including threats to close the facilities; by the end of 1986 the LLRWPA had been amended and seven compacts, incorporating 37 states, were ratified. The amendments sought a compromise designed to provide LLRW producers with a disposal pathway in the short term and assure the existing disposal states that Beatty, Barnwell and Hanford would not become, by default, the nation's permanent LLRW disposal sites. Three provisions are key (Low-Level Radioactive Waste Policy Act of 1985 [1986]):

- Existing disposal sites would continue to accept waste for another 7 years and an emergency clause extending beyond 7 years in the event of "an immediate and serious threat to the public health and safety or the common defense and security."

- Nondisposal states/compacts must reach a series of milestones (from joining a compact to siting a disposal facility) by specific dates in order to continue disposing of LLRW at the three existing sites.
- Waste volume reduction strategies were encouraged, augmented by the promise of DOE technical assistance.

However, one of the most powerful sticks contained in the amendments was successfully challenged by New York. The 'take-title' provision held that if states or compacts failed to provide for the disposal of all waste generated within their borders by 1 January 1996, they were required, upon request, to take title to and possession of that waste and become liable for damages suffered by the generators. In 1992, the US Supreme Court ruled that while Congress had the power to preempt state regulation or to encourage states to provide suggested regulatory systems for disposal of the waste they generated, it did not have the power to compel the states to do so in a particular way.[5]

Negotiating the compacts and finding new disposal sites

While geographic contiguity determined the organization of most compacts, three – Southwest (California/Arizona/North Dakota/South Dakota), Atlantic (New Jersey/Connecticut/South Carolina) and Texas (Texas/Vermont) – were not so intuitive. Over time, states changed compacts (Wyoming from Rocky Mountains to Northwest), withdrew from compact membership (Maine, Nebraska, North Carolina) or were expelled from a compact (Michigan). Others (Massachusetts, New York, New Hampshire, Puerto Rico, Rhode Island and Washington, DC) have not joined any compact. For the District of Columbia, at least, it was not for lack of trying. District officials tried twice to join the Southeast Compact but were rejected by the Commission because of its volunteer hosting requirement for new members.[6]

Michigan and the Midwest compact

The Act's deadline led to some unintended, but hardly surprising, behavior by designated host states. For example, Michigan was eventually expelled from the Midwest Compact "because members decided that the Michigan Low Level Waste Authority had unreasonable criteria that essentially precluded the state from finding a suitable site." This was a reasonable contention given that screening criteria eliminated over 95 percent of the state during the first phase of the siting process. James Cleary, commissioner of the Michigan LLRW Authority, certainly suggested as much: "I doubt that any location in Michigan can meet the strict siting criteria for a low-level waste facility under State law. . . . Our siting criteria go beyond the Federal requirements, and they may be prohibitive" (GAO 1999, p. 28).[7] Another tactic was slow-rolling. For example, in response to a threat from South Carolina that continued failure to comply with LLRWPA obligations would lead to its exclusion from Barnwell, Massachusetts officials blamed "inaction by the state legislature to approve bonds to finance site identification and characterization" (Petrella 2011, p. 125).

The Northeast Compact

In general, large waste generators whose volumes all but guaranteed that they would host tended to look for small volume partners in order to minimize the out-of-state waste burden the compact formation demanded, and small to medium volume generators tended to partner with large volume generators or existing disposal states to delay hosting themselves – or avoid it if possible. The fate of the now defunct Northeast Compact is instructive. Under the guidance of the Coalition of Northeastern Governors, it was envisioned that the compact would consist of 11 states and the District of Columbia. However, no one was thrilled about the possibility of being designated the host for what would have been the largest compact in the country; only Connecticut, Delaware, Maryland and New Jersey enacted the compact legislation (Newberry 1993, p. 50). New York and Pennsylvania, wary of being chosen to host because of the large volumes they produced and fearing that a one-state/one-vote arrangement would allow the small volume producers to form a majority to ensure this outcome, withdrew from negotiations (GAO 1995, p. 27; Gershey, Klein, Party and Wilkerson 1990, p. 121; United States Congress, Office of Technology Assessment [OTA] 1989, p. 45; Branson 1997, p. 532). To provide some context: in 1986 (the first year of DOE electronic records), out of a total of 1,805,142 cubic feet of LLRW disposed of at Barnwell, Beatty and Hanford, New York accounted for 107,018 cubic feet and Pennsylvania 191,073 cubic feet – good for sixth and second most in the nation, respectively (DOE n.d.a.). As a result, Pennsylvania formed the Appalachian Compact with Delaware, Maryland and West Virginia (Commonwealth of Pennsylvania 1985), preferring to be selected as the host state for a group of relatively small waste generators, while Vermont and Maine joined the Texas Compact. New York has remained unaffiliated, after having failed to join a compact; Governor Mario Cuomo wrote to all nine compacts enquiring about access to their operating or planned facilities, and all said no (Marks 1992). Further splintering the group, Massachusetts was suspected of devising siting criteria that ensured it would never host a facility and it has been unaffiliated ever since. New Hampshire and Rhode Island, small volume producers concerned that they might be forced to accept enormous quantities of waste from their larger compact neighbors, have also remained unaffiliated.

Connecticut and New Jersey, producers of roughly the same volumes of waste and "united largely by similarly ambivalent feelings about their proximity to New York," ended up as the only remaining members of the Northeast Compact (Weingart 2001, p. 34). Because they could not decide who would host their joint disposal facility, it was agreed that each would build one.[8] The compact commission had looked into other siting alternatives such as: one state accepting Class A waste and the other accepting Classes B and C; one state treating the waste and the other disposing of it; and one state accepting mixed hazardous waste and the other accepting all other types of LLRW (Berlin and Stanton 1989, p. 433).[9] But even this compromise proved problematic.[10] However, events in the Carolinas proved fortuitous for the rump Northeast Compact members.

The Southeast/Atlantic Compact

The Southeast Compact formed in 1983 with the operating Barnwell, South Carolina facility as its disposal site. However, Barnwell was scheduled to close in 1992. In 1986, North Carolina was selected as the second host state for the compact based on criteria that included volume and radioactivity of waste generated in past years, projected future volumes and transportation distances. The siting process did not advance very far, even as the North Carolina LLRW Management Authority costs blew out – they were $50 million over budget by 1 January 1992 (OTA 1989, p. 35; Bremen and Visocki 1992, p. 3). In 1994, Barnwell closed to non-Southeast Compact members. A year later, South Carolina withdrew from the compact (charging that North Carolina was "not acting in good faith" to develop a new facility[11]), reopened Barnwell to the rest of the country except North Carolina and tripled the surcharge on waste received (Weingart 2001, pp. 141–142). North Carolina withdrew from the compact in 1999 and was subsequently sued by the remaining compact members for "receiving approximately $80 million from the Commission with the full knowledge that in return the state was expected to develop a facility for the Compact" (Southeast Compact Commission 2000). The failed North Carolina siting effort was controversial for other reasons as well (see Box 2.3).

**Box 2.3   Economic distress and 'windshield surveys':
controversial analysis in the Tar Heel State**

In 1987, the North Carolina Low-Level Radioactive Waste Management Authority (NCLLRWMA) was created to oversee the siting process. Five sites were chosen in Richmond, Wake/Chatham, Union, Rowan and Wayne Counties for preliminary field studies. In April 1990, Ghio in Richmond County and Cokesberry, on the Wake/Chatham County line and adjacent to Carolina Power & Light's Shearon Harris nuclear plant, were chosen for detailed characterization work. After receiving input from the three counties and holding public hearings near each site, the NCLLRWMA held a televised 2-day meeting in early 1993 and voted unanimously in favor of Cokesberry – lower construction costs and minimal community disruption were particularly important considerations for the Authority members. Less than a week later, Chem-Nuclear submitted a license application to the Department of Health and Human Services' Division of Radiation Protection (Walker and MacMillan 1994, pp. 1305–1307).

One of the methods used to narrow the list of potential sites was 'windshield surveys'; that is, driving to the sites and visually inspecting them. Notes from those surveys "ran the gamut from physical topography of the site to the type and cost of housing present, race of inhabitants, identity and temperament of local officials and other criteria apparently unrelated to technical suitability." One independent consultant who participated in these surveys later explained that a guiding principle for his work with Chem-Nuclear was that the facility should be located in an "economically distressed" county (*Summary of Significant Findings Regarding the Process of Site Selection for the North Carolina Low-Level Radioactive Waste Facility* 1992).

In October 1989, Epley Associates was commissioned to assess the five sites based on such statistical data as demographics, income and education. More controversial was the inclusion of an assessment by a North Carolina political consultant of the feasibility of siting the facility in each county. When the report leaked, Richmond County filed suit against the NCLLR-WMA and Chem-Nuclear claiming the company broke state law by considering factors other than the purely technical. Opponents would describe some of the company's work as "environmental racism" (Pflieger 1992). The consultant's analysis provides an unvarnished and consequently fascinating glimpse into a siting study. For example:

Ghio, Richmond Co. – Might be among the less difficult of the potential sites.

- Relatively poor and underdeveloped with a less-than-thriving economy, it would benefit immensely from the economic rewards of hosting.
- Has no apparent history of environmental controversies or environmental group activism and none of the newspaper clips collected in the previous year indicate activities by CACTUS in Anson County or ORM-RADS in Moore County received any coverage in Richmond.
- Sheriff Goodman is far more important than the legislative delegation and if he is against the facility Chem-Nuclear will have a battle on its hands.

Cokesberry, Wake Co. – May be the most doable county in the state.

- Environmentalists will support siting at Shearon Harris as will much of the legislature and the utilities; the argument that the county benefits more than almost any other from industry and research and thus should host the facility will be very popular.
- The legislative delegation does not have a great deal of influence and the County Commissioners may be more open-minded than their counterparts elsewhere.

- Residents in the south, a region which remains rural, generally feel left out of the county's prosperity and might find an attractive economic package appealing.
- The county's high educational level as well as its ties to local universities and the Research Triangle Park indicate a public information campaign would be more effective here than other regions.
- Support from the Greater Raleigh Chamber of Commerce is a must.
- *The News and Observer* proved once again in the NC State University affair that it can wield enormous negative power when it perceives that public leaders are acting in a secretive and unresponsive way.[12] When Claude Sitton [*News and Observer* editor and winner of the Pulitzer Prize for coverage of the civil rights movement] takes on a crusade, he is a powerful opponent; we cannot have him crusading against this site.
- Members of Citizens Against Shearon Harris will be able to generate a great deal of opposition amongst neighborhood groups and opposition will be strong in Chatham and perhaps Lee, two counties that must be included in any socioeconomic package.

Williams, Wayne Co. – While this site may be dubious technically, Wayne is a potentially friendly host.

- Wayne is rock-ribbed conservative but still a Democratic county. It is not likely to welcome outsiders stirring up environmental objections.
- Wayne is very aggressive on economic development and industry recruitment and it would be possible to get the county to volunteer. The economy is doing pretty well but Seymour Johnson Air Force Base has been identified as vulnerable to closing before, and that makes folks nervous.

(*Summary of Significant Findings* 1992)

According to the LLRWPA, an unaffiliated state could not form a compact by itself, and thus could not exclude waste from outside its borders.[13] So South Carolina went looking for partners. And as John Weingart has explained, Connecticut and New Jersey were attractive to the Palmetto State for two reasons. First, through "an accident of legislative drafting," compact statute language was not uniform. While congressional consent was required for each compact to be created, not every compact required congressional (or even state legislature) consent to add new members. For the Northeast Compact, all that was needed was the approval of its two commissioners (Weingart 2001, pp. 318–319). Second, the other compacts that did not require congressional consent to increase membership already had at least five members; Connecticut and New Jersey offered fewer members and less total waste (Weingart 2001, p. 319).[14] Thus, in July 2000, the three formed the Atlantic Compact out of the disintegration of the Northeast Compact and the fracturing of the Southeast Compact. Then in 2001, South Carolina legislation again closed Barnwell's gates to non-compact waste, this time after mid-2008, and the restriction has been maintained (GAO 2004, p. 10). Further west, two compacts were cooperating very much as Congress had intended.

The Rocky Mountain and Northwest Compacts

As the largest waste generator in the Rocky Mountain Compact as approved by Congress in January 1986, Colorado was chosen to succeed Nevada when Beatty closed. Later the same year, the Colorado Geological Survey released a report identifying six candidate areas, and a representative site within each area, that might be suitable for locating a waste disposal facility (Eakins, Junge and Hynes 1986). In 1988, Umetco Minerals Corp., a subsidiary of Union Carbide, proposed developing an above-grade disposal facility at an old Union Carbide uranium mining site near the town of Uravan for radium waste from Denver's Superfund sites, as well as a mined cavity LLRW disposal facility for the compact if the company determined that compact members generated enough waste to make the operation financially viable (OTA 1989, p. 34).[15] Umetco's plans were strenuously opposed by neighboring Utah – Uravan is roughly 20 miles east of the Utah border. In October 1988, Utah Governor Norman Bangerter wrote a letter to Colorado Governor Roy Romer decrying the lack of consultation and raising specific concerns about the geology of the site, transportation safety and the risk of contaminating the Colorado River. According to the *Deseret News*, Colorado officials green-lighted the project without even doing Bangerter the courtesy of replying to his letter ("Colorado Should Become a Better Neighbor to Utah" 1989). Utah officials wrote to Romer again in 1993. Representative Kelly Atkinson summed up the legislature's frustration: "To have a neighboring state license an operation without consulting Utah leaves us totally unarmed in a war against unwanted environmental contamination" (Israelsen 1993). While Utah officials had legitimate environmental concerns, they also had an incentive to accentuate any technical uncertainty; the same year Umetco proposed building near Uravan, Envirocare was busy licensing a facility west of Salt Lake City to accept the same waste. Despite Colorado licensing the radium disposal facility, the Environmental Protection Agency (EPA), which is responsible for determining where Superfund waste is sent, contracted with Envirocare in Utah, effectively undercutting Umetco's plans (OTA 1989, p. 34). In 1990, mine owner Dave Blake lamented that the uranium-filled hills were probably 'hotter' than much of the waste that would have been imported: "People around here don't have the fear of radioactivity like most Americans do. I guess you could even say that we wish we had a little bit more of it" (Coates 1990).

In 1992, the Rocky Mountain Compact solved its Beatty-succession problems by reaching agreement with the Northwest Compact (Alaska, Hawaii, Idaho, Montana, Oregon, Utah, Washington and Wyoming) and the State of Washington to send up to 6,000 cubic feet of LLRW to Hanford annually. The agreement included a growth factor of 3 percent per annum. This was not expected to be a huge additional burden on Hanford because the Rocky Mountain Compact's only nuclear power plant – Fort St. Vrain, Colorado – had been decommissioned the same year and the compact would henceforth generate a relatively small volume of waste (GAO 2004, p. 36; Low-Level Radioactive Waste Forum 2006, p. 2).

The Northwest Compact adopted a restrictive approach to contracting with unaffiliated states: prospective partners could not generate more than 1,000 cubic feet of waste each year and had to be contiguous with a compact member state (OTA 1989, p. 33). However, the Northwest Compact also expanded beyond radioactive waste to embrace a more comprehensive disposal philosophy. As the compact legislation explains:

> in consideration of the State of Washington allowing access to its low-level waste disposal facility by generators in other party states, party states such as Oregon and Idaho which host hazardous chemical waste disposal facilities will allow access to such facilities by generators within other party states.
>
> (Berlin and Stanton 1989, pp. 430–431)

The Southwest Compact

South Dakota had been actively considering compact membership since at least 1983 when Governor Bill Janklow proposed that the state join the Midwest Compact. A year earlier, the Edgemont Development Committee invited Chem-Nuclear Systems to develop a LLRW disposal facility in Edgemont, a mining town of 1,500 residents in the southwest of the state.[16] As initially conceived, the facility would handle up to one-third (estimated at 1 million cubic feet) of the nation's annual waste production, create 100 jobs and generate $16 million in revenue for the state ("Plan for Nuclear Dump Divides Dakota Town" 1984; Brokaw 1985). On 5 June 1984, two-thirds of Fall River County voted in favor of a nonbinding referendum supporting construction of the facility – a not altogether surprising result in a community acclimatized to the risks of radiation.[17] According to real estate agent Harold Wyatt, head of the Edgemont Development Committee and president of the Chamber of Commerce, this should have been sufficient:

> We fail to see why the people in Watertown, Brookings, Sioux Falls or any other area in the eastern part of the state should have the power to determine what kind of industry we can attract here in the southwestern corner of the state.
>
> ("Plan for Nuclear Dump" 1984)

Chem-Nuclear chose the shuttered Black Hills Ordnance Depot 8 miles south of Edgemont. In 1985, the legislatures in North and South Dakota approved a Dakota Low Level Radioactive Waste Compact. However, the Nuclear Waste

Vote Coalition spearheaded a successful push for a statewide special election, and on 12 November 1985 South Dakotans overwhelmingly rejected membership in the compact.

The Dakotas did not have to wait long for a seemingly ideal solution to present itself, one that offered the possibility that they might never have to host.[18] However, local, state and federal politics would conspire to frustrate this plan as well. In September 1983, motivated in large part by the creation of the Northwest and Rocky Mountain compacts that left California isolated and without a guaranteed disposal path, Governor George Deukmejian signed legislation committing the Golden State to developing a LLRW disposal facility. California also entered into compact negotiations with Arizona but initial talks did not lead to an agreement.[19] As a result, Arizona formed the Western Compact with South Dakota in 1986 and commenced preparations to serve as the disposal host (North Dakota was eligible to join but could not officially do so at the time because its legislature did not meet that year). However, in 1987 California enacted the Southwest Compact and committed to hosting for the first 30 years. Arizona promptly repealed the Western Compact and joined the Southwest Compact, which was ratified by Congress in 1988. The Dakotas joined in early 1989 (Woolfenden 1999).[20]

The California Department of Health Services (DHS) conducted the initial statewide site screening, then chose US Ecology to complete the site characterization work and prepare to design, license and operate a disposal facility – despite having previously recommended against the firm because of its safety record (Hubler 1991). In 1988, Ward Valley, a 1,000-acre site in the Mojave Desert 22 miles west of Needles in San Bernardino County, was selected (OTA 1989, 47–48; Pasternak 1999, p. 19). In the fall of 1989, US Ecology submitted a license application for a near-surface disposal facility. However, because the site was on federal Bureau of Land Management (BLM) land, construction was contingent on Department of Interior (DOI) land transfer. In April 1991, the BLM and the State of California issued an environmental impact statement (EIS) determining that the facility would not cause significant adverse environmental effects. In July 1992, California asked DOI to sell the Ward Valley land to the state under the Federal Land Policy Management Act (FLPMA). In January 1993, outgoing DOI Secretary Manuel Lujan Jr. agreed and US Ecology, acting on behalf of the state, paid DOI $500,000.

This decision was promptly challenged in state court as being noncompliant with the FLPMA and National Environmental Policy Act and failing to protect the threatened desert tortoise under the Endangered Species Act. The Committee to Bridge the Gap (CBG), a Los Angeles–based nonprofit antinuclear group, focused its opposition on the risk that waste from power plants, particularly plutonium, would leak into the Colorado River.[21] CBG and other environmental and antinuclear activists also argued that the emergency clause of the Low-Level Radioactive Waste Policy Act Amendments (LLRWPAA) was in fact a thinly disguised loophole that would be invoked to bail out states that failed to build their own disposal facilities (Hubler 1991). Additionally, opponents expressed concern that US Ecology was utilizing the same trench design that had been used, and had leaked, at Sheffield in Illinois (Hubler 1991).

Meanwhile, in September 1993, California issued a construction and operating license to US Ecology for the proposed facility. Three months later, three US Geological Survey (USGS) geologists (the Wilshire group) warned that "groundwater at the Ward Valley site likely connects hydrologically to the Colorado River . . . [and] that bedrock above a major fault system underlying the entire region of the disposal site is highly fractured and probably capable of transmitting water. Rather than being a barrier against water movement as assumed by the site evaluation, these rocks may act as aquifers" (GAO 1998, p. 17). To settle this controversy and the questions raised by environmentalists and anti-nuclear groups, DOI created a National Academy of Sciences (NAS) special committee to review the USGS findings. Given the uncertainty, the new DOI Secretary Bruce Babbitt rescinded the land transfer, returned US Ecology's payment and deferred a decision until 1996.

In May 1995, the NAS special committee rebutted the Wilshire group's findings, concluding that the geologists' concerns were "highly unlikely" but recommended that additional tritium sampling be undertaken to establish base levels for subsequent monitoring (GAO 1997, p. 5). Later the same month, the Secretary of the Interior announced that the transfer would proceed if California agreed to adopt the site monitoring recommendations in the NAS report; not amend the volume and radiation limits set down in the license; and place specific limits on plutonium received. California refused "such an intrusion by an agency that lacks the authority and regulatory expertise" (DOE 1996, pp. 11–12). DOI responded by undertaking a second supplement to the 1991 EIS, addressing the NAS report, evidence of radioactive element migration in the soil at Beatty (which US Ecology was using as a 'conceptual analog') as well as Native American issues that had been considered previously (GAO 1998, pp. 31, 33; GAO 1997, p. 2).[22] As a result, the state and US Ecology sued DOI for exceeding its authority on radiation safety issues, and Republican Governor Pete Wilson requested that Congress intervene to transfer the land (United States Senate Committee on Energy and Natural Resources 1996).

On 31 March 1999, a federal judge ruled that DOI was not obligated to turn the land over to the state, and Secretary Babbitt called for all stakeholders to explore alternatives to the land transfer. US Ecology, after a decade of fighting, decided not to appeal. Politics played an important role in the company's decision: in January 1999 Governor Wilson was replaced by Democrat Gray Davis who, as lieutenant governor, had opposed the land transfer (Clifford 1999; GAO 1998). More controversially, during the discovery process in the case California and US Ecology brought against DOI, an internal Council on Environmental Quality memo written by Associate Director for Natural Resources Tom Jensen surfaced that read in part:

Interior Department officials, relying on the NAS analysis and recommendations, believe that the site can be operated and used with complete safety.

Interior would like very much to move ahead with the transfer and put the Ward Valley conflict behind the Administration. That said, they believe that, as a political matter, the Administration simply cannot of its own volition agree to hand the site over in exchange for a check and an unpopular governor's promise to do the right thing.

(Romano and Nagel 1999)

Explaining the lack of new disposal sites

As the preceding discussion suggests, siting new disposal facilities has been more difficult than the Act's authors envisaged. There are a number of reasons for this.

The legacy of earlier disposal practices and siting strategies

As discussed in the previous chapter, the performance of first generation burial trenches did not inspire a great deal of confidence. In addition, the top-down screening process adopted by most states exacerbated the stigma associated with hazardous facility siting. As William Newberry observed, the approach suggests that the "proposed development would present an unacceptable risk in all but the handful of areas pinpointed through the process . . . [and] the use of top-down GIS [geographic information mapping] for siting controversial facilities is considered inherently coercive" (Newberry 1993, pp. 61–62).

Imprecise science

Making the task even more difficult, because the science is imprecise, the perfect can become the enemy of the good and can lead to siting guidance that is, at best, confusing. For example, according to the North Carolina Radiation Protection Act, "low-level radioactive waste disposal facilities shall incorporate engineered barriers for all waste classifications." Yet in the next subsection, the Act requires that the site "meet all hydrogeological and other criteria and standards applicable to disposal site suitability as though engineered barriers were not required. Engineered barriers shall not substitute for a suitable site or compensate for any deficiency in a site" (North Carolina Radiation Protection Act 1975 § 104E-25 (c), (d)). Equally tough to over-come, a "simple consultant's report was often all that was needed to discredit the million-dollar screening exercise as biased, arbitrary, or technically flawed" (Newberry 1993, p. 63).

Poor program management

In multiple cases, state agencies have denied license applications, largely due to safety concerns, and opposition has proved tenacious, although it should be noted that more often than not the local town/community is supportive and most of the opposition comes from surrounding areas. However, sometimes those organizations charged with managing the projects have proved to be their own worst enemies. In 1987, the Illinois Department of Nuclear Safety (DNS) hired Battelle Memorial Institute to find potential hosts sites for the Central Midwest Compact disposal facility and invited the state's county boards to learn more about its radioactive waste disposal program. Based on statewide site character- ization work, locations in Clark County (near Martinsville) and Wayne County were deemed the most suitable for detailed characterization. In July 1989, DNS selected Chem-Nuclear Systems to design, build and operate a disposal facility (Karwath 1989). Chem-Nuclear was already well known to the Prairie State but for all the wrong reasons: in 1987, the company built a LLRW compactor near the town of Channahon, 50 miles southwest of Chicago, without informing the community.[23] Compounding the problem, DNS authorized Chem-Nuclear to move the compactor to whichever site was eventually chosen to host the compact disposal facility; at first the agency and company denied reports of the arrangement but eventually acknowledged that an agreement did in fact exist (Jones 1991). So in October 1989, when it was discovered that the word 'aquifer' had been deleted several times in a geology report on Martinsville in order to make the site appear more suitable, Illinoisans had reason to be concerned. During his Senate confirmation hearing earlier in the year, DNS director Terry Lash had maintained that there were no aquifers beneath the proposed site despite having allegedly seen the report the day before testifying. Indeed, accord- ing to the law firm hired by the state to investigate, Lash ordered the deletions. The director was forced to concede that two aquifers might partially exist beneath the site in the wake of the altered report revelations, and he resigned in 1990. Despite all of this controversy, Martinsville was selected, Chem-Nuclear submit- ted a license application for an aboveground facility in 1991 and the Martinsville City Council approved the siting of the facility in 1992 (Corpstein 1992).[24] However, the independent three-member Illinois Low-Level Radioactive Waste Disposal Facility Siting Commission ruled the location neither safe nor suitable, effectively killing the agreement. A subsequent Martinsville appeal was denied by the Commission. The entire process took 8 years and cost the state roughly $85 million (Weingart 2001, pp. 57–58; GAO 1999, pp. 64–65).

Brown field sites are not a magic bullet

Except for the Clive facility in Utah – which was developed outside the compact framework but with the acceptance of the Northwest Compact and is discussed later – not one new disposal site was successfully licensed as a result of the compact system until Andrews County, Texas, in 2009 (see chapter 4). It is instructive that both of these locations were brown fields: the Clive site had been licensed for naturally occurring radioactive waste since 1988 and Waste Control Specialists had been accepting hazardous waste at the Andrews site since 1992. Brown field siting is not, however, a magic bullet and may prompt feelings of victimization in the host community. As a result, some states have deliberately taken the opposite approach. For example, New Jersey's Regional Low-Level Radioactive Waste Disposal Facility Siting Act exempts the host municipality from being considered as a site for a solid or major hazardous waste facility; similarly, any municipality hosting a solid or hazardous waste facility is exempt from hosting a LLRW disposal facility (OTA 1989, p. 47).

Financial incentives/compensation cannot overcome committed political opposition

Financial and other incentives have been key to local community participation, but they have not guaranteed siting success. For example, when US Ecology submitted its license application in California, the company also opened an office in the town of Needles, hired a former high school teacher to act as a liaison, bought $3,000 worth of science books for the school district, sponsored a $2,500 annual scholarship for graduating high school seniors and paid for tours of the Beatty facility to anyone interested (Hubler 1991). Yet they had quite the opposite effect on Needles Mayor Roy Mills, who fumed: "I consider that a bribe" ("Has US Ecology Cleaned Up Its Act?" 1993). In Illinois, a disposal fee levied on nuclear utilities paid for a wide variety of goods and services in Martinsville, including $200,000 for the school district to buy computers and repair the high school roof, $24,000 for new police cars, $3,000 for the American Legion to buy a new freezer and $100 to each Martinsville citizen in December 1990 to put toward last winter's utility bills ("What This Town Needs Is . . . Nuclear Waste?" 1991). It should be noted that in both of these cases, the towns remained relatively supportive throughout the siting process but the proposed disposal facilities were terminated for reasons beyond the local communities' control.

Waste volumes and disposal rates

For facility operators, demand for their service has been a little difficult to predict. While disposal costs have risen ($1/cubic foot of LLRW in 1979 to over $400/cubic foot in 2004 [GAO 2004, p. 20] and roughly $1,625/cubic foot in 2012[25]), waste volumes have fluctuated wildly. In 1979, when Beatty and Hanford were closed temporarily, disposal pathway concerns were well founded. But the sites reopened a few weeks later and waste volumes decreased from 3.7 million cubic feet in 1980 to 1.1 million cubic feet in 1990 due in part to effective waste volume reduction techniques (GAO 1992, p. 9).[26] Yet, according to a 2004 GAO report: "Annual LLRW disposal volumes have increased significantly in recent years, primarily the result of cleaning up of DOE sites and decommissioning nuclear power plants." And this trend is increasing. In August 2013, Entergy Corp. announced that it would shut down the Vermont Yankee plant in 2014, adding to the 16 reactor sites the NRC has listed as undergoing decommissioning and the fifth reactor slated for decommissioning within the last 12 months (NRC updated 2013; Wingfield 2013).

For Entergy Corp., this cost is defrayed somewhat by Vermont's membership in the Texas Compact. However, low level waste disposal is significantly more expensive for generators that need to ship to a facility in another compact. To provide some context, the following are proposed maximum disposal rates submitted to the Texas Commission on Environmental Quality by Waste Control Specialists for the Andrews facility in 2010. Actual prices vary but the ratios are representative of the cost differential between compact members and out-of-compact customers (Chandrasoma 2010, p. 20):[27]

Waste Class	*FT³*	
	Compact	*Non-compact*
A – Non-compactable	$82.53	$210.94
A – High Dose Rate	$193.98	$457.38
B/C – Routine	$2,652.49	$5,872.48
B/C – High Activity	$7,957.46	$17,617.43

Quantifying the LLRW 'market' is difficult because DOE only keeps records on disposal rates; it does not track waste generation, so only ballpark estimates of how much waste is being stored around the country by generators and brokers are possible. Thus, the closest thing to a comprehensive picture available is the amount of waste that arrives at the disposal facilities' gates each year. The following snapshot is taken from DOE's records (the Manifest Information Management System) and illustrates the difficulty in trying to predict waste volumes:

- 1,805,142 cubic feet in 1986;
- 3,369,897 cubic feet in 1992;
- 1,065,617 cubic feet in 1998;
- 3,864,401 cubic feet in 2004;
- 2,146,351 cubic feet in 2010 (DOE n.d.a.).

For years, the market was made even less predictable by South Carolina's on again–off again approach to accepting out-of-compact waste.

Construction costs and regulatory guidance

For prospective disposal service providers, this waste stream volatility and the rising costs of developing such facilities (site screening, licensing, construction and operation, days/weeks/months in court and other delays caused by opponents) made the economics of new builds uncertain.[28] And given that disposal fees are the primary method to defray such costs, developing new facilities tended to be more expensive than continued operation of existing facilities for both operators and customers.[29] The practical approach to LLRW management taken by the regulator also contributed to the lack of progress on siting new facilities. According to the GAO: "While NRC policy favors disposal rather than storage over the long-term, since the mid-1990s the Commission has allowed on-site storage of LLRW without a specified time limit as long as it is safe." In what was something of a self-fulfilling prophecy, the commission "took this approach in part because LLRW can be stored and the states were not developing any new disposal facilities" (GAO 2004, p. 21).

The critical role of brokers[30]

Underlying all of this is the fact that there has not been a disposal space crisis like 1979 again. And the reason is quite simple, if often overlooked in the literature on LLRW disposal. If the disposal states enforced the exclusionary provisions of the LLRWPA as rigidly as the language suggests, many non-compact states would be awash in radioactive waste. This is not the case. New York provides a clear illustration of why. Despite not being a member of a compact or having any disposal facilities of its own, the Empire State disposed of 23,267.13 cubic feet of LLRW in 2000: 8,535.9 cubic feet at Barnwell, 5.75 cubic feet at Richland and 14,725.48 cubic feet at the Clive facility. These transactions were facilitated by brokers who prevent "an immediate and serious threat to the public health and safety" or undermine the fabric of the compact system, depending on your point of view (e-mail communication with James Voss, Senior Partner at Predicus LLC, 16 January 2015). Four brokers – Radiac Research Corporation and NDL Organization Inc. in state; ADCOM Express Inc. and Teledyne-Brown Engineering out of state – collected LLRW from generators in New York as well as New Jersey, Connecticut, Pennsylvania, Massachusetts, Vermont, Maine, Rhode Island, New Hampshire, Delaware and Illinois and transported the waste to storage facilities in New York or transited it through New York to storage facilities elsewhere. At the storage sites, the waste packages were consolidated and then shipped either by the broker or another transporter to a disposal or waste compaction/treatment facility. The length of storage (which could last up to a year) depended, in part, on the accumulation of sufficient quantities of waste to constitute full loads (New York State Department of Environmental Conservation, 2001). Networks of brokers performed, and continue to perform, the same service all over the country.

The unusual case of Clive

While $1 billion had been spent collectively by states and compacts on siting efforts in the 25 years since the LLRWPA was passed, not a single new disposal facility had been built within the framework of the Act (GAO 2004, p. 40). There was, however, one partial exception. In 1978, Congress passed the Uranium Mill Tailings Radiation Control Act that, amongst other things, tasked DOE to remediate 22 inactive uranium ore-processing sites around the country. Two of those sites were associated with the Vitro Corporation's idle uranium mill in south Salt Lake City (DOE n.d.b.). DOE identified and investigated 29 possible locations in Utah for disposal of the waste, eventually settling on a site 75 miles west of Salt Lake City in the unincorporated community of Clive, Tooele County. From 1984 to 1988, 1,666,000 tons of tailings were moved from the mill to Clive and placed in an aboveground disposal cell. In 1988, Envirocare purchased the land adjacent to the DOE site, which the state promptly licensed to accept naturally occurring radioactive waste in order to dispose of the Vitro tailings and waste from similar cleanup operations (Duncan and Eadie 1974, p. 1). In 1991, the license was amended to permit the disposal of some LLRW and the Northwest Compact agreed to allow Envirocare to accept these wastes from non-compact states. The exception was intended to cover 'orphan' LLRW; that is, wastes not addressed by federal law (DOE 1996, p. 9). Over the next 10 years, the site's license was amended multiple times, including in 2001 when Clive was approved to accept all types of Class A waste (GAO 2004, pp. 32–33).

A glimpse was also provided into the seamier side of the waste disposal business. In 1998, after stepping down as company president a year earlier, Khosrow Semnani pled guilty to a misdemeanor tax charge and received a $100,000 fine for paying Utah Bureau of Radiation Control Director Larry Anderson $600,000 in cash, gold coins and real estate between 1987 and 1994. Anderson had originally sued Semnani in 1996, claiming he was owed $5 million on top of the $600,000 already paid for helping to set up Envirocare. Semnani countersued, claiming extortion, and ended up testifying against Anderson, who went to jail for 2.5 years for income tax evasion; Anderson was acquitted of the extortion charge. When the payments became publicly known, Envirocare competitors Umetco Mineral Corp. and Nuclear Fuel Services (NFS) filed suits. Envirocare reached confidential out-of-court financial settlements with Umetco in 1998 and NFS in 1999 (Robinson 2002; "$600 Million Suit Targets Envirocare" 1997; Cates 1997a; Cates 1997b; Costanzo 1998; "Envirocare, NFS Settle Conspiracy Suit" 1999).

However, the company did not get everything it wanted. After striking out in Texas (see chapter 4), Envirocare received a license in 2001 from the state regulatory authority to accept Class B and C waste subject to approval by the Utah legislature and governor. In October 2004, a state task force recommended that Envirocare not be allowed to accept such waste, and in 2006 the application was withdrawn (League of Women Voters in Utah 2005, p. 11).

While the LLRWPA did not produce any of the "six to eight regional disposal facilities" envisioned during the Act's first three decades, it did function as "an essential vehicle of protection for existing host states to exercise authority over [low level radioactive waste] management" (Sherman 2011, p. 189). There was, however, one important exception to the lack of new disposal facilities taking shape during this period. But before examining developments in west Texas, we will take a closer look at the compact system's most spectacular failure, in northern Nebraska.

Notes

1 The medical community also pushed hard for the original language in the belief that nationalization represented the best defense against another disposal space crisis, a situation the hospitals could not afford.

2 William Newberry – former radioactive waste policy analyst to South Carolina Governor Richard Riley, manager of DOE's LLRW program and executive director of Vermont's LLRW program – unfairly described the two state compacts (of which there have been three temporarily and one permanently) as "a ruse to gain the member states exclusionary authority without the political burden of establishing disposal 'regions'" (Newberry 1993, p. 50).

3 Had Congress been explicit on this point in the LLRWPA, it would likely have been overstepping its authority just as it did with the 'take-title' provision discussed later.

4 At the time of compact formation, GAO estimated that Illinois produced 98 percent of the low level radioactive waste total (GAO 1999, p. 64).

5 The challenge, led by the State of New York and two of its counties (Allegany and Cortland), was supported by 17 other states. Washington, South Carolina and Nevada joined the federal government as defendants. See *New York v. United States* 1992.

6 On 21 November 1986 the Compact adopted a policy that "unless a potential party state volunteers to become the host state succeeding South Carolina, the Compact Commission will consider no application for Compact membership." As William Newberry has observed, Washington, DC's waste volume was not the problem: "The entire annual waste inventory from the District could be accepted by Barnwell in one normal day's operation" (Newberry 1993, p. 56).

7 Cleary is cited in Sherman 2001, p. 165.

8 Connecticut's first, failed attempt to site a facility has been described as "a classic example of the decide/announce/defend siting approach" (Forcella, Gingerich and Holeman 1994). It is worth noting that the state's follow-on strategy, a volunteer approach, did not fare much better.

9 When Arizona was still a likely member, the Rocky Mountain Compact envisioned the same type of division of labor:

> Both Arizona and Colorado could fulfill their host state roles concurrently by locating a disposal facility in one state and another type of management facility [such as collection, consolidation, storage, treatment and/or incineration] in the other state, contingent upon approval by the Rocky Mountain Compact Board.
>
> (Whitman and Slosky 1983, p. 91)

10 For an excellent explanation of New Jersey's inability to site a disposal facility see Weingart 2001.

11 The recent past had not inspired confidence in Raleigh's ability (and possibly willingness) to deliver on its LLRW commitment. In 1990, North Carolina failed "to fulfill its part of a regional agreement for the management of hazardous waste" (Bremen and Visocki 1992, p. 8).

12 The NC State 'affair' involved academic eligibility and players selling shoes and game tickets as well as receiving loans from boosters (all National Collegiate Athletic Association rules violations) for the men's basketball team. The scandal forced Chancellor Bruce Poulton to resign, stripped Jim Valvano of his athletic directorship and shortly thereafter prompted his resignation as coach; in addition, the basketball program was on probation for two years (Cart 1989; Miller 1989; Johnson 1990).

13 During the 1985 LLRWPAA debate, an amendment was introduced to authorize single-state compacts. However, it was "overwhelmingly defeated" (Testimony of Ray Peery 1987).

14 This did not, however, mean that the waste produced by South Carolina's new partners was insignificant. Connecticut and New Jersey combined produced approximately 7% of the national LLRW total (Rabe 1994, p. 143).

15 In 1982, Chem-Nuclear Systems Inc. was invited by the West End Business Development Committee to search for a LLRW disposal site in Montrose County, Colorado, a mining/milling region in the 'uranium belt.' Early the following year, Chem-Nuclear determined that the risk of geological faulting and flash flooding was too great and they terminated the project. The disappointment of local officials and business leaders was captured by West End Business Development Committee chairman Dan Crane: "It seems like we are coming out losers when we can't even attract a nuclear waste site that no one else wants" (Salisbury 1983).

16 At the time, South Dakota's uranium mines were suffering from a 50% drop in the price of uranium. The state's only uranium mill, in Edgemont, was constructed in 1956 and operated by Mines Development Inc. until 1972. In 1974, the Tennessee Valley Authority bought the mill but after conducting engineering, economic and environmental studies, chose not to restart operations (DOE 2009, p. 1).

17 The head of the Edgemont Development Committee, Harold Wyatt, described the prevailing view as follows: "People who live here a while know they're not going to turn green or glow or come down with cancer tomorrow." A less typical vote of confidence came from banker and Edgemont Development Committee member Don Hanson: "I tend to trust the government [in reference to the NRC]. If we don't, what kind of country are we going to have?" But support was not unanimous. Two skeptical South Dakotans living within 25 miles of the proposed facility, Baptist minister Russ Daniels and his rancher son-in-law Ray Lautenschlager, demonstrated an unusual commitment to understanding by conducting their own fact-finding mission during a family vacation that included visiting the Barnwell facility and Washington, DC, to speak with officials from the NRC. They remained unconvinced (Brokaw 1984; Imrie 1983).

18 Compact language was silent on how host selection would take place after California and the second largest waste generator (Arizona) had fulfilled their responsibilities.

19 Arizona, with several power plants scheduled to begin operation in the late 1980s, was 'provisionally designated' as a member of the Rocky Mountain Compact. However, because of the complex transportation routes required to move waste from major generating centers in Phoenix, Tucson and the Palo Verde nuclear plant to the disposal facility in Colorado that was slated to succeed Beatty, the Grand Canyon State withdrew and entered into discussions with California (Woolfenden 1999).

20 The Dakotas did not have any nuclear plants; the only plant to operate, in Sioux Falls, South Dakota, was shut down in 1967.

21 CBG President Dan Hirsch claimed, somewhat plausibly: "If the waste were solely medical and biomedical, I believe there would have been no fight" (Clifford 1994).

22 Revisiting impacts on Native Americans was prompted, in part, by the issuance of two executive orders after the EIS was conducted: Executive Order 13007 – the executive branch agency with statutory or administrative responsibility for the management of Federal lands shall, to the extent practicable, accommodate access to and ceremonial use of Indian sacred sites by Indian religious practitioners and avoid adversely affecting the physical integrity of such sacred sites; and Executive Order 12898 – each Federal agency shall make achieving environmental justice part of its mission by identifying and addressing, as appropriate, "disproportionately high and adverse human health or environmental effects of its programs, policies and activities on minority populations and low-income populations" (Advisory Council on Historic Preservation 1996; EPA 1994).

23 Channahon Mayor Wayne Chesson spoke for outraged residents: "They are operating on the premise that it is easier to get forgiveness than permission. Even if it is a safe and properly operated business, the way they did this puts a question on their credibility and honesty" (Bukro 1987; Goozner 1987).

24 A 1991 article in *Businessweek* painted a stark picture of Martinsville:

> The once-bustling Clark County town has seen its fortunes slide since the mid-1970s, when Interstate 70 bypassed it. Unemployment has hovered at 14% for years. Two years ago, the town lost its bank; this year, the newspaper folded. Townsfolk fret that the high school, with an enrollment of 115 – 50% less than a decade ago – will go next. "If it goes, we're gone," says resident Joe Boyer, who wants the dump.
> ("What This Town Needs" 1991)

25 The 2012 figure is what the Calvert Cliffs nuclear plant was paying as of 9 August 2012. As the plant is located in Maryland, a member of the Appalachian Compact without its own disposal facility, operator Constellation Energy Group pays out-of-region disposal fees. The price was confirmed by one of the authors during a site visit to Calvert Cliffs. The Appalachian Compact members (Delaware, Maryland, Pennsylvania and West Virginia) send Class A waste to Clive and sent Class B and C waste to Barnwell until 2008, when South Carolina stopped accepting out-of-compact waste. According to the compact's most recent annual report, until generators are allowed access to B and C disposal they will store the waste on site (Pennsylvania Bureau of Radiation Protection n.d., p. 20).

26 Techniques include substitution of nonradioactive materials for radioactive materials, segregation of radioactive wastes from nonradioactive wastes, recycling, compaction, dilution and incineration (GAO 2004, p. 20). Waste generators have also simply reduced the number of articles exposed to radiation (Weingart 2001, p. 23). For an interesting discussion of the economics of waste reduction see Miller 2003.

27 This ratio – non-compact members paying more than double up to 255% of the compact member rate – has been quite consistent throughout the compact history. For example, in 1988 Beatty was charging an average of $30.11/cubic foot for compact waste and $70.11/cubic foot for non-compact waste, and Barnwell was charging $36.87/cubic foot for compact waste and $76.87/cubic foot for non-compact waste (*Directions in Low-Level Radioactive Waste Management* 1990, pp. 20, 58).

28 In 1987, the NRC estimated that reviewing a license application would take 8 staff-years and encompass 22 technical disciplines, from geology to sociology. This estimate did not factor in any delays (NRC 1991).

29 For the companies that built and operated disposal facilities, another level of uncertainty was introduced in 1987 when the two insurance pools that covered the nuclear industry (American Nuclear Insurers and Mutual Atomic Energy Liability Underwriters) suspended writing new policies for LLRW disposal facilities due to "expanding environmental liabilities and disagreement between the pools and their insureds over the coverage provided for environment impairment. Emerging environmental regulations, such as those creating the Superfund, had by 1987 created a new set of risks not anticipated when the Nuclear Energy Liability Policy was conceived and written" (Karner and Mullen 1991, p. 476).

30 The authors would like to thank James Voss, Senior Partner at Predicus LLC, for bringing the critical role of brokers to their attention.

References

Advisory Council on Historic Preservation, Executive Order No. 13007: Indian Sacred Sites (24 May 1996), www.achp.gov/EO13007.html

Appalachian States Low-Level Radioactive Waste Compact, reprinted in NRC, *Nuclear Regulatory Legislation*, NUREG-0980, Vol. 1, No. 10 (2012).

Barrett, R., "Ethics Board Says Official Had No Conflict in Waste Panel Vote," *News and Observer (Raleigh)* (14 August 1990), reprinted in *Summary of Significant Findings Regarding the Process of Site Selection for the North Carolina Low-Level Radioactive Waste*

Facility, prepared by James, McElroy & Diehl, P.A. (19 February 1992), http://infohouse. p2ric.org/ref/28/27585.pdf

Berlin, R., and Stanton, C., *Radioactive Waste Management* (New York: John Wiley & Sons, 1989).

Bradbury, R., "Nuclear Dump Panel 'In the Dark' on Compact," *Rapid City Journal* (10 June 1983), http://bhodian.com/nuclearwaste.html

Branson, M., "Should Maine Ship Its Low-Level Radioactive Waste to Texas? A Critical Look at the Texas Low-Level Radioactive Waste Disposal Compact," *Maine Law Review*, Vol. 49, No. 2 (1997).

Bremen, S., and Visocki, K., "In Search of Equity: Development of a Regional System for Managing Low-Level Radioactive Waste in the United States," for publication in the *Forum for Applied Research and Public Policy*, University of Tennessee (30 January 1992), http://secompact.org/speechestestimony/

Brokaw, C., "South Dakotans Vote Down Radioactive Waste Plan," *Associated Press* (12 November 1985), www.apnewsarchive.com/1985/South-Dakotans-Vote-Down-Radioactive-Waste-Plan/id-886c48abc491fd60654b3d3ebd84c53f

Brokaw, C., "What Do They Want in Edgemont? Low-Level Nuclear Waste," *Spokane Chronicle* (13 January 1984), http://news.google.com/newspapers?nid=1345&dat=198 40113&id=av1LAAAAIBAJ&sjid=f_kDAAAAIBAJ&pg=6979,2290451

Bukro, C., "Nuclear-Waste Plant Moves in without Whisper," *Chicago Tribune* (26 January 1987), http://articles.chicagotribune.com/1987–01–26/news/8701070195_1_radioactive-waste-low-level-nuclear-power-plants

Butterfield, F., "Idaho Firm on Barring Atomic Waste," *New York Times* (23 October 1988), www.nytimes.com/1988/10/23/us/idaho-firm-on-barring-atomic-waste.html

Camper, L., "Low-Level Radioactive Waste Management in the United States: Where Have We Been: Where Are We Going," *Waste Management 2010 Conference*, Phoenix, Arizona (7–11 March 2010), www.wmsym.org/archives/2010/pdfs/10417.pdf

Cart, J., "There's Smoke on Tobacco Road: N.C. State Tries to Cool Valvano Controversy," *Los Angeles Times* (31 August 1989), http://articles.latimes.com/1989–08–31/sports/sp-1885_1_jim-valvano

Cates, K., "Colorado, D.C. Fire Shots at Envirocare," *Deseret News* (27 June 1997a) www.deseretnews.com/article/568872/Colorado-DC-fire-shots-at-Envirocare.html?pg=all

Cates, K., "Envirocare Official Says Suit Is Merely Harassment," *Deseret News* (14 March 1997b), www.deseretnews.com/article/548718/Envirocare-official-says-suit-is-merely-harassment-html?pg=all

Central Midwest Interstate Low-Level Radioactive Waste Compact, reprinted in NRC, *Nuclear Regulatory Legislation*, NUREG-0980, Vol. 1, No. 10 (2012).

Chandrasoma, S., Texas Commission on Environmental Quality, "Low-Level Radioactive Waste Disposal Rate Setting Activities," *Texas Radiation Regulatory Conference*, Austin, Texas (3 September 2010), www.google.com/url?sa=t&rct=j&q=&esrc=s&source=web& cd=5&ved=0CEIQFjAE&url=http%3A%2F%2Fwww.dshs.state.tx.us%2FWorkArea% 2Flinkit.aspx%3FLinkIdentifier%3Did%26ItemID%3D8589936815&ei=eTM3Uv7EBO Xk4APa7IAg&usg=AFQjCNGgATq2eB6nTnBXo55eKIktAVICtw

"City Wants Radioactive Dump," *Boca Raton News* (27 February 1983), http://news. google.com/newspapers?nid=1291&dat=19830227&id=U-o0AAAAIBAJ&sjid=T40D AAAAIBAJ&pg=6746%2c7254700

Clifford, F., "Caught in Fallout of Waste War," *Los Angeles Times* (14 January 1994), http://articles.latimes.com/1994–01–14/news/mn-11695_1_ward-valley

Clifford, F., "Ruling Apparently Kills Ward Valley Nuclear Dump Plan," *Los Angeles Times* (3 April 1999), http://articles.latimes.com/1999/apr/03/news/mn-23861

Coates, J., "Still a Hot Time in the Old Town, but in Roentgens," *Chicago Tribune* (8 June 1990).

"Colorado Should Become a Better Neighbor to Utah," *Deseret News* (5 January 1989), www.deseretnews.com/article/29519/COLORADO-SHOULD-BECOME-A-BETTER-NEIGHBOR-TO-UTAH.html?pg=all

Commonwealth of Pennsylvania, Legislative Reference Bureau, *Appalachian States Low-Level Radioactive Waste Compact*, SB 417, Act 1985–120 (22 December 1985), www.palrb.us/pamphletlaws/19001999/1985/0/act/0120.pdf

Corpstein, P., "Major Considerations for Development of a License Application for a New Low-Level Radioactive Waste Disposal Facility in Illinois," *Waste Management 1992 Conference*, Tucson, Arizona (23–27 February 1992), www.wmsym.org/archives/1992/V2/134.pdf

Costanzo, J., "Envirocare Chief Pleads Guilty to Tax Charge," *Deseret News* (2 August 1998), www.deseretnews.com/article/644509/Envirocare-chief-pleads-guilty-to-tax-charge.html?pg=all

Dininny, S., "Hanford Initiative Spurs Legal Rematch," *Seattle Times* (13 December 2004), http://seattletimes.com/html/localnews/2002117556_hanfordside13m.html

Directions in Low-Level Radioactive Waste Management: A Brief History of Commercial Low-Level Radioactive Waste Disposal, prepared at the Idaho National Engineering Laboratory by the National Low-Level Waste Management Program for the Department of Energy, DOE/LLW-103 (10 January 1990), www.osti.gov/scitech/servlets/purl/6161759

Duncan, D., and Eadie, G., *Surveys of the Uranium Mill Tailings Pile and Surrounding Areas: Salt Lake City, Utah*, EPA-520/6–74–006 (Las Vegas: EPA, 1974).

Eakins, W., Junge, W.R., and Hynes, J.L., *Candidate Area Evaluation Report: Low-Level Radioactive Waste Disposal, Colorado*, Open File 86–7, Colorado Geological Survey, Department of Natural Resources, State of Colorado (1986), http://geosurvey.state.co.us/pubs/online/Documents/1986%20OF%2086-07.pdf

EnergySolutions, *Bulk Waste Disposal and Treatment Facilities: Waste Acceptance Criteria*, Revision 6 (March 2006), www.doeal.gov/SWEIS/OtherDocuments/534%20EnergySolutions_of_Utah_WAC_R6.pdf

"Envirocare, NFS Settle Conspiracy Suit," *Deseret News* (25 August 1999), www.deseretnews.com/article/714480/Envirocare-NFS-settle-conspiracy-suit.html?pg=all

Forcella, D., Gingerich, R., and Holeman, G., "LLRW Disposal Facility Siting Approaches: Connecticut's Innovative Volunteer Approach," *Waste Management 1994 Conference*, Tucson, Arizona (27 February–3 March 1994), www.wmsym.org/archives/1994/V2/100.pdf

General Accounting Office, *Low-Level Radioactive Waste: Disposal Availability Adequate in the Short Term, but Oversight Needed to Identify Any Future Shortfalls*, GAO-04–604 (June 2004), www.gao.gov/new.items/d04604.pdf

General Accounting Office, *Low-Level Radioactive Waste: States Are Not Developing Disposal Facilities*, GAO-RCED-99–238 (September 1999), www.gao.gov/assets/160/156717.pdf

General Accounting Office, *Nuclear Waste: Slow Progress Developing Low-Level Radioactive Waste Disposal Facilities*, GAO/RCED-92–61 (January 1992), www.gao.gov/assets/160/151432.pdf

General Accounting Office, *Radioactive Waste: Answers to Questions Related to the Proposed Ward Valley Low-Level Radioactive Waste Disposal Facility*, GAO/RCED-98–40R (22 May 1998), www.gao.gov/assets/90/87895.pdf

General Accounting Office, *Radioactive Waste: Interior's Review of the Proposed Ward Valley Waste Site*, Testimony of Gary Jones Before the Committee on Energy and Natural

Resources, U.S. Senate, GAO/T-RCED-97–212 (22 July 1997), www.gao.gov/assets/110/106999.pdf

General Accounting Office, *Radioactive Waste: Status of Commercial Low-Level Waste Facilities*, GAO/RCED-95–67 (May 1995), www.gpo.gov/fdsys/pkg/GAOREPORTS-RCED-95–67/pdf/GAOREPORTS-RCED-95–67.pdf

Gershey, E., Klein, R., Party, E., and Wilkerson, A., *Low-Level Radioactive Waste: From Cradle to Grave* (New York: Van Nostrand Reinhold, 1990).

Gillam, J., "Capitol Political Bombshell Fused by Nuclear Dump," *Los Angeles Times* (20 May 1985), http://articles.latimes.com/1985–05–20/news/mn-16536_1_nuclear-waste

Glicksman, R., "Interstate Compacts for Low-Level Radioactive Waste Disposal: A Mechanism for Excluding Out-of-State Waste," in Michael E. Burns (ed.), *Low-Level Radioactive Waste Regulation: Science, Politics and Fear* (Chelsea, MI: Lewis, 1988).

Goozner, M., "Judge Blocks Use of Nuclear Waste Compactor," *Chicago Tribune* (4 June 1987), http://articles.chicagotribune.com/1987–06–04/business/8702110132_1_nuclear-power-plants-waste-processing-plant-chem-nuclear-systems

Government Printing Office, Texas Low-Level Radioactive Waste Disposal Compact Consent Act, Pub. L. No. 105–236 (20 September 1998), www.gpo.gov/fdsys/pkg/PLAW-105publ236/pdf/PLAW-105publ236.pdf

Haddow, E., "Depressed Colorado Town Recruits Low-Level Radioactive Dump," *Lawrence Journal-World* (27 February 1983), http://news.google.com/newspapers?nid=2199&dat=19830227&id=idBeAAAAIBAJ&sjid=g-gFAAAAIBAJ&pg=6838,4833551

Harf, J., "Recommendations for Siting, Development, and Operation of a Regional Low-Level Radioactive Waste Disposal Facility in Ohio," *Waste Management 1994 Conference*, Tucson, Arizona (27 February–3 March 1994), www.wmsym.org/archives/1994/V2/102.pdf

"Has US Ecology Cleaned Up Its Act?" *Businessweek* (7 November 1993), www.businessweek.com/stories/1993–11–07/has-us-ecology-cleaned-up-its-act

Hubler, S., "Only California Is on Track for Nuclear Dump," *Los Angeles Times* (20 May 1991), http://articles.latimes.com/1991–05–20/news/mn-1454_1_nuclear-waste

Imrie, B., "Igloo Area Men Protest Proposed Nuclear Dump," *Rapid City Journal* (29 April 1983), http://bhodian.com/nuclearwaste.html

"Iredell, Rowan Residents Blast Waste Officials," *Dispatch (Lexington)* (1 June 1990), http://news.google.com/newspapers?nid=1734&dat=19900601&id=VeYbAAAAIBAJ&sjid=aFIEAAAAIBAJ&pg=5930,4707323

Israelsen, B., "Utah Officials See Red over Plans to Expand Colorado N-waste Site," *Deseret News* (27 October 1993), www.deseretnews.com/article/317366/UTAH-OFFICIALS-SEE-RED-OVER-PLANS-TO-EXPAND-COLORADO-N-WASTE-SITE.html?pg=all

Johnson, R., "Take the V out of TV, Please," *Sports Illustrated* (18 June 1990), http://sportsillustrated.cnn.com/vault/article/magazine/MAG1136788/1/index.htm

Jones, D., "Nuclear-Waste Firm Has Checkered Past," *Hartford Courant* (7 July 1991), http://articles.courant.com/1991–07–07/news/0000214343_1_radioactive-waste-disposal-site-radioactive-waste-low-level-radioactive-waste

Junkert, R., Dressen, A.L., Siefken, D.L., Serie, P.J., and Jennrich, E.A., "Licensing the California Low-Level Waste Disposal Facility – Charting a New Course," *Waste Management 1991 Conference*, Tucson, Arizona (24–28 February 1991), www.wmsym.org/archives/1991/V2/40.pdf

Karner, D., and Mullen, J., "Financial Risk Management Issues for Low-Level Radioactive Waste Disposal Facilities," *Waste Management 1991 Conference*, Tucson, Arizona (24–28 February 1991), www.wmsym.org/archives/1991/V2/74.pdf

Karwath, R., "Deal Ok'd to Build Nuclear Waste Dump In Illinois," *Chicago Tribune* (26 July 1989), http://articles.chicagotribune.com/1989-07-26/news/8902200414_1_low-level-nuclear-waste-nuclear-plants-chem-nuclear-systems

League of Women Voters in Utah, *Political Decisions and Nuclear Waste in Utah* (January 2005), www.lwvutah.org/Studies/Political%20Decisions%20and%20Nuclear%20Waste%20Storage%20in%20Utah.pdf

Letter from South Carolina Water Resources Commission Executive Director Alfred Vang to North Carolina Low-Level Radioactive Waste Management Authority Executive Director John MacMillan (6 November 1991), reprinted in *Summary of Significant Findings Regarding the Process of Site Selection for the North Carolina Low-Level Radioactive Waste Facility*, prepared by James, McElroy & Diehl, P.A. (19 February 1992).

"Low-Level Radioactive Waste Disposal Company Shows Interest in Locating Here in West End," *San Miguel Basin Forum* (29 April 1982).

Low-Level Radioactive Waste Forum, Discussion of Issues Statement, "Management of Commercial Low-Level Radioactive Waste" (adopted 22 September 2005; amended 18 September 2006), www.llwforum.org/pdfs/ForumPolicyAmended10-18-06FINALFOR PUBLICATION.pdf

Low-Level Radioactive Waste Policy Act of 1985, Amended, Pub. L. No. 99-240 (15 January 1986), www.gtcceis.anl.gov/documents/docs/LLRWPAA.pdf

Maine Legislature, "An Act to Withdraw from the Texas Low-level Radioactive Waste Disposal Compact," Chapter 629, H.P. 1666-L.D. 2171 (effective 5 April 2002), www.mainelegislature.org/ros/LOM/lom120th/4pub601-650/pub601-650-28.htm

Marks, P., "State Finding Few Takers for Its Low-Level Nuclear Waste," *Hartford Courant* (24 May 1992), http://articles.courant.com/1992-05-24/news/0000201589_1_radioactive-waste-low-level-waste-disposal-low-level-nuclear-waste

Miller, C., "Looking to the STARS to Reduce Class B/C Waste," *Radwaste Solutions* (November/December 2003).

Miller, S., "N.C. State Rethinks Its Affairs with Valvano," *Daily Press (Newport News)* (22 November 1989), http://articles.dailypress.com/1989-11-22/sports/8911210486_1_jim-valvano-wolfpack-academic-improprieties

Mutchler, T., "Contender for Nuclear Safety Job Resigned Under Fire in Illinois," *Associated Press* (10 December 1993), www.apnewsarchive.com/1993/Contender-for-Nuclear-Safety-Job-Resigned-Under-Fire-in-Illinois/id-ddf57e241a9f39aedce6f69a20bc02cc

Newberry, W. F., "The Rise and Fall and Rise and Fall of American Public Policy on Disposal of Low-Level Radioactive Waste," *South Carolina Environmental Law Journal* (Winter 1993).

New York v. United States, 488 U.S. 1041 (1992), www.law.cornell.edu/supct/html/91-543.ZS.html

New York State Department of Environmental Conservation, Division of Solid & Hazardous Material, *2000 New York State Low-Level Radioactive Waste Transportation Report* (October 2001), www.dec.ny.gov/docs/materials_minerals_pdf/llwrpt00.pdf

North Carolina Radiation Protection Act 1975, § 104E-25 (c), (d), www.ncga.state.nc.us/EnactedLegislation/Statutes/HTML/ByChapter/Chapter_104E.html

Northwest Interstate Compact on Low-Level Radioactive Waste Management, reprinted in NRC, *Nuclear Regulatory Legislation*, NUREG-0980, Vol. 1, No. 10 (2012).

Pasternak, A., "The California and Southwestern Compact Low-Level Waste Disposal Program: Waste Generators' Perspective, 1983-1999," *Waste Management 1999 Conference* (28 February-4 March 1999), www.wmsym.org/archives/1999/16/16-1.pdf

Pearson, R., "Rock Tells Thompson to Oust State's Nuclear Safety Director," *Chicago Tribune* (1 November 1989), http://articles.chicagotribune.com/1989–11–01/news/8901270317_1_nuclear-safety-director-james-thompson-site

Pennsylvania Bureau of Radiation Protection, *2010 Annual Low-Level Radioactive Waste Program Report to the Pennsylvania General Assembly and the Appalachian Compact Commission* (n.d.), www.elibrary.dep.state.pa.us/dsweb/Get/Document-87697/2930-BK-DEP4322%202010.pdf

Petrella, M.E., "Wasting Away Again: Facing the Low-Level Radioactive Waste Debacle in the United States," *Fordham Environmental Law Review*, Vol. 5, No. 1 (2011).

Pflieger, M., "State's Disposal Firm Had Run-In over Bias Chem-Nuclear Sites Questioned in N.C.," *Morning Call (Lehigh Valley)* (9 April 1992), http://articles.mcall.com/1992–04–09/news/2863029_1_radioactive-waste-disposal-site-chem-nuclear-systems-dump

Piot, D.K., "States Seek Control of Atomic Waste Sites," *Christian Science Monitor* (5 August 1980), www.csmonitor.com/1980/0805/080541.html

"Plan for Nuclear Dump Divides Dakota Town," *New York Times* (4 November 1984), www.nytimes.com/1984/11/04/us/plan-for-nuclear-dump-divides-dakota-town.html

Rabe, B., *Beyond NIMBY: Hazardous Waste Siting in Canada and the United States* (Washington, DC: Brookings Institution, 1994).

Rabin, J., "L.A., San Diego Split on Ward Valley Dump," *Los Angeles Times* (24 April 1996), http://articles.latimes.com/1996–04–24/news/mn-62166_1_ward-valley

Robinson, D., "Semnani Living American Dream," *Deseret News* (11 November 2002), www.deseretnews.com/article/440014760/Semnani-living-American-dream.html?pg=all

Rocky Mountain Low-Level Radioactive Waste Compact, Pub. L. No. 99–240, 99 Stat. 1903 (15 January 1986), www.rmllwb.us/documents/rocky-mtn-compact-statute.pdf

Romano, S., and Nagel, J., "White House Involvement in Ward Valley Land Transfer Delays," *Waste Management 1999 Conference* (28 February–4 March 1999), www.wmsym.org/archives/1999/16/16–4.pdf

Salisbury, D., "This Town Wanted a Nuclear Dump," *Christian Science Monitor* (18 March 1983), www.csmonitor.com/1983/0318/031864.html

Schneider, K., "Idaho Governor Blocks Shipments of Atom Waste to U.S. Dump Site," *New York Times* (8 February 1991), www.nytimes.com/1991/02/08/us/idaho-governor-blocks-shipments-of-atom-waste-to-us-dump-site.html

Schneider, K., "Idaho Shuts Border to Nuclear Waste from Colorado Weapons Plant," *New York Times* (1 September 1989), www.nytimes.com/1989/09/01/us/idaho-shuts-border-to-nuclear-waste-from-colorado-weapons-plant.html

Sherman, D., *Not Here, Not There, Not Anywhere: Politics, Social Movements, and the Disposal of Low-Level Radioactive Waste* (Washington, DC: Resources for the Future, 2011).

"$600 Million Suit Targets Envirocare," *Deseret News* (11 March 1997), www.deseretnews.com/article/548113/600-million-suit-targets-Envirocare.html?pg=all

Solomon, B., *Review of Colorado Department of Health Hearing Exhibits Related to a Proposed Low-Level Radioactive Waste Disposal Facility, Montrose County, Colorado*, Utah Division of Environmental Level Health, Bureau of Radiation Control, Job No. (R-6) 89–03 (1 March 1989), reprinted in *Technical Report for 1989–1990: Applied Geology Program*, compiled by Bill D. Black, Utah Geological and Mineral Survey, Utah Department of Natural Resources (May 1990), http://ugspub.nr.utah.gov/publications/reports_of_investigations/RI-220.pdf

Southeast Compact Commission, "Southeast Compact Commission Takes Legal Action in U.S. Supreme Court Against North Carolina," News Release (10 July 2000).

Southeast Interstate Low-Level Radioactive Waste Management Compact, reprinted in NRC, *Nuclear Regulatory Legislation*, NUREG-0980, Vol. 1, No. 10 (2012).

Southwestern Low-Level Radioactive Waste Disposal Compact Consent Act, reprinted in NRC, *Nuclear Regulatory Legislation*, NUREG-0980, Vol. 1, No. 10 (2012).

Spent Fuel Test-Climax: An Evaluation of the Technical Feasibility of Geologic Storage of Spent Nuclear Fuel in Granite, Final Report (UCRL-53702), compiled by W.C. Patrick, Lawrence Livermore National Laboratory (30 March 1986).

State of Washington, Office of the Secretary of State, *Initiatives to the People: Initiative Measure No. 383* (n.d.), www.sos.wa.gov/elections/initiatives/statistics_initiatives.aspx

Summary of Significant Findings Regarding the Process of Site Selection for the North Carolina Low-Level Radioactive Waste Facility, prepared by James, McElroy & Diehl, P.A. (19 February 1992), http://infohouse.p2ric.org/ref/28/27585.pdf

Swanson, S., and Pearson, R., "Caution Flag up in Nuclear Dump Search," *Chicago Tribune* (18 October 1989), http://articles.chicagotribune.com/1989–10–18/news/8901230252_1_radioactive-waste-nuclear-safety-siting-process

Testimony of Ray Peery in Nebraska LB 426, Senator Sandra Scofield (Principal Introducer), Introducer's Statement of Intent, Ninetieth Legislature, First Session (19 February 1987), in Nebraska State Historical Society, Government Records, RG/41, Series 8, Central Interstate Low-Level Radioactive Waste Compact (LLRW-NE), Misc. Files, Committee/State/Legislature, 1987–2005, Box 1 of 2.

Texas Compact Low-Level Radioactive Waste Generation Trends and Management Alternatives Study: Technical Report, RAE-42774–019–5407–2, prepared by Rogers & Associates Engineering Branch, URS Corporation (August 2000), www.tceq.state.tx.us/assets/public/permitting/llrw/entire.pdf

United States Congress, Office of Technology Assessment, *Partnerships under Pressure: Managing Commercial Low-Level Radioactive Waste*, OTA-O-426 (Washington, DC: U.S. Government Printing Office, November 1989), www.fas.org/ota/reports/8923.pdf

United States Department of Commerce, National Oceanic and Atmospheric Administration, *Natural Disaster Survey Report, Hurricane Hugo: September 10–22, 1989* (May 1990), www.nws.noaa.gov/om/assessments/pdfs/hugo1.pdf

United States Department of Energy, *Manifest Information Management Systems* (n.d.a.), http://mims.doe.gov/GeneratorData.aspx

United States Department of Energy, Office of Environmental Management, *Report to Congress: 1995 Annual Report on Low-Level Radioactive Waste Management Progress*, DOE/EM-0292 (June 1996), www.nirs.org/radwaste/llw/annual95.pdf

United States Department of Energy, Office of Legacy Management, *Edgemont, South Dakota, Disposal Site: Fact Sheet* (4 April 2009), www.lm.doe.gov/Edgemont/edgemont-factsheet.pdf

United States Department of Energy, Office of Legacy Management, *Programmatic Framework: UMTRCA Title I Disposal and Processing Sites* (n.d.b.), http://energy.gov/lm/sites/lm-sites/programmatic-framework

United States Environmental Protection Agency, *Executive Order 12898: Federal Actions to Address Environmental Justice in Minority Populations and Low-Income Populations* (11 February 1994), www.epa.gov/region2/ej/exec_order_12898.pdf

United States Nuclear Regulatory Commission, *Licensing Requirements for Land Disposal of Radioactive Waste*, 10 CFR § 61.56 (1982), www.nrc.gov/reading-rm/doc-collections/cfr/part061/part061-0056.html

United States Nuclear Regulatory Commission, *Locations of Power Reactor Sites Undergoing Decommissioning* (updated 17 September 2013), www.nrc.gov/info-finder/decommissioning/power-reactor/

United States Nuclear Regulatory Commission, *NRC Regulations*, 10 CFR §61.55, Waste classification (updated July 2014), www.nrc.gov/reading-rm/doc-collections/cfr/part061/part061-0055.html

United States Nuclear Regulatory Commission, *Review Process for Low-Level Radioactive Waste Disposal License Application under Low-Level Radioactive Waste Amendments Act*, NUREG-1274 (reprinted April 1991), http://pbadupws.nrc.gov/docs/ML1321/ML13217A156.pdf

United States Nuclear Regulatory Commission, Advisory Committee on Nuclear Waste White Paper, *History and Framework of Commercial Low-Level Radioactive Waste Management in the United States*, NUREG-1853, Washington, DC (January 2007), www.nrc.gov/reading-rm/doc-collections/nuregs/staff/sr1853/sr1853.pdf

United States Senate Committee on Energy and Natural Resources, *Ward Valley Land Transfer Act*, Report 104–247, 104th Congress, 2nd Session (28 March 1996), www.gpo.gov/fdsys/pkg/CRPT-104srpt247/html/CRPT-104srpt247.htm

Walker, C., and MacMillan, J., "Siting the North Carolina Low-Level Radioactive Waste Facility," *Waste Management 1994 Conference*, Tucson, Arizona (27 February–3 March 1994), www.wmsym.org/archives/1994/V2/96.pdf

Washington State Bldg. and Constr. Trades Council v. Spellman, 684 F.2d 627 (9th Cir. 1982), http://openjurist.org/684/f2d/627/washington-state-building-and-construction-trades-council-v-c-spellman-united-states

Washington State Legislature, Chapter 43.145 RCW, *Northwest Interstate Compact on Low-Level Radioactive Waste Management*, Article VI, http://apps.leg.wa.gov/rcw/default.aspx?cite=43.145&full=true

Weingart, J., *Waste Is a Terrible Thing to Mind: Risk, Radiation, and Distrust of Government* (Princeton, NJ: Center for Analysis of Public Issues, 2001).

"What This Town Needs Is . . . Nuclear Waste?," *Businessweek* (18 August 1991), www.businessweek.com/stories/1991-08-18/what-this-town-needs-is-dot-dot-dot-nuclear-waste

Whitman, M., and Slosky, L., "A Regional Low-Level Waste Management System: The Siting Process," *Waste Management 1983 Conference*, Tucson, Arizona (27 February–3 March 1983), www.wmsym.org/archives/1983/V1/19.pdf

Wingfield, B., "Nuclear Trashmen Gain from Record U.S. Reactor Shutdowns," *Bloomberg* (4 September 2013), www.bloomberg.com/news/2013-09-04/nuclear-trashmen-gain-from-record-u-s-reactor-shutdowns.html

Winkley, N., "Area Minister Studies Igloo Nuclear Site Plan," *Rapid City Journal* (16 April 1983), http://bhodian.com/nuclearwaste.html

Womeldorf, D., Junkert, R., and Huck, R., Jr., "California's Review of US Ecology's Low-Level Radioactive Waste License Application," *Waste Management 1990 Conference*, Tucson, Arizona (25 February–1 March 1990), www.wmsym.org/archives/1990/V2/26.pdf

Woolfenden, J., "Arizona's Need for a Low-Level Radioactive Waste Disposal Site," *Waste Management 1999 Conference*, Tucson, Arizona (28 February–4 March 1999), www.wmsym.org/archives/1999/16/16-2.pdf

3 From Central Compact solution to $146-million bad-faith settlement

Low level radioactive waste disposal in Nebraska

Introduction

Boyd County, frontier land located in the sand hills of northern Nebraska, was established in August 1891. It is 545 square miles in size and bordered by South Dakota to the north, Holt County to the south, Knox County to the east and Keya Paha County to the west. The county seat is Butte. By the time US Ecology was invited to find a suitable LLRW disposal location, the county had a population of roughly 2,800, with Butte accounting for 452 and Spencer 10 miles east accounting for 535 (United States Census Bureau 1990).

Nebraska's two nuclear reactors have been operating since the early 1970s: Cooper in the southeast of the state, commissioned in July 1974 and owned by the Nebraska Public Power District (NPPD); and Fort Calhoun close to the Iowa border, commissioned in August 1973 and operated by the Omaha Public Power District (OPPD). The state had a ringside seat at a 1980s low level radioactive waste (LLRW) disposal facility siting controversy. As discussed in chapter 2, the town of Edgemont, in the southwest corner of South Dakota near the Wyoming and Nebraska borders, seriously considered a national LLRW disposal facility until the plan was rejected by a statewide special election in November 1985.

Creation of the Central Compact

In 1982, Arkansas, Kansas, Louisiana, Oklahoma and Nebraska formed the Central Interstate Compact

> to cooperate in the protection of the health, safety and welfare of their citizens and the environment; . . . to limit the number of facilities needed to effectively and efficiently manage low-level radioactive wastes and to encourage the reduction of the generation thereof; and to distribute the costs, benefits and obligations among the party states.
>
> (United States Nuclear Regulatory Commission [NRC] 2011, p. 310)

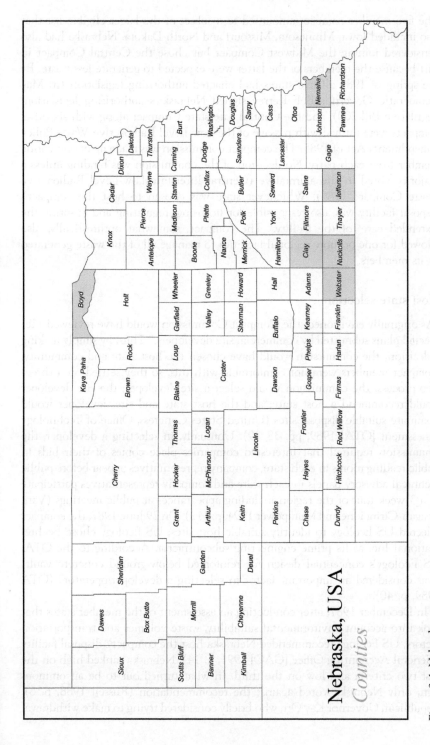

Figure 3.1 Nebraska map

The five-member compact amounted to a subset of the larger eligible list that also included Iowa, Minnesota, Missouri and North Dakota. Nebraska had also considered joining the Midwest Compact but chose the Central Compact in part because the members of the latter were expected to generate less waste. By the spring of 1983 all five states had enacted authorizing legislation (in May Democratic Governor Bob Kerrey signed Nebraska's authorizing legislation, Legislative Bill 200), and the Central Interstate Compact along with six other compacts were ratified with passage of the Low Level Radioactive Waste Policy Amendments Act of 1985. The compact commission was made up of one voting member from each party. No decision of the commission was binding unless a majority voted in the affirmative (Central Interstate Low-Level Radioactive Waste Compact 1986). Whichever state was chosen to host the compact's disposal facility was also responsible for licensing, regulating and ensuring the 'extended care' of the facility.[1] The compact, somewhat optimistically, also allowed for one or more regional facilities to manage all of the waste generated by its members.

Host state selection

"As originally envisioned, the Compact Commission would have reviewed site-specific plans submitted by commercial site developers." Thus, by simply making a decision, the commission would have chosen the host state and community. Compact members were not comfortable with this, so they settled on a three-step process: the commission would select a site developer; the site developer would recommend a host state; and the host state and site developer would nominate suitable disposal sites (United States Congress, Office of Technology Assessment [OTA] 1989, pp. 38–39). Unusually, in selecting a developer, the commission required that interested companies place copies of their bids in public reading rooms in each state, company representatives appear before public technical advisory panels in each state and company representatives participate in a 3-week tour of the region including appearances at public meetings (Vari, Reagan-Cirincione and Mumpower 1994, p. 112). On 29 June 1987, the compact selected US Ecology to identify suitable host sites; US Ecology chose Bechtel National Inc. as its prime engineering subcontractor. According to the OTA, US Ecology's conceptual design for reinforced below-ground concrete vaults "was considered an important factor in selecting a developer/operator" (OTA 1989, p. 40).

In December 1987, after conducting an assessment of the member states that took into account environmental suitability, waste volumes and transportation factors, US Ecology recommended Nebraska host the compact's disposal facility (General Accounting Office [GAO] 1991, p. 14). Nebraska ranked high on the first two criteria and low on the third. In what turned out to be an ominous sign, only Nebraska voted against the recommendation (Russell 1988, p. 6). Republican Governor Kay Orr, who briefly considered trying to make withdrawal from the compact contingent upon having already hosted a disposal facility, was philosophical, explaining on Christmas Eve: "Although Nebraska's commissioner voted against, the State of Nebraska recognizes its responsibility as a member of the Compact and accepts such designation as host state" (Statement of Orr 1987; *Entergy Arkansas, Inc. v. Nebraska* 1999). This ambivalence also prompted the governor to enter discussions with California officials on the use of the proposed Ward Valley facility. Opponents were convinced that far less objective factors were at play in the selection process. Specifically, the Cornhuskers were targeted because Nebraska was the weakest state politically in the compact and its 49-member unicameral legislature was relatively easy to lobby; the state had the weakest liability laws in the country; and state regulators possessed no particular expertise in the area of hazardous/nuclear waste (Kaufman and Moorer 1991).

The Nebraska Low-Level Radioactive Waste Disposal Act

In April 1988, the legislature enacted the Nebraska Low-Level Radioactive Waste Disposal Act (LLRWDA). The Department of Environmental Control (DEC – subsequently renamed the Department of Environmental Quality, or DEQ) would serve as the lead agency overseeing siting and licensing; the Radiological Health Division of the Department of Health (DOH) would regulate. The two agencies would jointly monitor once the facility was operational. This bifurcated arrangement proved problematic during the licensing process; as US Ecology later noted, the agencies' site suitability and performance criteria regulations were *almost* identical. For example, DEC required that the facility not contain a 100-year floodplain, but the equivalent DOH regulation required that "the site shall not be in an area which has a greater than one percent chance of flooding" – a much more difficult determination to make (DeOld, Neal, Sabbe and Bagchi 1994, pp. 1339, 1341). Questions of jurisdiction between the two agencies played a prominent role in the ensuing court cases between the state and US Ecology and by 1996 they were deliberately provoked by Governor Nelson's staff, who realized that DOH probably lacked the statutory power to act as a coequal decision-maker to DEQ. And this was a problem for opponents because the "DOH staff was perceived by the Nelson administration to be much more willing to be hard on [US Ecology]" (*Entergy Arkansas, Inc. v. Nebraska* 2002).

Prior to Nebraska's selection, Governor Orr had announced 10 conditions – according to state senator Merton 'Cap' Dierks, "we called them the Ten Commandments" (Statement of Dierks 1999, p. 25) – that would need to be met before the state would agree to host a facility. These included the defrayal of local monitoring committee costs; state control of the facility design and right to refuse decommissioning waste; retrievability of Class C waste; compensation for the state and host community (including communities involved in the site selection process); and a local property value guarantee. But the most controversial concerned community consent. Much was made of Orr's explicit rejection of a vote on consent. In letter after letter replying to Boyd County residents and others asking, demanding and/or begging that she make any further site work contingent on a referendum, Orr explained: "Unfortunately, the issue of a local vote is not in my power to deliver. A governor has absolutely no constitutional or statutory authority to call an election of any sort" (Letter from Governor Kay Orr to Jane Vogt 1990). This position was entirely consistent with her powers and the relevant legislation (LB 1092) according to US District Judge Richard Kopf:

> When announcing the condition of community consent it was specifically stated that a local referendum was not anticipated. Rather, community consent would be manifest through the actions of locally elected officials. The closest consolidated community to the site is Butte. The Butte Town Board has had in place, and continues to have, a resolution which supports and invites the facility.
>
> (*Nebraska v. Central Interstate Low-Level Radioactive Waste Commission* 1993)

Needless to say, the finer points of jurisprudence were lost on most residents.

Orr's conditions were reflected in the LLRWDA and a series of amendments that were passed in May 1989. For the purposes of this study, the most important provisions of the act were as follows (Nebraska Legislative Bill 761 [1989], p. 5):[2]

- The developer must select three proposed sites by 1 January 1989; a local monitoring committee must be established for each site within 30 days; and the host site monitoring committee must continue to exist.
- A $300,000 Local Site Selection Cash Fund was created, funded by the four nonhost members of the compact, to be shared equally by all local monitoring committees for social, economic and technical studies as well as planning, construction and maintenance monitoring.
- A Local Monitoring Committee Cash Fund was created with a $100,000 annual budget.
- A Community Improvements Cash Fund was created, to be paid by US Ecology through a levy on operations. Unlike many other such levies that were pegged to a percentage of the revenue generated by the facility, this levy specified $2 million plus increases in line with the Consumer Price Index (CPI) to be paid each year.
- Owners within a 3-mile radius would be compensated if their property values declined.
- The disposal facility would operate for 30 years or until 5 million cubic feet of waste had been received, whichever came first.

Local monitoring committees (LMCs) were established to "represent the citizens of the proposed site areas and maintain communication with the developer and the Department to assure protection of public health and safety and the protection of the air, land, and water resources of the area." The LMCs were to be given access to all monitoring data and authority to contract independent technical experts during characterization. The committees were intended to

> provide significant input concerning local needs and resources regarding all relevant aspects of the site selection and, after a site is selected, that the remaining local monitoring committee provide significant input concerning local needs and resources regarding all relevant aspects of the construction, operation, monitoring, closure, and custodial care of the facility.
>
> (Nebraska Legislative Bill 761 [1989], p. 5)

Each monitoring committee was to consist of 10 Nebraska residents: two from municipalities with zoning jurisdiction within 15 miles of the proposed site or from the closest municipality; two from the county of the proposed site (the owner of property within a 3-mile radius of the proposed site and an at-large member); two to be appointed by the board of directors of the natural resources district in which the site is proposed; and four who reside within 50 miles of the proposed site to be appointed by the governor. These four were to be a conservation representative, an agriculture representative, the chief of a fire department located within 15 miles of the proposed site, and an at-large member.

Site selection

The first stage of the screening process used existing records – geography, geology and water resources – to develop an understanding of the state that would enable the company to "identify progressively smaller and more technically suitable geographic areas" (GAO 1991, p. 14). In April 1988, US Ecology presented the results of its first-phase work and its phased screening strategy to a 12-member Citizens Advisory Committee (CAC). The Committee had been established by the company and the Nebraska League of Women Voters on 3 March 1988 as a mechanism for public involvement in the screening/selection process and facility design concepts (Letter from Richard Paton to Vera May Lutz 1988; DeOld et al. 1994, p. 1339).[3] Membership was selected by the Nebraska County Officials Association (two members), the League of Municipalities (two members), the Natural Resources Districts (two members), farm organizations (two members), the Sierra Club (one member), the Nebraska Medical Association (one member), the Nebraska Academy of Sciences (one member) and the Nebraska Association of Commerce and Industry (one member). Noting some criticism that the selection criteria excluded major opponents – seemingly overlooking the Sierra Club but likely referring to the ineligibility for membership of groups like Save Boyd County because they were not "statewide" organizations – the CAC final report explained that the criteria served a balancing function because they also excluded major supporters such as the waste generators (current employees at least) and the American Nuclear Society (Kerr and McDonald 1989, pp. 5–7). The members included a former US Department of Interior official, a Little Blue Natural Resources District Board member and past president of the Sierra Club; the president of the Howell Lumber Company; a professor emeritus in the University of Nebraska's Department of Chemistry; the president of the Wayne County Farm Bureau; a retired first assistant general manager of NPPD; a farmer, rancher and Sheridan County commissioner; the director of nuclear medicine at the Nebraska Medical Center; a rancher and founder of Bull Barn Genetics; the chairman of the Big Nemaha Watershed Board; a CT technologist at Mary Lanning Memorial Hospital; the president of the Nebraska Association of Resource Districts; and a member of the Lower Republican National Resource District (Committee on Judiciary 1989, pp. 23–24).

The CAC held six public meetings between April and November of 1988 as well as two sets of public workshops. An additional meeting was held in April 1989 so US Ecology could update the committee on the selection of the three candidate sites and facility design changes. These meetings were moderated by Dr. Robert Furgason, vice chancellor of academic affairs at the University of Nebraska, with participation from DEC, DOH, US Ecology, Bechtel and the compact commission as well as independent radiologists and geologists. The Committee provided input in various areas that resulted in regulatory requirements and design changes, including: decommissioning waste could only be disposed of with DEC's special approval; managing Class C waste separately and storing or disposing of it in retrievable form; creating more space between Class A cells as originally designed; and provisioning facility access from a central corridor to enhance monitoring. Other suggestions, such as placing movable steel caps on the cells to prevent excess rain from intruding when they were being filled, were not instituted (OTA 1989, p. 40; Kerr and McDonald 1989, pp. 33, 65). While relatively short-lived, the CAC was broad-based, knowledgeable and actively involved with US Ecology – all attributes that typically help to build public trust. However, after its work had been completed, the committee expressed disappointment in the public's lack of interest in its meetings (Kerr and McDonald 1989, p. 40).

In June 1988, US Ecology solicited expressions of community interest, defined by the CAC as that expressed by a county board (Kerr and McDonald 1989, p. 2). Twenty-one counties and 54 communities passed resolutions asking to be considered in the preliminary screening process; both Boyd County and the Village of Butte were amongst those (GAO 1991, p. 8; OTA 1989, p. 39). Local agents were used to identify landowners in potential siting areas willing to grant purchase options for their land "and forego income from either agricultural or ranching sources for a year to permit site characterization work to take place" (DeOld et al. 1994, p. 1339). Areas without receptive landowners were excluded from further consideration (GAO 1991, p. 4).

Box 3.1   US Ecology's aboveground disposal facility design

The conceptual design that US Ecology originally submitted, and the compact commission accepted, was for a shallow land burial facility. How-ever, CAC-hosted public workshops revealed a "strong preference for an above-grade facility, concrete engineered barriers, and extensive monitor-ing requirements to ensure immediate detection of any releases from the disposal unit" (OTA 1989, p. 40). As a result, LB 761 of 1989 prohibited shallow land burial as practiced prior to 1979.[4] LB 761 also required that the facility meet the state's zero-release objectives and mandated a design that allowed for the waste to be retrieved if necessary. DEC regulations required the site developer to design an above-grade facility incorporat-ing one or more engineered barriers to isolate the waste (OTA 1989, pp. 39–40). The company responded with a design, based on concepts first used in France, for an aboveground, reinforced concrete, vault-type facility consisting of 20 Class A waste disposal cells and one Class B/C cell (GAO 1991, pp. 3, 21; *Entergy Arkansas, Inc. v. Nebraska* 2002). According to a US Ecology handbook distributed throughout the state:

> through the judicious selection of a site that meets or exceeds the siting standards and the concept of multiple engineered barriers built into our design, the situations that occurred at below-ground disposal facilities built in the 1960s are very unlikely to occur at the Nebraska facility.
>
> (Bartimus 1989)

However, in the event of a total system failure, a ring of monitoring wells was designed to detect radionuclide movement so the plume could be intercepted (Testimony of University of Nebraska Law Professor Norm Thorson 1989, p. 35).

This would be the first above-grade facility in the US to get to the licensing stage and, like all new technologies, was not as well understood as shallow land burial by regulators. Adding to the challenge, it was more complex to design, requiring additional engineering and scientific disci-plines (Ringenberg and Jacobson 1991). Making US Ecology and Bechtel's jobs even tougher, opponents claimed that the French facility the design was being modeled on had been leaking (Worthington 1990; *Key Issues and Problems Requiring Resolution Prior to Siting and Operating Nuclear and Hazardous Waste Facilities in the State of Nebraska* 1990, p. 24).[5]

Interested counties were screened against county-specific criteria such as ground and surface water, geology, land use, population, urban growth and biological and cultural resources. This screening phase produced smaller areas ranging from 0.5 to 18 square miles that were designated "potential siting areas." Three counties withdrew their expressions of interest during the county-level screening process and six more withdrew after "potential areas" had been identified. According to one report, the Jefferson County Board of Commissioners withdrew from consideration after some residents threatened to boycott businesses owned by people in favor of a disposal facility. Chairman Ivan Zimmerman was quoted as saying: "There's so much hostility that it seemed like the community could be torn apart" (Russell 1988). In November, US Ecology asked the CAC to rank 27 unidentified potential sites. While most of the 13 sites ranked highest were in Boyd and Nemaha Counties, areas in Boyd, Clay, Nemaha and Nuckolls Counties were all viewed as being licensable (GAO 1991, p. 19).

On 6 December 1988, about 1 month before US Ecology announced its selection of three candidate sites, the Butte Village Board of Trustees – which US Ecology viewed as the 'host community' (DeOld et al. 1994, p. 1339) – reaffirmed its support for the project.[6] The board also noted that it reserved the right to withdraw. Then, in a 22 December letter, the Boyd County Board of Supervisors requested that US Ecology agree to several conditions related to community support, public health and safety, and economic compensation and reimbursement. The board also requested that a study of economic impacts be conducted and that $1 million for public improvement projects in the county be guaranteed. US Ecology responded that it did not have authority to agree to all of the requests and explained that the conditions were already part of the siting process. On 18 January 1989, US Ecology announced its selection of the three candidate sites in Boyd, Nemaha and Nuckolls Counties. Purchase option agreements in all three counties were signed the same month (DeOld et al. 1994, p. 1339). The day of the announcement, the company was informed of resolutions passed a week earlier by the Boyd County Board of Supervisors withdrawing support for the disposal facility because US Ecology was unwilling or unable to meet the conditions imposed by the board. US Ecology's position was that the board's action could not stop the process because the compact and US Ecology had complied with the community support (i.e., the town of Butte, not the county) provision of Nebraska law (GAO 1991, p. 8).

Community consent

Determining what constituted 'the community' and whether it had consented to the disposal facility was never resolved. Community consent was not defined by law and this allowed everyone with an interest in the subject to assert the legitimacy of their own definition and, in a sense, no one was wrong. The *Los Angeles Times* reported in March 1989 that Governor Orr believed there would be "a great danger" in allowing county voters to make siting decisions and, because there was no agreed upon definition of an 'affected community,' legislators would have to determine "what constitutes support by the people of that area" (Bartimus 1989). However, lawmakers were similarly disinclined to be tied to anything specific. Legislation that was considered and rejected included an area within a specific radius of the site, the host county, and "one bill went so far as to suggest that the community should encompass the Local Natural Resources District, which includes portions of several counties" (DeOld et al. 1994, p. 1340).

In January 1988, Senators Schellpeper, Conway, Scofield and Bernard-Stevens introduced LB 882 proposing a 'special election' in the affected county to ensure community consent (Legislative Journal of the State of Nebraska 1988, p. 135). The senators then requested an attorney general's opinion as to whether the bill conflicted with existing law and the compact's provisions. The attorney general found that the bill did not conflict, unless the procedure resulted in a construction delay, at which time the federal courts would need to decide whether the vote could be construed as arbitrary and capricious. The attorney general also had two specific concerns. First, while neither the governor nor the compact defined 'community,' LB 882's definition was the host county and any county with a boundary that falls within a 20-mile radius of the proposed site. In "almost all cases in Nebraska this would involve more than one county and in some instances may involve as many as six or seven counties" – well beyond the reasonable limitations of the ordinary meaning of community. Second, the bill proposed that a supermajority be required for consent; that is, if 40 percent or more of electors voted no, the facility could not be built. This left open the possibility of rule by the will of the minority (Spire and Willard 1988).

With the demise of LB 882, committee members turned to LB 1092 introduced by Senators Schellpeper, Hefner, Coordsen, Scofield and Dierks. LB 1092 also included the county vote provision but with a simple majority. Schellpeper and Scofield maintained that to forgo a county vote would send the message that the local voters did not know enough to make the right decision, but most of their colleagues disagreed. The counterarguments fell into three main categories. First, other hazardous facilities had been built in the state without first obtaining community consent, and those nearby learned to live with them.[7] Second, it was bad public policy: if every public good – roads, schools, pipelines and car washes were used as examples – was subject to a community referendum, then nothing would ever get built. Third, a vote might create a popularity contest or bidding war. While it may seem highly implausible now, several legislators argued that there might be too much interest, with counties volunteering based on the lure of financial rewards, and US Ecology tempted to choose the most popular site rather than the safest (Nebraska Legislature n.d., pp. 10958–10960, 10962, 11221, 11402). The final bill did not include a county vote and extended property liability to a 3-mile radius of the facility. The final consent definition read as follows:

> To the extent possible, consistent with the highest level of protection for the health and safety of the citizens of the state and protection of the environment, the developer shall make every effort to locate the facility where community support is evident.
>
> (Nebraska Revised Statute 81–1579 n.d.)[8]

In an attempt to short-circuit the compact and US Ecology's plans, McCulley Township (the proposed site was 2.5 miles west of Butte, technically in McCulley) passed ordinances prohibiting the siting of a disposal facility. The commission and US Ecology successfully brought a federal suit declaring the ordinances unconstitutional (Central Interstate Low-Level Radioactive Waste Commission 1999). Rose Selle wrote to the governor in May 1990 about how unfair it was that McCulley Township residents (of which she was one) could not vote for Butte board members but those same members could, and did, decide to put a disposal facility in McCulley (Letter from Rose Selle to Governor Orr 1990). The compact's answer ran as follows:

> Although the LLRW site is located on the eastern edge of McCulley Township, this township has no true communities (i.e. towns and villages). It is made up of farmsteads. The township also has no formal services that will be provided to the site.
>
> (Memorandum to Governor-Elect Ben Nelson from
> Central Interstate Low-Level Radioactive Waste
> Compact Commission 1990, p. 13)

Even if a definition of 'affected community' had been agreed upon, the question of irrevocability remained. Barring the discovery of a serious safety issue, at what point did the community become the 'designated' host site? Nebraska's commissioner to the compact Norm Thorson explained:

> A point in time [must] be set when a community must indicate whether they are willing to be considered or not, and that then becomes their decision. You obviously can't have a situation where people are opting in and opting out of the process.
>
> (Thorson cited in Memorandum to
> Governor-Elect Ben Nelson 1990, p. 3)

Like US Ecology, the compact commission proceeded according to the principle that local support was demonstrated through formal resolutions passed by the community or population center nearest the proposed site with a sufficiently developed infrastructure to provide vital services to the facility during construction and operation (Memorandum to Governor-Elect Ben Nelson 1990, p. 7). When he succeeded Kay Orr in 1991, Governor Ben Nelson disputed both the contention that the county was the only body that could legitimately give consent and the commission's understanding of Boyd County infrastructure, given that the town of Lynch (more than 20 miles from Butte) would provide emergency medical care (Letter from Governor Nelson to the Central Interstate Compact Commissioners 1992).

In December 1992, an informal LMC-sponsored poll of Boyd County residents' attitudes to the facility was conducted. Project supporters boycotted. Few independent observers predicted any sort of resolution would be forthcoming.

For example, the *Philadelphia Inquirer* reported that "the nonbinding vote next month is expected to accomplish little more than provoking more litigation – and maybe more trouble" (Mayer 1992). However, Governor Nelson believed the results of the special poll "will be an accurate measurement of community consent." The poll result was a 1,107 to 86 landslide victory for the opposition (Letter from Loren Sieh to Governor Nelson 1992). On 13 January 1993, Governor Nelson, citing the results of that poll, filed suit against the compact and US Ecology to stop work due to lack of community consent. In October 1993, the suit was dismissed. Nebraska appealed, only to have the Eighth Circuit Court affirm the decision in June 1994, and then doubled down by petitioning the US Supreme Court. The petition was denied in November 1994 (DeOld et al. 1994, p. 1340; Central Interstate Low-Level Radioactive Waste Commission 1999).

The emergence of opposition

Opponents were quick to denounce both US Ecology and its choice of candidate sites. Much was made of the history of radionuclide leakage at US Ecology–operated LLRW disposal facilities in Illinois, Kentucky and Nevada. There were accusations that companies such as US Ecology working in both the construction and cleanup businesses "have no incentive to do the job right. They are just perpetuating their livelihood because they can make enough money cleaning up the mess they've created" (Testimony of Lynn Moorer 1989, pp. 182–183). Assistant to the Director of the Hazardous Waste Site Control Division of the US EPA Hugh Kaufman and Lynn Moorer of Save Boyd County argued that the three counties were chosen because residents fit the profile of people likely to be least resistant to waste projects and inadequate news coverage contributed to residents' confusion (Kaufman and Moorer 1991). Spencer rancher Lowell Fisher made a similar point: the counties are

> rural and sparsely populated, have low incomes, are mostly above middle age, politically conservative, free-market oriented, have a high school education or less and [are] staunchly patriotic. But we're not stupid. We've got a lawyer, we're raising money, and we're getting smarter every day.
> (Bartimus 1989)

Hugh Kaufman's opinion is important because he was much more than simply a Washington, DC, bureaucrat expressing support for the Nebraska opposition.[9] The Village of Nora appointed Kaufman as its representative to the Nuckolls County LMC. However, the attorney general delivered an opinion, based on a provision of LB 761, requiring that LMC members be Nebraska residents; thereby Kaufman was ineligible to serve. Several newspaper editorials depicted the opinion as an attempt to stifle public input. The village responded by making Kaufman an honorary resident, and while the matter was decided in court he continued to serve on the LMC – where, according to one consultants' report, "his personal efforts centered on berating committee members during meetings and alleging legal violations" (Kerr and Neal 1995, p. 8).[10] But before a ruling could be handed down, Boyd County was selected, removing Nuckolls from consideration. It was a measure of the level of distrust that had built up by that point that although the state instructed the Nuckolls and Nemaha LMCs to disband in January 1990, the Nuckolls committee members claimed that the selection of Butte was in fact a smokescreen and continued their activities for another year (Kerr and Neal 1995, p. 8).

Kerr and Neal observed that the Nemaha LMC – representing the county least isolated from metropolitan centers, with the highest population and host to a nuclear power plant – was the most harmonious of the LMCs. By contrast, the LMCs in Boyd and Nuckolls "struggled with their charges." Members were harassed at meetings, at work and at home, and their businesses were boycotted. Major membership and leadership changes took place and neither "ever achieved the balance necessary to gain credibility with persons on both sides of the siting issue" (Kerr and Neal 1995, pp. 7–8). For example, in 1990, the Nuckolls LMC accused federal, state, compact and industry officials of "threatening the democratic underpinnings of our society . . . [by presenting] evasive, nonresponsive, misleading, and, in some cases, mendacious" information to the committee. The LMC disputed just about everything, including: the selection of the county; the qualifications of responsible state officials and their financial ties to the radioactive waste industry; radioactive waste classifications; the disposal technology; the shipping containers; and licensing and insurance issues (*Key Issues and Problems* 1990, pp. 22–39).

From site characterization to license application: the selection of Boyd County

In April 1989 characterization field work began, and at around the same time the state hired engineering firms HDR and JHC to provide consulting services on the license application (*Entergy Arkansas, Inc. v. Nebraska* 2002). In February 1990 the legislature was informed that, based on superior geology and groundwater, surface water and water drainage patterns, the site in Boyd County had been selected. In July 1990 the company submitted a license application – of over 4,200 pages – to build a facility on a 320-acre tract of agricultural land that it had purchased 2.5 miles west of the Village of Butte and less than 5 miles from the South Dakota border.[11] However, as opponents would regularly remark, the site was not close to an interstate, meaning that heavy semitrailer trucks would be traversing state and county roads to deliver waste to the facility (Di Tullio and Resnikoff 1992). US Ecology countered that the facility could expect an average of one truck per day throughout its 30-year life based on the Central Compact's projected waste volumes. More appealing, the company hoped, were its economic development estimates: a minimum of $1.5–2 million generated annually by surcharge rates to be split between the state, county and host community; up to 40 local jobs with a payroll of up to $1 million plus the

purchase of associated goods and services; and the provision of additional training and support for local emergency response personnel (United States Department of Ecology n.d.).

Disputed science would play a central role in the fight between supporters
and opponents. According to GAO, the geologists hired by each LMC
concluded:

> Notwithstanding some concerns that they raised [relating to geologic and
> hydrologic characterization], that US Ecology and its site contractors had
> performed their work in a technically correct and proficient manner and
> had reached appropriate conclusions about each site on the basis of the
> information collected. They also agreed that the work performed provided
> a sufficient basis on which to select the Boyd County site.
>
> (GAO 1991, pp. 1–2, 5)

However, GAO advised that because geologic and hydrologic data were collected during a dry year, US Ecology would need to show that the site was
"generally well drained and free of areas of flooding or frequent ponding . . .
[and] that sufficient depth to the water table exist[s] so that ground water
intrusion into the waste will not occur" during a heavy wet period (GAO
1991, p. 6). State licensing officials had similar concerns and requested additional information in order to evaluate the license application. US Ecology
studies determined that flooding from a stream on the property could reach
the facility and wetlands could receive groundwater and surface drainage
during wet years. As a result, the facility design was modified to include
drainage structures (GAO 1991, p. 6). Opponents were not convinced, describing the site as more like a swamp than a suitable location for LLRW disposal.
One of the more entertaining and inventive tactics employed was the staging
of a canoe race in a ditch near the site in June 1994 to demonstrate how
much rainfall was likely at the site (Committee on Natural Resources 1997).
John DeOld valiantly yet unconvincingly tried to make a virtue out of neces-
sity, arguing:

> We recognized right from day one the advantage of having that wetland
> up there because that wetland forms essentially a sink or a basin. We knew
> actually where any potential leak from that facility would end up and that
> would be underneath or into that particular wetland. It makes it very simple
> and easy to model and also to monitor in the event there is a release.
>
> (Reiman and Nelson 1996)

Dr. Harold Pierce was the consulting geologist for most of Boyd County's investigation and concurred with the consensus view that Butte was the most suitable
site.[12] However, two South Dakota geologists – Perry Rahn and Arden Davis –
hired by the monitoring committee expressed concern that groundwater runoff
during wet years would contaminate the Ponca Creek. As a result, they doubted

that the site would meet regulatory requirements for contaminated groundwater discharges from the site boundaries.[13]

The license consisted of two documents: a safety analysis report and an environmental report. US Ecology submitted its application in July 1990. Following a series of back-and-forth information exchanges – four rounds of comments totaling more than 2,200 technical questions, requests for additional information as well as overcoming "a breakdown in communications between the project and the state's review team" – the license was deemed complete in December 1991 (DeOld et al. 1994, pp. 1342–1343). State officials estimated that the review process would take about 15 months and cost about $6 million (GAO 1991, p. 3). In fact, it would take more than six times as long and cost almost 15 times as much.

"No M'Orr nukes": Governor Kay Orr and LLRW disposal[14]

Organized opposition actually predated the selection of the three candidate sites. In February 1988, Nebraskans for the Right to Vote launched a petition (Initiative 402) requiring community consent for the siting of any facility and the state's withdrawal from the compact. However, the referendum was defeated in November 1988 by a margin of 64 percent to 36 percent (OTA 1989, p. 39). It was reported that the nuclear utilities – NPPD, OPPD, Kansas's Wolf Creek Nuclear Operating Corp., Arkansas Power and Light, Louisiana's Gulf States Utilities and Louisiana Power & Light – outspent Nebraska for the Right to Vote $1.5 million to $25,000. It was also reported that advertisements warning that power plants could be shut down and hospital radiation treatments cut back if Initiative 402 passed were particularly effective in convincing undecided voters (Bartimus 1989).[15] Despite being defeated, Initiative 402 caught the attention of the other compact members; it was reported that then Arkansas governor Bill Clinton indicated that if Nebraska withdrew from the compact, Arkansas would follow suit the next day (Russell 1988). Not surprisingly, the result failed to appease opponents and their tactics escalated.

Businesses owned by project supporters were boycotted, but things would get nastier. On 17 October 1990, Governor Orr wrote a letter to David Beliles, thanking the editor-publisher of the *Grand Island (NE) Independent* for writing a balanced article on nuclear waste disposal and confessing: "The problem of low-level radioactive waste disposal has, for too many folks, gone beyond the rational and completely into the emotional realm" (Letter from Governor Kay Orr to David Beliles 1990). Two months earlier, she had received a letter containing 'implied threats' from someone she knew but would not disclose. As a result, the governor refused to campaign in Boyd County ("Nebraska Governor Curbs Campaign after Threat" 1990).

Promoters of the disposal facility "were greeted by ranchers toting buckets of feathers and hot tar" (Hubler 1991). Opponents staged mock funerals for state and compact officials who attended a meeting in Butte (O'Hanlon 2011).

A dead black cat stuffed in his letterbox convinced one commissioner to change his vote on LLRW disposal in Webster County (Bartimus 1989).[16] Harassing phone calls were common. Compact chairman Ray Peery kept changing his unlisted number, but anonymous and often threatening callers kept ringing him at all hours of the night (Cragin 2007, p. 146). US Ecology Vice President Richard Paton was threatened by one phone caller: "We'll take you out feet first" (Bartimus 1989). Road signs played a prominent role in the protest movement, ranging from humorous to ominous: "Nebraska is a Breadbasket, not a Wastebasket"; "Dump the Dump Queen"; "PinnochiOrr"; "Dope Pusher, Dump Pusher, Same Thing"; and "Remember Ruby Ridge" on the horizontal plank of a makeshift white wooden cross (Worthington 1990; Cragin 2007, p. 86; Schmidt 1990).[17] Lowell Fisher, who lived 8 miles from the proposed site, staged a month-long hunger strike in the lead up to the 1990 gubernatorial election.[18] Orr received dozens of letters blaming her for forcing Fisher resort to such extreme tactics and pleading with her to stop the project in the interests of Fisher's health. After several years of constant protest, US Ecology erected a fence around the site and hired a firm to provide 24-hour security. Protesters responded by harassing the guards, cutting the fence and laying tire spikes on work roads ("Nuclear Dump Still in Limbo" 1994, p. 3B; Schmidt 1990). Boyd County LMC chairman Marcum's house was shot up in April 1990 (Cragin 2007, p. 114). Tension remained high after Orr's defeat. In October 1991, the compact commission cancelled a tour of the site due to safety concerns. Two months later, a US Ecology representative attended an LMC meeting with six bodyguards, sparking accusations from both sides that concealed weapons were being brought into meetings (Vari et al. 1994, p. 127). In August 1992, Charles Zidko of Spencer and Paul Allen of Bristow resigned as cochairmen of Save Boyd County. Referencing *Boyd County Sociocultural Assessment*, a Rocky Mountain Social Science Association of Utah report commissioned by the Boyd County LMC (which found that many residents expected violence in Boyd County over the proposed facility and a number were "almost certain that some lives would be lost"), Zidko and Allen explained in a press release: "We (the leadership) can no longer assume responsibility for potential actions by individual citizens nor can the Save Boyd County organization" ("Co-chairmen of Anti-nuclear Waste Dump Group Resign" 1992, p. 6). The announcement was both a reflection of how volatile the situation had become and an effective way to communicate an implied threat. US Ecology spokesman Jim Neal responded: "I don't know what Save Boyd County is doing, but the potential that you have a splinter group taking control I think is pretty conceivable" ("Boyd County Residents Expect Violence" 1992, p. 9).

This is not to say that public support was nonexistent outside of Butte. Kay Orr's files include about a dozen letters of support and at least two offers to sell land (Letter from Dan Meyer to Governor Orr 1988; Letter from Alan Woods 1987). And groups like Concerned Citizens of Nebraska and Boyd County's People for Progress, the latter funded by the compact, worked to promote community acceptance but the opposition was more motivated and willing to go further to win (Worthington 1990).

The 1990 gubernatorial election pitted Orr against Ben Nelson. In a campaign speech to a "cheering crowd of Boyd County residents," Nelson promised that, if elected, "it is not likely that there will be a nuclear dump in Boyd County or in Nebraska" (*Entergy Arkansas, Inc. v. Nebraska* 2002). On 13 December 1990, Kate Allen (a lawyer who would start working on LLRW issues in the Governor's Policy Research Office within a month) and University of Nebraska at Lincoln economics professor Gregory Hayden (who would become Nebraska's commissioner to the compact) met with lawyers at Nelson's firm, Kennedy, Holland. Allen's notes list the governor-elect's goals:

> withdraw from Compact; prevent a facility from being built in Nebraska; make community consent a condition of licensure; grant a license only if shared liability language is amended into the Compact; delay the granting of a license until all other states/compacts have submitted a license or until a majority have granted licenses.
>
> (*Entergy Arkansas, Inc. v. Nebraska* 2002)

Not surprisingly, low level waste proved to be a factor, albeit difficult to quantify. Boyd County's Republican Party refused to endorse Orr and came out in support of Nelson. In addition, Boyd County LMC chairman Marcum was not helping. The doctor likely made few friends when, in 1989, he told a reporter:

> Outside rabble-rousers have teamed up with local kooks to coerce people into being against the waste site. These farmers don't read very much, they aren't educated on the issue. They think their property values will be lower, but, in fact, they'll be higher, and we may get as many as 40 new jobs out of it.
>
> (Bartimus 1989)

Then in early October 1990, Marcum was charged by a Boyd County grand jury with 10 misdemeanor counts of violating Nebraska's public meetings law, including failure to follow a published agenda, refusal to recognize critics and failure to give reasonable advance notice of a meeting (Worthington 1990; Letter from Jerry Heermann et al. to Carl Schuman and Governor Kay Orr 1990). Nelson won Boyd County by 310 votes en route to winning the gubernatorial election by the slim margin of 4,030 votes (Robbins 1990).[19]

Promises to keep: Governor Ben Nelson and LLRW disposal

Upon taking office, the governor started acting on the promises he made during the campaign: he opened an inquiry into community consent issues and replaced Marcum as chairman of the Boyd County LMC. At the same time, the Lower

Niobara Natural Resources District, which includes Boyd County, changed membership and replaced its LMC members with opponents. By the time retired school administrator Marvin Humpal resigned in August 1991, the Boyd County LMC had effectively become an opposition group; Butte mayor Ron Schroetlin was the lone supporter on the committee. On the LMC shake-up, Nelson offered: "I don't want to stack the deck, but I do want to send a clear signal that it won't be business as usual for the committee" (GAO 1991, p. 9; Kerr and Neal 1995, p. 8; "Committee Member Quits in Boyd County" 1991). For the company and its consultants, the effect was dramatic. As described by John DeOld of US Ecology:

> Although in the past the atmosphere of the public attending monitoring committee meetings had at times been tense, the developer and committee had some opportunities to exchange ideas and information. After the committee adopted a position opposing the project, citizens supporting the project stopped attending meetings, and the atmosphere became more hostile. Committee members made it clear that they were unable or unwilling to control the crowds. The new chairman [Jim Selle] (who had previously helped organize the county opposition group) made frequent public statements that seemed sympathetic to those individuals harassing and threatening project staff. Ultimately, the project made the decision that, for reasons of personal safety, attendance at the meetings could not continue.
>
> (DeOld et al. 1994, p. 1340)

The LMC and many Nebraska officials shared a widely held view that if the facility was developed before similar facilities in other states, Nebraska might become the host for "a major part of the low-level and hazardous waste generated in the United States" (GAO Letter to the Honorable J. James Exon 1992). Back in 1985, Congress had set 1 January 1993 as the date when Nevada, South Carolina and Washington could begin denying out-of-compact waste shipments. The worry was that the NRC would invoke the 'emergency access' provision of the Low-Level Radioactive Waste Policy Act Amendments (LLRWPAA) in order to provide continued disposal services for those generators who no longer had access to Beatty, Barnwell and Hanford. The GAO explained that the NRC did not "anticipate any situation where the lack of access would create a serious and immediate threat to the public health and safety" (NRC 1991, pp. 2, 4). However, the GAO's assurances did little to satisfy opponents. Indeed, it was precisely this concern that prompted suggestions during a confidential planning session amongst state officials that a decision to grant the license be delayed until all other states/compacts had either submitted license applications or until the majority had granted licenses to try to ensure Nebraska was not the first or second licensee, "in case the feds decide we only need a few facilities nationwide" (Options Meeting between Burke, Harsh, Hayden and Allen, n.d.). In July 1991 the governors of Nebraska and Michigan unsuccessfully proposed an amendment to the National Governors Association's nuclear policy calling for a reexamination of the LLRW facility development process, including costs and number of sites (GAO 1992, p. 21).

There was widespread concern about the uncertain compact economics and how key stakeholders might react. A number of legislators feared that if disposal prices were too high, members (states and/or generators) would defect and ship their waste somewhere cheaper. At the admittedly extreme end of this debate, Senator Chambers asked whether the compact provided for the use of federal troops to enforce its provisions at a 1989 hearing (Committee on Judiciary 1989). Nebraska's former compact commissioner Gregory Hayden was particularly vocal, arguing that the waste generated by the Central Compact would not provide an adequate revenue stream, putting pressure on US Ecology and the state to raise disposal fees.[20] Alternative strategies to drive disposal fees back down were no more palatable: the other compact members could force Nebraska to accept new members or several compacts could be consolidated.

There was also a symbiotic relationship between the governor's office and the Boyd County LMC. Ostensibly, the "purpose of the LMC was to facilitate communications between US Ecology, Nebraska, and the residents of Boyd County. In fact, the LMC [had] served as a vigorous site opponent and an aggressive litigator" since 1991 (*Entergy Arkansas, Inc. v. Nebraska* 2002). Not only that, in a 2 September 1992 e-mail to her supervisor, Allen asserted that the LMC could "be used by the Governor to do things he cannot do directly" (*Entergy Arkansas, Inc. v. Nebraska* 2002). Indeed, in its affirmation of the dismissal of the Boyd County and Boyd County LMC suit against US Ecology claiming lack of community consent, the Court of Appeals for the Eighth Circuit held that "Boyd County and the LMC are for preclusion purposes one and the same as Nebraska" (*Entergy Arkansas, Inc. v. Nebraska* 2002).

This is not to suggest that the LMC was simply a creature of the governor's office; both groups wanted the same thing and worked together to achieve their goal. For example, in 1992 Kate Allen received a briefing from DEQ legal counsel Mike Linder and then discussed his analysis with LMC lawyer Pat Knapp; Allen also provided Knapp with internal DEQ documents. If evidence was needed of where the governor's sympathies lay, it was provided in 1997. In August, the governor's office coordinated a LLRW summit. Shortly before the event was scheduled to occur, Town of Butte chairman Harold Reiser wrote to Nelson asking why the city had only just found out about it and why no one had been asked to participate. Steve Moeller replied that he had announced the summit at an LMC meeting in July. "As you know, the State of Nebraska views the county as the host community. . . . At this time, we have no plans of having villages and townships in Boyd County participate directly on any of the summit panels." Moeller did express his hope that all villages and townships sent people to attend. Tellingly, both Loren Sieh and Charles Zidko were invited to speak (Letter from Steve Moeller to Harold Reiser 1997; Letter of Invitation from Governor Nelson to Loren Sieh 1997; Letter of Invitation from Governor Nelson to Charles Zidko 1997).

While the Boyd County LMC was being remade in the opposition's image, the compact commission was undermining its own credibility. Opposition groups and Nebraska officials had been questioning why the commission had not allowed an audit in 3 years, and on 23 April 1991 the reason became clear. Based on evidence provided by commission bookkeeper Audrey Richert, chairman Ray Peery was taken into custody by Lincoln police and the FBI on suspicion of stealing from the commission ("Chief of Waste Panel Is Charged with Theft" 1991; Governor's Office News Release 1991). In January 1992, Peery was found guilty of one count of theft and three counts of money laundering for stealing almost $800,000 and was sentenced to 4 years and 2 months in prison ("Former Compact Director Given Four Years" 1992, p. 1).[21]

The attorney general's office is asked to weigh in . . . then isn't

In addition to 'local' politics, state officials were paying close attention to developments in other states. Kate Allen had spoken with a California Department of Environmental Health lawyer in April 1992 about the problems US Ecology was having getting licensed in Ward Valley. Allen had also been in contact with Vermont LLRW officials in August 1992 regarding a lawsuit that had been brought against their contractor for "missing a fatal flaw of wetlands on the selected site." Shortly after the Vermont consultation, Allen spoke with a member of the governor's staff about how DEQ director Randy Wood's mind might be changed if he determined that wetlands on the site were not a 'fatal flaw.' Allen's concern was that if DEQ determined that the floodplains and wetlands did not constitute a 'fatal flaw' and the attorney general agreed with this assessment – an outcome considered likely given both the merits of the case and the fact that Attorney General Don Stenberg was a political rival of Nelson – then "hello waste dump and send the National Guard to Boyd County." In retrospect, this may not have been too much of an exaggeration.

On 14 October 1992, Wood requested an attorney general's opinion on the position that as long as the waste disposal structure – as opposed to the larger 320-acre site – was not in a wetland, then the site suitability requirements would not be violated. And less than a month later, many state officials' worst fears were about to be realized. On 5 November, Steve Moeller called Assistant Attorney General Linda Willard, who was preparing her opinion. Willard informed Moeller that she would find DEQ's position as outlined in the request legally defensible. Moeller then met with the directors of DEQ and DOH and Kim Robak, Nelson's legal counsel and, as per Robak's instruction, called Willard to inform her that the request would be withdrawn. The opinion was never issued.

"Hit-and-run guerilla warfare": the opposition strategy of litigation

In February 1990, opponents launched what would be the first of many legal challenges. Concerned Citizens of Nebraska filed suit against the NRC, Nebraska DEC, Central Compact Commission and US Ecology to prevent the establishment of a disposal site on a variety of constitutional and fundamental rights grounds. In finding the NRC waste regulations valid and the rest of the claims lacking merit, Judge Urbom dismissed the case against the commission and US Ecology in October 1990 and dismissed the case against the NRC in April 1991. The Court of Appeals for the Eighth Circuit ruled that Urbom did not have the jurisdiction to consider NRC regulations but affirmed the remainder of the decision in July 1992 (*Concerned Citizens of Nebraska v. United States Nuclear Regulatory Commission* 1992; *Entergy Arkansas, Inc. v. Nebraska* 2002). Hot on the heels of this defeat, Diane Burton and Dawneane Munn sued the commission claiming that the body increased their taxes unconstitutionally. On 24 February 1993 the case was dismissed. This did not prevent an unsuccessful appeal followed by an unsuccessful petition to the US Supreme Court (Central Interstate Low-Level Radioactive Waste Commission 1999). The entire legal process took 2 years to play out. In April 1992 the LMC filed suit, claiming that the compact commission failed to provide information on a funding arrangement in which the major generators provided $16.9 million toward the licensing process. Judge Urbom dismissed the case in June (*Entergy Arkansas, Inc. v. Nebraska* 2002).

On 30 December 1992, Boyd County and the Boyd County Local Monitoring Committee filed suit against US Ecology, asserting again that community consent had not been obtained. The suit was dismissed in July 1994 and affirmed on appeal in February 1995. When handing down his July decision, US District Judge for the District of Nebraska Richard Kopf advised:

> While the State of Nebraska and its constituent political bodies are entitled to fully and fairly litigate their legitimate claims, they are not entitled to wage what might be characterized as hit-and-run guerilla warfare by filing multiple lawsuits on the same claim in order to frustrate performance of the compact.
>
> (*Entergy Arkansas, Inc. v. Nebraska* 2002)

On 3 February 1995, Nebraska filed suit against the commission claiming it was wrongly withholding federal rebate funds. The commission filed a counterclaim contending that Nebraska failed to provide a proper accounting for use of the funds. Both claims were dismissed with prejudice in July. This case is also notable because it is the only one that the state did not lose. In addition to the questions of rebates, Nebraska also filed suit contending that the state had the right to a second voting compact commissioner and a third nonvoting commissioner. That case was dismissed in October 1995. Senior state officials were fully supportive of the opposition strategy and even had some ideas of their own about how to make it more effective. In a meeting with site opponents, Governor Nelson explained: "Let's talk about litigation [without] giving our plan to the other side – we want to keep them off balance" (*Entergy Arkansas, Inc. v. Nebraska* 2002). Indeed, "off balance" may have been an understatement. According to Kate Allen's notes of 23 January 1991, at least some staff "want USEcol[ogy] to think EBN [Earl Benjamin Nelson] is deranged."[22]

In 1996 the Boyd County Board of Equalization almost tripled its valuation of the 320 acres US Ecology had purchased in 1990. A higher valuation would, of course, result in more tax revenue for the state. In 1997, the company took the board to court. On 5 May 1998, the Nebraska Court of Appeals ruled in favor of US Ecology, finding the board's valuation "arbitrary and capricious" (*US Ecology v. Boyd County Board of Equalization* 1998). On 22 August 1997, Nebraska filed suit against the commission asserting that it had the right to veto waste exports and imports. The case was dismissed in November 1998 and the decision upheld on appeal in April 2000 (*Entergy Arkansas, Inc. v. Nebraska* 2002).

In response to this barrage of lawsuits, the compact commission created a litigation committee. However, when opponents found out it would meet in executive session (in accordance with the compact's bylaws), they accused the commissioners of acting contrary to the compact's commitment to transparency (Letter from Phyllis Weakly to the Central Interstate Compact Commissioners 1997).

License denial: round one

On 22 January 1993, DEQ issued a Notice of Intent to Deny the license application due to poor drainage and 42 acres of wetlands at the proposed site. In response, US Ecology initiated a contested case. According to the company, DEQ's position was based on its interpretation of the terms 'unit,' 'site,' 'facility' and 'buffer zone.' Federal and state regulations required that no waste be disposed of in a wetland.

> Even though waste would be placed in a disposal unit (part of the disposal site), the definitional path of the agencies led to the conclusion that, in essence, the presence of wetlands in the buffer zone (part of the facility) would preclude disposal of the waste in the facility.
>
> (DeOld et al. 1994, p. 1341)

Shortly after the Notice of Intent to Deny was issued, Barnwell closed its doors to Central Compact generators, citing lack of progress toward licensing a facility.

In August 1993, US Ecology redrew the site boundaries, eliminating "all but one very small [less than one acre] wetland" and reducing the site from 320 acres to 110 acres, resulting in the withdrawal of the Notice of Intent to Deny by DEQ (DeOld et al. 1994, p. 1340). US Ecology also scaled back its plans in accordance with the diminished real estate: 12 Class A waste cells and one Class B/C cell. State officials responded on two fronts. First, US Ecology was prevented from carrying out any mitigation work at the site. The Army Corps of Engineers had granted the company permission to plow and fill the wetland. However, state officials made clear that any attempt to do so without a license would constitute 'construction,' resulting in denial of the license. Second,

Nebraska filed a suit claiming that community consent had not been obtained for the smaller site, even though it was fully contained within the original 320 acres. This suit was also dismissed. In a sign of how fraught relations had become, the commission and US Ecology filed a motion of sanctions against the state. In an effort to defuse the situation, the presiding judge brokered a compromise in December: "Although I find that the motion for sanctions is generally meritorious, at my specific request counsel for both defendants have graciously agreed to withdraw their motion" (*Entergy Arkansas, Inc. v. Nebraska* 2002).

License denial: round two

In mid-1992, the Nebraska Auditor of Public Accounts recommended that DEQ adopt a budget and timetable for the project. DEQ never did.[23] After 6 years of delay, the nonhost members of the compact had had enough. On 27 August 1996, the commission held a special meeting to determine an appropriate schedule for Nebraska to process the license. The directors of DEQ and DOH declined to attend or participate. On 30 September, after giving the state the opportunity to object, the commission ordered Nebraska to issue the Draft Environmental Impact Analysis and Draft Safety Evaluation Report and set 14 January 1997 as the hard deadline for the license review to be completed. Two months later, the state filed suit contending the commission had no right to set a deadline. Judge Urbom found for the commission in October 1998, a decision that was upheld on appeal in August 1999.[24]

In late August 1997, HDR and JHC presented their groundwater, surface water and financial assurance findings to state officials. The consultants found that the application complied with the license requirements. Given concerns over the financial condition of American Ecology (US Ecology's parent company), they recommended that a conditional license be issued, requiring the company to provide construction financing documentation within 120 days.[25]

In October 1997, the state's Draft Safety Evaluation Report (DSER) and the Draft Environmental Impact Analysis (DEIA) were released. The state also conducted its own Independent Performance Assessment (IPA) – an analysis of long-term structure performance postclosure conducted by an independent consultant. The DSER found the license (including financial assurance) acceptable and the IPA determined that annual human exposure doses would be less than the regulatory limits. And while the DSER indicated that the facility would impact several environmental resources, the DEIA countered that all potentially adverse environmental impacts could be mitigated except for sociocultural impacts. The draft documents also explained that these impacts were expected to decline during the period of facility operation, assuming the facility operated without radiological accidents. The release triggered a 90-day public comment period ending with public hearings that were held from 2–5 February 1998 in Naper and Butte – more than 2,000 comments were received (Central Interstate Low-Level Radioactive Waste Commission n.d., pp. 5–6).

In June 1998, Marvin Carlson, a University of Nebraska geology professor and the state's review manager for site characteristics, submitted his draft responses to public comments. The bottom line: "The disposal facility is above any potential groundwater level, is not in a wetland, and no part of the site lies within a 100-year floodplain. . . . There are no flowing wells or springs on site" (*Entergy Arkansas, Inc. v. Nebraska* 2002). However, by this time, powerful political forces were at play. An 18 July e-mail from Craig Osborn of HDR to his fellow consultants, apprising them of a surprise visit by DEQ officials the day before, instructed:

> Please call all RMs [review managers] and notify them of a mandatory mtg. on July 27th at Mahoney Lodge. We need to also advise them that *they may be asked to meet with Randy [Wood] during the remainder of that week . . . to reconsider their response to comments.*
>
> (*Entergy Arkansas, Inc. v. Nebraska* 2002, emphasis added)

At a press conference on 6 August 1998, Nebraska regulators announced their Intent to Deny US Ecology's license application. Seven reasons were provided:

- The site lacked sufficient depth to the water table.
- The site lacked an adequate buffer zone beneath the waste for environmental monitoring and mitigative measures.
- Engineered barriers were planned substitutes for a suitable site.
- Groundwater discharged to the surface within the disposal site.
- The high groundwater table would intercept the leachate collections system and site deficiencies would require continuing active maintenance after site closure.
- US Ecology and American Ecology had not demonstrated that they were financially qualified to finance the project.
- The Radiation Safety Program did not adequately address accidents or off-site consequences.

Public hearings were again held in Naper and Butte in November 1998 and US Ecology rebutted the proposed denial. In particular, the company relied on testimony from Princeton hydrology professor Stewart Taylor, who had prepared groundwater models for the DSER. Despite what it believed was a strong technical case for licensing the site as then configured, US Ecology attempted to scale back the facility footprint again. This time, the company offered to build only four Class A waste cells and one Class B/C cell (*Entergy Arkansas, Inc. v. Nebraska* 2002). Whatever the hydrologic merits of this solution, US Ecology had conceded actual, or at the very least potential, problems with the site. This compromise failed to satisfy opponents and on 18 December the license application was formally denied (Nebraska DEQ 1998a; Nebraska DEQ 1998b).

"A complete lack of performance": the final court case

On 30 December 1998, the major regional waste generators (Entergy Arkansas/ Gulf States/Louisiana and Wolf Creek Nuclear Operating Corporation, who had collectively spent a reported $90 million trying to get a facility built [O'Hanlon 2011]), filed suit against the state, its agents and the commission, claiming injury due to the 'bad faith' review by the state's regulators. All environmental monitoring activities ceased the next day, although that did not stop DEQ from demanding, on 25 January 1999, $100,000 from US Ecology by 1 February to pay the LMC. The same month, the commission realigned itself as a plaintiff (Central Interstate Low-Level Waste Commission n.d., p. 6). When the other compact members joined, Nebraska Commissioner Gregory Hayden railed: "This is an attempt to strip Nebraska of its statehood. It's an attack on our state" ("States Join Nuclear Waste Suit against Nebraska" 1999). The Eighth Circuit Court of Appeals dismissed the generators as plaintiffs but allowed the commission to continue. US Ecology's Lincoln and Butte offices were closed on 31 March. In April, the US District Court issued a preliminary injunction against Nebraska and others, finding good reason to believe that Nebraska's denial, on safety and environmental grounds, of a license to construct and operate a disposal facility was "politically preordained." The final break came on 6 May when the legislature adopted LB 530 withdrawing Nebraska from the compact. Six days later Governor Johanns signed the bill, which became effective 27 August 1999 (Nebraska Unicameral Legislature 1999; Nebraska Legislature 1999, p. 82).[26] However, according to the compact statute, unless permitted by unanimous approval of the commission, withdrawal would only take effect 5 years after a governor had given notice in writing (Public Law 99–240 1986). The rest of the commissioners were in no mood to do Nebraska any favors.

The trial began in July 2001, concluded 14 months later and cost Nebraska $25 million in legal fees to fight – and lose (O'Hanlon 2011). It would cost almost six times that figure to settle. In a scathing 2002 decision, US District Judge Richard Kopf of Lincoln found:

> Governor Nelson either directly or through his subordinates, influenced the process in order to fulfill a campaign promise, which required that the license be denied without regard to the technical merits. . . . Frankly, I cannot conceive of a stronger case of bad faith in the performance of a contract.[27]

The commission also sought equitable relief; that is, an independent body to conduct a relicensing process and, if the license was granted, independent supervision over Nebraska's regulation of the facility. Judge Kopf determined that this was inappropriate for two reasons: first, he had

> no confidence that the staff of DOH or DEQ could be restored to an objective state of mind by a mere court order even should I impose the supervision

of a special master. Still further, many of the key consultants . . . have been put in the position of having to defend Nebraska in this litigation. . . . Like water in a well laced with poison, the only alternative is to look elsewhere.

(*Entergy Arkansas, Inc. v. Nebraska* 2002)

Second, Nebraska had withdrawn from the compact for all intents and purposes, creating "a fog of uncertainty about this court's ability to effectively enforce an equitable order during any necessary remedial period" (*Entergy Arkansas, Inc. v. Nebraska* 2002).

In 2004, the Court of Appeals for the Eighth Circuit affirmed a federal district court decision that Nebraska, as the designated host state, was liable for more than $151 million in damages for reneging on its obligations. In his 2002 opinion, Judge Kopf was blunt: "There was a complete lack of performance on the part of Nebraska such that the Commission received nothing of value from its dealing with Nebraska." Subsequently, the Central Interstate Compact voted 3 to 1 to accept a settlement with Nebraska for $141 million plus interest.[28] Under the settlement, if Nebraska and the other compact members negotiated access to the proposed disposal facility in Texas, the amount Nebraska would have to pay would be reduced to $130 million plus interest (GAO 2004, p. 9). As will be discussed in the next chapter, Texas would not be ready to offer this service for about a decade. Nebraska had earlier offered to pay the Lone Star State a flat $25 million, plus another $5 million to cover any unforeseen storage expenses, to take the compact's waste. On 1 August 2005, the state treasurer's office wire-transferred $145,811,367.11 to the compact commission; it was "the single largest payment ever made in the state" at that time.[29]

Conclusion

In July 2005, the Central Interstate Compact Commission, based on "the availability and adequacy of options for the processing, storage and disposal of LLRW, . . . determined that no need currently exists for the siting, construction and operation of a disposal facility in the Compact region." As a result, the commission would "defer active efforts to site a disposal facility until such time as it determines that the needs of the LLRW generators in the region and the public interest justify pursuit of such a facility" (Central Interstate Low-Level Radioactive Waste Commission n.d.). There was also a feeling that the Boyd County experience had so poisoned the atmosphere that the Central Compact might be broken. Ron Hammerschmidt of the Kansas Department of Environment observed: "It's improbable that anyone could force the development. We sure couldn't make it happen in Nebraska" (O'Hanlon 2011). This brought to a close the most contentious chapter in US LLRW compact history. Nebraska is the poster child for how badly things can go wrong in hazardous waste disposal siting. Some of the reasons are fairly obvious; others are more subtle.

To begin with the most obvious, it is extraordinarily difficult for any project to move forward when most state officials, following the governor's lead, are actively opposed. According John Weingart, director of New Jersey's Low Level Radioactive Waste Disposal Facility Siting Board from September 1994 to August 1998, "Nebraska was never treated as a serious contender" at the national siting board meetings he attended. "In fact, the Central Compact Commission director frequently had to deny reports of his own program's death" (Weingart 2001, p. 341).

Just as important, the public opposition was organized, energized and prepared for a long fight. Individuals and groups felt strongly about radioactive waste and a small but significant minority was willing to take rather extreme measures to ensure the facility was never built. The unwillingness to define 'host community' or 'consent' clearly also hurt siting efforts and aided the opponents' cause. Some of this has been traced back to Boyd's history of intertown rivalries and the resulting lack of a countywide sense of community.[30] According to Boyd County Board member Robert Classen: "How far do you go with community consent: One mile away? Five miles? The whole county? Not the way they fight, it's not a community" (Worthington 1990). For sure, any definition would have been controversial. But by settling on the ambiguous characterization "the developer shall make every effort to locate the facility where community support is evident," legislators (and Governor Orr) allowed opponents to lay claim to their own definitions. Without any firm guidance from Lincoln, US Ecology's position – that Butte was the 'host community' and it had given consent – was not necessarily any more legitimate than anyone else's formulation.

It is also worth noting that seemingly small misunderstandings can have important cumulative effects in these highly charged situations. For example, the *Lawrence World-Journal* reported in June 1994 that US Ecology's project director told the Central Compact Commission that a state official had asked him to keep the weeds down at the site, so he contracted with a local farmer to plow a section of the site and plant grain sorghum. However, because US Ecology did not have a written order, the commission refused to pay the $9,000 for the work ("Nuclear Dump Still in Limbo" 1994, p. 3B). Even if not true (and the authors have no reason to doubt its veracity), these sorts of stories chip away at the credibility of the developer and the siting authorities in the eyes of the public, further inflaming an already toxic relationship.

The opposition benefited from the makeup of the host county's economy, if not its health. A predominantly farming community, there were no nuclear power plants in Boyd County or similar industries that could have created powerful constituencies for LLRW disposal as they have in other states and countries. The locus of support was the town of Butte but it was far from unanimous. While supporters boycotted the LMC's informal 1992 poll of Boyd County, more than a quarter of Butte residents did participate and voted against the disposal facility. Similarly, the Butte Village Board of Trustees was a key project supporter, while the Boyd County Board of Supervisors passed resolutions in January 1989 withdrawing support for the facility. It is significant that the former is predominantly a business association; the latter is responsible for public policy more broadly defined. Opponents also controlled the LMC after mid-1991, which served as an interface between US Ecology and the county, and made little attempt to carry out their work objectively. Whether the Citizens Advisory Committee would have mitigated some of the community distrust had it served for the duration of Nebraska's compact membership is an open question, but nothing short of the cancellation of the project would satisfy the dedicated opponents such as Save Boyd County and the Boyd County LMC, and they were receiving plenty of support from government officials in Lincoln.

Opponents were also assisted by meteorology. The disposal facility was to be built in a high rainfall area that required some relatively complicated modeling, in particular hydrology. It is much easier to make the safety case for a facility in the desert where there is very little water to contend with. To many members of the public, rain plus complex engineering seemed to suggest that the site was not ideal. Opponents made the most of this, memorably holding a canoe race in a ditch near the site in 1994 to highlight the amount of water that would surround and possibly penetrate the facility. US Ecology scaled back the facility design twice, to no avail. Further, engineered barriers were portrayed as evidence that the site was unsuitable rather than as redundant safety measures. Charles Zidko's observation was representative: "The site has been extensively engineered to cover up poor site selection" (Committee on Natural Resources 1997, p. 51). This is a common opposition strategy and was used to great effect in Nevada where opponents contemptuously described the engineered barriers for Yucca Mountain such as titanium drip shields as "ever-more-exotic engineering 'fixes' " and offered them up as proof that the geological science was flawed (Breslow 2010, p. 2). While engineered barriers are considered best practice for a defense-in-depth approach to disposal, the proposition that they are covering up for flawed real estate can be very difficult to rebut, particularly when there is no definitive scientific 'answer' to the question of safety; geologists and hydrologists could be found to show that the facility would be safe or unsafe or anywhere in between. This is even tougher when the public is already skeptical, and folks in Boyd County had reason for pause. Opponents had made much of US Ecology's poor operational record in Illinois, Kentucky and Nevada and, while not a US Ecology employee, Ray Peery's money laundering activities certainly didn't help matters.

Like many other states considering LLRW disposal in the 1980s and 1990s, there was a fear amongst members of the public as well as in the government and legislature that if the proposed facility became operational before other states/compacts developed new disposal facilities, Nebraska might be forced to accept LLRW from all over the country. This proved difficult to dispel. While federal law protected Nebraska from being forced to accept out-of-compact waste, there was a large amount of skepticism that this would hold up if tested. After all, Nebraska had been forced by the other four compact commissioners to host a disposal facility back in 1987. There were also legitimate questions about the economics of LLRW disposal in a compact that generated a relatively small amount of waste and whether out-of-compact waste would be necessary to keep disposal prices affordable for the compact generators.

For the government and the opposition, the courts served a very important purpose just as they did in many other places around the US and around the world. Between 1993 and 1997, Nebraska filed six lawsuits, losing five and settling one. Boyd County also filed suit and lost. Viewed in isolation, the court cases were a complete failure. From a strategic perspective, however, they were wildly successful. They served as a highly effective delaying tactic, in some cases taking years as they wound their way to the Supreme Court. Indeed, Governor Nelson argued in June 1995 "our best bet is to be the underdog who has been taken advantage of by the bad power companies" (*Entergy Arkansas, Inc. v. Nebraska* 2002). The longer these cases dragged on, the more reasonable this explanation appeared.

The experience has left lasting scars in Boyd County. According to Senator Merton 'Cap' Dierks, the fight "broke families apart. One family wouldn't hold a funeral in Butte where they had attended church for years. A widow asked that her husband be buried in South Dakota" ("Nuclear Dump Still in Limbo" 1994, p. 3B). A local farm owner confirmed to one of the authors in 2014 that this was, and continues to be, the case in Butte and other parts of the county (Boyd County resident, Bonesteel, South Dakota, personal communication, 25 October 2014).

Notes

1 Senator Schmit offered a compelling reason for compact membership: independently it was certain that Nebraska would have to provide a disposal facility for its waste; in the Central Compact there was only a 20% chance that Nebraska would host. "[T]his is about as good as we can do to assure the citizens of Nebraska that we will not just automatically become a dumping ground for this type of waste" (Nebraska Legislature n.d., p. 4455).

2 The authors would like to thank Nebraska Legislative Records Historian Diana Bridges for providing a copy of this legislation.

3 The League provided support services to the committee with a grant from US Ecology.

4 By prohibiting "shallow-land burial as practiced prior to 1979," the legislature was instructing US Ecology to design a facility incorporating the most advanced engineered barriers in order to prevent the leakage problems that plagued first generation trench disposal (Bedinger 1989).

5 Opponents referred to the French facility CSM but meant CSA. The CSM disposal facility, adjacent to AREVA's La Hague spent fuel reprocessing facility, was commissioned in 1969 for short-lived LLRW and intermediate level radioactive waste (ILRW) and operated until 1994.

> In the mid-1980s, in preparation for closure of the CSM, Andra designed a new surface disposal facility, the CSA, located 250 km (155 miles) east of Paris. . . . Its design took stock of the lessons learnt at the CSM and it was commissioned in January 1992.
> (Nuclear Energy Agency [NEA] 2014, p. 11–12; Dupuis 2006)

6 A mid-1990s Butte house income survey provides clear insight into why the financial benefits of a disposal facility might be so attractive to the town: 15 households earned less than $10,000/year; 14 between $10,000 and $15,000; 6 between $15,000 and $20,000; 6 between $20,000 and $25,000; 10 between $25,000 and $35,000; 5 between $35,000 and $45,000; and 3 over $45,000 ("Butte Community Survey" n.d.).

7 Senator Remmers noted that he and his neighbors were not consulted when the Cooper nuclear power plant, 'a greater danger than a LLRW disposal facility,' was built and no one complained. Senator Schmit made an unfortunate comparison with the "unauthorized, unsupervised, nonmonitored [sic] dumping of low-level [radioactive] waste" at the University of Nebraska's Agricultural Research and Development Center near Mead in Saunders County. "I believe the people have just decided that they are going to have to rely upon the good judgment of those individuals who are qualified to know what best to do in this regard." Formerly an ordnance plant, the EPA would later discover that residential water supply wells had been contaminated by volatile organic compounds, requiring extensive cleanup operations (Nebraska Legislature n.d., pp. 10960, 10964; EPA 2009).

8 Senator Dierks blamed the demise of the county vote on utility, compact and US Ecology lobbyists "working the rotunda" (Committee on Natural Resources 1997, p. 27).

9 Kaufman was a long-time government whistleblower. See McCardle 2011.

10 After initially refusing to fill its two positions on the LMC, arguing that to do so implied support for the project, the Boyd County Board of Supervisors tried to get an associate of Kaufman's in Nebraska state government on the committee.

11 The South Dakota Senate passed a resolution praising Nelson's efforts to stop the project in 1993 (South Dakota Legislature Release 1993).

12 Harold Pierce's tenure was not a pleasant one. His wife wrote a letter to Governor Orr in 1990 explaining that the veteran of two wars and Silver Star awardee was being sued by Jim Selle for defamation of character and the loss of Selle's wood stove business, and he had been repeatedly threatened to the point that he had obtained a permit to carry a concealed weapon (Letter from Beatty Pierce to Kay Orr 1990).

13 Arden Davis submitted a highly critical final report to the South Dakota government in 2002 (Expert Report of Arden D. Davis 2002).

14 Robbins 1990.

15 In 1990, the *Omaha World-Herald* reported that the Central Compact Commission planned to pay Los Angeles firm Winner Wagner & Mandabach $989,000 to develop a public education campaign to "offset negative attacks on the project." Winner Wagner & Mandabach also helped defeat Initiative 402. Senator Schmit thought it a big waste of money:

> It is just doggone silly to pay some outfit from Los Angeles to come here and tell us what a lucky bunch of hay shakers we are to have this thing put in our back yard. . . . The facility is going to be located here, three sites have already been identified. Ninety nine percent of the people in the state . . . do not care if it is here or not, and the one percent who do might just as well beat their head against a brick wall.
>
> ("Schmit Attacks Waste Site Publicity Funds," 1990)

16 Webster County is in the south of the state and shares a border with Kansas. With Nuckolls County to the east and Clay County to the northeast, Webster was located in the heart of a potential host region.

17 "Ruby Ridge" refers to the 1992 siege at the Ruby Ridge property of Randy Weaver in northern Idaho. The resulting confrontation between the family, a friend and federal authorities resulted in the deaths of Weaver's wife and son and a federal marshal.

18 Fisher ended his hunger strike about a week before the election, explaining that while his goal of making Boyd County consent a formal part of the siting process was not achieved, he did succeed in making more people in Nebraska and across the United States aware of what was going on. "Never did I say that I would starve to death or that I would continue until November 6th." However, he certainly alluded to this a year earlier: "I told my children, they're going to build this waste site in Boyd County over my dead body. I don't lie to my children" (Press Statement of Lowell Fisher 1990; Testimony of Lowell Fisher Before the Committee on Natural Resources 1989).

19 Don Walton provides good perspective on Governor Orr's 4-year term and the reasons for her defeat in Walton 2013.

20 Despite the facility's capacity of 5 million cubic feet, a US Ecology spokesman estimated in 1989 that the facility would only receive 50,000–70,000 cubic feet of compact waste during its 30-year operating life. Hayden maintained that this situation would be exacerbated by increasingly effective waste reduction strategies and the cheaper option of sending the compact's Class A waste to the Envirocare facility in Utah. Envirocare owner Khosrow Semnani sent a letter to Governor Nelson in May 1995 offering precisely this service (Schmidt 1989; Trip Report and Meeting Notes 1996; Letter from Khosrow Semnani to Governor Nelson 1995).

21 Peery, who had been carrying on an affair with his office manager Kelly Gold, used the money to buy furniture, jewelry, vacations and cars (including a Mercedes, a BMW and a Jaguar). He also gave car loans to two University of Nebraska basketball players in violation of National Collegiate Athletic Association rules (Cragin 2007, p. 147; "Huskers' Probe Turns up New Violations" 1991).

22 Nelson admitted that he sometimes used the 'deranged governor' phraseology, but stated that when he used those words he only intended to refer to some future governor (*Entergy Arkansas, Inc. v. Nebraska* 2002).

23 According to court documents, Kate Allen also tried to convince the auditor to change his findings (*Entergy Arkansas, Inc. v. Nebraska* 2002).

24 The Court of Appeals did not make a determination on the deadline because the license had been denied by that point. However, in a footnote to its decision, the court noted: "Without addressing the issue directly, we believe, in any event, that the deadline established by the Commission was reasonable" (*Entergy Arkansas, Inc. v. Nebraska* 2002).

25 The financial health of American Ecology was a major source of controversy between supporters and opponents of the project. See *Entergy Arkansas, Inc. v. Nebraska* 2002.

26 This was not the first time the legislature had considered pulling out of the compact. In January 1990, Senator McFarland introduced LB 1025 proposing Nebraska's withdrawal; Senator Schmit prevented the bill from going to a floor vote (Statement of Dierks 1999, pp. 61–62).

27 Kopf added:

> First, I am firmly convinced that Governor Nelson believed his conduct to be justified, and that he honestly thought he was acting in the best interests of his constituents. The evidence shows that from the beginning of the process, Nelson thought the Commission's method of selecting a site was terribly flawed, and that Nebraskans had been deprived of their right to community consent. Second, and this point cannot be overemphasized, subjective beliefs that one's conduct is justified do not diminish the obligation imposed under the compact to exercise objective good faith.
>
> (*Entergy Arkansas, Inc. v. Nebraska* 2002)

28 Nebraska could not vote; Kansas was the lone no-vote. Kansas officials said they rejected the settlement because it represented a failure of the compact system (O'Hanlon 2004). Greg Hayden had likely not endeared himself to colleagues in Topeka when, 4 years earlier, he suggested that the compact needed to look to another state to host a disposal facility, then added "We all know it's going to be Kansas" ("Nebraska Wants Nuclear Waste Dump to Be in Kansas" 1998).

29 According to State Accounting Administrator Paul Carlson, the payment amounted to roughly $83 for each resident (Laukaitis 2005).

30 Susan Cragin's *Nuclear Nebraska*, an unabashedly partisan retelling of the LLRW story from the opponents' perspective, does provide some interesting insight into the centrality of schools to small town life and offers a credible explanation for some of the bad blood between Butte and its neighbors (Cragin 2007, pp. 15–18).

References

Bartimus, T., "Plan for Nuclear Dump Stirs Rancor in Rural Nebraska," *Los Angeles Times* (26 March 1989), http://articles.latimes.com/1989-03-26/news/mn-778_1_nuclear-waste-dump

Bedinger, M. S., *Geohydrologic Aspects for Siting and Design of Low-Level Radioactive-Waste Disposal*, U.S. Geological Survey Circular 1034 (1989), http://pubs.usgs.gov/circ/1989/1034/report.pdf

Beliles, D., "Nuclear Waste Isn't Going Away," *Grand Island Independent* (13 October 1990).

Boyd County, Nebraska. "About Boyd County" (n.d.), www.boydcounty.ne.gov/webpages/about/about.html

"Boyd County Residents Expect Violence," *McCook Daily Gazette* (29 July 1992).

Breslow, B., "Yucca Mountain – Lessons to Be Learned and a Strategy for the Future," *Blue Ribbon Commission on America's Nuclear Future – Disposal Subcommittee* (7 July 2010), http://brc.gov/Disposal_SC/docs/Bruce%20Breslow-NV%20Agency%20for%20NP-Final.pdf

"Butte Community Survey" (n.d.) in Nebraska State Historical Society, Government Records, RG/41, Series 8, Central Interstate Low-Level Radioactive Waste Compact (LLRW-NE), Misc. Files, Committee/State/Legislature, 1987–2005, Box 1 of 2.

Cawley, C., Sabbe, M., Bisese, P., et al., *An Approach to the Licensing of a Mixed Waste Unit* (n.d.), in Nebraska State Historical Society, Government Records, RG/41, Series 1, Central Interstate Low-Level Radioactive Waste Compact (LLRW-NE), Research Files, Misc. Reports, 1989–2003, Box 5 of 5.

"Central Compact Issues Export Authorizations over Nebraska's Objection," LLW Notes, LLW Forum (July 1997), in Nebraska State Historical Society, Government Records, RG/41, Series 1, Central Interstate Low-Level Radioactive Waste Compact (LLRW-NE), Research Files, Articles and Books, 1961–2006, Box 2 of 5.

Central Interstate Low-Level Radioactive Waste Commission, *Actions in Which the Commission Is or Was a Party* (1999), www.cillrwcc.org/Legal_Action/SumLit_A.html

Central Interstate Low-Level Radioactive Waste Commission, *Annual Report 2004–2005* (n.d.), www.cillrwcc.org/2004-2005%20Annual%20Report.pdf

Central Interstate Low-Level Radioactive Waste Commission, *Resolutions of the Central Interstate LLRW Commission* (14–15 July 2005), www.cillrwcc.org/2005-07-14-15_Resolutions.pdf

Central Interstate Low-Level Radioactive Waste Commission, *Rules* (amended 12 June 2013), www.cillrwcc.org/CIC%20Rules%202013-June.pdf

Central Interstate Low-Level Radioactive Waste Compact, Pub. L. No. 99–240, 99 Stat. 1864 (15 January 1986), www.cillrwcc.org/PL99-240-CICsection.pdf

"Chief of Waste Panel Is Charged with Theft," *New York Times* (24 April 1991), www.nytimes.com/1991/04/24/us/chief-of-waste-panel-is-charged-with-theft.html

"Co-chairmen of Anti-nuclear Waste Dump Group Resign," *McCook Daily Gazette* (18 August 1992).

"Committee Member Quits in Boyd County," *Lincoln Journal* (14 August 1991), in Nebraska State Historical Society, Government Records, RG1-Gov. Nelson (SG44).

Committee on Judiciary, *LB 761* (23 October 1989), pp. 33, 35, in Nebraska State Historical Society, Government Records, RG/41, Series 1, Central Interstate Low-Level Radioactive Waste Compact (LLRW-NE), Research Files, Misc. Reports, 1989–2003, Box 5 of 5.

Committee on Natural Resources, *LR 202 Transcript* (13 December 1997), in Nebraska State Historical Society, Government Records, RG/41, Series 8, Central Interstate Low-Level Radioactive Waste Compact (LLRW-NE), Misc. Files, Committee/State/ Legislature, 1987–2005, Box 1 of 2.

Concerned Citizens of Nebraska v. United States Nuclear Regulatory Commission, 970 F.2d 421 (8th Cir. 1992), http://openjurist.org/970/f2d/421/concerned-citizens-of-nebraska-v-united-states-nuclear-regulatory-commission

Cragin, S., *Nuclear Nebraska: The Remarkable Story of the Little County That Couldn't Be Bought* (New York: AMACOM, 2007).

Crump, A.E., "Prepared Testimony: The History of the Central Interstate Low-Level Radioactive Waste Compact Commission," *Natural Resources Committee* (20 March 1997), in Nebraska State Historical Society, Government Records, RG/41, Series 8, Central Interstate Low-Level Radioactive Waste Compact (LLRW-NE), Misc. Files, Committee/State/Legislature, 1987–2005, Box 1 of 2.

DeOld, J., Neal, J., Sabbe, M., and Bagchi, M., "Low-Level Radioactive Waste Disposal: Status of the Central Interstate Compact Nebraska Project," *Waste Management 1994 Symposium*, Tucson, Arizona (27 February–3 March 1994), www.wmsym.org/archives/1994/V2/103.pdf

Di Tullio, L., and Resnikoff, M., Radioactive Waste Management Associates, *Review of Safety Analysis Report, Part 1 – Geology and Hydrology, Proposed Low-Level Waste Facility, Butte, Nebraska* (29 June 1992), in Nebraska State Historical Society, Government Records, RG/41, Series 1, Central Interstate Low-Level Radioactive Waste Compact (LLRW-NE), Research Files, Misc. Reports, 1989–2003, Box 5 of 5.

Dupuis, M.C., "Current Status of the French Radioactive Waste Disposal Programme," European Nuclear Society (2006), www.euronuclear.org/events/topseal/transactions/Paper-Session-I-Dupuis.pdf

Entergy Arkansas, Inc. v. Nebraska, 46 F. Supp. 2d 977 (D. Neb. 1999), http://law.justia.com/cases/federal/district-courts/FSupp2/46/977/2488216/

Entergy Arkansas, Inc. v. Nebraska, 226 F. Supp. 2d 1047 (D. Neb. 2002), http://law.justia.com/cases/federal/district-courts/FSupp2/226/1047/2323080/

Expert Report of Arden D. Davis (South Dakota: No. 4663) (30 January 2002), in Nebraska State Historical Society, Government Records, RG/41, Series 1, Central Interstate Low-Level Radioactive Waste Compact (LLRW-NE), Research Files, Misc. Reports, 1989–2003, Box 5 of 5.

Expert Report of Dr. John Osnes (January 2002) in Nebraska State Historical Society, Government Records, RG/41, Series 1, Central Interstate Low-Level Radioactive Waste Compact (LLRW-NE), Research Files, Misc. Reports, 1989–2003, Box 5 of 5.

"Former Compact Director Given Four Years," *McCook Daily Gazette* (24 January 1992).

Freudenburg, W., and Grevers, J., *Nebraska Statewide Attitudes toward Nuclear Waste Facilities: A Preliminary Analysis*, Social Science Research Associates (1990), in Nebraska State Historical Society, Government Records, RG/41, Series 1, Central Interstate Low-Level Radioactive Waste Compact (LLRW-NE), Research Files, Misc. Reports, 1989–2003, Box 5 of 5.

General Accounting Office, *Low-Level Radioactive Waste: Future Waste Volumes and Disposal Options Are Uncertain – Statement of (Ms.) Robin Nazzaro, Director, Natural Resources and Environment before the Senate Committee on Energy and Natural Resources*, GAO-04–1097T (30 September 2004), www.gao.gov/assets/120/111273.html

General Accounting Office, *Nuclear Waste: Extensive Process to Site Low-Level Waste Disposal Facility in Nebraska*, GAO/RCED-91–149 (July 1991), www.gao.gov/assets/220/214543.pdf

General Accounting Office, *Nuclear Waste: Slow Progress Developing Low-Level Radioactive Waste Disposal Facilities*, GAO/RCED-92–61 (January 1992), www.gao.gov/assets/160/151432.pdf

Governor's Office News Release (23 April 1991), in Nebraska State Historical Society, Government Records, RG1-Gov. Nelson (SG44).

Hubler, S., "Only California Is on Track for Nuclear Dump," *Los Angeles Times* (20 May 1991), http://articles.latimes.com/1991–05–20/news/mn-1454_1_nuclear-waste

"Huskers' Probe Turns up New Violations," *Tulsa World* (14 June 1991), www.tulsaworld.com/archives/huskers-probe-turns-up-new-violations/article_c3f6df2e-922f-5c7d-8541-c704be0f9964.html

Interim Council, Ponca Tribe of Nebraska, Resolution 5–93 (4 January 1993), in Nebraska State Historical Society, Government Records, RG1-Gov. Nelson (SG44).

Kaufman, H., and Moorer, L., "The Nuke Dump NIMBY Game: Why Nebraska Was Targeted," *Public Utilities Fortnightly*, Vol. 128, No. 2 (15 July 1991), in Nebraska State Historical Society, Government Records, RG141, Series 1, Central Interstate Low-Level Radioactive Waste Compact (LLRW-Nebraska), Research Files, Articles and Books, 1961–2006, Box 2 of 5.

Kerr, K., and McDonald, C., *Final Report on the Citizens Advisory Committee on Low-Level Radioactive Waste*, League of Women Voters of Nebraska (May 1989).

Kerr, T., and Neal, J., *What Makes an Effective Citizens Advisory Group? An Analysis of the Effectiveness of Local Citizens Advisory Groups in Siting Low-Level Radioactive Waste Disposal Facilities in the United States*, Afton Associates (5 September 1995), in Nebraska State Historical Society, Government Records, RG/141, Series 1, Central Interstate Low-Level Radioactive Waste Compact (LLRW-NE), Research Files, Reports/Printed Publications, 1992–2006, Box 4 of 5.

Key Issues and Problems Requiring Resolution Prior to Siting and Operating Nuclear and Hazardous Waste Facilities in the State of Nebraska, 1990 Annual Report of the Nuckolls County, Nebraska Nuclear and Hazardous Waste Monitoring Committee, in Nebraska State Historical Society, Government Records, RG/41, Series 1, Central Interstate Low-Level Radioactive Waste Compact (LLRW-NE), Research Files, Misc. Reports, 1989–2003, Box 5 of 5.

Laukaitis, A., "Call Finally Ends Nuke Waste Dispute," *Lincoln Star Journal* (1 August 2005), http://journalstar.com/news/local/call-finally-ends-nuke-waste-dispute/article_d45d3c67-cf09–5053–98df-8ab5a7f8eeb6.html

Legislative Journal of the State of Nebraska, Vol. 1, 90th Legislature, 2nd Session (convened 6 January 1988, adjourned 8 April 1988), Lincoln, Nebraska, www.nebraskalegislature.gov/FloorDocs/90/PDF/Journal/r2journal.pdf

Letter from Alan Woods (offering 235 acres in Blue Hill) (30 December 1987), in Nebraska State Historical Society, Government Records, RG001, Government, SG43, Orr, Kay, S1 Correspondence, Public Opinion, LLRW, Box 42.

Letter from Beatty Pierce to Kay Orr (3 May 1990), in Nebraska State Historical Society, Government Records, RG001, Government, SG43, Orr, Kay, S1, Correspondence, Public Opinion, LLRW, Box 42.

Letter from Dan Meyer to Governor Orr (offering 160 acres in Wisner) (14 January 1988), in Nebraska State Historical Society, Government Records, RG001, Government, SG43, Orr, Kay, S1 Correspondence, Public Opinion, LLRW, Box 42.

Letter from Eugene Crump to Governor Nelson (12 September 1997), in Nebraska State Historical Society, Government Records, RG1-Gov. Nelson (SG44).

Letter from Eugene Crump to Loren Sieh (2 December 1992), in Nebraska State Historical Society, Government Records, RG1-Gov. Nelson (SG44).

Letter from Governor Kay Orr to David Beliles (17 October 1990), in Nebraska State Historical Society, Government Records, RG001, Government, SG43, Orr, Kay, S1, Correspondence, Public Opinion, LLRW, Box 42.

Letter from Governor Kay Orr to Jane Vogt (22 October 1990), in Nebraska State Historical Society, Government Records, RG001, Government, SG43, Orr, Kay, S1, Correspondence, Public Opinion, LLRW, Box 42.

Letter from Governor Nelson to Loren Sieh (13 November 1992), in Nebraska State Historical Society, Government Records, RG1-Gov. Nelson (SG44).

Letter from Governor Nelson to the Central Interstate Compact Commissioners (23 December 1992), in Nebraska State Historical Society, Government Records, RG1-Gov. Nelson (SG44).

Letter from Governor Nelson to the Secretary of the Commission, Docketing and Service Branch, Nuclear Regulatory Commission (28 November 1994), in Nebraska State Historical Society, Government Records, RG1-Gov. Nelson (SG44).

Letter from Harold Reiser to Governor Nelson (12 December 1994), in Nebraska State Historical Society, Government Records, RG1-Gov. Nelson (SG44).

Letter from Jerry Heermann et al. to Carl Schuman (Boyd Attorney) and Governor Kay Orr re: Potential Criminal Violations of Nebraska Public Meetings Law (23 February 1990), in Nebraska State Historical Society, Government Records, RG001, Government, SG43, Orr, Kay, S1, Correspondence, Public Opinion, LLRW, Box 42.

Letter from Khosrow Semnani to Governor Nelson (12 May 1995), in Nebraska State Historical Society, Government Records, RG1-Gov. Nelson (SG44).

Letter from Loren Sieh to Governor Nelson (11 December 1992), in Nebraska State Historical Society, Government Records, RG1-Gov. Nelson (SG44).

Letter from Norma Boettcher to Governor Kay Orr (2 April 1990), in Nebraska State Historical Society, Government Records, RG001, Government, SG43, Orr, Kay, S1, Correspondence, Public Opinion, LLRW, Box 42.

Letter from Nuckolls County Nuclear and Hazardous Waste Monitoring Committee Chairman Mick Karmazin to John DeOld (21 June 1990), in Nebraska State Historical Society, Government Records, RG001, Government, SG43, Orr, Kay, S1, Correspondence, Public Opinion, LLRW, Box 42.

Letter from Phyllis Weakly (Co-chair, Save Boyd County) to the Central Interstate Compact Commissioners (25 June 1997), in Nebraska State Historical Society, Government Records, RG/41, Series 8, Central Interstate Low-Level Radioactive Waste Compact (LLRW-NE), Misc. Files, Committee/State/Legislature, 1987–2005, Box 1 of 2.

Letter from Richard Paton (US Ecology) to Vera May Lutz (Nebraska League of Women Voters) (3 March 1988), in Nebraska State Historical Society, Government Records, RG001, Government, SG43, Orr, Kay, S1, Correspondence, Public Opinion, LLRW, Box 42.

Letter from Rose Selle to Governor Orr (15 May 1990), in Nebraska State Historical Society, Government Records, RG001, Government, SG43, Orr, Kay, S1 Correspondence, Public Opinion, LLRW, Box 42.

Letter from Steve Moeller to Harold Reiser (18 August 1997), in Nebraska State Historical Society, Government Records, RG1-Gov. Nelson (SG44).

Letter of Invitation from Governor Nelson to Charles Zidko (31 July 1997), in Nebraska State Historical Society, Government Records, RG1-Gov. Nelson (SG44).

Letter of Invitation from Governor Nelson to Loren Sieh (31 July 1997), in Nebraska State Historical Society, Government Records, RG1-Gov. Nelson (SG44).

Marks, P., "State Finding Few Takers for Its Low-Level Nuclear Waste," *Hartford Courant* (24 May 1992), http://articles.courant.com/1992-05-24/news/0000201589_1_radioactive-waste-low-level-waste-disposal-low-level-nuclear-waste

Mayer, C., "Neighbors Become Enemies over Toxic Dump," *Philadelphia Inquirer* (26 November 1992), http://articles.philly.com/1992-11-26/news/26009053_1_radioactive-waste-butte-boyd-county

McCardle, J., "No Retreat for Veteran EPA Whistleblower in Era of 'Harsher and Vicious' Retaliation," *New York Times* (6 January 2011), www.nytimes.com/gwire/2011/01/06/06 greenwire-no-retreat-for-veteran-epa-whistleblower-in-er-76194.html

Memorandum to Governor-Elect Ben Nelson from Central Interstate Low-Level Radioactive Waste Compact Commission re: Community Consent, Cline, Williams, Wright, Johnson and Oldfather – Counsel (7 December 1990), in Nebraska State Historical Society, Government Records, RG1-Gov. Nelson (SG44).

Nebraska v. Central Interstate Low-Level Radioactive Waste Commission, 834 F. Supp. 1205 (D. Neb. 1993), http://elr.info/sites/default/files/litigation/24.20434.htm

Nebraska Department of Environmental Quality, *Before the Nebraska Department of Environmental Quality and the Nebraska Department of Health and Human Services Regulation and Licensure, in the Matter of the Application by US Ecology, Inc. for a License to Construct, Operate, and Close a Commercial Low-Level Radioactive Waste Disposal Facility, Denial of Application for a License* (18 December 1998a), www.deq.state.ne.us/Priority.nsf/pages/denial

Nebraska Department of Environmental Quality, *Proposed License Decision* (revised 30 December 1998b), www.deq.state.ne.us/Priority.nsf/23e5e39594c064ee852564ae004fa 010/6df9ad234fe147458625665d0059d07d?OpenDocument

"Nebraska Governor Curbs Campaign after Threat," *New York Times* (10 October 1990), www.nytimes.com/1990/10/10/us/nebraska-governor-curbs-campaign-after-threat.html

"Nebraska Is Wary on Proposed Site for Nuclear Waste," *Seattle Times* (25 November 1990), http://community.seattletimes.nwsource.com/archive/?date=19901125&s lug=1106030

Nebraska Legislative Bill 761, "An Act to Amend the Low-Level Waste Disposal Act," (approved by the Governor May 25, 1989).

Nebraska Legislature, *Floor Debate Transcript for the 90th Legislature* (n.d.), http://nebraskaleg-islature.gov/transcripts/browse_past.php?leg=90

Nebraska Legislature, Legislative Research Division, *A Review: Ninety-Sixth Legislature, First Session, 1999* (August 1999), http://nebraskalegislature.gov/pdf/reports/research/review99.pdf

Nebraska Revised Statute 81–1579 (n.d.), http://nebraskalegislature.gov/laws/statutes.php?statute=81-1579

Nebraska Unicameral Legislature, Seq. No. 420, Final Reading, LB 530 Dierks (6 May 1999), in Nebraska State Historical Society, Government Records, RG/41, Series 8, Central Interstate Low-Level Radioactive Waste Compact (LLRW-NE), Misc. Files, Committee/State/Legislature, 1987–2005, Box 1 of 2.

"Nebraska Wants Nuclear Waste Dump to Be in Kansas," *CJ Online* (21 September 1998), in Nebraska State Historical Society, Government Records, RG1-Gov. Nelson (SG44).

Nelson Campaign, "The Issues" (print), in Nebraska State Historical Society, Government Records, RG/41, Series 1, Central Interstate Low-Level Radioactive Waste Compact (LLRW-NE), Research Files, Articles and Books, 1961–2006, Box 2 of 5.

"Nuclear Dump Still in Limbo," *Lawrence Journal-World* (27 June 1994).

Nuclear Energy Agency, *Radioactive Waste Management Programmes in OECD/NEA Member Countries, France Profile 2014* (March 2014), www.oecd-nea.org/rwm/profiles/France_profile_web.pdf

O'Hanlon, K., "Epilogue: Nuke Dump Battle Peaked 10 Years Ago This Month," *Lincoln Journal Star* (4 July 2011), http://journalstar.com/special-section/epilogue/epilogue-nuke-dump-battle-peaked-years-ago-this-month/article_8fe7f462–7662–5c03–8d03–7f4cc4729a0f.html

O'Hanlon, K., "Nebraska to Pay for Blocking Nuclear Waste Dump," *Topeka Capital Journal* (10 August 2004), www.cjonline.com/stories/081004/bus_nebraskawaste.shtml

Options Meeting (Dec. 13 notes) between Tom Burke, Michael Harsh, Greg Hayden and Kate Allen at Kennedy, Holland (n.d.), in Nebraska State Historical Society, Government Records, RG/41, Series 8, Central Interstate Low-Level Radioactive Waste Compact (LLRW-NE), Misc. Files, Committee/State/Legislature, 1987–2005, Box 1 of 2.

Press Statement of Lowell Fisher (20 October 1990), in Nebraska State Historical Society, Government Records, RG001, Government, SG43, Orr, Kay, S1 Correspondence, Public Opinion, LLRW, Box 42.

Reiman, J., and Nelson, P., "Report Notes for LLRW Forum" (received 5 June 1996), in Nebraska State Historical Society, Government Records, RG/41, Series 8, Central Interstate Low-Level Radioactive Waste Compact (LLRW-NE), Misc. Files, Committee/State/Legislature, 1987–2005, Box 1 of 2.

Ringenberg, J., and Jacobson, C., "Lessons Learned during Review of the First Above-Grade Concrete Facility for LLRW Disposal," *Waste Management 1991 Symposium*, Tucson, Arizona (24–28 February 1991), www.wmsym.org/archives/1991/V2/39.pdf

Robbins, W., "Politics Overtake Selecting Nuclear Dump Sites," *New York Times* (30 September 1990), www.nytimes.com/1990/09/30/us/politics-overtake-selecting-nuclear-dump-sites.html

Russell, D., "Dumping the Dump: Nebraskans Use Ballot to Fight Nuclear Industry," *In These Times* (31 August 1988), www.unz.org/Pub/InTheseTimes-1988aug31–00006

Schmidt, J. L., "Developer Picks Northern Nebraska for Nuclear Waste Dump," *Associated Press* (29 December 1989), www.apnewsarchive.com/1989/Developer-Picks-Northern-Nebraska-For-Nuclear-Waste-Dump/id-3b87fba16f6ff42ff734e98e3c52885b

Schmidt, J. L., "Hunger Strike, Politics, Nuclear Waste Cloud Scenic Hillsides," *Associated Press* (22 October 1990), www.apnewsarchive.com/1990/Hunger-Strike-Politics-Nuclear-Waste-Cloud-Scenic-Hillsides/id-c964d4a5fbca969d75a6a68189f92adb

"Schmit Attacks Waste Site Publicity Funds," *Omaha World-Herald* (5 July 1990).

South Dakota Legislature Release, "South Dakota Senate Offers Support to Nebraska in Rejecting Waste Site" (28 January 1993), in Nebraska State Historical Society, Government Records, RG1-Gov. Nelson (SG44).

Spire, R., and Willard, L., *Identification and Election Relative to Low-Level Radioactive Waste Facility Site*, Department of Justice, State of Nebraska (23 February 1988), www.ago.ne.gov/resources/dyn/files/632471zbe/ae23f/_fn/88012_2–24–88.pdf

Statement of Dierks, Committee on Natural Resources, LB 606 (rough draft) (17 February 1999), in Nebraska State Historical Society, Government Records, RG/41, Series 8, Central Interstate Low-Level Radioactive Waste Compact (LLRW-NE), Misc. Files, Committee/State/Legislature, 1987–2005, Box 1 of 2.

Statement of Governor Orr (24 December 1987) in RG/41, Series 1, Central Interstate Low-Level Radioactive Waste Compact (LLRW-NE), Research Files, Misc. Reports, 1989–2003, Box 5 of 5.

Statement of Senator Chris Beutler in Committee on Natural Resources, LR 202 (transcript) (13 December 1997).

State of Nebraska, Department of Health and Human Services, Division of Public Health, Office of Radiological Health, *Statutes Relating to Radiation Control Act* (2008), http://dhhs.ne.gov/publichealth/Documents/RADACT.pdf

"States Join Nuclear Waste Suit against Nebraska," *Amarillo Globe News* (14 January 1999), http://amarillo.com/stories/1999/01/14/wtf_LO0732.002.shtml

Testimony of Lowell Fisher before the Committee on Natural Resources (18 December 1989), in Nebraska State Historical Society, Government Records, RG001, Government, SG43, Orr, Kay, S1 Correspondence, Public Opinion, LLRW, Box 42.

Testimony of Lynn Moorer, Committee on Judiciary, LB 761 (23 October 1989).

Testimony of Tom Grube, Nemaha County LMC, Committee on Judiciary, LB 761 (23 October 1989), and Save Boyd County Association (25 June 1997), in Nebraska State Historical Society, Government Records, RG/41, Series 8, Central Interstate Low-Level Radioactive Waste Compact (LLRW-NE), Misc. Files, Committee/State/Legislature, 1987–2005, Box 1 of 2.

Testimony of University of Nebraska Law Professor Norm Thorson, Committee on Judiciary, LB 761 (23 October 1989), in Nebraska State Historical Society, Government Records, RG/41, Series 1, Central Interstate Low-Level Radioactive Waste Compact (LLRW-NE), Research Files, Misc. Reports, 1989–2003, Box 5 of 5.

Trip Report and Meeting Notes, Boyd County Local Monitoring Committee (19 August 1996), in Nebraska State Historical Society, Government Records, RG/41, Series 8, Central Interstate Low-Level Radioactive Waste Compact (LLRW-NE), Misc. Files, Committee/State/Legislature, 1987–2005, Box 1 of 2.

United States Census Bureau, "Boyd County 1990," www.census.gov/population/cencounts/ne190090.txt

United States Congress, Office of Technology Assessment, *Partnerships under Pressure: Managing Commercial Low-Level Radioactive Waste*, OTA-O-426 (Washington, DC: U.S. Government Printing Office, November 1989), www.fas.org/ota/reports/8923.pdf

United States Department of Ecology, *Low-Level Radioactive Waste Disposal: Information for Nebraskans* (n.d.), in Nebraska State Historical Society, Government Records, RG/41, Series 1, Central Interstate Low-Level Radioactive Waste Compact (LLRW-NE), Research Files, Articles and Books, 1961–2006, Box 2 of 5.

United States Environmental Protection Agency, *Former Nebraska Ordnance Plant* (13 March 2009), www.epa.gov/region7/cleanup/npl_files/ne6211890011.pdf

United States General Accounting Office Letter to the Honorable J. James Exon, "Nebraska Low-Level Waste," GAO/RCED-93-47R (14 October 1992), www.gao.gov/assets/90/82665.pdf

United States Nuclear Regulatory Commission, Information Notice 91-65, *Emergency Access to Low-Level Radioactive Waste Disposal Facilities* (16 October 1991), www.nrc.gov/reading-rm/doc-collections/gen-comm/info-notices/1991/in91065.html

United States Nuclear Regulatory Commission, Office of the General Counsel, *Nuclear Regulatory Legislation – 5. Low Level Radioactive Waste,* "Central Interstate Low-Level Radioactive Waste Compact," NUREG -0980, Vol. 1, No. 9 (January 2011), www.nrc.gov/reading-rm/doc-collections/nuregs/staff/sr0980/v1/sr0980v1.pdf

US Ecology, Inc. v. Boyd County Board of Equalization, Boyd County, Nebraska, No. A-97–802 (decided 5 May 1998), http://caselaw.findlaw.com/ne-court-of-appeals/1261651.html

Vari, A., Reagan-Cirincione, P., and Mumpower, J. *LLRW Disposal Facility Siting: Successes and Failures in Six Countries* (Boston, MA: Kluwer Academic, 1994).

Walton, D., "Opening the History Books on Kay Orr's Legacy," *Lincoln Journal Star* (10 February 2013), http://journalstar.com/news/state-and-regional/statehouse/opening-the-history-books-on-kay-orr-s-legacy/article_0feb29de-0d35–5495–93a5–14a7a2f6ce2f.html

Weingart, J., *Waste Is a Terrible Thing to Mind: Risk, Radiation, and Distrust of Government* (Princeton, NJ: Center for Analysis of Public Issues, 2001).

Worthington, R., "Nebraska County Split over Nuclear Dump," *Chicago Tribune* (22 October 1990).

4   From Lone Star solution to Texas Compact

Low level radioactive waste disposal in Texas

Introduction

As a massive oil and natural gas producer, it is not surprising that Texas was a latecomer to nuclear energy. Construction began in 1974–75 on four reactors at two sites: Comanche Peak 1 and 2 in Somervell County, 55 miles southwest of Fort Worth, which began operating in April 1990 and 1993, respectively; and South Texas Project 1 and 2 in Matagorda County, 90 miles southwest of Houston, which began operating in March 1988 and 1989, respectively. According to state law, reactors must have at least 5 years of on-site storage capacity for low level radioactive waste (LLRW; Jacobi 1992). The state also had some experience with nuclear waste. Two counties – Deaf Smith and Swisher, both in the central Panhandle – were amongst nine sites under consideration as the nation's commercial spent fuel repository. Deaf Smith made the short list of three, along with Hanford, Washington, and Yucca Mountain, Nevada. Already a divisive issue, substantial opposition arose when it became clear that site characterization involved drilling a shaft through the Ogallala and Dockum Group aquifers into the salt bed to dig tunnels for technical studies.[1] Water supply integrity was and remains particularly sensitive in the Southwest where severe shortages are common. For Texans and Washingtonians, the repository became a moot point in 1987 when the US Congress directed the Department of Energy (DOE) to limit its site characterization work to Yucca Mountain only.

Formation of the Texas Low Level Radioactive Waste Disposal Authority: 1981

In response to the Low-Level Radioactive Waste Policy Act (LLRWPA), Texas decided to build its own disposal facility. Given the belief that, as a large waste generator, Texas would serve as the host for any compact that it created or joined, there was little interest in cooperating with other states. At the time, Texas had roughly 1,500 licensed users of radioactive material, was the third largest national generator of institutional LLRW in the country, the seventh largest generator of industrial LLRW and, when its nuclear plants started operation, was expected to be the seventh largest generator of all LLRW (Texas House

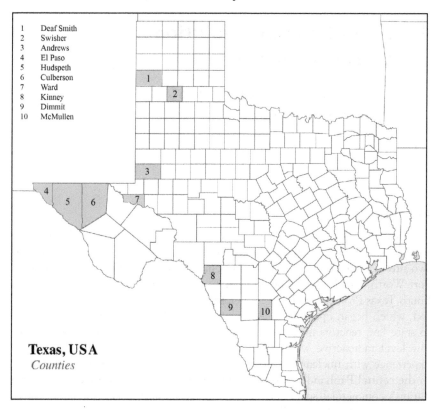

1   Deaf Smith
2   Swisher
3   Andrews
4   El Paso
5   Hudspeth
6   Culberson
7   Ward
8   Kinney
9   Dimmit
10 McMullen

Texas, USA
Counties

Figure 4.1 Texas map

Study Group 1981, pp. 2, 4). June 1981 enabling legislation – Texas was the first state to enact legislation in response to the Act – created the Texas Low Level Radioactive Waste Disposal Authority (TLLRWDA) (H.B. 1533 [1981]; S.B. 1177 [1981]). The TLLRWDA's board of directors was required to include a doctor licensed to practice in Texas, a certified health physicist, an attorney licensed to practice in Texas, a geologist and two members of the public, including a resident of the host county (House Group Bill Analysis 1981; Smyrl n.d.).

The TLLRWDA was directed to study two or more potential sites and determine key disposal requirements such as waste volumes by source and category, transport costs and motor vehicle and rail access to each site. Socioeconomic impacts on emergency services, utilities and other government services as well as the perceived risks of the disposal sites were to be analyzed in consultation with county officials. After selecting the most suitable site, a hearing in the host county would be held and a draft report detailing the site selection process would be made available to the public. The TLLRWDA was also empowered – but not required – to hold informational seminars for the public and appoint a mediator to meet with delegates (whom the Authority would select) from groups of interested parties before the public hearing (S.B. 1177 [1981], p. 10). Controversially, a 1984 report written for the TLLRWDA by two Texas A&M professors surveying siting opportunities and challenges concluded:

> The findings of this survey suggest that a broad-based public information campaign designed to familiarize the general public with all aspects of waste disposal siting might prove detrimental. A preferred methodology might be to develop public information campaigns targeted at special populations. One population that might benefit from such a campaign is Hispanics. This group is the least informed of all segments of the population. The Authority should be aware, however, that increasing the level of knowledge of Hispanics might simply increase opposition to the site.
>
> (Ivins 1997)

The original legislation did provide specific instruction to the TLLRWDA on several subjects that attracted controversy as the site selection process progressed. First, the bill included the power of eminent domain. Although removed in conference, the legislature would wrestle with condemnation until 2003 when the power was finally granted. Second, the state would retain ownership over the facility, maintaining "maximum responsiveness of the site operators to input from citizens and state regulatory agencies" and reinforcing the "legal grounds for excluding waste generated outside the state" (Texas House Study Group 1981, p. 4). Third, while only disposal of waste generated in Texas was authorized, the board could recommend to the legislature that it be authorized to "enter into a contract with a regional compact of states or with states individually." A report that accompanied the bill noted conflicting opinions about the economics of in-state disposal. The Texas Energy and Natural Resources Advisory Council staff indicated that disposal of Texas waste only was economically feasible but cautioned: "No other state does it. Texas produces less than 3 percent of the nation's total low-level waste. At the current rate, it would take several years to generate enough waste to fill even one trench in an existing burial ground." A representative from Chem-Nuclear Systems' LLRW site in Barnwell, South Carolina – Chem-Nuclear was considered the prime candidate to operate a Texas facility – was less reserved, informing the House Committee on Urban Issues that the costs of such a facility would be prohibitive (Texas House Study Group 1981, pp. 4–5).[2] Fourth, the board was authorized to make 'impact assistance' grants to a city, county, hospital district, school district, water district or other political subdivision to reimburse them for project-related expenses (S.B. 1177 [1981], p. 31). The House Study Group report also painted a damning, and fairly accurate, picture of the radioactive waste disposal legacy that the siting agency would have to contend with: "The record in other states has been one of consistent failure to provide adequately for the cost of site clean-up, and perpetual care and monitoring" (Texas House Study Group 1981, p. 5).

False starts at Tilden and Fort Hancock: 1981–1991

The first priority for the TLLRWDA was to determine which parts of the state could potentially host a facility and which should be excluded. In the initial screening, areas were eliminated where tectonic process could significantly affect site performance; surface geological processes could adversely affect site performance; 100-year floodplains, coastal high hazard zones or wetlands existed; recharge zones of aquifers were present; recovery of significant natural resources could affect site performance; future population growth could affect site performance; counties had population densities over 400 persons per square mile; national/state parks, monuments or wildlife management regions were present; and characterization, modeling or monitoring was not possible.[3] The most promising sites were found in the west, south and northwest of the state (Newberry 1994, pp. 94, 102). Out of 15 potential regions, eight 'preferred siting areas' were selected for stage two regional screening (Newberry 1994, pp. 94, 98). Within those eight areas, 57 sites were identified and a weight-scoring system was developed to help the TLLRWDA narrow the search further.

Of those 57 sites, 26 in 11 counties were recommended for field investigation. In May 1983, the TLLRWDA started soliciting landowners through local real estate brokers to identify parcels of land available for purchase.[4] After failing to gain access to several sites, and lacking the power of eminent domain, the TLLRWDA settled on five: northwest McMullen County, central Dimmit County, southwest of Dell City in Hudspeth County, the Diablo Plateau in Hudspeth County and near Encinal in LaSalle County. After precharacterization, all five were deemed potentially suitable (Newberry 1994, pp. 98–99).

The TLLRWDA created a six-member Citizens' Advisory Panel that provided input on site selection criteria and introduced a conflict resolution process in Dimmitt and Hudspeth Counties. It does not appear that the panel generated much public support and the conflict resolution did not go as planned; increasing awareness simply reinforced many participants' resolve to fight. The Authority reached out to the Texas Advisory Commission on Intergovernmental Relations for advice on involving local governments in the siting process. The commission recommended mitigation, negotiation and incentives. The Authority also began studying financial assistance packages and a rangeland improvement and wildlife management program. Several years later, in 1987, the legislature passed a law directing contractors to source local goods, services and workforce whenever possible during construction and operation of the facility (Vari, Reagan-Cirincione and Mumpower 1994, pp. 139–141, 156, 158; Mathews and Bowmer 1986, p. 59). But in late 1983 the TLLRWDA's siting process began to unravel.

In the majority Hispanic/Latino community of Dell City, local opposition – driven largely by concerns that radioactive waste would contaminate the water supply – prompted the TLLRWDA to stop its investigation ("Radioactive Waste Dump Proposal Hit Dell City" 1983, p. 6).[5] The Authority came into conflict with the university system over the Diablo Plateau site and the LaSalle site "became unavailable for purchase" (Mathews and Bowmer 1986, p. 57). As a result, in August 1984, the board designated 465 acres near Asherton in Dimmit County and 365 acres near Tilden in McMullen County for further study. Based on a unanimous staff recommendation, the Tilden site was selected ("Boundary Shift Due on Texas Dump Sites" 1984, p. 5C). However, local opposition combined with lobbying from Corpus Christi city officials, state legislators and Governor Mark White (who appointed four of the six TLLRWDA board members) helped to convince the board to ignore the advice of its staff and reject the McMullen site. On 22 February 1985, the board voted unanimously to restart the search focusing on state-owned land ("State Board Rejects McMullen" 1985).

Meanwhile, the legislature, led by the powerful south Texas delegation, was amending the TLLRWDA statute (Mathews 1997). Hugo Berlanga (D-Corpus Christi) introduced H.B. 449 in January 1985. The bill gave preference to state-owned land, which resulted in the focus of site selection moving to West Texas where most such land was located (Texas Compact Low-Level Radioactive Waste Generation Trends and Management Alternatives Study 2000, pp. 2–10; United States Congress, Office of Technology Assessment [OTA] 1989, p. 51; Smyrl n.d.; Newberry 1994, p. 92). It prohibited siting within 20 miles of certain reservoirs, effectively eliminating Dimmit and McMullen (Newberry 1994, p. 101), encouraged consideration of alternative waste management techniques such as aboveground isolation and mandated a licensing moratorium until 6 July 1987.[6] H.B. 449 became law on 14 June 1985 (H.B. 449 [1985]).

TLLRWDA staff returned to the original screening results to determine how much state-owned land had not been excluded (Newberry 1994, p. 93; "State Board Rejects McMullen" 1985). Unlike its western neighbors, Texas was an independent nation from 1836 to 1846; as a result the state, rather than the federal government, held title to almost all of its public land.[7] Twenty potential sites were reduced to four: two in Hudspeth County and two in Culberson County. In February 1987, the TLLRWDA selected a Hudspeth site, 11 miles northeast of Fort Hancock; opened a field office in town offering community services and public information programs; and hosted tours of the Beatty disposal facility and the DOE's Nevada Test Site (OTA 1989, p. 52). The Authority proposed creating a West Texas Policy Makers Forum, chaired by the West Texas Council of Governments, to facilitate the involvement of all major stakeholders in the site evaluation (Vari et al. 1994, p. 149). However, El Paso County (which abuts Hudspeth's western border) obtained a temporary injunction halting siting activities by asserting that the facility would adversely impact the county, was too close to a reservoir and was not the most suitable site. The injunction was overturned by the El Paso County Court of Appeals, allowing the TLLRWDA to resume its characterization work. By 1989, El Paso County had spent more than $500,000 hiring geologists and lawyers to review the site selection process. For opponents, this would be money well spent. Engineering firm Sergent, Hauskins & Beckwith examined the site and delivered a report to county officials the same year that formed the technical basis for a successful legal challenge and prompted charges of environmental racism in Sierra Blanca a few years later. The 'smoking guns' included the existence of a thrust fault or complex terminus of a thrust fault underlying the site based on the structure of the surrounding region (El Paso and Sierra Blanca), making the geology extremely difficult to characterize; the existence of several major tectonic fault zones in the area; and the location of virtually the entire site within the 100-year floodplain (LeMone, Xie, Keller and Dodge 2001). The existence of Indian petroglyphs was also cited as an exclusionary factor (Hubler 1991). The host county was conflicted. For a period of time, the Hudspeth County commissioners withdrew from an agreement with El Paso County to cooperate in pursuing the lawsuit and planned to use lawyers provided by the DOE's Low Level Waste Management Program to review the TLLRWDA's site characterization work (OTA 1989, p. 52).

The site was officially designated in May 1990 as the preferred location. However, protests and court actions by El Paso and Hudspeth Counties continued to delay progress and, following a 2-week trial in September, Presiding Judge for the Sixth Judicial Region William Moody issued a permanent injunction against the site in January 1991 (United States Nuclear Regulatory Commission [NRC] 2007, p. 26; LeMone et al. 2001, endnote 10). As a result, the TLLRWDA, prompted by Governor Ann Richards, began looking for alternatives.

Creation of the Texas Compact: 1987–1998

Meanwhile, frustration in Nevada, South Carolina and Washington at the lack of progress in creating alternative disposal facilities forced Congress to amend the Low-Level Radioactive Waste Policy Act in 1985 to accelerate compliance. Of particular import: states and compacts without disposal facilities were obligated to reach a series of milestones by specific dates in order to continue disposing of waste at the three operating sites (Low-Level Radioactive Waste Policy Act of 1985 [1986]). This prompted Texas lawmakers to rethink their approach. The legislature instructed the TLLRWDA to prepare background material on joining a compact. A report was presented to the legislature in 1988, and officials from Maine and Vermont testified at a House Committee on Environmental Affairs hearing in October. While endorsing the long-established Texas policy of taking care of only its own waste, the Committee noted that the policy could be reviewed if other states offered significant fiscal incentives to cover the costs of facility construction. In early 1989, both Maine and Vermont submitted compact membership proposals. The TLLRWDA also discussed the possibility of forming a compact with Puerto Rico (OTA 1989, pp. 49, 51, 54).

By 1993, Texas licensees were producing roughly 52,000 cubic feet of LLRW containing 11,000 curies of radioactivity. Utilities produced 63 percent of the volume and more than 90 percent of the radioactivity (Jacobi 1992). The Texas legislature approved the Texas-Maine-Vermont Compact in May 1993 and established a Low-Level Radioactive Waste Disposal Compact Commission consisting of six Texans and one member from each other compact state to administer the agreement; the bill was signed into law by Governor Richards in June (S.B. 1206 [1993]). Maine joined the compact in November 1993 and

Vermont in April 1994. Under the terms of the compact, Maine and Vermont would each pay $25 million toward the development, operation and closure of the disposal facility and an additional $2.5 million each to pay for community development projects designated by the host county (S.B. 1206 [1993]). In return, they would receive access to 20 percent of the disposal volume of the facility.

In Washington, DC, however, things were more complicated. In January 1995, legislation was introduced for Congressional consent to the creation of the Texas Compact: H.R. 558 in the House sponsored by Jack Fields (R-TX) of Houston and cosponsored by eight members of the Texas delegation and two members of the Maine delegation; and S. 419 by Olympia Snowe (R-ME) and cosponsored by the remaining Maine and Vermont senators (H.R. 558 [1995]; S. 419 [1995]). The staunchest opposition came from West Texas, in particular Republican Representative Henry Bonilla. Dallas Democrat John Bryant also voiced his opposition, arguing that the compact would legitimize a siting decision that violated at least the spirit of the La Paz Agreement ("This Congress would not tolerate any such action if taken by a Mexican state government"[8]) and necessitated the transport of radioactive waste over thousands of miles. Bryant maintained that the decision was flawed in any event given its proximity to the Rio Grande and within an earthquake zone ("Dissenting Views of Hon. John Bryant (H.R. 558)" 1995). Ultimately the legislation was held up on a procedural vote.

In 1997, the legislation was reintroduced by Olympia Snowe and her Maine and Vermont colleagues in the Senate and by Texas Republican Joe Barton and 23 cosponsors, predominantly fellow Texans, in the House (S. 270 [1997]; H.R. 629 [1997]). Again the opposition came from West Texas, most vocally Representatives Bonilla and Silvestre Reyes, whose concerns included environmental justice, relations with Mexico and the stress on an area already burdened with Merco's large biosolids disposal project (see Box 4.1) (American Geological Institute 1998).

The most passionate opponent outside of Texas and Mexico was Minnesota Democratic Senator Paul Wellstone. Wellstone unsuccessfully attached an amendment to the Texas Compact legislation specifying that the compact not be implemented in any way that discriminates against any community by reason of the composition of the community in terms of race, color, national origin or income level.[9] But the senator's efforts were not exactly welcomed outside the ranks of opponents. For example, Ray Sullivan, spokesman for Governor George Bush, observed testily: "The people who are best able to decide for Texas are Texans" (Mittelstadt 1997).

Finally, on 20 September 1998 Congress ratified the compact (Government Printing Office 1998). Other states, some of whom generated large amounts of radioactive waste, such as Connecticut and New Jersey, offered millions of dollars to join but Texas declined. TLLRWDA spokeswoman Susan Odom explained:

What the compact allows us to do is find some states that generate low volumes [of waste, enter a] compact and then protect ourselves within the confines of federal law. Connecticut, simply by virtue of waste volume, probably would not be eligible.

(Marks 1992)[10]

False start in Spofford: 1988–1993

In June 1988, Texcor Industries Inc. president Charles Salsman, a geologist and MBA "by way of El Paso and San Antonio," and George Borkorney, a public relations specialist from New Braunfels, began meeting with county commissioners, business leaders and civic organizations in Brackettville, the seat of Kinney County in south Texas, to solicit support for their plan to site a naturally occurring radioactive material (NORM)[11] disposal facility 10 miles south near the town of Spofford. The Texas oil and gas industry and industrial plants were major NORM producers. The amount of radioactivity was small but the volume was large, more than 1.3 million cubic feet according to one estimate (Jacobi 1992).

Texcor promised to commit $100,000 per year to Brackettville civic projects if the facility was approved and estimated that the facility would generate at least 75 jobs during the construction phase, 25 full-time jobs, more than $100,000 in annual goods and services purchases from area merchants as well as property taxes (Siegel 1991; Nixon 1990). Salsman and his family rented a house in a community less than a mile from downtown Brackettville. Salsman bought the champion hog at the county livestock show auction one year and the champion steer the next; he contributed to the county Little League, Firemen's Association and high school's 'Project Graduation'; and he donated $250 toward the Miss Kinney County scholarship (Siegel 1991). Texcor ran editorials in local newspapers and even published *N.O.R.M. News*. Indeed, as Siegel remarked, "even the most contentious folks in Kinney County . . . now agree on one point: If you wrote a checklist of what a fellow should do to make himself welcome, Charles Salsman followed it to the letter" (Siegel 1991).

Yet, the 'big city' Texans struggled to shake the image of interlopers and, despite 29 percent of the county living below the poverty line, the promise of financial benefits was not sufficient and the public reception soon turned sour.[12] Opposition from Spofford residents, spearheaded primarily by Citizens Against a Radioactive Environment (CARE) and its leader Madge Belcher, with support from neighboring communities in Texas and Mexico, was fervent. CARE collected about 1,600 signatures in the county (out of a population of approximately 2,500) opposing Texcor's plan and hired a San Antonio lawyer by selling goats, holding bake sales and running tamale cook-offs (Siegel 1991). Belcher's view of why Texcor was in Spofford was clear and heartfelt, if a little hyperbolic:

The money to be made from this is tremendous and the political clout is nil. It's a write off area, politicians have been writing it off for centuries [the county was founded in 1850 and the town in 1882]. This is political.

You find them going to remote areas with a low level of education and low political clout.

(Nixon 1990)

Mexican officials also protested, claiming that Spofford and a planned hazardous waste landfill in Dryden violated the La Paz Agreement on contamination in the border zone and asked to participate in the public hearings then underway for both facilities.[13]

Adding fuel to the fire, opponents came across a report written for the California Waste Management Board in 1984 by Cerrell Associates on waste-to-energy conversion plant siting (Siegel 1991). The so-called 'Cerrell strategy' outlined in the report had been brandished ever since it became public by environmental groups as evidence that siting of hazardous facilities is "99 percent politics and 1 percent science" ("Targeting 'Cerrell' Communities" n.d., p. 1). Using public opinion literature and questionnaire and telephone surveys, the report observed that certain groups are less resistant to hosting "toxic chemical dumps, landfills, offshore oil rigs, nuclear power plants, and other unpopular facilities." These groups included conservatives/Republicans; rural (South and Midwest) communities; small communities (usually 25,000 or less); ranchers, farmers and 'nature exploitive' jobs; low income earners; those with high school or lower educations; 'old-timer' residents of 20+ years; and those open to significant economic benefits. ("Targetings 'Cerrell' Communities" n.d., pp. 50–53). Kinney County ticked all of these boxes.

While Bureau of Radiation Control director David Lacker observed that public opinion had no impact – "Legally, we can't use it as a basis for dismissal" (Nixon 1990) – and the Department of Health recommended licensing the facility in May 1991, the Texas Water Commission rejected the application on 30 June 1993, citing a failure to adequately describe what sorts of waste the facility would receive, the presence of an active fault line and concerns that the facility might contaminate the Edwards Aquifer and the Rio Grande (Smith 1993; Landa 2013).

False start at Sierra Blanca: 1991–1998

The search for LLRW alternatives to Fort Hancock led to a novel solution. Rather than commence another expensive and time-consuming statewide screening, the legislature simply designated 400 square miles in southeastern Hudspeth County, further from El Paso and thus less objectionable to that county, as the area in which a disposal facility would be sited. According to one report, one of El Paso County's primary concerns with Fort Hancock was that the county wanted to pump water from two ranches it had bought in Hudspeth County that were located east of the site (Pfeiffer 1998, p. A6). In June 1991, investigation began at five potentially suitable tracts of land and in August 1991, a 16,000-acre site – Faskin Ranch – near Sierra Blanca was selected (Newberry 1994, p. 107; McCutcheon 1991, pp. G1, G5; "Texas Regulators Vote against

Sierra Blanca Nuke Waste Dump" 1998). With a population of 700, two-thirds of which was Latino and 39 percent lived below the poverty line, Sierra Blanca was located 16 miles from the Rio Grande, in a county with a per capita income of $8,000 (Texas-Maine-Vermont Compact 1998). Preliminary investigation began in fall 1991. The TLLRWDA approved the land purchase for just under $1 million in February 1992 and submitted a license application to the Texas Department of Health a month later.

Sending a clear message to prospective opposition, Texas officials warned that, unlike two private waste management projects – Texcor's NORM facility and the hazardous waste facility Chemical Waste Management Inc. was proposing near Dryden – the facility slated for Sierra Blanca needed to be built *somewhere* by 1996 to comply with federal requirements (Golden 1992; Shannon 1992). Design work was undertaken on the interstate highway exchange to improve access to the site and the TLLRWDA planned to offer grazing leases on more than 14,000 acres of the land while it continued studying the remaining 2,000 acres. By 1998, the more than $3.3 million in tax money that accrued to the county following its selection had bought a new football field, a library, a community park, school computers, a medical clinic, a fire truck and ambulances (de la Garza 1998; Pfeiffer 1998, p. A6). However, once again the site proved to be unpopular.

The Mexican Foreign Ministry sent a diplomatic note to the Department of State requesting that the facility be relocated; Mexican congressmen from bordering states protested that the selection was in fact environmental and economic racism; governors from bordering states sent letters urging Governor George W. Bush to move the facility; protests were held on both sides and across the border; and a city councilman from Ciudad Juarez and several supporters even staged a hunger strike on the bridge linking Juarez and El Paso. In 1998, a Permanent Commission of the Mexican Congress passed a resolution describing the project as "an aggression" to Mexican national dignity and Environment Minister Julia Carabias, an early supporter, observed that the facility would "not be helpful to good neighbor relations."[14]

Opponents in Texas did not simply claim environmental racism;[15] in April 1997, a complaint was filed under Title VI of the 1964 Civil Rights Act alleging discriminatory practices by state and federal agencies (Betancourt 1998, p. 15; DOE 1996, p. 18). And these claims were not limited to 'environmental' groups. As far back as January 1993 Representative Pete Gallego (D-Alpine) had complained to Governor Ann Richards of "a recognizable pattern by state government in general . . . of dumping every form of waste near the Rio Grande and its people" (Blakeslee 1997). TLLRWDA general counsel Lee Mathews responded that the racism charge was "fashionable" and the "least meritorious of all the arguments."[16] The Sierra Blanca Legal Defense Fund (SBLDF) also led more traditional forms of protest, including a series of 'No Nukes' concerts in various parts of the state featuring Bonnie Raitt and Texas musicians including Jimmie Dale Gilmore, Joe Ely and Jimmie Vaughn (Ivins 1997). The SBLDF also argued in 1999 that none of the licensing documents – such as the Texas Natural Resources Conservation

Commission's (TNRCC) Environmental Assessment, the license application and communications from the State Office of Hearings Examiners – had been translated into Spanish despite the fact that it is the first language for many potentially affected parties (Sierra Blanca Legal Defense Fund 1999).

In January 1998, a contested case hearing on the permit began before the State Office of Administrative Hearings, and in July the two presiding judges recommended that the application be rejected because of failure to include a comprehensive geological survey or socioeconomic impact assessment (Senate Interim Committee on Natural Resources 2000, pp. 10–11). The ruling was sufficient for Governor Bush to urge the TNRCC to "thoroughly review this recommendation and the facts to make their decision on sound science and the health and safety of Texans" (Lyman 1998). In October, the commission voted 3–0 to deny the license application on the grounds that the Authority failed to adequately analyze the potential risk of an earthquake fault, paid insufficient attention to the socioeconomic effects on the host community as well as concerns that the site sat above the West Texas Bolson aquifer supplying several communities ("Texas Agency Denies Permit for Waste Site" 1998; Runyon 1999).

Box 4.1   Poisoning the well? The 'Poo Poo Choo Choo' arrives in West Texas, 1992–2001[17]

In 1992, New York–based Merco Joint Venture was awarded a 6-year contract to dispose of 225 tons per day of 'biosolids' – the remaining waste after sewerage has been treated that can act as a powerful fertilizer – at the Mile High Ranch, a 128,000-acre failed housing development and golf course in Sierra Blanca. That the contract only required 32 days of review by state officials raised some eyebrows (De la Garza 1998; Myerson 1995; Kohout n.d.). The dumping operation divided the community. One local joke went: "When people flush in New York, they say 'Viva Texas.' " Merco gave Texas Tech $1.5 million over the life of the contract to study the operation's environmental impact and became the town's largest employer (Myerson 1995). The contract was terminated in June 2001 by the New York City officials ("Disposing NY Sewage in Region to End" 2001). In 1998 the New Jersey–based EPIC began negotiating a 15-year contract to establish a second dump site 10 miles east of the Merco site. However, Merco had become increasingly unpopular over the years – the smell and declining property values were commonly cited as important contributing factors (Knight 1998) – and the prospect of EPIC expanding the waste footprint proved too much for even some supporters of the original contract (Montes 1997; Lyman 1998). Suggestions in 2007 that biosolids dumping might return to Sierra Blanca met with similarly negative reactions in the community (Grissom 2007).

Andrews County and Waste Control Specialists

By the 1970s, Andrews County was eager to diversify from the boom-and-bust cycle of nonrenewable oil. But it was not until the early 1980s under Andrews Industrial Foundation president James Roberts that an aggressive campaign was launched to bring new industries to town, most of which were controversial: the spent nuclear fuel repository that Nevada would be designated to host by Congress in 1987; the Superconducting Super Collider that went to Waxahachie (30 miles south of Dallas) but was cancelled by Congress in 1993; a state prison; and a LLRW disposal facility.[18] None materialized, and the 1986 oil crash devastated the county (Quirk 2013; Wilder 2009).[19] Today roughly three-quarters of the county's more than 16,000 residents live in the city of Andrews.[20] Three state highways intersect the county but no interstate highway. Not surprisingly, there is a strong community bond. James Roberts explained: "From those who remained sprung a peculiar oneness, a striking cohesiveness, an almost built-in hereditary togetherness not repeated elsewhere in the state." Mayor Robert Zap added: "We've lived in isolation out here and if we don't cooperate and work as a unit we're in big trouble" (Wilder 2009). Just as important, Andrews is built on 'nature exploitive' jobs that depend on engineered solutions:

> Unlike George W. Bush's Midland, 40 miles away and home to corporate offices and Mercedes dealers, Andrews is made up of people who get their hands dirty. . . . "People here don't own the oil wells, they work on 'em – they're the drillers, the pulling unit people, the pumpers." In this rough and tumble corner of the oil patch, hazards are a fact of life.
>
> (Wilder 2009)

Waste Control Specialists (WCS) has been disposing of industrial solid waste at its Andrews County facility – located roughly 30 miles west of the city of Andrews and 6 miles east of Eunice, New Mexico – since 1994 and received a license in 1997 to treat and temporarily store radioactive by-product material from DOE's uranium production facilities. In May 2008, the company was granted a license to dispose of 750,000 cubic feet of this material (WCS n.d.). Radioactive waste that the state deemed exempt from regulation is also buried at the hazardous waste facility. WCS is also permitted for a host of other waste types, including the treatment, storage and disposal of waste contaminated with polychlorinated biphenyls (PCBs) and NRC exempt/exempt-mixed waste disposal, including selected NORM waste on what is now a 15,215-acre tract sitting on top of 800–1,000 feet of red-bed clay.[21]

By the time the company received its LLRW disposal license in 2009, the county occupied the eastern flank of what was being referred to as the 'nuclear corridor,' a zone of civilian and military nuclear operations that stretched from West Texas to eastern New Mexico, including:

- Los Alamos National Laboratory (LANL), 400 miles northwest of Andrews in New Mexico, established in 1943;[22]

- Sandia National Laboratory, 360 miles northwest of Andrews in New Mexico, established in 1945;
- the Waste Isolation Pilot Plant (WIPP) for transuranic waste from US military programs, 30 miles west of the WCS site in Carlsbad, New Mexico, operating since March 1999;
- Pantex, the primary nuclear weapons assembly, disassembly and modification center, 230 miles north of Andrews in Texas, operating since 1975;
- URENCO USA's enrichment plant, literally across the road from WCS, which would begin operation in June 2010.

"The willing buyer gets it": the private sector solution

Reflecting on the victory in Sierra Blanca, SBLDF lawyer David Frederick offered: "The place had no future with a dump. It may not have a great future now, but at least there won't be a dump" ("Texas Agency Denies Permit" 1998). Then opponents began bracing for another fight. According to an October 1998 report in *Livestock Weekly*: "Some advocates are pushing for Andrews County [but the Sierra Blanca Legal Defense Fund] vows it will get involved again if that is the case" ("Texas Regulators Vote" 1998).

At the same time, Representatives Warren Chisum (R-Pampa), Norma Chavez (D-El Paso) and Pete Gallego all introduced bills removing the restriction that the disposal facility be located in Hudspeth (H.B. 1910 [1999]; H.B. 3320 [1999]; H.B. 674 [1999]). For Gallego and others, Andrews appeared to be the perfect substitute: "If you have a willing buyer and a willing seller, the willing buyer gets it." Added cosponsor Representative Gary Walker (R-Plains): "That's the only place I've known that has shown a willingness to have low-level radioactive waste" (Robbins 1999c; Wise 1999d). The legislature also wrestled with the Texas Health and Safety Code to correct a slew of perceived problems. These can be divided into three broad categories.

Shallow land burial versus aboveground storage

In March 1999, H.B. 1910 proposed that all references to 'waste disposal' be changed to 'waste management' in order to authorize a long-term storage option – aboveground, accessible concrete vaults, referred to as 'assured isolation' – in addition to disposal (H.B. 1910 [1999]). Chisum argued that if "you can go above ground, you can build it earthquake-proof, tornado-proof, storm-proof, and you don't have to worry about underground water" (Robbins 1999c). West Texas Representative Gary Walker worried that while a number of communities would likely be interested in hosting an aboveground facility – a prediction that turned out to be incorrect[23] – 'assured isolation' might not meet the compact's definition of 'disposal,' and if that was the case, Andrews County would not receive the $27.5 million that it was entitled to from Vermont as the compact's designated disposal site. Professing his faith in shallow land burial, Walker argued that there was "absolutely no possibility" of groundwater contamination at the WCS site (Robbins 1999b; Robbins 1999c). Chisum's bill was also sensitive to several of the points of contention that had stymied previous siting attempts, prohibiting the siting of the facility in a county adjacent to an international boundary, giving preference to a site approved by county voters in a nonbinding referendum and limiting the amount of out-of-compact waste to 10 percent of the total expected by Texas generators (H.B. 1910 [1999]). The bill was left pending in the Natural Resources Committee but not before gaining some popularity amongst lawmakers (Wise 1999b).

Lacking a clear understanding of the acceptability of long-term storage as a waste management solution for the compact, the legislature asked Attorney General John Cornyn to weigh in. On 18 May 1999, Cornyn delivered his opinion: because assured isolation did not permanently isolate or dispose of LLRW, it did not satisfy the state's obligation to dispose of the waste (Office of the Attorney General 1999). However, this did not stop legislators from continuing to push for assured isolation as a temporary or permanent solution. None of these bills became law, but the willingness to continue to advocate a waste management approach that the attorney general had determined would not fulfill Texas's obligation under the compact is representative of a widespread concern with burying radioactive waste in the ground, the same ground that supports the state's aquifers.

State versus private operation of the disposal facility

WCS pursued the LLRW market piece by piece, and the first target was mixed (hazardous and low level radioactive) waste. In May 1995 Senators Teel Bivins (R-Amarillo) and Gary Walker obliged by introducing S.B. 1697. The bill, permitting a private entity to dispose of mixed waste, was extraordinarily WCS-friendly, specifying that the private entity must have been permitted by 1 January 1995 to "operate a commercial hazardous waste landfill in a county that has a population of less than 25,000 and average rainfall of less than 18 inches per year." A House report accompanying the bill even noted that "Waste Control Specialists . . . would fit the bill's description of a private entity" (S.B. 1697 [1995]; House Research Organization Bill Analysis, S.B. 1697 [2015]). Ultimately S.B. 1697 was left to die in committee amid accusations of lies and attempted bribery ("Nuclear Bill Gets Derailed" 1995; Blakeslee 1997).

Despite the inability of the TLLRWDA to find a willing host, the legislature was not quite ready to privatize LLRW disposal. In February 1999, Chisum introduced H.B. 1171 authorizing the TNRCC to license a private entity for disposal or assured isolation (Senate Research Center, Bill Analysis: C.S.H.B. 1171 [1999]). An amendment by Senator Robert Duncan was adopted limiting the possible disposal location to Andrews County (Duncan Amendment to H.B. 1171 [1999]).[24] His logic – to prevent 'prospecting' for disposal sites – was both dismissive of proponents' strongest selling point and wildly optimistic about the political acceptability of such facilities: "Low-level nuclear waste disposal is not an economic development issue. I fear that if we allow multiple sites that we will have a proliferation of these sites in West Texas." The bill was passed by the House then passed by Senate with amendments but was not conferenced to reconcile the language before the end of the legislative session (H.B. 1171 [1999]).

A House report accompanying H.B. 1910 provided an exhaustive analysis of the fault lines in the debate over state ownership versus private ownership. Proponents of state ownership maintained that government would better protect public health and safety while the private sector was a more efficient builder/operator – "the best of both worlds." As the license-holder, the state would ensure proper facility construction and maintenance from the start rather than inheriting "problems from private contractors who had no incentive to plan for the very long term," change operators in the event of substandard performance and determine the volume and type of waste that would be accepted. Uppermost in legislators' minds was the massive DOE waste stream – estimated at 100–300 million cubic feet versus 2–3 million cubic feet of compact waste over 50 years – and the fear that a private company left to its own devices would mingle federal and compact waste to reduce disposal costs. While this might be lucrative it was deemed poor public policy, as any future accident could not be traced to the responsible party. The arguments in favor of private ownership were primarily financial, in particular the expectation that a company would use its own money rather than taxpayer dollars (House Research Organization Bill Analysis, H.B. 1910 [1999]).

Opposition to privatizing LLRW disposal came from a variety of sources. Conservative State Representative Robert Talton (R-Pasadena) argued: "We should have learned from the Superfunds that privates didn't clean up their mess. We'll get a super mess. Who paid for it last time? Taxpayers. I don't want taxpayers to pay again" (De Rouffignac 1996b). Utility lobbyists Advocates for Responsible Dumping in Texas (ARDT), fearing that a private operation might not be bound by compact rules, also opposed a legislative change. According to ARDT spokesman Eddie Selig, "Our position is that the state needs to follow through on its policy direction of the past fifteen years" (Blakeslee 1997).[25]

Supporters of a private operation benefited from the historical record: the state simply could not get the job done. By 31 May 1999 the TLLRWDA had been abolished and its functions transferred to the TNRCC due in large part to legislators' frustration that a disposal site had not been found after spending 18 years and $53 million trying (Senate Interim Committee on Natural Resources 2000, p. 13; Parker 1999; H.B. 2954 [1999]). In September 2002, the TNRCC was renamed the Texas Commission on Environmental Quality (TCEQ).

Disposal of DOE waste

As mentioned previously, WCS had been originally permitted to manage industrial waste at Andrews in 1994. However, that market grew "fiercely competitive" as generators reduced waste volumes so the company decided to pursue "the more lucrative and robust radioactive waste market" (De Rouffignac 1996a). Given that the TLLRWDA was still trying to get a disposal facility licensed in Sierra Blanca at this stage, WCS went after the radioactive waste market piece by piece. And the largest and most valuable piece was the DOE's LLRW stream. WCS argued that its hazardous waste operations made the site particularly attractive for DOE in its sales pitch: "Various studies have shown that the long-lived toxicity of RCRA waste is comparable to low-level radioactive waste." Combined with operational facilities that could accommodate radioactive waste, direct rail access, nearby interstates and a history of safe storage and disposal, the Andrews site provided "the opportunity for significant savings for government disposal operations" (Statement of Eric C. Peus, Waste Control Specialists LLC in "Disposal of Low-Level Radioactive Waste" 2000). But WCS was not the only game in town. In the fall of 1996 Envirocare purchased 880 acres of ranchland roughly 7 miles east of WCS – a "modern-day land rush" – and filed a preliminary application with the TNRCC for a disposal facility that would also accept DOE waste. Envirocare Executive Vice-President Charles Judd explained: "We searched around the country and found what we think is the best site – in Andrews County. . . . The key element is public acceptance of a facility. We think we found a place where there is local support." WCS spokesman Bill Miller was nonplussed: "We consider it a ploy. We don't take it seriously" (De Rouffignac 1996b). This was a not entirely accurate statement.

WCS received a LLRW treatment and storage license on 3 November 1997 after being granted a NORM disposal license 2 months earlier, but in 1998 the Fifth Circuit Court of Appeals dismissed a federal district court decision allowing WCS to bid for DOE disposal contracts despite only having a treatment/storage license (Statement of Eric C. Peus 2000; De Rouffignac 1998b). WCS had submitted an application to dispose of DOE waste in December 1996, with Texas Tech providing the oversight lead (Blakeslee 1997). While the TNRCC had taken the position that it was not empowered to grant or deny a license to dispose of federal LLRW, the company's approach put it on a collision course with the state's top law enforcement officer. Texas Attorney General Dan Morales filed a brief with the Fifth Circuit Court of Appeals in New Orleans arguing that DOE should not be able to bypass state jurisdiction when contracting with private parties: "Public policy requires that all wastes generated by DOE be subject to independent oversight and enforcement preferably by qualified state regulatory agencies." Morales was not the only one – 16 other state attorneys general had already filed briefs challenging the ruling (De Rouffignac 1998a). Texas lawmakers were making the same point. Gary Walker opined: "It's not going to just go there because somebody wants it to go there. It's got to be licensed and regulated through the state of Texas" (Robbins 1999c).

Despite this setback, WCS was awarded a reported $90 million contract from the Department of Defense (DOD) to dispose of DOD and Army Corps of Engineers NORM and very low activity waste, both exempt from state regulation. The contract was a zero-sum game for WCS and its West Texas competitor Envirocare. Envirocare had previously received some of the waste at its Tooele

County, Utah, facility but had sued the government over a waste separation dispute. Envirocare lost the suit and DOD recontracted with WCS (Wise 1999a). Even the state of Texas was not big enough for both companies, but federal and state courts would be required to determine who would stay and who would leave.

**Box 4.2   The battle of West Texas: WCS and
Envirocare, 1997–2000**

On 2 May 1997, WCS filed a $500 million libel and business disparagement suit against Envirocare, alleging that Envirocare used its monopoly power in the LLRW and mixed waste disposal markets to prevent WCS from obtaining government authorizations; engaged in improper communications with government officials; used unwitting state legislators to attack WCS; spread defamatory information about WCS; and created a sham disposal operation in Andrews County (*Waste Control Specialists LLC v. Envirocare et al.* 1997). WCS claimed that Envirocare representatives told state officials that WCS would not be allowed to send its waste to Clive for disposal in order to undermine the application (De Rouffignac 1997). On 13 March 1998, the suit was increased to $1 billion as WCS "learned more about the things they've done" (Wise 1998b). In June 1998 a federal judge dismissed the suit, ruling that Envirocare's tactics were "protected petitioning activities" under the First Amendment. WCS appealed the decision and the Fifth Circuit Court of Appeals sent the suit back to back to Andrews County ("Judge Dismisses $1 Billion Waste Lawsuit" 1998; Kane 2000a).

In April 2000, Envirocare fired back, filing a federal defamation lawsuit for unspecified damages against WCS, former WCS President Kenneth Bigham and private investigator Paul Byerly, alleging these parties (and others it intended to name as the suit progressed) defamed and disparaged Envirocare and its owner Khosrow Semnani in order to undermine the company's efforts to license a facility in Andrews County. As reported in The *Deseret News*, the suit made some salacious claims (Spangler 2000):

- that the company was illegally trading arms, diverting radioactive waste to weapons brokers, financing Middle East terrorists and threatening to kill anyone who opposed it;
- that Semnani maintained illicit sexual relationships with female regulators for the purpose of obtaining inside regulatory information and to obtain favorable treatment;
- that Envirocare accepted wastes it was not legally permitted to take, including high-level wastes from Kuwait;
- that Semnani was a bigamist.

While the suits bounced between courts, WCS contracted with South Texas Project and Texas Utilities to dispose of their LLRW at a massive discount from the price being charged at Barnwell, bringing two of the three stars into alignment for WCS: customers ready to do business and a willing host community. Now all that was needed was legislative authorization – the contract would not take effect until the legislature authorized WCS to construct and operate a disposal facility – and the Gallego and Chisum bills then being debated appeared to put this within reach (De Rouffignac 1999).[26] And in August 1999, WCS moved its base of operations from Pasadena to Andrews. Finally, in November 2000, the two companies reached a confidential out-of-court settlement and Envirocare began closing down its offices in Andrews and Monahans (the seat for Ward County) (Kane 2000b; Flores 2001).

Lloyd Eisenrich provided a fair assessment of the situation: The facility "never would have happened if somebody like Harold Simmons hadn't gotten involved, who had the pockets to fight the legal battles and the long-term legislative process, the permitting process, and all that. Anybody else would've folded at the table and walked away" (Homans 2012).

Controversy over geology

According to *Livestock Weekly*, a 1987 TLLRWDA report on one site in Andrews County considered the location "marginal" because of rainfall levels, sandy soil that encouraged water table recharge and the existence of windmills near the site that suggested shallow ground water. TLLRWDA general counsel Lee Mathews confirmed that several holes had been drilled and maps had been consulted: "We saw that there were issues that might require more time or money to investigate." And TLLRWDA general manager Lawrence 'Rick' Jacobi – who, after 18 years with TLLRWDA would take a job as Envirocare's vice president of operations in February 1999 – explained that if it was found that the Ogallala Aquifer recharged from or through the site, state law precluded any further consideration of the location. However, Envirocare Director of Permitting Norm Sunderland maintained that Andrews was suitable precisely because of its clay deposits and low rainfall ("Texas Regulators Vote" 1998).

In 1993, oil and gas consulting firm Terra Dynamics conducted survey work at the proposed Andrews site for WCS, finding that the "Ogallala formation does not appear to be water bearing at the proposed WCS landfill site . . . [and the] local groundwater system will be insulated from proposed landfill activities at the WCS facility by the aquitard characteristics of the upper Dockum Group, and by the proposed landfill design and engineering controls" (*RCRA Permit Application for a Hazardous Waste Storage, Treatment and Disposal Facility: Andrews County, Texas* 1993, pp. VI.B.-2, VI.B.-9). In March 1999, Alan Dutton of the

University of Texas's Bureau of Economic Geology released a report, commissioned by the TLLRWDA, indicating that the Ogallala Aquifer might lie beneath Envirocare's proposed LLRW treatment and storage site and that High Plains water formations might also reach beneath the WCS site. Dutton, who relied primarily on past geological studies, recommended further study before licensing any facilities. State Water Development Board maps also indicated that the WCS site was very close to the aquifer (Homans 2012). While neither company stopped work in Andrews County, Envirocare began looking in Ward County (south of Andrews) and, in November 1999, settled on land near Barstow (Flores 2001). WCS had no such reservations. The company disputed Dutton's findings, citing a 1996 study by Texas Tech scientists Ken Rainwater and Thomas Lehman commissioned by the Andrews Industrial Foundation. Using information from the Terra Dynamics survey, core samples and other site data, Rainwater and Lehman had determined that the WCS location was safe (Wise 1999f).

In 2003, a LLRW bill was drafted that proved acceptable to the majority. Authored by George 'Buddy' West (R-Andrews/Ector/Winkler Counties), Chisum and Wayne Smith (R-Harris County), H.B. 1567:

- authorized a private entity to hold a 35-year disposal license with 10-year extensions;
- granted the attorney general power of eminent domain;
- prohibited burial in an unlined disposal unit without technical enhancements;
- prohibited siting in a county located within 62 miles of the US–Mexican border, in a county with more than 20 inches of annual rainfall, in a county adjoining certain segments of the Devils or Pecos Rivers, in a 100-year floodplain and less than 20 miles upstream of a reservoir built by the Bureau of Land Management, Army Corps of Engineers or as part of a state water plan;
- mandated physical separation of the federal facility from the compact facility with a stipulation that the federal facility could only begin operation once the compact facility started receiving waste;
- placed capacity and volume limits on the federal facility with a caveat that if, after 5 years, the commission found that the facility did not pose "a significant risk to human health, public safety, or the environment," capacity and volume could be increased;
- limited out-of-state waste to compact members only;
- required the licensee to transfer 5 percent of gross receipts from both facilities to the host county and 10 percent to the state each quarter;
- instructed the Texas Department of Health (TDH) to issue only one license for a compact waste disposal facility – this, combined with a requirement that license applications be lodged within a year of the bill taking effect, virtually guaranteed that a WCS application would be the only paperwork crossing TDH's desks.[27]

Thus, with a process stacked heavily in its favor, WCS submitted a license application to construct and operate a near-surface disposal facility in August 2004 (House Research Organization Bill Analysis: H.B. 1567 [2003]; General Accounting Office [GAO] 2004, p. 9; NRC 2007, p. 31).

After reviewing the WCS application, TCEQ staffers recommended rejecting it. The application was then reviewed by a TCEQ technical team. The second review, completed in August 2006, found the application "very, very deficient" (Wilder 2008). In August 2007, a memo from four of the team members – two geologists and two engineers – stated that the proximity of a water table "makes groundwater intrusion into the proposed disposal units highly likely . . . [and] natural site conditions cannot be improved through special license conditions." The memo also expressed concern that a second water table was closer to the bottom of the landfill than the 14 feet WCS claimed (Wilder 2008). Two of the four, an engineer and a geologist, resigned over concerns about the site that they felt had been ignored, and in December the team's technical writer and spokesman also resigned in protest (Polk 2010). The review team also ultimately recommended that the commission deny the application. However, in 2008, then Executive Director Glenn Shankle over-ruled his staffers and recommended that the commissioners approve the license, which they did.

In 2007, the Sierra Club, which had experienced had extreme difficulty finding Andrews residents willing to file for contested case hearings, challenged the company's environmental licenses because of the discovery of groundwater in some of the site's 520 monitoring wells. WCS president Rodney Baltzer responded: "Any of the water they're talking about out there isn't groundwater; it's infiltration from rain, and it's not connected to the Ogallala Aquifer or some kind of well someone's drinking from. The red-bed clays underneath are like concrete." Andrews County responded by suing the Sierra Club on 12 August and was soon joined by the Andrews Industrial Forum. Sierra Club lawyers claimed unsuccessfully that the action amounted to a strategic lawsuit against public participation (SLAPP), which was illegal in Texas (Swartsell 2012b).

On 1 July 2008, the Barnwell disposal facility closed its doors to all non-Atlantic compact waste. The next month, TCEQ issued a draft license for the near-surface disposal of Class A, B and C LLRW at Andrews. WCS Vice President Bill Dornsife asserted, not unreasonably: "Considering our political support, considering our local support, if a new facility cannot be licensed in Texas, it probably can't be licensed anywhere" (Wilder 2008).

The contrast between the support in Andrews and the opposition elsewhere in Texas and around the country was marked. A large part of the reason why is risk perception. Andrews Industrial Foundation president Lloyd Eisenrich explained:

> Nobody's going to build a Toyota plant in west Andrews County. . . . You've got a county with over ten thousand holes poked in the ground and H_2S

[hydrogen sulfide] gas out there that could wipe out this whole community with one leak and the wind blowing in the right direction. They understand hazard.

(Homans 2012)[28]

WCS President Eric Peus made the same point, observing that the large amount of support for the facility was

> due in significant part to the fact that the industry base of the region is oil and gas production, and the citizens are thus comfortable with and accepting of the risks of technology. They also fully understand the superior geological characteristics of the site.
>
> (Statement of Eric C. Peus 2000)[29]

In January 2009, the TCEQ issued a license to WCS to dispose of LLRW from two distinct streams: waste from compact members in a 2.31 million cubic foot and 3.89 million curie capacity facility; and waste from DOE in a 26 million cubic foot and 5.6 million curie capacity facility (WCS n.d.; Van Villet 2012). Greater-Than-Class-C waste was prohibited and on 6 March 2012 the license was amended to specifically prohibit waste of international origin (TCEQ 2012, p. 2). The TCEQ commissioners voted 2–0 on the license with one abstention. Construction began the same year after the county narrowly (642–639) passed a bond issue to loan WCS $75 million (Swartsell 2012a; Polk 2010).

On the need for a disposal facility, the Texas Senate Interim Committee on Natural Resources noted that several small generators and one broker had recently gone out of business or bankrupt, leaving the LLRW on site in need of appropriate management. In some instances, waste had been discovered by unknowing public citizens or stolen and sold for scrap metal. Some sources have never been recovered. As a last resort, the TDH took possession of more than 150 sources because there were no in-state or out-of-state disposal options but they had limited capacity and had to stop accepting new material. Thus, the "location where radioactive material is discovered or abandoned in Texas becomes a long-term storage facility by default" (Senate Interim Committee on Natural Resources 2000, p. 6). In 2001, a House Research Organization report estimated that LLRW was being stored at more than 900 locations, including universities, hospitals, closets, garages, rooftops and nuclear plants (House Research Organization Bill Analysis, H.B. 85 [2001], p. 2).

Disposal of compact versus out-of-compact waste

The WCS LLRW disposal license was for all waste classes. However, the more radioactive (B and C) – and more lucrative – waste classes were always the main objective, in large part because Envirocare had captured the Class A market at Clive. The company's next priority was to obtain a license for out-of-compact waste. At a waste conference in 2008, Bill Dornsife provided some insight into the company's plans: "For political reasons, we don't want anyone to come knocking on the door until we get this up and operating, but I think there are some capabilities there" (Wilder 2008). In fact, as early as October 2001 WCS entered into an agreement with Utilities Service Alliance, representing 15 utilities and 27 reactors ("US Nuclear Fuel Cycle" updated 2014). In June 2009 WCS began importing Class B and C waste from the radioactive waste processor Studsvik in Tennessee for interim storage under an agreement signed in 2007 (Campbell 2009; "Studsvik Signs Teaming Agreement" with Waste Control Specialists LLC [WCS] 2007; Wilder 2010).[30] Another small but significant step was taken on 10 September 2009 when the company submitted a letter to the NRC stating: "We are optimistic that the WCS facility will eventually be open for disposal of Class A, B and C LLW by non-regional generators" (Camper 2010, p. 13).

Speculation about WCS's intention with respect to out-of-compact waste had been swirling for more than a decade. On 7 October 1997, Representative Lloyd Doggett introduced an amendment to the compact legislation mandating that only LLRW from Maine and Vermont would be imported into Texas under the compact. The amendment passed in the House but was defeated in conference committee (H.AMDT.419, 105th Congress 1997). In November, Molly Ivins reported that Rick Jacobi had stated in an interview with the *Houston Business Journal* that the "site is designed for 100,000 cubic feet per year, which would cost about $160 per cubic foot. But if only 60,000 cubic feet per year of waste arrives, the price would be $250 per cubic foot" (Ivins 1997). Thus it was in the company's best interest to receive as much waste as possible and in the customers' best interests to support this position in order to keep disposal costs as low as possible. Senator Wellstone quoted economist and Central Compact Commissioner Gregory Hayden, who made the same point but with a much broader brushstroke: "The small volume of waste available for any new site would not allow the facility to take advantage of economies of scale. Thus it would not even be able to operate at the low-cost portion of its own cost functions" (Texas/Maine/Vermont Compact 1998; Hayden and Bolduc 1997). It should be noted that Hayden was from Nebraska and, as discussed in the previous chapter, the time of writing marked the final stages of an ugly battle between US Ecology/the Boyd County Monitoring Committee and many local residents as well as between Nebraska and the rest of the compact over Nebraska's LLRW hosting obligations, so some skepticism about the efficacy of the compact system should not be surprising. But the math was sound and supported by analysis carried out by engineering firm Rogers and Associates in 2000 (Texas Compact Low-Level Radioactive Waste Generation Trends and Management Alternatives Study 2000, pp. 1–5, 4–103, 4–104).

In January 2011, the Texas Low Level Radioactive Waste Disposal Compact Commission (TLLRWDCC) passed a rule allowing the facility to accept out-of-compact waste, subject to the granting of an import license by the commission.[31] Generators from out-of-compact states would pay a 20 percent surcharge and out-of-compact waste was limited to 30 percent of the facility's licensed capacity.[32] As a result, in July 2012 Studsvik signed a disposal contract with the TLLRWDCC, allowing WCS to dispose of the material it had been storing for the processor since 2009 (Texas Low-Level Radioactive Waste Disposal Compact Commission 2012). The legislature concurred in May. However, that was not the end of the story. In September, *Reuters* reported that Governor Rick Perry had tried to head off opposition to the acceptance of out-of-compact waste within the TLLRWDCC by offering one of the commissioners a plum board of regents job in order to remove him and his 'no' vote.[33]

In April 2012 the first shipment of compact waste, from Bionomics Inc., was received at the facility and 5 months later the first shipments from Vermont – from the Vermont Yankee nuclear plant, the University of Vermont and Fletcher Allen Health Care Hospital – arrived (WCS Press Release 2012; "Vt. Begins Shipping Radioactive Waste to Texas" 2012). This was not without controversy. In the lead up to the first shipment, the director of the San Antonio-based Sustainable Energy & Economic Development (SEED) Coalition Karen Hadden remarked that while all radioactive waste operations were dangerous, "we are very concerned about highway accidents. There could be accidents in downtown Fort Worth and Houston" (Blaney 2012). Conversely, Scott Kovac of NukeWatch New Mexico was quoted as being "impressed with their low-level waste cell" (Wald 2014). At a ribbon-cutting ceremony celebrating the opening of WCS's federal facility and the receipt of first shipment of waste (from Los Alamos National Laboratory) on 6 June 2013, President Rod Baltzer remarked: "We wanted to be a one-stop shop with everything in. We're proud to have a large and very robust complex" (Blaney 2013). Since then the legislature has been busy drafting bills on out-of-compact waste incorporating volume/curie limits and category restrictions as well as encouraging compact generators to export Class A waste.[34]

Conclusion

With the partial exception of the Clive facility in Utah – which was developed outside the compact framework but with the acceptance of the Northwest Compact – the WCS facility was the first disposal site to be successfully licensed as a result of the compact system. First and foremost, the successful siting in Andrews is demonstrative of the benefits of a brown field site versus a green field site where the community is exposed to, and comfortable with, industrial hazard. This risk perception creates a natural constituency for projects like radioactive waste disposal that does not exist in, say, farming communities like Boyd County, Nebraska. While the provision of money and social services are necessary, particularly in an area where new jobs are highly sought after, but not sufficient to successful siting, the strong support waste disposal received from the powerful Andrews Industrial Forum was important. Without this, WCS would have had a harder time convincing residents that radioactive waste disposal was in their interests. It certainly also helps that West Texas is arid, the sort of climate generally associated with safe long-term waste isolation, where moving water is the most effective method of radionuclide transportation. From a layman's point of view, it makes more sense to dispose of radioactive waste in the dry Texas climate than a high rainfall area like Nebraska. And Andrews is not an isolated outpost; the county sits on the eastern flank of a burgeoning 'nuclear corridor' surrounded by like-minded communities that also benefit from hazardous industries (oil and natural gas) in general and the nuclear industry in particular. This is why definitions of 'affected community' were far less of an issue in West Texas than in northern Nebraska. As a result, environmental organizations struggled to gain traction. The Sierra Club found little support amongst the local population – indeed, the county sued the environmental group in 2007 – and the Sierra Blanca Legal Defense Fund lamented that it had been unable to elicit support from most national, mainstream environmental groups or funding from major foundations (Wilder 2009; Sierra Blanca Legal Defense Fund 1999).

That being said, communities beyond the host town or county did make their preferences felt. El Paso County played a large role in the rejection of the Fort Hancock site and Mexican officials fought successfully against several proposed sites. Indeed, according to US and Mexican officials, "border communities that once kept their distance have begun to find themselves frequently allied, or at least in consultation, over the mutual environmental problems" (Golden 1992). But while there was controversy over where the facility would be located, as a big LLRW generator with a history of solving its own problems, there was never any dispute that Texas would be building a disposal facility somewhere. Unlike in Nebraska, where the compact commissioner was outvoted by his fellow com-missioners and there was always simmering resentment that the state had been 'forced' to host, Texas officials created a waste solution on their own terms – that is, a compact that accepted a small amount of out-of-state waste in order to ensure Texas would not be forced to accept waste from all over the country – unless the price was right.

Public engagement is critical at all stages of the siting process, and words are important so should be chosen carefully. At a town meeting in Dell City, Direc-tor of Special Programs for the TLLRWDA Tom Blackburn was quoted as saying that LLRW is "just not that hazardous" ("Radioactive Waste Dump Proposal" 1983, p. 6). Most LLRW waste is not very hazardous, but some is. Similarly, Representative Gary Walker's statement that there was "absolutely no possibil-ity" of groundwater contamination at the site is patently not true. Blanket statements designed to gloss over inconvenient details are not helpful in the long run, undermining proponents' credibility and suggesting that the public cannot be trusted to make informed decisions. But overemphasizing 'neutral language' also runs the risk of being interpreted as trying to put lipstick on a pig. When Texcor's president Charles Salsman was selling NORM disposal to Spofford, some residents noted suspiciously that he always used the words 'waste facility' rather than 'dump' (Siegel 1991).

Who is speaking can be just as important as what is being said. In 1984 the TLLRWDA hired a public relations firm to help make its messaging more effective. The firm advised: "A more positive view of safe disposal technologies should be engendered by the use of medical doctors and university faculty scientists as public spokesmen for the Authority. Whenever possible the Authority should speak through these parties" (Texas/Maine/Vermont Compact 1998). While Senator Wellstone was using this example pejoratively, it is true that trusted professionals like doctors can be very effective emissaries with the public, particularly when, as is often the case, government officials and representatives from the radioactive waste industry are suspected of having ulterior motives.

Just as in Nebraska and several other states considering new LLRW facilities, there was fear amongst legislators and the Texas public that because siting efforts had failed so spectacularly elsewhere, and despite explicit protection against just such preemption in the LLRWPA, if Texas opened a facility then Congress might be tempted to designate it as the nation's dump and ignore or abandon the compact system. Apprehension over federal incursion into states' rights is a theme that runs deep in American politics and certainly should not be surprising in Texas. But of course, the WCS facility now accepts waste from 34 states around the country that do not have access to a compact disposal facility.

While certainly not applicable everywhere, in certain circumstances a couple of siting failures may actually increase confidence by showing that unsuitable locations will be rejected, thus demonstrating the integrity of the siting process. In more contentious situations like Nebraska, investigating sites that turn out to be unsuitable might well be viewed as a sign of desperation but, as mentioned previously, officials were siting a LLRW disposal facility somewhere so this is not an unreasonable contention in the Texas case. And with a disposal facility now up and running in Andrews, Texas is also serving as a test case for the proposition that LLRW disposal might lead to spent nuclear fuel solutions. In a 28 March 2014 letter to Lieutenant Governor David Dewhurst and House Speaker Joe Straus, Governor Rick Perry explained that, with the Court of Appeals for the District of Columbia Circuit determining that the federal government has "no credible plan" to dispose of the nation's spent fuel and high level waste, it was time for the state to start looking for its own solution (Office of the Governor 2014). Straus instructed the House Environmental Regulation Committee to make "specific recommendations on the state and federal actions necessary to permit a high-level radioactive waste disposal or interim storage facility in Texas" (Malewitz 2014a). AFCI Texas LLC has been pursuing spent fuel storage and looked at lessons learned from Yucca Mountain in Nevada and the failed Private Fuel Storage project in Utah, and has been holding discussions with WCS about their approach in Andrews County before pitching the idea to interested county officials, including commissioners in Loving (population: 95) and Howard (population: 36,000). The Eddy-Lea Energy Alliance is also pursuing aboveground interim spent fuel storage at a proposed site between Carlsbad and Hobbs in New Mexico (Walker 2012). However, WCS is interested in spent fuel storage as well and has the inside running. In February 2014, WIPP was closed following a radiation leak from a waste drum incorrectly packaged at Los Alamos National Laboratory (LANL). Since April 2014, WCS has been providing temporary storage for LANL transuranic waste at Andrews until the New Mexico repository is reopened. Not only is WCS providing an important public service, but safe stewardship of the TRU waste further demonstrates the company's expertise in radioactive waste management and makes it more likely that the state will look favorably on a WCS application to store spent fuel. While there have certainly been complaints in the media about 'mission creep,' an incremental approach to waste disposal that builds a track record of safety is clearly an effective way to earn public trust.

Notes

1 Frito Lay and Holly Sugar indicated that a repository might force them to move their operations; health food company Arrowhead Mills said that a repository was incompatible with its operation (Salisbury 1985).
2 According to the DOE's Manifest Information Management System (MIMS), Texas disposed of 71,718 cubic feet of LLRW in 1987; 53,091 cubic feet in 1991; 39,680 cubic feet in 1995; 130,228 cubic feet in 1999; 151,357 cubic feet in 2003; 69,759 cubic feet in 2007; and 23,197 cubic feet in 2011 (DOE n.d.).
3 Sensitive to the fragile ecosystem, the TLLRWDA included impact on flora and fauna as one of the general siting criteria.
4 Complicating any possible purchase, all surface and mineral rights – which were often owned separately – were required for the disposal site (Newberry 1994, pp. 100–101).
5 The now-defunct University of Texas at Austin student activist organization UT Watch reported in December 1994 that the attendance of 200 angry ranchers and farmers at a TLLRWDA meeting was particularly effective in conveying Dell City's sentiment to siting officials (Rogers 1994).
6 The moratorium was motivated in large part by a concern that if Texas licensed a facility before other states/compacts, it ran the risk of becoming a national disposal site.
7 Less than 2% of Texas is federal land. By way of comparison, Nevada is 86% federally owned and Utah 64% ("A Spread of One's Own" 1998).
8 Article 2 of the 1983 La Paz Agreement called on both the US and Mexico to prevent, reduce and eliminate sources of contamination in the border zone area extending 62 miles on either side. The facility was to be built roughly 16 miles from the Rio Grande (Betancourt 1998, p. 15; Lyman 1998; De la Garza 1998).
9 The amendment was adopted by the Senate but dropped in conference (Wellstone Amendment No. 2277 [1997]).
10 Maine withdrew from the compact in April 2002, effective April 2004 due to the impending completion of decommissioning of Maine Yankee, the state's only nuclear plant and its largest waste generator.
11 Naturally occurring radioactive material (NORM) consists of radionuclides that have been present in the earth's crust since it was formed, such as uranium, thorium, radium and their decay products. The term NORM is usually used in specific situations where human activity – oil and gas production, coal mining, in construction and in recycling – increases the potential for exposure. Where human activity increases the concentration of radionuclides, the term technologically enhanced naturally occurring radioactive material (TENORM) is often used ("Naturally-Occurring Radiation: Overview" updated 2015; "Naturally-Occurring Radioactive Materials" updated 2015). Texcor would primarily have disposed of NORM from oil field slag and sand from in situ leeching uranium mines.

12 Young mother and St. Andrew's Episcopal Church organist Lisa Conoly, whose family had built the first house in Kinney County four generations earlier, observed that Salsman was "Real down-home country, trying to be a homeboy. When you're from here, though, you can tell" (Siegel 1991). Spofford is roughly 460 miles southeast of El Paso and 125 miles west of San Antonio; Borkorney's home in New Braunfels is roughly 160 miles east of Spofford.

13 On 2 April, Mexico revoked Illinois-based Chemical Waste Management's license to build a toxic waste incinerator near Tijuana, describing the decision as a 'signal' that it was complying with the La Paz Agreement and expected the US to do the same (Scott 1992).

14 The Permanent Commission resolution was supported by the governing Institutional Revolutionary Party, the Party of the Democratic Revolution, the National Action Party, the Green Party and the Workers Party (Betancourt 1998, p. 15).

15 General store and ranch owner Bill Addington's description was representative: "We're the path of least resistance. We have few voters, we're far, far away from the centers of power and 70 percent of us happen to be Mexican. It's a classic case of environmental racism" (Pfeiffer 1998, p. A6).

16 Mathews was reported as making several other observations that must have set off alarms bells amongst opponents. Responding to concerns that the site was in an earthquake zone, he explained that scientists characterized the area as an 'inferred fault' rather than an 'active fault.' And as to possible contamination of the Rio Grande, Mathews asserted that any contamination would be over tens of thousands of years, "not any time soon" (De la Garza 1998).

17 The 'Poo Poo Choo Choo' was how some locals referred to the train that delivered the biosolids to Texas (Blakeslee 1997).

18 The *Texas Observer* reported that, according to the Sierra Club and Nuclear Information and Resource Service (another antinuclear group), WCS offered them the use of company geologists to help kill the Sierra Blanca project (Wilder 2009).

19 It is worth noting that Nevada, home to the first commercial LLRW disposal facility in the country, also unsuccessfully pursued the repository during the 1970s and early to mid-1980s and the Super Collider. See Newman 2012.

20 Figures taken from United States Census Bureau, *State and County QuickFacts*, www.census.gov/.

21 There are very tight restrictions on the amount of liquid allowed in waste packages. Eric C. Peus stated: "Waste containing liquid must contain as little free-standing and non-corrosive liquid as is reasonably achievable but in no case must the liquid exceed one percent of the volume" (TCEQ 2009, p. 26).

22 LANL and University of Texas Permian Basin proposed building a high-temperature teaching and test reactor (HT³R) in Andrews. According to UTPB, "with the election of President Obama, DOE ceased all talks with regard to support of the HT³R and we decided to shelve the HT³R project until a more favorable political environment comes back to Washington, DC" (Campbell 2010; University of Texas of the Permian Basin 2014; Wright 2006).

23 In addition to Andrews, Envirocare considered Childress, Borden, Loving and Ward Counties for its Assured Isolation Storage Facility but backed down in the face of local opposition (Kane 1999; Wise 1999c; Wise 1999e).

24 Somewhat counterintuitively, in March Chisum also introduced H.B. 1910 (1999) that maintained the state's licensing authority.

25 ARDT's executive board is made up of representatives from S.T.P. Nuclear Operating Company in Texas, Comanche Peak Nuclear Power Plant in Texas, Vermont Yankee and health physics, medical and university research communities in Texas and Vermont. See www.ardt.org.

26 As discussed in chapter 2, Illinois was a particularly stark reminder of the burden a host state might be left with.

27 H.B. 1567 passed the House 107–34 and the Senate 23–7. The conference committee report passed the House 92–42 and was adopted by voice vote in the Senate (H.B. 1567 [2003]).

28 Of course, not all of the neighbors were happy. Rose Gardner of Eunice, New Mexico, took exception in 2012: "Waste Control Specialists has been described as a remote location. Remote from Dallas? Okay. Remote from New York? Okay. But it's right here. It's close to my town" (Swartsell 2012). According to the article, Gardner had undergone radiation therapy for thyroid problems and was concerned about further exposure.

29 Andrews hydrologist Darrell Jackson offered: "We think we're doing a service for the nation and the state" (Wilder 2009).

30 Wilder incorrectly asserted that WCS did not have a license to receive the Studsvik waste.

31 Provision was also made for new members to join the compact, provided Texas officials accepted them, at a cost of $30 million before 2018 and $50 million after 2018 (Blaney 2011).

32 In August 2014, TCEQ voted unanimously to allow WCS to accept 'Greater-Than-Class-C' waste and expand the facility's capacity (Malewitz 2014b).

33 The commissioner in question was Texan Bob Gregory. According to the story, Gregory was known to be one of two opponents of out-of-compact waste on the eight-member commission. While a 6–2 vote was still a comfortable majority, the two Republican commissioners from Vermont who supported out-of-compact waste were scheduled to be replaced in early 2011. Fearing that the incoming commissioners might not be so accommodating, the governor's office angled to ease Gregory out, in part to reward Harold Simmons who had donated more than $1 million to Perry's gubernatorial campaigns. Gregory refused the offer and, despite a plea that it was "beyond preposterous" to make a decision without having read the 5,000 public comments that had been submitted, the commission voted early before the incumbent Vermonter's term ended (Baltimore, Henderson and Brooks 2011; Texas Disposal Systems 2011; Blakeslee 1997).

34 See, for example, S.B. 791 (2013); S.B. 347 (2013).

References

"An Act to Withdraw from the Texas Low-level Radioactive Waste Disposal Compact," Public Laws of Maine, 2nd Regular Session of the 120th, Ch. 629, H.P.1666 – L.D.2171 (5 April 2002), www.mainelegislature.org/ros/LOM/lom120th/4pub601–650/pub601–650–28.htm

American Geological Institute, *Texas Compact Legislative Background* (23 October 1998), www.agiweb.org/legis105/lownuke.html

"Andrews Residents Leary [sic] of Possible Radioactive Waste Facility," *Lubbock Avalanche-Journal* (18 January 1999), http://lubbockonline.com/stories/011899/LD0638.shtml

Baltimore, C., Henderson, P., and Brooks, K., "Perry Sought to Sideline Nuclear Waste Site Critic," *Reuters* (1 September 2011), www.reuters.com/article/2011/09/01/us-usa-campaign-perry-dump-idUSTRE78053Z20110901

Barer, D., "Radioactive Waste Site Fees Push Texas Users Out-of-State," *Statesman* (29 November 2012), www.statesman.com/news/news/radioactive-waste-site-fees-push-texas-users-out-o/nTJpP/

Betancourt, A., "Border Skirmish," *Bulletin of the Atomic Scientists*, Vol. 54, No. 3 (1998): 14–16.

Blake, M., "The GOP's Nuke Dump Donor," *Salon* (5 April 2012), www.salon.com/2012/04/05/the_gops_nuke_dump_donor/

Blakeslee, N., "The West Texas Waste Wars," *Texas Observer* (28 March 1997), www.texasradiation.org/andrews/wastewar.html

Blaney, B., "Loving County Wants to Store Spent Nuclear Fuel," *Washington Times* (15 March 2014), www.washingtontimes.com/news/2014/mar/15/loving-county-wants-to-store-spent-nuclear-fuel/

Blaney, B., "Texas Company Could Bury First Nuclear Waste in April," *Lubbock Avalanche-Journal* (19 March 2012), http://lubbockonline.com/texas/2012–03–19/texas-company-could-bury-first-nuclear-waste-april#.Uzmsz6hdW7w

Blaney, B., "Texas House OK's Taking in More Radioactive Waste," *Businessweek* (17 May 2011), www.businessweek.com/ap/financialnews/D9N9GCT81.htm

Blaney, B., "Texas Site Begins Taking Federal Nuclear Waste," *ABC News* (7 June 2013), http://abcnews.go.com/US/wireStory/texas-site-begins-taking-federal-nuclear-waste-19343196#.UbJBx-dgS8A

Bonfield, T., "Fernald: History Repeats Itself," *Cincinnati Enquirer* (11 February 1996), www.enquirer.com/fernald/stories/021196c_fernald.html

"Boundary Shift Due on Texas Dump Sites," *Victoria Advocate* (1 December 1984).

Burrough, B., *The Big Rich: The Rise and Fall of the Greatest Texas Oil Fortunes* (New York: Penguin, 2009).

Campbell, B., "Andrews' Nuclear Reactor Progresses, Albeit Slowly," *Midland Reporter-Telegram* (1 May 2010), www.mrt.com/news/top_stories/article_0e94744d-c92c-51bb-acf5-f5e6afc038b2.html

Campbell, R., "Waste Control Specialists to Begin Storing Waste from Tennessee Company," *Midland Reporter-Telegram* (3 June 2009), www.mrt.com/news/top_stories/article_eec0090f-ed79-5e9e-bf68-146729883828.html

Camper, L., "Low-Level Radioactive Waste Management in the United States: Where Have We Been: Where Are We Going," *Waste Management 2010 Conference*, Phoenix, Arizona (7–11 March 2010), www.wmsym.org/archives/2010/pdfs/10417.pdf

City of Andrews, " 'Father' of Andrews: R.M. 'Bob' Means" (2011), www.cityofandrews.org/history/father_of_andrews.html

Congressional Record: Proceedings and Debates of the 105th Congress, 2nd Session, Vol. 144, Part 8 (2–15 June 1998).

County of Andrews, "Andrews County History" (n.d.), www.co.andrews.tx.us/about.php

De la Garza, P., "A Nuclear Waste Dump Becomes a Border Issue," *Chicago Tribune* (19 October 1998), http://articles.chicagotribune.com/1998–10–19/news/9810190189_1_sierra-blanca-border-issue-gas-station

Department of Energy, Office of Environmental Management, *Report to Congress: 1995 Annual Report on Low-Level Radioactive Waste Management Progress*, DOE/EM-0292, June 1996, http://www.nirs.org/radwaste/llw/annual95.pdf

De Rouffignac, A., "Attorney General Takes Action in Radioactive Waste Dispute," *Houston Business Journal* (1998a), www.bizjournals.com/houston/stories/1998/04/06/story8.html

De Rouffignac, A., "Firm Files Lawsuit in Dispute over Radioactive Waste Site," *Houston Business Journal* (1997), www.bizjournals.com/houston/stories/1997/06/09/story4.html

De Rouffignac, A., "Houston Firm Loses Legal Round in Federal Waste Disposal Fight," *Houston Business Journal* (1998b), www.bizjournals.com/houston/stories/1998/05/25/story7.html

De Rouffignac, A., "Nuclear Plants Contract with WCS to Store Waste at West Texas Site," *Houston Business Journal* (7 March 1999), www.bizjournals.comhouston/stories/1999/03/08/story6.html

De Rouffignac, A., "Small Firm Sees Bonanza in DOE Waste," *Houston Business Journal* (1996a), www.bizjournals.com/houston/stories/1996/09/09/story1.html

De Rouffignac, A., "Utah Firm Joins Rush to Dump Radioactive Waste in West Texas," *Houston Business Journal* (1996b), www.bizjournals.com/houston/stories/1996/10/07/story2.html

"Disposing NY Sewage in Region to End," *Lubbock Avalanche-Journal* (20 June 2001), http://lubbockonline.com/stories/062001/sta_062001108.shtml

"Dissenting Views of Hon. John Bryant (H.R. 558)," *House Report 104–148 – Texas Low-Level Radioactive Waste Disposal Compact Consent Act* (20 June 1995).

"Dump Battle Can Move to Federal Court," *Lubbock Avalanche-Journal* (3 June 1998), http://lubbockonline.com/stories/060398/053-0714.001.shtml

Flores, R., "Envirocare Dumps Barstow Waste Site Plan," *Pecos Enterprise* (30 January 2001), www.pecos.net/news/arch2001/013001p.htm

General Accounting Office, *Low-Level Radioactive Waste: Future Waste Volumes and Disposal Options Are Uncertain – Statement of (Ms.) Robin Nazzaro, Director, Natural Resources and Environment Before the Senate Committee on Energy and Natural Resources*, GAO-04-1097T (30 September 2004), www.gao.gov/assets/120/111273.html

Golden, T., "Dump Bid Assailed along Rio Grande," *New York Times* (29 March 1992), www.nytimes.com/1992/03/29/world/dump-bid-assailed-along-rio-grande.html

Gonzalez, S., "More Talks Held on Possible Nuclear Site in Howard County," *NewsWest 9* (8 April 2013), www.newswest9.com/story/21913262/more-talks-on-possible-nuclear-site-in-howard-county

Government Printing Office, H.R. 629, Report No. 105–181, 105th Congress, 1st Session (6 February 1997), www.gpo.gov/fdsys/pkg/BILLS-105hr629rh/BILLS-105hr629rh.pdf

Government Printing Office, Texas Low-Level Radioactive Waste Disposal Compact Consent Act, Pub. L. No. 105–236 (20 September 1998), www.gpo.gov/fdsys/pkg/PLAW-105publ236/pdf/PLAW-105publ236.pdf

Grissom, B., "Sierra Blancans Again Debate Possible Sludge Dump," *El Paso Times* (15 July 2007), www.elpasotimes.com/news/ci_6379497%22

H.AMDT.419, 105th Congress (1997–1998) (7 October 1997).

Hayden, F.G., and Bolduc, S.R., "Political and Economic Analysis of Low-Level Radioactive Waste," *University of Nebraska – Lincoln Economics Department Faculty Publications*, Paper 17 (1 June 1997), http://digitalcommons.unl.edu/cgi/viewcontent.cgi?article=1016&context=econfacpub

H.B. 449: Relating to Disposal Sites of the Texas Low-Level Radioactive Waste Disposal Authority, Texas Legislature Online (14 June 1985), www.lrl.state.tx.us/LASDOCS/69R/HB449/HB449_69R.pdf#page=60

H.B. 674: Relating to the Texas Low-Level Radioactive Waste Disposal Authority, the Disposal of Low-Level Radioactive Waste, and the Site for That Disposal (8 March 1999), www.capitol.state.tx.us/BillLookup/History.aspx?LegSess=76R&Bill=HB674

H.B. 1171: Relating to Regulation of Radioactive Materials and Other Sources of Radiation (22 May 1999), www.capitol.state.tx.us/BillLookup/History.aspx?LegSess=76R&Bill=HB1171

H.B. 1533: Relating to the Creation, Administration, Powers, Duties, Operations, and Financing of the Texas Low-Level Radioactive Waste Disposal Authority (14 May 1981), www.lrl.state.tx.us/legis/billSearch/text.cfm?legSession=67-0&billtypeDetail=HB&billNumberDetail=1533&billSuffixDetail=&startRow=1&IDlist=&unClicklist=&number=50

H.B. 1567: Relating to the Disposal of Low-Level Radioactive Waste; Authorizing the Exercise of the Power of Eminent Domain (1 September 2003), www.lrl.state.tx.us/legis/billSearch/text.cfm?legSession=78-0&billtypeDetail=HB&billNumberDetail=1567&billSuffixDetail=&startRow=1&IDlist=&unClicklist=&number=50

H.B. 1910: Relating to the Disposal or Assured Isolation of Low-Level Radioactive Waste (13 May 1999), www.capitol.state.tx.us/BillLookup/History.aspx?LegSess=76R&Bill=HB1910

H.B. 2589: Relating to the Assured Isolation of Low-Level Radioactive Waste (13 March 2003), www.legis.state.tx.us/BillLookup/History.aspx?LegSess=78R&Bill=HB2589

H.B. 2905: Relating to the Regulation and Management of Low-Level Radioactive Waste (3 April 2001), www.lrl.state.tx.us/legis/billSearch/text.cfm?legSession=78-0&billtypeDetail=HB&billNumberDetail=1567&billSuffixDetail=&startRow=1&IDlist=&unClicklist=&number=50

H.B. 2954: Relating to the Application of the Sunset Review Process to Certain State Agencies (30 May 1999), www.lrl.state.tx.us/legis/billSearch/text.cfm?legSession=67-0&billtypeDetail=HB&billNumberDetail=1177&billSuffixDetail=&startRow=1&IDlist=&unClicklist=&number=50

H.B. 3320: Relating to the Selection of the Disposal Site Designated by the Texas Low-Level Radioactive Waste Disposal Authority (16 March 1999), www.capitol.state.tx.us/BillLookup/History.aspx?LegSess=76R&Bill=HB3320

Homans, C., "The Operator," *New Republic* (20 April 2012), www.newrepublic.com/article/politics/magazine/102778/harold-simmons-campaign-donor-2012-gop#

House Committee on Environmental Affairs, *Committee Report: SB1177*, 67th Regular Session, Legislative Reference Library of Texas (12 May 1981), www.lrl.state.tx.us/

House Group Bill Analysis, *S.B. 1177 by Brooks (C.S.S.B. 1177 by Bock)* (14 May 1981), www.lrl.state.tx.us/scanned/hroBillAnalyses/67-0/SB1177.pdf

House Report 105–630 to the Texas Low-Level Radioactive Waste Disposal Compact Consent Act (n.d.), http://thomas.loc.gov/cgi-bin/bdquery/z?d105:HR00629:@@@K

House Research Organization Bill Analysis, H.B. 85, by Gallego (10 April 2001), www.hro.house.state.tx.us/pdf/ba77r/hb0085.pdf#navpanes=0

House Research Organization Bill Analysis, H.B. 1567 by West, Chisum, W. Smith (CSHB by West) (22 April 2003), www.lrl.state.tx.us/scanned/hroBillAnalyses/78-0/HB1567.PDF

House Research Organization Bill Analysis, H.B. 1910 by Chisum (29 April 1999), www.lrl.state.tx.us/scanned/hroBillAnalyses/76-0/HB1910.pdf

House Research Organization Bill Analysis, S.B. 1697 by Bivins (Walker) (23 May 2015), www.lrl.state.tx.us/scanned/hroBillAnalyses/74-0/SB1697.pdf

H.R. 558: Texas Low-Level Radioactive Waste Disposal Compact Consent Act (18 January 1995).

H.R. 629: Texas Low-Level Radioactive Waste Disposal Compact Consent Act (6 February 1997), www.congress.gov/bill/105th-congress/house-bill/629/text?q=%7B%22searc h%22%3A%5B%22cite%3A%28hr629%29%22%5D%7D&resultIndex=2

H.R. 1681: Relating to the Lease and Sale of Certain Land by the Texas Low-Level Radioactive Waste Disposal Authority (17 May 1995), www.lrl.state.tx.us/legis/billSearch/text.cfm?legSession=67-0&billtypeDetail=HB&billNumberDetail=1177&billSuffixDetail=&startRow=1&IDlist=&unClicklist=&number=50

Hubler, S., "Only California Is on Track for Nuclear Dump," *Los Angeles Times* (20 May 1991), http://articles.latimes.com/1991-05-20/news/mn-1454_1_nuclear-waste

Ivins, M., " 'Environmental Racism' in West Texas," *Abilene Reporter-News* (1 November 1997), www.texnews.com/opinion97/molly110197.html

Jacobi, L., "Texas Approach to the Management of Low Level Radioactive Waste After 1992," *Waste Management 1992 Conference*, Tucson, Arizona (22–26 February 1992), www.wmsym.org/archives/1992/V1/52.pdf

"Judge Dismisses $1 Billion Waste Lawsuit," *Lubbock Avalanche-Journal* (2 September 1998), http://lubbockonline.com/stories/090298/0902980016.shtml

Kane, L., "Childress County Ruled Out as Nuclear Waste Dump," *Lubbock Avalanche-Journal* (27 August 1999), http://lubbockonline.com/stories/082799/sta_0827990072.shtml

Kane, L., "Waste Case Must Stay in Andrews," *Lubbock Avalanche-Journal* (2000a), http://lubbockonline.com/stories/012000/sta_012000063.shtml

Kane, L., "Waste Firms Settle Differences," *Lubbock Avalanche-Journal* (2000b), http://lubbockonline.com/stories/112800/upd_075-5309.shtml

Knight, D., "Nuclear Waste Dump Planned on U.S.–Mexican border," *Albion Monitor* (1 July 1998), www.monitor.net/monitor/9807a/copyright/texmexdump.html

Kohout, M.D., *Sierra Blanca, TX*, Texas State Historical Association (n.d.), www.tshaonline.org/handbook/online/articles/hls47

Landa, J., "Eagle Ford Shale Oil Company Seeks Permit to Dispose Oil & Gas Waste Underground in Maverick County," *Eagle Pass Business Journal* (7 January 2013), www.epbusinessjournal.com/2013/01/eagle-ford-shale-oil-company-seeks-permit-to-dispose-oil-gas-waste-underground-in-maverick-county/

LeMone, D., Xie, H., Keller, G.R., and Dodge, R., "Remote Sensing Analysis of the Fort Hancock Low-Level Radioactive Waste Disposal Site: Hudspeth County, Texas," *Waste Management 2001 Conference*, Tucson, Arizona (25 February–1 March 2001), www.wmsym.org/archives/2001/21C/21C-21.pdf

Lomenick, T.F., *The Siting Record: An Account of the Programs of Federal Agencies and Events That Have Led to the Selection of a Potential Site for a Geologic Repository for High-Level Radioactive Waste*, Oak Ridge National Laboratory, ORNL/TM-12940 (March 1996).

Low-Level Radioactive Waste Policy Act of 1985, Amended, Pub. L. No. 99–240, 99 Stat. 1864 (15 January 1986), www.gtcceis.anl.gov/documents/docs/LLRWPAA.pdf

Lyman, R., "For Some, Texas Town Is Too Popular as Waste Disposal Site," *New York Times* (2 September 1998), www.nytimes.com/1998/09/02/us/for-some-texas-town-is-too-popular-as-waste-disposal-site.html

Maine.gov, Division of Environmental Health, "Radioactive Waste Section" (updated 2011), www.maine.gov/dhhs/mecdc/environmental-health/rad/hp-waste.htm

Malewitz, J., "Nuclear Waste Storage on Texas Lawmakers' Agenda," *Texas Tribune* (12 February 2014a), www.texastribune.org/2014/02/12/strauss-puts-nuclear-waste-texas-lawmakers-agenda/

Malewitz, J., "Texas' Nuclear Waste Dump Gets Wriggle Room," *Texas Tribune* (20 August 2014b), www.texastribune.org/2014/08/20/texas-nuclear-waste-dump-poised-get-wiggle-room/

Marks, P., "State Finding Few Takers for Its Low-Level Nuclear Waste," *Hartford Courant* (24 May 1992), http://articles.courant.com/1992-05-24/news/0000201589_1_radioactive-waste-low-level-waste-disposal-low-level-nuclear-waste

Mashhood, F., "District Judge Grants Hearing in Fight against West Texas Radioactive Waste Dump," *Austin American-Statesman* (8 May 2012), www.statesman.com/news/texas/district-judge-grants-hearing-in-fight-against-west-2346916.html

Mathews, L., "A Low-Level Radioactive Waste Disposal Site in Texas – Will It Become a Reality?" *Waste Management 1997 Conference*, Tucson, Arizona (23–27 February 1987), www.wmsym.org/archives/1997/sess_8/08–03.htm

Mathews, L., and Bowmer, W., "The Texas Situation," *Waste Management 1986 Conference*, Tucson, Arizona (22–26 February 1986), www.wmsym.org/archives/1986/V3/11.pdf

McCutcheon, C., "N-Dumps Trigger Opposite Reactions," *Albuquerque Journal* (24 February 1991).

Mittelstadt, M., "Wellstone Will Seek to Amend Texas Low-Level Radioactive Compact," *Abilene Reporter-News* (23 October 1997), www.texnews.com/texas97/waste102397.html

"The Modern Texas Economy," in *Texas Politics*, University of Texas at Austin (2009), http://texaspolitics.laits.utexas.edu/9_3_0.html

Montes, E., "Texas Opposition Mounting to Further Shipments of New York Sludge," *Abilene Reporter-News* (18 May 1997), www.texnews.com/texas97/sludge051897.html

Mount, P., "Texcor Talks to Witnesses," *Del Rio News Herald* (15 August 1992), www.newspapers.com/newspage/6340541/

Myerson, A., "Buying an Uneasy Home for New York City Waste," *New York Times* (16 July 1995), www.nytimes.com/1995/07/16/nyregion/buying-an-uneasy-home-for-new-york-city-waste.html

"Naturally-Occurring Radiation: Overview," Environmental Protection Agency (updated 29 June 2015), www.epa.gov/radiation/natural-radiation-overview.html

"Naturally-Occurring Radioactive Materials," World Nuclear Association (updated May 2015), www.world-nuclear.org/info/Safety-and-Security/Radiation-and-Health/Naturally-Occurring-Radioactive-Materials-NORM/

Newberry, W. F., Idaho National Engineering Laboratory, *Comparative Approaches to Siting Low-Level Radioactive Waste Disposal Facilities*, DOE-LLW-199 (July 1994), www.osti.gov/scitech/servlets/purl/114010

Newberry, W. F., "The Rise and Fall and Rise and Fall of American Public Policy on Disposal of Low-Level Radioactive Waste," *South Carolina Environmental Law Journal* (Winter 1993).

Newman, A., " 'An Area Previously Determined to Be the Best Adapted for Such Purposes': Nevada, Nuclear Waste and Assembly Joint Resolution 15 of 1975," *Journal of Policy History*, Vol. 24, No. 3 (2012): 432–465.

Newton, C., "Chisum Debates Low Level Nuclear Dump for Andrews County," *Lubbock Avalanche-Journal* (21 March 1999), http://lubbockonline.com/stories/032199/reg_LD0787.001.shtml

Nixon, P., "NORM Waste Dump Shakes Brackettville," *Del Rio News Herald* (15 April 1990), www.newspapers.com/newspage/9726310/

"Nuclear Bill Gets Derailed," *Brownsville Herald* (24 May 1995).

Office of House Bill Analysis, C.S.S.B. 1541 by Duncan (17 May 2001), in S.B. 1541 Relating to the Permanent Management of Low-Level Radioactive Waste (20 May 2001).

Office of the Attorney General – State of Texas (John Cornyn), Opinion No. JC-0052 (18 May 1999), www.texasattorneygeneral.gov/opinions/opinions/49cornyn/op/1999/htm/jc0052.htm

Office of the Governor, Letter to the Honorable David Dewhurst and the Honorable Joe Straus, Austin (28 March 2014), http://media.cmgdigital.com/shared/news/documents/2014/03/31/SKMBT_36314033117180.pdf

Parker, P., "Senate OKs Andrews Waste Site," *Lubbock Avalanche-Journal* (22 May 1999), http://lubbockonline.com/stories/052299/reg_052299125.shtml

Permanent Management of Low-Level Radioactive Waste, Committee Substitute for S.B. No. 1541 by Duncan (20 April 2001), www.capitol.state.tx.us/BillLookup/Text.aspx? LegSess=77R&Bill=SB1541

Pfeiffer, B., "Burial Plan Brings Cash, Fear to Poor Desert Town," *Bangor Daily News* (31 January–1 February 1998).

Polk, L., "Harold Simmons Is Dallas' Most Evil Genius," *D Magazine* (2010), www. dmagazine.com/publications/d-magazine/2010/february/harold-simmons-is-dallas-most-evil-genius?single=1

Quirk, T., "How Texas Lost the World's Largest Super Collider," *Texas Monthly* (21 October 2013), www.texasmonthly.com/story/how-texas-lost-worlds-largest-super-collider

"Radioactive Waste Dump Proposal Hit Dell City," *Galveston Daily News* (12 November 1983), www.newspapers.com/newspage/14548726/

RCRA Permit Application for a Hazardous Waste Storage, Treatment and Disposal Facility: Andrews County, Texas, Section VI. Geology Report, prepared for Waste Control Specialists, Inc. by Terra Dynamics Incorporated, Project No. 92–152 (March 1993), http://pbadupws.nrc.gov/docs/ML0419/ML041910484.pdf

Robbins, M.A., "House Debates Nuclear Waste Dump Bill," *Lubbock Avalanche-Journal* (7 May 1999a), http://lubbockonline.com/stories/050799/sta_050799053.shtml

Robbins, M.A., "Opinion Sought on Waste Disposal," *Lubbock Avalanche-Journal* (16 March 1999b), http://lubbockonline.com/stories/031699/sta_031699094.shtml

Robbins, M.A., "Radioactive Waste Disposal Discussed," *Lubbock Avalanche-Journal* (4 May 2000), http://lubbockonline.com/stories/050400/sta_050400069.shtml

Robbins, M.A., "Texas Legislature Set to Battle Radioactive Waste Site Issue," *Lubbock Avalanche-Journal* (1999c), http://lubbockonline.com/stories/020799/AST-3177.shtml

Rogers, E., "Run to the Border: Nuclear and Toxic Industries Find Opposition Where They Least Expected It," *UT Watch*, Vol. 1, No. 44 (December 1994), www.utwatch. org/archives/subtex/toxic_issue4.html

Runyon, L.C., "Low-Level Radioactive Waste Legislative Activity Update," National Conference of State Legislators – Environment, Energy and Transportation Program (July 1999), www.texasradiation.org/andrews/LegisActupdate.html

S. 270, Texas Low-Level Radioactive Waste Disposal Compact Consent Act (5 February 1997).

S. 419, Texas Low-Level Radioactive Waste Disposal Compact Consent Act (15 February 1995), http://thomas.loc.gov/cgi-bin/bdquery/D?d104:30:./temp/~bdLq8V::|/home/ LegislativeData.php?n=BSS;c=104

Salisbury, D., "Storing Nuclear Waste/The Deaf Smith Site: Prospect of Nuclear Waste Dump Draws Scowls from Farmers in Texas Panhandle," *Christian Science Monitor* (25 June 1985), www.csmonitor.com/1985/0625/arad2.html

S.B. 62: Relating to the Reporting of Waste Volumes and the Study, Selection, Acquisition, and Operation of Disposal Sites by the Texas Low-Level Radioactive Waste Disposal Authority (3 August 1987), www.lrl.state.tx.us/LASDOCS/70CS2/SB62/ SB62_70CS2.pdf

S.B. 347: Relating to Funding for the Operations of the Texas Low-Level Radioactive Waste Disposal Compact Commission and to the Disposal of Certain Low-Level Radioactive Waste (14 June 2013), http://openstates.org/tx/bills/83/SB347/

S.B. 791: Relating to the Regulation of Low-Level Radioactive Waste Disposal Facilities and Radioactive Substances (20 May 2013), http://openstates.org/tx/bills/83/SB791/

S.B. 1177: Relating to the Creation, Administration, Powers, Duties, Operations, and Financing of the Texas Low-Level Radioactive Waste Disposal Authority, Providing for Civil Penalties; Making an Appropriation (1 June 1981), www.lrl.state.tx.us/legis/billSearch/text.cfm?legSession=67-0&billtypeDetail=HB&billNumberDetail=1177&billSuffixDetail=&startRow=1&IDlist=&unClicklist=&number=50

S.B. 1206: Relating to the Texas Low-Level Radioactive Waste Disposal Compact (9 June 1993), www.capitol.state.tx.us/BillLookup/History.aspx?LegSess=73R&Bill=SB1206

S.B. 1418: Relating to the Texas Low-Level Radioactive Waste Disposal Authority and the Transportation of Radioactive Materials and Waste (23 April 1993), www.capitol.state.tx.us/BillLookup/Text.aspx?LegSess=73R&Bill=SB1418

S.B. 1697: Relating to the Storage, Processing and Disposal of Radioactive Waste, Low-Level Waste and Mixed Waste (23 May 1995), www.lrl.state.tx.us/legis/billSearch/text.cfm?legSession=67-0&billtypeDetail=HB&billNumberDetail=1177&billSuffixDetail=&startRow=1&IDlist=&unClicklist=&number=50

Scott, D.C., "US Waste-Dump Proposals Bring Protests from Mexico," *Christian Science Monitor* (6 April 1992), www.csmonitor.com/1992/0406/06013.html

Senate Interim Committee on Natural Resources, Interim Report to the 77th Legislature, *Storage and Disposal Options for Low-Level Radioactive Waste* (November 2000), www.senate.state.tx.us/75r/senate/commit/archive/c580/pdf/LLRWreport.pdf

Senate Research Center, Bill Analysis: C.S.H.B. 1171 by Chisum (Brown), Natural Resources, Committee Report [Substituted] (14 May 1999), www.capitol.state.tx.us/BillLookup/Text.aspx?LegSess=76R&Bill=HB1171

Senator Judith Zaffirini, *Summary of Legislation Passed, 1987–2011* (n.d.), http://107.20.245.137/zaffirini/wp-content/uploads/2012/09/Senator-Judith-Zaffirini-Summary-of-Legislation-Passed-1987-201116.pdf

Shannon, K., "South Texans Battle over Proposed Hazardous Dumps," *Kerrville Daily Times* (12 April 1992).

Sheehy, S., *Texas Big Rich: Exploits, Eccentricities, and Fabulous Wealth Won and Lost* (New York: William Morrow, 1990).

Shevory, K., "Waste Operator Donates to Senator," *Amarillo Globe News* (2 April 2001), http://amarillo.com/stories/2001/04/02/tex_waste.shtml

Siegel, B., "A Perfect Place for a Waste Dump," *Los Angeles Times* (22 December 1991), http://articles.latimes.com/1991-12-22/magazine/tm-1262_1_waste-dump-county-seat-grand-champion

Sierra Blanca Legal Defense Fund, "Environmental Justice Case Study: The Struggle for Sierra Blanca, Texas against a Low-Level Nuclear Waste Site" (1999), www.umich.edu/~snre492/blanca.html

Sierra Blanca Legal Defense Fund Press Release (30 September 1997), in Nebraska State Historical Society, Government Records, RG141, Series 1, Central Interstate Low-Level Radioactive Waste Compact (LLRW-Nebraska), Research Files, Articles and Books, 1961–2006, Box 2 of 5.

Smith, D., "Victory: No Dump in Spofford," *Del Rio News Herald* (1 July 1993), www.newspapers.com/newspage/7652208/

Smyrl, V., "Texas Low-Level Radioactive Waste Disposal Authority," *Texas State Historical Society* (n.d.), www.tshaonline.org/handbook/online/articles/metur

Spangler, J., "Owner of Envirocare Files Defamation Lawsuit," *Deseret News* (15 April 2000), www.deseretnews.com/article/812945/Owner-of-Envirocare-files-defamation-lawsuit.html?pg=all

"A Spread of One's Own," *Economist* (19 November 1998), www.economist.com/node/176738

"State Board Rejects McMullen for Waste Disposal Site," *Victoria Advocate* (23 February 1985).

Statement of Eric C. Peus, Waste Control Specialists LLC in "Disposal of Low-Level Radioactive Waste," Hearing before the Committee on Environment and Public Works, U.S. Senate Hearing 106–959 (25 July 2000), www.gpo.gov/fdsys/pkg/CHRG-106shrg71521/html/CHRG-106shrg71521.htm

"Studsvik Signs Teaming Agreement with Waste Control Specialists LLC (WCS)," Studsvik Press Release (7 September 2007), http://investors.studsvik.com/files/press/studsvik/1152103en1.pdf

Swartsell, N., "Harold Simmons' Waste Company Pays County, State," *Texas Tribune* (12 September 2012a), www.texastribune.org/2012/09/12/wcs-pays-andrews-county-and-texas/

Swartsell, N., "Texas Sierra Club Fight over Radioactive Waste Heats Up," *Texas Tribune* (21 October 2012b), www.texastribune.org/2012/10/21/texas-sierra-club-fights-wcs-radioactive-waste-sit/

"Targeting 'Cerrell' Communities," *Energy Justice Network* (n.d.), www.ejnet.org/ej/cerrell.pdf

"Texas Agency Denies Permit for Waste Site," *New York Times* (23 October 1998), www.nytimes.com/1998/10/23/us/texas-agency-denies-permit-for-waste-site.html

Texas Commission on Environmental Quality, *Radioactive Material License*, Amendment 00 (10 September 2009), www.tceq.state.tx.us/assets/public/permitting/rad/wcs/20090910%20License%20R04100%20issued%20CCO.pdf

Texas Commission on Environmental Quality, *Radioactive Material License*, Section 9, "General Requirements" (18 September 2012), www.wcstexas.com/PDF_downloads/WCS%20LLW-Disposal%20License%20R04100%20Amend%2018.pdf

Texas Compact Low-Level Radioactive Waste Generation Trends and Management Alternatives Study: Technical Report, RAE-42774–019–5407–2, prepared by Rogers & Associates Engineering Branch, URS Corporation (August 2000), www.tceq.state.tx.us/assets/public/permitting/llrw/entire.pdf

Texas Department of Agriculture, "Texas Ag Stats" (n.d.), www.texasagriculture.gov/About/TexasAgStats.aspx

Texas Disposal Systems, "About Us" (2011), www.texasdisposal.com/our-history

Texas House Study Group, *Bill Analysis, CSHB 1533 by Bock* (11 May 1981), www.lrl.state.tx.us/scanned/hroBillAnalyses/67–0/HB1533.pdf

Texas Low Level Radioactive Waste Disposal Compact Commission, *Agreement for Importation of Nonparty Low-level Radioactive Waste for Disposal in the Texas Low-Level Radioactive Waste Disposal Compact Facility* (1 July 2012), www.tllrwdcc.org/wp-content/uploads/2012/08/Studsvik-Signed-Agreement-TLLRWDCC-2–0009–00.pdf

Texas/Maine/Vermont Compact, *Congressional Record*, Vol. 144, No. 42 (3 April 1998), www.gpo.gov/fdsys/pkg/CREC-1998-04-03/html/CREC-1998-04-03-pt1-PgS3233-2.htm

Texas-Maine-Vermont Compact, Statement of Senator Paul Wellstone, *Congressional Record*, Vol. 144, No. 77 (15 June 1998), www.gpo.gov/fdsys/pkg/CREC-1998-06-15/html/CREC-1998-06-15-pt1-PgS6349.htm

"Texas Regulators Vote against Sierra Blanca Nuke Waste Dump," *Livestock Weekly* (29 October 1998), www.livestockweekly.com/papers/98/10/29/whlnukedump.asp

Texas State Historical Association, "Ranching" (n.d.), www.tshaonline.org/handbook/online/articles/azr02

United States Census Bureau, *State-County QuickFacts: Howard County* (2013 Estimate), http://quickfacts.census.gov/qfd/states/48/48227.html

United States Census Bureau, *State-County QuickFacts: Loving County* (2013 Estimate), http://quickfacts.census.gov/qfd/states/48/48301.html

United States Congress, Office of Technology Assessment, *Partnerships Under Pressure: Managing Commercial Low-Level Radioactive Waste*, OTA-O-426 (Washington, DC: U.S. Government Printing Office, November 1989), www.fas.org/ota/reports/8923.pdf

United States Department of Energy, *Manifest Information Management Systems* (n.d.), http://mims.doe.gov/GeneratorData.aspx

United States Environmental Protection Agency, *Fernald Preserve* (June 2010), www.epa.gov/reg5sfun/redevelop/pdfs/Fernald_Preserve.pdf

United States Nuclear Regulatory Commission, Advisory Committee on Nuclear Waste White Paper, *History and Framework of Commercial Low-Level Radioactive Waste Management in the United States*, NUREG-1853, Washington, DC (January 2007), www.nrc.gov/reading-rm/doc-collections/nuregs/staff/sr1853/sr1853.pdf

University of Texas of the Permian Basin, "HT^{3}R" (2014), www.utpb.edu/research-grants/ht3r/

"US Nuclear Fuel Cycle," *World Nuclear Association* (updated April 2014), www.world-nuclear.org/info/Country-Profiles/Countries-T-Z/USA – Nuclear-Fuel-Cycle/

"Valhi, Inc. Announces Low-Level Radioactive Waste Disposal License Decision," *iStock-Analyst.com* (12 August 2008), www.istockanalyst.com/article/viewiStockNews/articleid/2506754

Van Vliet, J., "Construction, Startup and Operation of a New LLRW Disposal Facility in Andrews County, Texas," *Waste Management 2012 Conference*, Phoenix, Arizona (26 February–1 March 2012), www.wmsym.org/archives/2012/papers/12151.pdf

Vari, A., Reagan-Cirincione, P., and Mumpower, J. *LLRW Disposal Facility Siting: Successes and Failures in Six Countries* (Boston, MA: Kluwer Academic, 1994).

"Vt. Begins Shipping Radioactive Waste to Texas," *Associated Press* (27 September 2012), http://fuelfix.com/blog/2012/09/27/vt-begins-shipping-radioactive-waste-to-texas/

Wald, M., "Texas Company, Alone in U.S., Cashes in on Nuclear Waste," *New York Times* (20 January 2014), www.nytimes.com/2014/01/21/business/energy-environment/texas-company-alone-in-us-cashes-in-on-nuclear-waste.html

Walker, T., "Eddy-Lea Energy Alliance Envisions Southeastern New Mexico Home for Spent Nuclear Fuel," *Carlsbad Current-Argus* (4 October 2012), www.currentargus.com/ci_21697228/eddy-lea-energy-alliance-envisions-southeastern-new-mexico

Waste Control Specialists, "Providing a Solution for Every Disposal Need" (n.d.), www.texassolution.com/documents/wcsoverview.pdf

Waste Control Specialists LLC v. Envirocare, Khosrow B. Semnani, Charles A Judd, Frank C. Thorley, George W. Hellstrom, Billy W. Clayton and Nancy M. Molleda, No. 14,580, Plaintiff's Original Petition in the District Court of Andrews County, Texas (2 May 1997), http://pbadupws.nrc.gov/docs/ML0301/ML030130112.pdf

Waste Control Specialists Press Release, "WCS Commences Low-Level Radioactive Waste Disposal Operations: Texas Compact Operator Safely Disposes of First Shipment of Low-Level Radioactive Waste" (27 April 2012), www.wcstexas.com/PDF_downloads/WCS%20Press%20Release%20First%20LLRW%20Disposed.pdf

Wellstone Amendment No. 2277, 1 April 1998, H.R. 629RH, *Texas Low-Level Radioactive Waste Disposal Compact Consent Act* (15 July 1997), http://thomas.loc.gov/cgi-bin/query/D?c105:6:./temp/~c105g293KK

Wilder, F., "Good to Glow," *Texas Observer* (4 April 2008), www.texasobserver. org/2729-good-to-glow-despite-its-own-scientists-objections-state-regulators-are-green-lighting-a-massive-nuclear-waste-dump-in-west-texas/

Wilder, F., "TCEQ Rolls Over for Harold Simmons," *Texas Observer* (10 September 2010), www.texasobserver.org/tceq-rolls-over-for-harold-simmons/

Wilder, F., "Waste Texas," *Texas Observer* (6 March 2009), www.texasobserver.org/2978-waste-texas-why-andrews-county-is-so-eager-to-get-dumped-on/

Wise, J., "Andrews Cleans Up on Vacuum Cleaners," *Lubbock Avalanche-Journal* (1997), http://lubbockonline.com/news/040697/andrews.htm

Wise, J., "Andrews Company Lands Federal Nuclear Waste Disposal Contracts," *Lubbock Avalanche-Journal* (1999a), http://lubbockonline.com/stories/070199/loc_070199100. shtml

Wise, J., "Andrews Still Courting Waste Facility," *Lubbock Avalanche-Journal* (1999b), http://lubbockonline.com/stories/061299/loc_0612990089.shtml

Wise, J., "Borden Commissioners Ask to Be Dropped from Waste List," *Lubbock Avalanche-Journal* (1999c), http://lubbockonline.com/stories/101299/loc_101299074.shtml

Wise, J., "Ex-radioactive Waste Regulator Joins Envirocare," *Lubbock Avalanche-Journal* (1999d), http://lubbockonline.com/stories/020399/053-1524.shtml

Wise, J., "Nuclear Waste Company Considering Area Sites," *Lubbock Avalanche-Journal* (1999e), http://lubbockonline.com/stories/072899/loc_072899037.shtml

Wise, J., "Officials Survey Andrews County for Nuke Dump Site," *Lubbock Avalanche-Journal* (1998a), http://lubbockonline.com/stories/111998/053-1269.shtml

Wise, J., "Radioactive Waste Site Questioned," *Lubbock Avalanche-Journal* (1999f), http://lubbockonline.com/stories/031999/reg_031999103.shtml

Wise, J., "Waste Control Removes Hance from Lineup," *Lubbock Avalanche-Journal* (1999g), http://lubbockonline.com/stories/102999/loc_1029990121.shtml

Wise, J., "Waste Control Ups Ante by Seeking $1 Billion from Envirocare," *Lubbock Avalanche-Journal* (1998b), http://lubbockonline.com/stories/032798/053-0659.shtml

Wright, J., "High-Temperature Teaching and Test Reactor (HT^{3}R): Program Objectives," Presentation to the NRC, Rockville, MD (11 May 2006), http://pbadupws.nrc.gov/ docs/ML0613/ML061320066.pdf

Yergin, D., *The Prize: The Epic Quest for Oil, Money & Power* (New York: Free Press, 1991).

5 "A long way short of having broad community support"

Low level radioactive waste disposal in Australia

Introduction

Australia is the third largest global producer of uranium, all of which it exports.[1] While the nation does not utilize nuclear power for electricity generation or have a nuclear weapons capability – although Maralinga in South Australia and the Montebello Islands off the Western Australian coast hosted British nuclear weapon tests during the 1950s and 1960s – the Australian Nuclear Science and Technology Organisation (ANSTO) operates the Open Pool Australian Lightwater (OPAL) research reactor in the south Sydney suburb of Lucas Heights in New South Wales (NSW). The OPAL reactor produces radioactive sources for use in medical procedures, research and by industries such as mining all over the country (James and Rann n.d., p. 1). The federal government maintains that a central repository to dispose of the waste generated by these essential activities is in the national interest and the government must lead the way (Lloyd 2006, p. 6).[2]

The Commonwealth Department of Resources, Energy and Tourism is charged with implementing the federal government's policy on radioactive waste management, in particular overseeing the waste storage/disposal siting process.[3] While the federal system is designed to diffuse decision-making since several jurisdictions must consent, the federal government can override state objections as per section 108 of the Australian Constitution (Holland 2002a, pp. 76–86).

Radioactive waste totals

Each year Australia produces approximately 1,400 cubic feet of low level radioactive waste (LLRW) and 177 cubic feet of short- and long-term intermediate level radioactive waste (IRLW).[4] As of 2011, approximately 157,000 cubic feet of waste had been accumulated: 135,000 cubic feet of LLRW waste and 15,000 cubic feet of ILRW waste generated mainly by ANSTO with significant contributions from the Commonwealth Science and Industry Research Organisation (CSIRO) and the Defence Department that are the responsibility of the federal government; and approximately 7,000 cubic feet of LLRW distributed amongst the states and territories (James and Rann n.d.; Department of

Resources, Energy and Tourism 2009, p. 3; ANSTO 2011, p. 3; Department of Industry n.d.). In addition, it is anticipated that decommissioning of the HIFAR (High Flux Australian Reactor) research reactor, beginning in 2016, will generate up to 16,000 cubic feet of LLRW and 17,000 cubic feet of ILRW while the Moata training reactor, dismantled in 2010, will generate 2,150 cubic feet of LLRW and 5 cubic feet of ILRW during decommissioning (ANSTO n.d.a.).[5]

Federal Industry Minister Ian MacFarlane has acknowledged that there is no complete inventory of where and how Australia's nuclear waste is currently located (Selvaratnam 2014). Such wastes are stored in less than ideal conditions (for example, hospital car parks and university laboratories – and even in a disused incinerator room in the offices of the state government in Melbourne at one stage [Panter 1992] – at over 100 temporary sites nationwide [World Nuclear Association (WNA) updated 2014]). These sites were not designed for long-term storage, are nearing capacity and are considered a risk to people and the environment because such waste is "potentially subject to: vandalism, accidents, abandonment, the vagaries of climate and degradation of packaging" ("A Radioactive Waste Repository for Australia, Commonwealth Australia, Site Selection Study – Phase 3" ["Phase 3"] 1997 WNA updated 2014). Given these risks, the federal government has been trying for decades without success to build a federal facility to consolidate this waste.

Public attitudes to radioactive waste

Both scientific consensus and international experience have demonstrated that low and short-lived intermediate level waste can be safely packaged and disposed of in properly sited, near-surface facilities to decay to naturally insignificant levels over 100 to 300 years ("Phase 3" 1997). Historically a substantial majority of Australians have displayed great antipathy toward both nuclear power and radioactive waste disposal facility proposals. Some of the reasons for this antipathy include:

- fears of radiation – some rational, some irrational – exacerbated by scientific controversy regarding the effects of radiation;
- a false assumption that accidents at Australian nuclear facilities (including storage and disposal sites) could have similarly serious consequences as accidents such as Chernobyl;
- concern over a possible fall in property values near a disposal site and not-in-my-backyard (NIMBY) attitudes of elected officials and government bureaucrats;
- fear that any interim storage site will become a permanent national repository;
- fear that the very isolation of a rural site may lead to vandalism, or a site near a population center may threaten the health of large numbers of people and critical sources of community income such as tourism;
- a belief that disposing of radioactive waste only encourages more to be produced;

- concerns about waste being transported long distances from the source, particularly interstate (and possibly overseas), motivated by beliefs that the further the wastes are taken away from the source, the more dangerous they must be or that they are "other people's" wastes;
- a history of poor environmental management by the government (Panter 1992, p. 6).

Combined, these reasons have made it extremely difficult for decision-makers to overcome local fears about the safety of radioactive waste disposal facilities. They have also led to demands from local communities for radioactive waste to be removed from existing storage locations. For example, the objections of the Sutherland Shire Council to the storage of lightly contaminated soil from the CSIRO's Fisherman's Bend site in Victoria at Lucas Heights and the objections by local residents to the storage of Department of Defence radioactive waste at the Australian Defence Industries (ADI) St Marys site in NSW ("National Radioactive Waste Repository Site Selection Study, Phase 1" ["Phase 1"] 1993).

While Australia currently has two LLRW disposal facilities – Esk, Queensland, and Mount Walton East, Western Australia – these sites only accept only waste

Figure 5.1 Australia map

generated in-state (Nicholson 2013).[6] With the exception of the Australian Capital Territory, every other state and territory in the country has, at one time or another, refused to allow a federal radioactive waste facility to be located within its boundaries (Panter 1992, p. 7).

Attempts to site a federal LLRW repository: a history

Initial siting efforts were made by the states rather than being orchestrated at the federal level. In early 1978, the NSW government planned to move approximately 3,000 tonnes of radioactive soil from a former uranium smelter at Hunters Hill in Sydney to Manara in the state's far west. However, local residents including the aboriginal people, graziers and councillors came together to oppose the plan (Aston 2011). NSW Premier Neville Wran then asked South Australia to accept the waste at Radium Hill, an old uranium mine, but the South Australian Premier David Tonkin refused (Panter 1992).

In March 1983, a wakeup call was sounded in Melbourne when a fire narrowly missed an office building in which radioactive waste had been temporarily stored since 1976. The Victorian government sought to establish a repository in late 1985 in Dutson Downs in the southeast of the state but was met with fierce opposition led by unions and the local government. By February 1986, the plan had been abandoned. Western Australia, Tasmania and Queensland all have similar stories. For example, the Queensland government built a storage bunker in 1989 for radioactive waste storage at Redbank, 18 miles west of Brisbane, to replace a 40-year-old tin shed in inner Brisbane but was forced to abandon it due to local opposition before eventually building the site in Esk (Panter 1992, p. 5).

In response to a 1975 National Health & Medical Research Council recommendation for a central repository for longer-lived radioactive wastes, a Commonwealth-State Consultative Committee (C/SCC) was set up in 1980 to better coordinate policies regarding radioactive waste generated by the medical profession, industry and research organizations. The C/SCC determined that LLRW needed a Code of Practice and recommended in 1985 that a federal program of site identification for near-surface disposal of radioactive waste be initiated. The Committee came up with a list of 16 sites to be considered over the next 12 months and there was ministerial agreement that it would be better to have one or two shared federal facilities rather than a site in each state or territory (Panter 1992, pp. 6–7; "Phase 1" 1993).

An initial desktop review was undertaken utilizing International Atomic Energy Agency (IAEA) guidelines and the results were collated by the Committee (Federal Parliament of Australia updated 2011; "Phase 1" 1993). In 1986 the C/SCC reported that a number of sites were potentially suitable and recommended that state governments advise the federal government on how to proceed with detailed investigations within their boundaries. In March 1986, the federal Minister for Resources and Energy wrote to state and territorial ministers seeking expressions of interest, but only the Northern Territory government responded positively ("Phase 1" 1993).

In April 1988, the Northern Territory Government, after carefully considering its position, agreed to a pilot study and was awarded $100,000 from the Commonwealth to that end (Holland 2002a, pp. 76–86; "Phase 1" 1993). The territory government appointed ANSTO to carry out the feasibility study, which was completed in March 1989. Officials considered the report for over 2 years but ultimately informed the federal government in May 1991 that they did not wish to proceed with the project for what appeared to be domestic political considerations rather than any technical deficiencies noted in the report (Panter 1992).

To further complicate the situation, on 5 February 1992 the Land and Environment Court of NSW ordered that ANSTO be prohibited from transporting radioactive waste to Lucas Heights. The Shire of Sutherland had brought the action because 70,600 cubic feet of radioactive soil from Victoria had been delivered to ANSTO and there were plans to relocate a further 600 cubic feet of defense waste from St Marys. The federal government responded to the ruling by introducing the Australian Nuclear Science and Technology Organisation Amendment Bill 1992, which gave ANSTO future immunity from court action and allowed the government to store radioactive waste as a temporary measure (Panter 1992, p. 1).

On 1 June 1992, the Minister for Primary Industries and Energy Simon Crean stated that the federal government was still committed to building a national repository and announced another countrywide site selection study. This commitment was supported by the state and territory governments and codified in the National Strategy for Ecologically Sustainable Development of December 1992 ("National Radioactive Waste Repository, Site Selection Study, Phase 2" ["Phase 2"] 1995).

On 7 October 1992, the discussion paper "A Radioactive Waste Repository for Australia: Methods for Choosing the Right Site" was released, providing background information on the issue and a methodology to identify potential sites after the first phase of the selection study was submitted for public comment ("Phase 2" 1995). Most of the submissions received were in favor of a repository but the majority of those opposed objected to the facility being located in or near their community ("Phase 2" 1995).

A month later, a Code of Practice for the Near-Surface Disposal of Radioactive Waste in Australia, based on IAEA guidelines, outlined the following siting criteria (Department of Resources, Energy and Tourism 2009, pp. 6–7; "Phase 3" 1997):

- The site should be located in an area of low rainfall, free from flooding, have good surface drainage features and be geomorphologically stable.
- The water table should be deep enough to ensure that groundwater is unlikely to rise to within 16 feet of the waste and large fluctuations in the water table should be unlikely.
- Geological structure and hydrogeological conditions should permit groundwater modeling and enable prediction of radionuclide migration.

- The site should be located away from known or anticipated seismic, tectonic or volcanic activity.
- The site should be in an area of low population density where projected population growth or the prospects for future development are very low.
- Groundwater should ideally not be suitable for human consumption, pastoral or agricultural use.
- The site should have suitable geochemical and geotechnical properties to inhibit radionuclide migration.

Underpinning these criteria was the importance of natural site characteristics in providing an effective barrier to the dispersal of radionuclides and human intrusion ("Phase 3" 1997). It was envisaged that the facility would include a surface or near-surface disposal trench for LLRW and short-lived ILRW and provide for deeper disposal of the smaller volume of long-lived ILRW.

In 1992, an area near Woomera, South Australia, was identified as a prime candidate for a repository (Federal Parliament of Australia updated 2011). Technical studies began the same year with the goal of a formal recommendation by 1994. However, local resistance was considerable. The Kalgoorlie-Boulder Council opposed constructing a facility within city limits, submitting a 700-signature public petition to this effect, and the City of Port Augusta opposed any construction near Woomera (Holland 2002a, pp. 76–86, 79; "Phase 2" 1995).

In May 1995, a Senate Select Committee on the Dangers of Radioactive Waste was created. Its mandate included examining the process required to develop a near-surface radioactive waste facility ("Phase 3" 1997). The ongoing federal repository siting study was postponed until the Committee could issue its findings so they could be incorporated into any final report. The Committee's report, "No Time to Waste," was given to the federal parliament on 30 April 1996. For the purposes of this book, the key recommendation was: "The Committee recommends a national above ground storage facility be established which has the capacity to take low, intermediate and high-level radioactive waste" (Holland 2002a, pp. 76–86, 80; "Phase 3" 1997).

However, the newly elected Liberal government rejected the report on the grounds that the Committee "had failed to maintain the distinction between the different categories of nuclear waste" and ignored international best practice that near-surface disposal was the most suitable approach for low and intermediate level waste rather than storage (Holland 2002a, pp. 76–86, 80). The federal government intended to continue its existing work to find a suitable site for LLRW and ILRW; a site requiring an "area of 2.25 square kilometers [8.68 square miles] . . . including a large [natural] buffer zone where access is controlled and conditions monitored" ("Phase 3" 1997).

In February 1998, an area of 67,000 square kilometers (roughly 25,900 square miles) was nominated: the Billa Kalina Region in South Australia. After meetings with regional stakeholders and site visits by aboriginal groups, 11 sites were selected for hydrogeological test drilling starting in the middle of 2000. Based on drilling results, five sites were selected for the next stage of characterization. However, after consultation between the federal government and local aboriginal groups, who raised heritage concerns, two sites were withdrawn from consideration. The three remaining sites were subjected to environmental assessment and in January 2001 the preferred site in Woomera, Evetts Field West, about 27 miles west of the Roxby Downs-Woomera road, was announced (Senator Warwick Parer 1998; Holland 2002a, pp. 80–81; Senator Nick Minchin 1999). An alternative site, east of the Roxby Downs-Woomera road, was also selected ("How Sites in South Australia Were Chosen" 2001).

Box 5.1   The Pangea proposal

While attempts were being made to site a federal low level waste repository, a proposal to investigate the feasibility of building an international spent fuel and high level waste disposal facility in Australia had a profound effect on the domestic debate. In 1998, Pangea Resources Australia, a commercial venture funded by British Nuclear Fuels Limited, the Swiss radioactive waste management authority Nagra and the Canadian company Enterra Holdings Limited, proposed that a permanent deep geological disposal site be developed in the rock formations underlying the desert regions of either South Australia or Western Australia (Holland 2002b, p. 285). Australia was considered a perfect site for such a repository given its large size, small population, geological stability, sophisticated transport network, mining expertise working in isolated regions and political stability (Kurzeme n.d., p. 67; Taylor 2006, p. 879).

Neither state government was happy with the idea. Western Australia passed a bipartisan motion stating "total opposition to any proposal from any person or company to situate an international nuclear waste repository in Western Australia on the grounds that such a repository poses a significant threat to Western Australia's environment and public safety" (Western Australia Parliamentary Debates, House of Assembly 1999, p. 644; Holland 2002b, p. 285). The state government then passed the Nuclear Waste Storage (Prohibition) Act 1999 with the "intention of prohibiting the establishment of a nuclear waste storage facility in this State or the use of any place in this State for the storage or disposal of nuclear waste" (Holland 2002b, p. 286).

The conservative South Australia government, under pressure from the Labor opposition, passed almost identical legislation to its Western Australia counterpart. The Nuclear Waste Storage Facility (Prohibition) Act 2000 only allowed for low level waste to be housed within its borders and prohibited funds from being spent on projects such as feasibility studies (Holland 2002b, p. 286).

The Australian Senate echoed these sentiments in a motion expressing

> its fundamental opposition to the proposal by Pangea to situate an international nuclear waste repository in Western Australia, or anywhere else within the territories of the Commonwealth of Australia, on the grounds that such a repository poses significant threats to Australia's environment, public safety and sovereignty.
>
> (Holland 2002b, p. 286)

Using deeply evocative language, environmental organizations charged that transnational corporations wanted to make Australia the "world's rubbish dump." Further, transporting waste over long distances would increase the potential environmental hazards. When a promotional advertisement leaked to the media, the public reaction was swift and extremely negative. The federal government chose not to act on the proposal and by 2000, after investing $15 million dollars, Pangea shelved the idea (Holland 2002b, pp. 283–301; Falk, Green and Mudd 2006, pp. 845–857).

In early 2001, the Australian National Store Advisory Committee developed a set of 'Site Selection Themes.' These themes, designed to meet state and international standards, were meant to ensure the safety of the radioactive waste in the storage facility; operational requirements for safe transport, handling, storage and retrieval of waste packages; the safety of humans and the environment; and the security of the facility.

In May 2003, the government announced that Woomera would be the definitive site. The repository would be 1,076 square feet, with long trenches up to 65 feet deep to hold the waste and encircled by a buffer zone of 0.86 square miles (WNA updated 2014). However, on 14 July 2004 Prime Minister Howard announced that the government was abandoning the 'National Repository Project' due to the intransigence of the state government that, fearing political blowback, was adamant that no repository would be built within its borders (Federal Parliament of Australia updated 2011). The South Australian government went so far as to take the federal government to court to block the compulsory acquisition of land needed for the preferred site by declaring the area a public park, with the Full Federal Court of Australia ultimately ruling against the Commonwealth (*South Australia v. Honourable Peter Slipper MP* 2004; Bennett 2007, pp. 79–93; Lloyd 2006, p. 6,7).

Unable to make any headway on siting a national repository, state governments were instructed by the federal government to set up their own facilities to 'international standards.' Policy-makers at both the state and federal levels agreed that while a single federal site was the preferred option, no state government was likely to host, so the Commonwealth government started looking for potential sites on federal government land (WNA updated 2014).

In 2005, the federal government passed the Commonwealth Radioactive Waste Management Act 2005. The Act gave the Science Minister extremely wide discretion to declare any site suitable and acquire land for that purpose. The Act also allowed for nominations by Northern Territory Aboriginal Land Councils for sites within their jurisdiction to be considered by the federal government. Problematically, the Act appeared written specifically to deter legitimate stakeholder consultation and ensure that legal challenges from aboriginal groups would be frustrated (Commonwealth Radioactive Waste Management Act 2005; Bonacci 2014). The Act removed rights for applicants to challenge decisions of the Minister on the grounds of procedural fairness and exempted the minister's declaration of a facility site from being considered a 'legislative instrument,' thus rendering the use of rights granted under the Administrative Decisions (Judicial Review) Act 1977 (Cth) null and void and making it extremely difficult for an objector to challenge the decision under administrative law processes (Lloyd 2006, p. 7).

Four new sites were selected, all in the Northern Territory: Fishers Ridge, east of Katherine; Mt Everard, northwest of Alice Springs and Harts Range, northeast of Alice Springs (both were on land where the Jindalee Over the Horizon Radar network was located); and Muckaty Station, a disused cattle station approximately 74 miles north of Tennant Creek (Department of Industry n.d.a.). On 15 July 2005, the federal government announced that the three defense sites where it had greater political sway over the territorial government – Mount Everard, Harts Ridge and Fishers Ridge – had been chosen for further characterization (Federal Parliament of Australia updated 2011). The sites would be subjected to "field assessments" and "environmental assessment and licencing" in preparation for disposing of both ILRW and LLRW (WNA updated 2014).

However, in June 2007 the Northern Land Council (NLC) nominated Muckaty on behalf of the traditional owners, the Ngapa clan, and the federal government accepted the nomination over the objections of the Northern Territory government.[7] If Muckaty became the preferred site, the owners would sign over 0.57 square miles of their land as a long-lasting lease (WNA updated 2014). Optimistically, the government planned to open the facility in 2011 (Northern Land Council 2014).

Once again, plans were changed with a change of federal government in December 2007. The Kevin Rudd–led Labor government decided to take radioactive waste management out of the science portfolio and placed it for the first time in the resources and industry portfolio (Ludlam 2012). The Greens – Australia's environmental political party – observed that the decision shifted responsibility to a department with no expertise in such a complex and delicate area, which is one reason why the government ran into problems subsequently (Ludlam 2012).

Introduced into parliament by the Federal Resources Minister Martin Ferguson in 2010, the National Radioactive Waste Management Bill 2010 was intended to repeal and replace the Commonwealth Radioactive Waste Management Act

2005 (National Radioactive Waste Management Bill 2010). The bill granted the federal government wide-ranging powers to override extant Commonwealth legislation (in particular aboriginal heritage and environment protection laws) and, pursuant to clauses 11 and 12, the Commonwealth could effectively exclude state and territory laws from operating if they were considered a hindrance to determining the suitability of a site. Again it allowed volunteer communities to be nominated by the NLC and, if there were no takers, then a nationwide search for volunteer communities would be initiated. Both processes, it was promised, would involve extensive consultation with all stakeholders and any selected site would be subject to all relevant environmental and heritage processes. This has turned out to be more promise than fact. The bill was justly criticized for its disregard of the Aboriginal Land Rights Act 1976 (ALRA; Green 2011, p. 1; Cole 2012). That Act requires that when a nomination is pending, the full council of the NLC must be convinced that the proper consent was obtained from the affected traditional owners of the land (Aboriginal Land Rights Act [NT] 1976). The bill also ignored the stated intention of the Nuclear Waste Transport, Storage, Disposal (Prohibition) Act 2004 NT, where the Northern Territory parliament sought to block the imposition of a repository against its citizens' wishes (Nuclear Waste Transport, Storage, Disposal [Prohibition] Act [NT] 2004).

The Bill was described as both "heavy-handed and undemocratic" and the government was criticized by the Northern Territory Central Land Council for pursuing "an approach characterized by the desire to find a politically expedient solution, contempt for state and Territory laws, and disregard for decision making processes enshrined in the Land Rights Act" (Green 2011, p. 1). Further, on 22 December 2010, the Climate Change, Environment and the Arts Standing Committee's report on the National Radioactive Waste Management Bill was tabled in the House of Representatives. Notwithstanding substantive concerns about the Bill that were identified in the report, critics claimed that the "timing was clearly a cynical attempt to avoid public scrutiny as the inquiry was not required to report until late March 2011" (Green 2011, p. 2).

The government attempted to ease the enactment of the Bill with an 11-day inquiry by the Legal and Constitutional Committee. After an outcry, the time frame was extended and the Committee received 238 submissions that were overwhelmingly critical of the legislation, particularly the extent to which it retained one nomination and shielded it from procedural fairness and judicial review. The Committee was repeatedly called upon to meet the affected communities at Tennant Creek but was unwilling to do so (Advisory Report on the Bill, Parliament of Australia n.d., chap. 1).

The Australian Conservation Foundation called for a broader public process incorporating best practice principles. The Foundation also claimed the Muckaty process was flawed because the landowners did not give 'proper consent' and they were not correctly informed about the potential risks or human rights principles (Australian Conservation Foundation Submission Inquiry of the

Senate Standing Committee on Legal and Constitutional Affairs into the National Radioactive Waste Management Bill 2010, p. 2).

The Australian Greens blocked the bill for 2 years but it eventually came into effect on 4 April 2012, replacing the 2005 Act after the Greens secured an amendment barring the storage of international nuclear waste (National Radioactive Waste Management Act 2012). While it did restore some procedural fairness rights lost under the 2005 Act, it is rightly considered to have not gone far enough to allow for a truly consultative process. Environmental nongovernmental organizations (ENGOs) and indigenous groups were particularly concerned that the act gave the Resources Minister Martin Ferguson powers that were too wide-ranging (Beck 2012).

The Act gave the federal government the power "to make arrangements for the safe and secure management of radioactive waste generated, possessed or controlled by the Commonwealth." However, no site could be "considered as a potential location for a radioactive waste management facility without the voluntary nomination of that site and agreement of persons with relevant rights and interests" (National Radioactive Waste Management Act 2012).[8]

The Act allowed for two potential pathways to nomination. A land council in the Northern Territory could volunteer aboriginal land on behalf of the traditional owners. If such a volunteered area could not be found, a countrywide volunteer process for siting a facility would be undertaken. Under either scenario, extensive consultations were to be undertaken by the relevant decision-makers. The new Act also overcame an egregious error committed by the 2005 Act and restored aggrieved persons' rights to challenge a decision under the Administrative Decisions (Judicial Review) Act 1977 thus increasing accountability by officials (National Radioactive Waste Management Act 2012).

A regional consultative committee was also established to communicate with local communities. This process was designed to raise awareness through dialogue, address local concerns and ensure government transparency (National Radioactive Waste Management Act 2012).

The Muckaty Station proposal

Muckaty Station is owned by the Aboriginal Land Trust[9] and is situated approximately 68 miles north of Tennant Creek, within the Tomkinson Creek Province in the central Northern Territory. It is a pastoral station utilized primarily for cattle and horse grazing and is under the guardianship of several aboriginal clans within the Land Trust agreement. The proposed site is a region under Ngapa clan guardianship and is not used for pastoral purposes (Department of Resources, Energy and Tourism 2009, p. 30).

Muckaty Station has four sites listed on the Australian Heritage Places Inventory,[10] has a total population of approximately 2,164, an area of 92,660 square miles (that is, 74 square miles per person) and is not considered a likely area of population growth in the future ("Suburban Profile: Muckaty Station" n.d.; Department of Resources, Energy and Tourism 2009, p. 86).

When Muckaty Station was formally returned to the traditional owners of the land, the Aboriginal Land Commissioner Justice Peter Gray decided that five traditional owner groups had joint and overlapping ownership of the region: the Ngapa, Wirntiku, Milwayi, Yapayapa and Ngarrka clans (Summary of Muckaty Station Legal Proceedings). The three Ngapa subgroups[11] bear "overlapping responsibilities" and thus "share responsibility for the portion of the Ngapa dreaming[12] track on the land claimed" for Muckaty (*Mark Lane Jangala & Ors v. Commonwealth of Australia & Ors*, Further Amended Statement of Claim 2012, p. 16).

As discussed above Muckaty Station was first nominated by the NLC[13] via the National Radioactive Waste Management Bill in 2007. At the time, the nomination was approved by one small family of traditional owners who are now considered by the majority of Muckaty Station residents to have acted contrary to wishes of the local community. The majority of traditional owners protested the bill with letters and petitions to federal Resources Minister Martin Ferguson, including a letter on 8 May 2009 signed by 25 Ngapa traditional owners and 32 traditional owners from other Muckaty groups (Cole 2012). The most significant concern outlined in the letter related to the fact that Muckaty Station is a sacred site and, because the nomination process failed to elicit the consent of many of the traditional owners, was in breach of the Aboriginal Land Rights Act and other laws, themes that were echoed in a federal court case brought by a number of Muckaty traditional elders.

Payment to utilize the site

To induce the senior members of the Lauda Ngapa, the Milwayi and other traditional owners on or near the Muckaty site to agree to the facility, the federal government was willing to pay the sum of $200,000 to the NLC, which would then give or use the monies for the benefit of Lauder Ngapa Group members and placed up to $11 million into a charitable trust. A further $1 million would be utilized for education scholarships (*Lorna Fejo, Dick Foster and Ronald Brown v. The Northern Land Council, the Minister for Resources and Energy and Minister for Tourism*, Third Further Amended Application 2010, p. 6). This type of 'sustainable development' is hardly unique. To take one example, BHP Billiton created the Olympic Dam Aboriginal Community Trust as part of a proposed expansion of its Olympic Dam mine in South Australia to support education, health care, aged care and employment amongst neighboring aboriginal groups.

In March 2008, $144,000 was paid to members of the Lauder Ngapa group, $15,000 was paid to members of the Milwayi group, $26,000 was paid to Foster Ngapa local members and $15,000 was paid to one member of the Yapayapa local descent group. From late 2006 until mid-2007, the NLC worked to gain the consent of the Lauda and Milwayi groups. They did so under the assumption that the Lauder Ngapa group had been designated by the NLC's anthropologists to be the legitimate and exclusive traditional aboriginal owners of the site and access road (*Fejo, Foster and Brown*, Third Further Amended Application 2010, p. 6).

The Muckaty nomination was approved by the NLC on 18 June 2007 and provided to the Science Minister. The approval of the ALRA Minister was given on 13 August 2007 and a Site Nomination Deed executed on 16 August 2007 (*Fejo, Foster and Brown*, Third Further Amended Application 2010, pp. 5, 8–9). In the middle of August 2008, the NLC certified that the traditional aboriginal owners understood the nature of the proposal, had been given adequate information and consulted (and given opportunities to express their views) and given their informed consent.

The federal court case

In June 2010, legal proceedings against both the federal government and the NLC were initiated by Mark Lane Jangala, a senior elder of the Ngapa clan, and other elders of Muckaty Station representing a coalition of four other traditional owner clans and some members of the Ngapa clan.[14] The elders argued that, despite being traditional owners of that land, they had been excluded from consultations. The applicants argued that the nomination should be ruled invalid because before the NLC nominated the Muckaty site, it had incorrectly identified the family of Amy Lauder (who had since died) as the owners of the land, who had no right to put forward the nomination and should not have received any compensation ("Date Set for Court Fight over Muckaty Nuclear Waste Dump" 2013; Beck 2012; Bonacci 2014; Wishart 2013, p. 1); failed to consult with the indigenous owners; and failed to ensure that the traditional owners sufficiently understood the consequences of the nomination (*Mark Lane Jangala v. The Commonwealth of Australia, the Northern Land Council & the Minister for Resources, Energy & Tourism*, Statement of Claim 2010, pp. 3–4). They further argued that a LLRW repository at Muckaty "would be incompatible with the traditional significance of the Muckaty land and would have serious adverse effects on the sacred sites and tracks on the Muckaty land" (*Jangala*, Statement of Claim 2010, p. 4).

The trial date was set for only a few weeks after Federal Resources Minister Gary Gray visited the proposed site and initiated meetings with the traditional owners at the Muckaty Station. The minister's visit was the first since the site's nomination 6 years prior (Brain 2013).

A sacred site

Elders alleged that the area included sacred aboriginal sites (including dreaming sites) and tracks sacred to all the descent groups that share the area. Further, one of the sites was a sacred male initiation site: Karakara and its concomitant waterhole (*Jangala*, Statement of Claim *Mark Lane Jangala v. The Commonwealth of Australia, the Northern Land Council & the Minister for Resources, Energy &*

Tourism 2010, pp. 1–2). For indigenous peoples, traditional ownership of the land subsumes within it responsibilities to protect such sites for both present and future generations (*Jangala*, Statement of Claim 2010, p. 2). Mr. Jangala saw it as his responsibility as a senior Ngapa elder to preserve the land for his people, their law and their culture. Further, as a senior elder he was also partly responsible for sacred male initiation ceremonies at the site.[15]

Legitimate consent not given

Failure to consult with and secure host community consent due to lack of consultation formed the main thrust of the legal argument (Summary of Muckaty Station Legal Proceedings). Further it was alleged that that the nomination had 'bypassed' the legal requirements of the ALRA; that is, the resource minister had unlawfully approved the site based on inaccurate advice that lawful consent had been given. For these reasons, the applicants asked the court to vacate the decision (Lee 2014).

Incorrect identification of the Lauder group as sole elders

The applicants alleged that the NLC, when making its nomination of the Muckaty site, "had no proper basis for determining that the Lauder subgroup were the exclusive Aboriginal traditional owners of nominated land, such determination being inconsistent with the findings in the Aboriginal Land Commissioner's Muckaty Station Report" (*Jangala & Ors*, Further Amended Statement of Claim 2012, p. 24).

Rather, when the NLC made the nomination of the site it had ignored advice from Dick Foster Jangala, considered a knowledgeable and prominent senior elder, that

> the nominated land was land through which several dreamings passed for which the Milwayi descent group were primarily responsible . . . that all the groups whose dreamings came through the nominated land would need to say yes or no before the area could be nominated as a potential site for a radioactive waste depository [sic].
>
> (*Jangala & Ors*, Further Amended Statement
> of Claim 2012, p. 14)

The government argued that as per the Aboriginal Land Commissioner's Muckaty Station Report, the traditional owners were "members of the Ngapa local descent group, the Yapayapa local descent group, the Ngarrka local descent group, the Wirntiku local descent group, the Kurrakurraja local descent group, the Walanypirri local descent group and the Milwayi local descent group" (*Jangala & Ors*, Further Amended Statement of Claim 2012, p. 2). They maintained that Amy Lauder and her siblings are members of the Ngapa (Lauder) group (also recognized as the Lauder family branch of the Ngapa group) and thus Amy Lauder and her clan were the traditional owners of Muckaty Station, or part thereof in the Muckaty Station Land Claim, and could give assent to the nomination (*Fejo, Foster and Brown*, Third Further Amended Application 2010, p. 3; *Mark Lane Jangala & Ors v. Commonwealth of Australia & Ors*, Amended Defence of Second and Fourth Respondents 2013, p. 7). The NLC and the federal government argued that they had made all reasonable enquiries in determining that the Lauder family members of the Ngapa descent group were the exclusive owners of the site and those interested in proceedings were given an opportunity to give their views (*Jangala & Ors*, Amended Defence of Second and Fourth Respondents 2013, pp. 11–12).[16]

The applicants alleged that Amy Lauder and 25 other indigenous persons from the Ngapa (Lauder), Ngapa (Foster), Wimtuku, Milwayi and Yapayapa local descent groups were paid $200,000 for their support of the nomination in February 2008 as per the Site Nomination Deed (*Jangala & Ors*, Amended Defence of Second and Fourth Respondents 2013, p. 17; *Jangala & Ors v. Commonwealth of Australia & Ors*, Fourth Further Amended Statement of Claim [20 June 2014], No. VID 433 of 2010, on file with the authors, p. 7).

In March 2012, the Commonwealth indicated that a disposal facility on aboriginal land should go ahead even if the land's traditional owners had been incorrectly identified. It was argued that even if the NLC gave the federal government incorrect information about the traditional owners of the Muckaty Station, it would not invalidate the government's 2007 approval (Beck 2012). According to the lawyers, the government's new radioactive waste law requires only that a land council present evidence of who the traditional owners are, not that the evidence be true.

Despite the clear opposition of the territorial government, a coalition of aboriginal clans and an ongoing federal court action, the federal government remained committed to the site and vowed to fight the court action. By October 2013, plans to build the facility were well underway with the government having received concept designs from Empresa Nacional de Residuos Radiactivos S.A. (ENRESA), the Spanish radioactive waste management organization (McCarthy 2013).

Collapse of the case

In a startling turn of events, in June 2014 the NLC announced that the site nomination was being withdrawn. The Council explained that the issue was proving too divisive amongst the clans of the Muckaty Aboriginal Land Trust ("Muckaty Station: Northern Land Council Withdraws Nomination of Site of First Nuclear Waste Dump" 2014; Akerman 2014). The federal court then ordered that the proceedings be dismissed with each party to bear their own costs (*Jangala & Ors*, Fourth Further Amended Statement of Claim 2014).

However, the federal government stated it would continue to seek to build a repository in the Northern Territory (Akerman 2014). According to Minister Macfarlane, "if a suitable site is not identified through these discussions the government will commence a new tender process for nominations for another site in accordance with the Act" (Akerman 2014).

In early November, one of the clan groups proposed that a second parcel of land at Muckaty Station be nominated (Davidson 2014). However, resistance from other local groups remained strong. One of the traditional owners, Dianne Stokes, stated: "We fought very hard before, and we started off talking. . . . It's the same fight about the waste in Muckaty. We said to the ministers . . . we don't want any waste coming to Muckaty Land Trust" (Davidson 2014).

To avoid any further nominations, many traditional owners are seeking to come under the aegis of the neighboring Central Land Council, which had recently met and chose not to nominate a site in the Tanami region. In a statement, the Council stressed that "Industry minister Ian Macfarlane's requirement of a site 'free from dispute' cannot therefore be met" (Davidson 2014).

Macfarlane stated in August 2014 that, as per the 2012 Act from 30 September the nomination process could be opened up again to all states and territories and in particular to pastoralists who own freehold land, and one cattleman in the Northern Territory, John Armstrong, indicated he might be interested ("Time Is Running Out to Find a Nuclear Waste Site in Australia" 2014). In December, Minister Macfarlane initiated another nation-wide call for volunteer sites with a 5 May 2015 deadline. According to news reports, at least three submissions were received, all in Western Australia: mining company Gindalbie Metals nominated Badja Station, roughly 310 miles north of Perth; Shire of Leonora Councillor Glenn Baker nominated land on his own property in Goldfields-Esperance roughly 515 miles northeast of Perth; and another nomination near Warburton, 932 miles east-north-east of Perth. The government is now evaluating the nominations in order to produce a short list of suitable sites for further examination. The Northern Territory chief minister, Adam Giles, has given tacit approval to any proposed nomination, arguing that it is an issue between the landowner and the federal government:

> A number of Territory traditional owners have expressed an interest in potentially nominating their land as a new site for a nuclear waste repository . . . [and this would] present an economic opportunity for landowners who might be interested in putting their hand up.
>
> (Davidson 2014)

Potentially tens of millions of dollars could be paid to any community that agrees to host (Davidson 2014; Whinnett 2014, p. 4).

The government appears confident that they can get a volunteer but nuclear campaigner Dr. Jim Green from Friends of the Earth is not convinced it will be easy:

> There's been various interest at various sites in the Northern Territory but no nomination. At least one site in Western Australia there's been some interest but I'm not at all convinced that there are going to be any nominations because while there are pockets of interest. . . . I'm not sure that there's

going to be broad community support in any of those sites in the Northern Territory or WA.

(Selvaratnam 2014)

Conclusion

With the withdrawal of the Muckaty nomination, the federal government's attempts to build a federal LLRW near-surface disposal facility appear to be in total disarray. Muckaty was the only site the government wanted and had invested heavily in making it work. The Australian Conservation Foundation (ACF) has argued that Western Australia would be a better location for any future repository, but that state government has made it clear in the past it has no desire to host a federal site (Nicholson 2013). State governments, both Labor and Liberal, fear of the political backlash volunteering would engender and the near-term prospects that this will change are not encouraging; licensing facilities in Queensland and Western Australia for in-state waste was difficult enough.

The federal government has not been able to solve its self-imposed radioactive waste Gordian knot because it has neglected to apply environmental justice to its decision-making processes. In the rush to license and build, flawed processes have marginalized community participation. Paying lip service to the idea of consultation is not the way to build public support for any siting decision. The community, broadly defined, needs to buy in to the process, to feel their concerns are being taken seriously.

The ACF, citing a 2006 UK expert committee on radioactive waste report, stated:

> It is generally considered that a voluntary process is essential to ensure equity, efficiency and the likelihood of successfully completing the process. There is a growing recognition that it is not ethically acceptable for a society to impose a radioactive waste facility on an unwilling community.

(Sweeney 2013)

Despite multiple failed siting attempts and reams of government reports, submissions, Acts of Parliament, Codes of Practice, Parliamentary Discussion Papers and Senate Select Committee Reports over four decades, no repository has been built. The federal government has failed to convince any of the state governments to host a facility on behalf of the rest of the country. Only the Northern Territory has shown any interest and the most recent siting effort there failed spectacularly.

The government has implemented a predominantly top-down approach rather than a consultative process, which would stand the best chance of success. Definitions of consent have tended to be selective rather than inclusive and methods such as withdrawing appeal rights from potential objectors do not engender public trust. Similarly, compensation packages have been somewhat narrow and, as occurred in Muckaty, this tends to breed resentment amongst those who miss out. This is commonly referred to as the donut effect. Clearly delineating the 'affected community' and incorporating a spatial distribution of compensation – that is, concentric circles around the facility, with compensation decreasing the further away from the site one lives out to a certain distance – should go some way toward alleviating this problem.

The attempt by Pangea to make the case for a multinational repository inflamed fears that Australia's geological advantages and stable political system would result in the country becoming the world's dumping ground for nuclear waste, and these suspicions appear to have bled into the debate about how to deal with Australia's domestic low and intermediate level waste, to the detriment of the disposal of the latter.

The latest attempt to build a site in Muckaty has been dogged not only by a flawed process but also by accusations that the federal government is failing to implement 'environmental justice' by disproportionately impacting historically disenfranchised races and lower socioeconomic groups, 'vulnerable postcodes,' with a preference for indigenous land (McGurty 1997, pp. 301–323).

The Muckaty process raises serious questions about Australian decision-makers honoring hard won aboriginal land rights, respecting aboriginal sacred sites and Australia's commitment to the United Nations Declaration on the Rights of Indigenous Peoples (United Nations General Assembly 2007). The Declaration under Article 29 Section 2 forbids the siting of hazardous materials in the lands or territories of indigenous peoples without proper consent. As Maurice Blackburn senior associate Martin Hyde observed:

> If you are going to take away people's land in perpetuity and fill it with radioactive waste, you have a legal and moral obligation to ask the owners first and seek their informed consent. It appears that simply did not happen.
>
> (Summary of Muckaty Station Legal Proceedings)[17]

George Newhouse, human rights lawyer with Surry Partners, one of the firms representing the Ngapa clan leaders, stated:

> This is an important case not only because it is about the dumping of nuclear waste on Aboriginal land but it will set out the principles that will guide the way that Indigenous Land Councils treat the people that they are supposed to represent.
>
> (Summary of Muckaty Station Legal Proceedings)

Seeking another site in the Northern Territory on aboriginal land will not work if environmental justice is not taken into account. Continuing to disrespect aboriginal land rights is no way to resolve the issue.

ENGOs and labor unions have called for an inquiry into the site nomination process and, given the problems experienced over the last four decades, it is clear that a new approach is needed (Davidson 2014). ACF spokesman Dave Sweeney has noted:

> Radioactive waste lasts far longer than any politician and we need to get its management responsible and right. The best way to do this is through an open, independent and evidence based approach that moves stakeholders from the trenches to the table.
>
> (Davidson 2014)

Whatever happens, 466 cubic feet of intermediate level waste from spent research reactor fuel reprocessed in France will be returned to Australia in 2015 (ANSTO n.d.b.; Wood 2014). Problematically, even with an agreement completed immediately, it would take "three to five years" under ideal circumstances to build a repository, so the French waste will need to be stored on an interim basis until a permanent solution can be found (Selvaratnam 2014).[18] At present the government lacks a comprehensive strategy that will achieve its radioactive waste management goals.

Notes

1 While the federal government has in the past supported the notion of utilizing nuclear power plants to meet the country's burgeoning electricity needs, there are currently no concrete plans to do so. See for example, Department of Prime Minister and Cabinet 2006.
2 Australia is further obligated under the Joint Convention on the Safety of Spent Fuel Management and on the Safety of Radioactive Waste Management 2001 to provide for the safe and secure management of its radioactive waste (Joint Convention on the Safety of Spent Fuel Management and on the Safety of Radioactive Waste Management 2001).
3 As the national regulator, the Australian Radiation Protection and Nuclear Safety Agency (ARPANSA) is the federal body responsible for ensuring the health and safety of Australian citizens and the environment from the deleterious effects of radiation (see ARPANS Act 1998; ANSTO 2011; Department of Industry n.d.).
4 Long-term ILRW is also referred to as Category S waste. The major source of Category S is reprocessing waste from research reactor spent fuel. In February 2001, the federal government proposed building a dedicated Category S facility but to date has made no progress toward this goal (Forum for Nuclear Cooperation in Asia [FNCA] n.d.).
5 HIFAR fuel (enriched to 60% uranium-235) was fabricated in the US and UK: US-origin spent fuel was sent back to the US for storage/disposal; UK-origin spent fuel was sent to the UK and France for reprocessing and the resultant ILRW will be returned to Australia for storage/disposal. All MOATA fuel (enriched to 80% uranium-235) was supplied by the US and the spent fuel has been returned to the US.
6 In December 1994, the Queensland government opened Esk, 46 miles west of Brisbane. It was opposed by local residents, particularly in the Wivenhoe Dam catchment area, who formed a community action group People Against Radioactive Dumps (PARD) but licensed nonetheless. Radioactive waste material that was in storage in Brisbane has been moved to the facility (Piro 1991; "Radioactive Waste Store

Feasibility Study – Stage Two" 2005, p. 4–4). The Western Australia LLRW site is at Mt Walton East (a goldfields area), 46 miles northeast of Koolyanobbing and was constructed in the 1990s. The facility was constructed over the objections of the Goldfields region ("Radioactive Waste Store Feasibility Study – Stage Two" 2005, pp. 4–12; Federal Parliament of Australia updated 2011).

7 The NLC is an Aboriginal Land Council established under section 21 of the *Land Rights Act*. Land Councils "function to supervise, and provide administrative or other assistance for, Land Trusts holding, or established to hold, Aboriginal land in its area" (*Mark Lane Jangala & Ors v. Commonwealth of Australia & Ors*, Amended Defence of Second and Fourth Respondents 2012, p. 4). In September 1999 "an Aboriginal Land Trust by the name of the Muckaty Aboriginal Land Trust (the Muckaty Land Trust) to hold title to land for the benefit of aboriginals entitled by aboriginal tradition to the use or occupation of the land concerned, whether or not the traditional entitlement is qualified as to place, time, circumstance, purpose or permission" was established (*Jangala & Ors*, Amended Defence of Second and Fourth Respondents 2013, p. 3).

8 The Act provides no definition of what are 'relevant' rights and interests. Doing so would be extremely beneficial for determining affected parties rights under the process.

9 Acting on the recommendations of Justice Peter Gray, the ALRA minister recommended to the governor-general that he grant a fee simple estate in land which had been the subject of the Muckaty Land Claim by the indigenous inhabitants of the land. The governor-general subsequently gave the land to the Muckaty Aboriginal Land Trust via a Deed of Grant on 25 November 1999. The Muckaty Aboriginal Land Trust is for the benefit of each of the traditional aboriginal owners of Muckaty Station (*Fejo, Foster and Brown*, Third Further Amended Application 2010, pp. 1–2).

10 The inventory is a searchable database that includes places registered on Australian State, Territory and Commonwealth Heritage Registers and Lists which are considered unique or valuable and should be preserved (Australian Heritage Places Inventory n.d.).

11 The Ngapa (Lauder) group is classified as a local descent group which has

common spiritual affiliations to sites on part of the Muckaty Land Trust Land, . . . [placing them] under a primary spiritual responsibility for those sites and for that land; and are entitled by Aboriginal tradition to forage as of right over that land; and that land includes the Nominated Land.

(*Jangala & Ors*, Amended Defence of Second and Fourth Respondents 2013, p. 6)

12 The aboriginal concept of 'dreaming' or 'dreamtime' has no direct English equivalent, but can be best understood as linked to indigenous conceptions of the creation process and spiritual links to ancestors and is considered to be outside of time. See www. creativespirits.info/aboriginalculture/spirituality/what-is-the-dreamtime-or-the-dreaming#axzz3ZDLiwDer.

13 The Northern Land Council (NLC) is a corporation auspiced under the ALRA to "supervise and administer Aboriginal land trusts in respect of areas in the Northern Territory." This includes the Muckaty Station site (*Fejo, Foster and Brown*, Third Further Amended Application 2010, p. 3).

14 The other applicants were Lorna Fejo Nangala, Dick Foster Jangala and Ronald Brown Japangarti, who all maintained they were traditional aboriginal owners of part of the Muckaty Station land. Mark Jangala is Kurtungurlu (membership of the descent group by a mother's father) of the Milwayi local descent group and is an aboriginal elder of the Ngapa group (*Fejo, Foster and Brown*, Third Further Amended Application 2010, pp. 2–3).

15 Mark Lane Jangala, Dick Foster Jangala and Robert Brown Japangarti all bear responsibility under indigenous tradition for the Karakara. Dick Foster Jangala conducts the male initiation ceremonies annually. In the Muckaty Land Claim Report, Justice

Gray also characterized Karakara as a site where male initiations were carried out (*Jangala*, Statement of Claim 2010, pp. 2, 8).

16 Amy Lauder and Jeffrey Dixon (her husband) were chosen as member representatives to the NLC and were at a meeting of the Full Council of the NLC on 24 May 2007 that nominated the Muckaty site and directed to enter into the Site Nomination Deed.

17 www.mauriceblackburn.com.au/about/media-centre/media-statements/2010/indigenous-owners-launch-federal-legal-challenge-over-australia-s-first-nuclear-waste-dump/

18 Selvaratnam's 3- to 5-year construction estimate was a quote from federal Minister for Industry and Science Ian Macfarlane.

References

The Aboriginal Land Rights Act 1976 (NT), www.austlii.edu.au/au/legis/cth/consol_act/alrta1976444/

Advisory Report on the Bill, Parliament of Australia [National Radioactive Waste Bill 2010], (Chapter 1) (n.d.), www.aph.gov.au/About_Parliament/Parliamentary_Departments/Parliamentary_Library/pubs/BN/2011–2012/RadioActiveWaste

Akerman, P., "Northern Territory Muckaty Waste Dump Plan Abandoned," *Australian* (9 June 2014), www.theaustralian.com.au/news/nation/northern-territory-muckaty-waste-dump-plan-abandoned/story-e6frg6nf-1226959705496?nk=dc2e9b1ed0711b612 3e6c33fdde05a39

"Alternative Location Sought on Muckaty Station for Nuclear Waste Dump," *SBS News Online* (26 August 2013), www.sbs.com.au/news/article/2012/11/08/alternative-location-sought-muckaty-station-nuclear-waste-dump

Aston, H., "Radioactive Waste Haunts Hunters Hill Residents," *Sydney Morning Herald* (30 October 2011), www.smh.com.au/environment/radioactive-waste-haunts-hunters-hill-residents-20111029–1mpb6.html

Australian Conservation Foundation Submission Inquiry of the Senate Standing Committee on Legal and Constitutional Affairs into the National Radioactive Waste Management Bill 2010, www.acfonline.org.au/sites/default/files/resources/ACF_National_Radioactive_Waste_Management_Bill_2010_Senate_Inquiry_Sub.pdf

Australian Heritage Places Inventory, *About the Australian Heritage Places Inventory* (n.d.), www.heritage.gov.au/ahpi/about.html

Australian Nuclear Science and Technology Organisation, *Decommissioning Earlier Reactors* (n.d.a.), www.ansto.gov.au/AboutANSTO/OPAL/Decommissioningearlierreactors/

Australian Nuclear Science and Technology Organisation, *Management of Radioactive Waste in Australia* (January 2011), www.ansto.gov.au/cs/groups/corporate/documents/webcontent/mdaw/mday/~edisp/acstest_040440.pdf

Australian Nuclear Science and Technology Organisation, *Managing Radioactive Waste* (n.d.b.), www.ansto.gov.au/NuclearFacts/ManagingRadioActiveWaste/index.htm

Australian Radiation Protection and Nuclear Safety Act (1998), www.austlii.edu.au/au/legis/cth/consol_act/arpansa1998487/

Beck, M., "Radioactive Dump – With 10 Days' Notice, Court Told," *Sydney Morning Herald* (28 March 2012), www.smh.com.au/environment/radioactive-dump – with-10-days-notice-court-told-20120328–1vxdz.html

Bennett, D., "The Constitutional Decisions of Justice Selway: (I) Nuclear Waste Dumps and Fire Brigades; (II) Low Flying Planes and (III) What Is State Insurance?" *2007 Adelaide Law Review*, www.austlii.edu.au/au/journals/AdelLawRw/2007/4.pdf

Bonacci, M., "Federal Court Goes to Muckaty," *Green Left Weekly* (14 June 2014), www.greenleft.org.au/node/56628

Brain, C., "Federal Minister Visits Muckaty Station," *ABS News Online* (1 August 2013), www.abc.net.au/news/2013–08–01/muckaty-resources-minister/4857690

Cole, F., "Indigenous Community Pleads with Minister on NT Nuclear Dump," *Crikey* (9 February 2012), www.crikey.com.au/2012/02/09/indigenous-community-pleads-with-minister-on-nt-nuclear-dump/

Commonwealth Radioactive Waste Management Act 2005 (Cth), www.comlaw.gov.au/Details/C2006C00710

"Date Set for Court Fight over Muckaty Nuclear Waste Dump," *ABC News Online* (26 August 2013), www.abc.net.au/news/2013–08–26/court-date-set-for-nuclear-waste-dump-fight/4912730

Davidson, H., "Muckaty Landowners Say Nuclear Dump Fight Is 'Back to Square One,'" *Guardian* (13 November 2014), www.theguardian.com/australia-news/2014/nov/13/muckaty-landowners-say-nuclear-dump-fight-is-back-to-square-one

Department of Industry, *Amounts of Radioactive Waste in Australia: About the Amounts of Australia's Radioactive Waste* (n.d.a.), www.industry.gov.au/resource/RadioactiveWaste/RadiationandRadioactiveWaste/Pages/Amounts.aspx

Department of Industry, *Managing Australia's Nuclear Waste, Australian Government* (n.d.b.), www.managingnuclearwaste.gov.au

Department of Industry, *Potential Sites under the 2005 Act* (n.d.), www.industry.gov.au/resource/RadioactiveWaste/RadioactivewastemanagementinAustralia/CommonwealthRadioactiveWasteManagementAct2005/Pages/Potentialsitesunderthe2005Act.aspx

Department of Prime Minister and Cabinet, *Uranium Mining, Process and Nuclear Energy Review* (2006), www.ansto.gov.au/__data/assets/pdf_file/0005/38975/Umpner_report_2006.pdf

Department of Resources, Energy and Tourism, "Proposed Commonwealth Radioactive Waste Management Facility Northern Territory: Synthesis Report" (13 March 2009), www.industry.gov.au/resource/Documents/radioactive_waste/radioactive-waste-management/08–0589–01–2145479A%20(Synthesis).pdf

Falk, J., Green, J., and Mudd, G., "Australia, Uranium and Nuclear Power," *International Journal of Environmental Studies*, Vol. 63, No. 6 (December 2006).

Federal Parliament of Australia, *Radioactive Waste*, www.aph.gov.au/About_Parliament/Parliamentary_Departments/Parliamentary_Library/Publications_Archive/online/RadioactiveWaste

Federal Parliament of Australia, *Radioactive Waste and Spent Nuclear Fuel Management in Australia* (updated 21 July 2011), www.aph.gov.au/About_Parliament/Parliamentary_Departments/Parliamentary_Library/pubs/BN/2011–2012/RadioActiveWaste#_Toc299022834

Forum for Nuclear Cooperation in Asia (FNCA), FNCA Consolidated Report on Radioactive Waste Management (Australia) (n.d.), www.fnca.mext.go.jp/english/rwm/news_img/rwm_cr03_01.pdf

Green, J., *Proposed Radioactive Waste Dump at Muckaty, NT*, Briefing Paper (February 2011).

Holland, I., "Consultation, Constraints and Norms: The Case of Nuclear Waste," *Australian Journal of Public Administration*, Vol. 61, No. 1 (2002a).

Holland, I., "Waste Not Want Not: Australia and the Politics of High Level Waste," *Australian Journal of Political Science*, Vol. 37, No. 2 (2002b).

How Sites in South Australia Were Chosen: Site Selection Study and Community Consultation, *The Facts, Not Fiction* (July 2001), www.aph.gov.au/About_Parliament/Parliamentary_ Departments/Parliamentary_Library/pubs/BN/2011–2012/RadioActiveWaste

James, M., and Rann, A., "Radioactive Waste and Spent Nuclear Fuel Management in Australia," Parliamentary Library, Department of Parliamentary Services, Parliament of Australia (n.d.), www.aph.gov.au/About_Parliament/Parliamentary_Departments/ Parliamentary_Library/pubs/BN/2011–2012/RadioActiveWaste

Joint Convention on the Safety of Spent Fuel Management and on the Safety of Radio- active Waste Management (2001), www.iaea.org/Publications/Documents/Infcircs/1997/ infcirc546.pdf

Kurzeme, M., "The Pangea Concept for an International Radioactive Waste Repository" (n.d.), www.iaea.org/inis/collection/NCLCollectionStore/_Public/31/033/31033869. pdf

Lee, J., "Federal Court Case Opens on Muckaty Station Nuclear Waste Dump," *Sydney Morning Herald* (3 June 2014), www.smh.com.au/federal-politics/political-news/federal- court-case-opens-on-muckaty-station-nuclear-waste-dump-20140602–39es9. html#ixzz3A3sNvAbq

Lloyd, B., *The National Radioactive Waste Facility,* Research Papers of the Parliamentary Library Service, no. 1 (2006), Northern Territory Library.

Lorna Fejo, Dick Foster and Ronald Brown v. The Northern Land Council, The Minister for Resources and Energy and Minister for Tourism Named in the Schedule, Third Further Amended Application, No. VID 433 of 2010, Federal Court of Australia (10 June 2014).

Ludlam, Scott, "This Land Is Not Nowhere, These People Are Not No-one." *Human Rights in Australia* (13 August 2012), http://rightnow.org.au/writing-cat/article/this-land-is- not-nowhere-these-people-are-not-no-one/

Mark Lane Jangala v. The Commonwealth of Australia, The Northern Land Council & The Minister for Resources, Energy & Tourism, Statement of Claim, No. VID 433 of 2010, The Federal Court of Australia Victorian District Registry (16 August 2010).

Mark Lane Jangala & Ors v. Commonwealth of Australia & Ors, Amended Defence of Second and Fourth Respondents, No. VID 433 of 2010, The Federal Court of Australia Victorian District Registry (19 April 2012).

Mark Lane Jangala & Ors v. Commonwealth of Australia & Ors, Amended Defence of Second and Fourth Respondents, No. VID 433 of 2010, The Federal Court of Australia Victorian District Registry (24 September 2013).

Mark Lane Jangala & Ors v. Commonwealth of Australia & Ors, Further Amended Defence of Second and Fourth Respondents, No. VID 433 of 2010, The Federal Court of Australia Victorian District Registry (26 February 2014).

Mark Lane Jangala & Ors v. Commonwealth of Australia & Ors, Further Amended Statement of Claim, No. VID433 of 2010, Federal Court of Australia (23 April 2012).

McCarthy, M., "Nuclear Waste Plans 'Progressing'," *ABC News* (8 October 2013), www. abc.net.au/news/2013–10–07/nuclear-dump/5002944

McGurty, E., "From NIMBY to Civil Rights: The Origins of the Environmental Justice Movement," *Environmental History,* Vol. 2, No. 3 (1997): 301–323.

"Muckaty Station: Northern Land Council Withdraws Nomination of Site of First Nuclear Waste Dump," *ABC News* (19 June 2014), www.abc.net.au/news/2014–06–19/ northern-land-council-withdraws-muckaty-creek-nomination/5535318

National Radioactive Waste Management Bill 2010 (Cth), www.comlaw.gov.au/Details/C2010B00042

National Radioactive Waste Management Act 2012 (Cth), www.comlaw.gov.au/Details/C2012A00029

National Radioactive Waste Repository, Site Selection Study (Australia), Phase 1 (August 1993).

National Radioactive Waste Repository, Site Selection Study, Phase 2, Australian Government Publishing Service Canberra (November 1995), www.industry.gov.au/resource/Documents/radioactive_waste/report_on_public_comment_phase_2.pdf

Nicholson, L., "Western Australia in Nation's Nuclear Waste Dump Sights," *Sydney Morning Herald* (12 November 2013), www.smh.com.au/federal-politics/western-australia-in-nations-nuclear-waste-dump-sights-20131112–2xdzn.html

Northern Land Council, "NLC Settles on Muckaty" (19 June 2014), www.nlc.org.au/media-releases/article/nlc-settles-on-muckaty

Nuclear Waste Transport, Storage, Disposal (Prohibition) Act 2004 (NT), http://notes.nt.gov.au/dcm/legislat/legislat.nsf/linkreference/NUCLEAR%20WASTE%20TRANSPORT,%20STORAGE%20AND%20DISPOSAL%20%28PROHIBITION%29%20ACT%202004

Panter, R., Science, Technology & Environment Group, Parliamentary Research Service, Issues Paper No. 6, *Radioactive Waste Disposal in Australia* (28 April 1992).

Piro, N., "Rural Queensland Fears Radioactive Dump," *Green Left Weekly* (25 September 1991), www.greenleft.org.au/node/574

"A Radioactive Waste Repository for Australia, Commonwealth Australia, Site Selection Study – Phase 3" (1997), www.industry.gov.au/resource/Documents/radioactive_waste/public_discussion_paper_phase_3.pdf

"Radioactive Waste Store Feasibility Study – Stage Two," URS, prepared for the Environmental Protection Authority (3 November 2005), www.epa.sa.gov.au/xstd_files/Radiation/Report/radioactive_stage2.pdf

Reynolds, W., *Australia's Bid for the Atomic Bomb* (Melbourne: Melbourne University Press, 2000).

Selvaratnam, N., "Government Searching for Nuclear Waste Site as Time Runs Out," *SBS News* (30 September 2014), www.sbs.com.au/news/article/2014/09/30/government-searching-nuclear-waste-site-time-runs-out

Senator Nick Minchin, Media Release, "Two Radioactive Repository Sites Withdrawn Following Community Consultation" (18 November 1999), http://parlinfo.aph.gov.au/parlInfo/search/display/display.w3p;query=%28Id:media/pressrel/aoi06%29;rec=0

Senator Warwick Parer, Media Release, "SA Region Selected for National Radioactive Waste Repository Site," DPIE 98/276P (18 February 1998).

South Australia v Honourable Peter Slipper MP (2004), ALR, 473.

"Suburban Profile: Muckaty Station NT, 0862," *Tomorrow Finance* (n.d.), www.tomorrowfinance.com.au/PropertyReports/NT/City+subs/Muckaty+Station-0862

Summary of Muckaty Station Legal Proceedings, Maurice Blackburn Solicitors (n.d.), on file with the authors.

Sweeney, D. "Plan to Use Aboriginal Land as a Nuclear Waste Dump Is Flawed and Misguided." *The Guardian*, (31 July 2013). www.theguardian.com/commentisfree/2013/jul/31/muckaty-aboriginal-land-nuclear-waste

Taylor, G., "Australia: Host for a Nuclear Waste Storage Site?," *International Journal of Environmental Studies*, Vol. 63, No. 6 (December 2006).

"Time Is Running Out to Find a Nuclear Waste Site in Australia," *ABC News* (9 October 2014), www.abc.net.au/radionational/programs/bushtelegraph/nuclear-waste/5798278

United Nations General Assembly, *United Nations Declaration on the Rights of Indigenous Peoples: Resolution Adopted by the General Assembly* (2 October 2007), A/RES/61/295, www.un.org/esa/socdev/unpfii/documents/DRIPS_en.pdf

Western Australia Parliamentary Debates, House of Assembly (7 September 1999).

Whinnet, E., "Nuke Waste Worry – Where Will We Bury It?" *Herald Sun* (18 August 2014).

Wishart, M., "Muckaty Traditional Owners Fighting Ferguson's Dump," *Chain Reaction* (17 June 2013).

Wood, D., "Australia Has Nowhere to Put French Nuclear Waste," *Vice News* (14 July 2014), https://news.vice.com/article/australia-has-nowhere-to-put-its-shipment-of-french-nuclear-waste

World Nuclear Association, *Radioactive Waste Repository and Store for Australia* (updated June 2014), www.world-nuclear.org/info/Country-Profiles/Countries-A-F/Appendices/Radioactive-waste-repository–store-for-Australia/

6 Ensuring El Cabril is not a "millstone for future generations"

Low level radioactive waste disposal in Spain

Introduction: a 'unique' inheritance

With the partial exception of South Korea, Spain differs from the other case studies examined in this book in two respects. First, like Korea, Spain transitioned to democracy relatively late in the post–World War II period – until 1975, the country was a fascist state under Francisco Franco – and with this transition came a vigorous civil society.[1] Second, unlike Korea, the nascent democracy inherited a functioning radioactive waste disposal facility – El Cabril in Córdoba – as well as neighboring communities willing to exercise their newly acquired democratic right to object to the facility. As a result, the challenges faced by waste management authorities have been unique, and this is reflected in the structure of the chapter. The first three sections outline the role of nuclear power in society, the production and management of radioactive waste as well as public attitudes to nuclear activities, including the integral role played by the Spanish antinuclear movement. The remainder of the chapter traces the history of radioactive waste disposal at El Cabril from the use of an abandoned uranium mine in 1961 to its most recent expansion, describes the motivations and tactics of those opposed to the facility and concludes with the siting authority's efforts to appease opponents and build public support for continued operations at El Cabril.

Spain and nuclear power

The generation of radioactive waste began during the 1950s when the infant nuclear industry began utilizing radioisotopes for industrial, medical and research purposes ("Radioactive Waste Management Programmes in OECD/NEW Member Countries: Spain" 2013, p. 2). Four research reactors helped to facilitate the country's development of nuclear power, which commenced in 1968 when the Jose Cabrera reactor near Madrid started operating. All of the research reactors have now been decommissioned (International Atomic Energy Agency [IAEA] n.d., p. 6; IAEA Research Reactor Database, n.d.). The Spanish nuclear power complex includes seven reactors, the Juzbado Fuel Manufacturing Facility in Salamanca northwest of Madrid and the Ministry of Science and Technology's

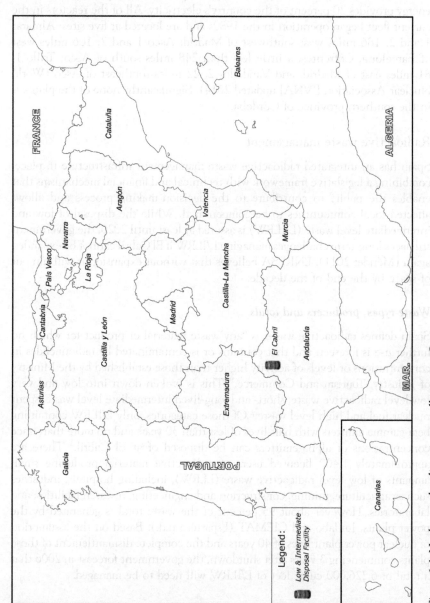

Figure 6.1 Nuclear and radioactive installations in Spain

energy and environmental research institute Centro de Investigaciones Energé-ticas, Medoambientales y Tecnologicas (CIEMAT) in Madrid (Empresa Nacional de Residuos Radiactivos S.A. [ENRESA] n.d., p. 59; IAEA Spain n.d.). Nuclear energy provides 20 percent of the country's electricity. All of the reactors in the current fleet began operation in the 1980s and are located at five sites: Almaraz 1 and 2, 186 miles west-southwest of Madrid; Asco 1 and 2, 106 miles west of Barcelona; Cofrentes, a little less than 248 miles south of Asco; Trillo 1, 81 miles east of Madrid; and Vandellós 2, 22 miles southeast of Asco (World Nuclear Association [WNA] updated 2014). Significantly, none of the plants is in the southern province of Córdoba.

Radioactive waste management

Spain has an integrated radioactive waste management infrastructure in place, combining a legislative framework with technical and financial mechanisms that enables the public to contribute to the decision-making process and allows affected local communities to be compensated. While the disposal of low and intermediate level waste (L/ILRW) is assured at least until 2020, the government still faces long-term challenges managing L/ILRW if El Cabril cannot be expanded again (Méndez 2011). ENRESA believes that without expansion it will run out of space by the end of the decade.

Waste types, producers and totals

Spain defines radioactive waste as "any waste material or product for which no further use is foreseen and that contains or is contaminated by radionuclides in concentrations or levels of activity higher than those established by the Ministry of Industry, Tourism and Commerce." This is broken down into low and very low level radioactive waste, short- and long-lived intermediate level waste, spent nuclear fuel and high level waste.[2] Of those categories, only L/ILRW containing beta-gamma emitters with half-lives of less than 30 years and no more than trace concentrations of alpha-emitters can be disposed of at El Cabril.[3] There are approximately 1,400 licensed users of radioactive material producing small amounts of low level radioactive waste (LLRW), including hospitals; industries such as agriculture, mining, construction and engineering; research facilities; and laboratories. However about 95 percent of the waste total is generated by the power plants, Juzdabo and CIEMAT (Espartero n.d.). Based on the assumption of nuclear power plant lives of 40 years and the complete dismantlement of those plants commencing 3 years after shutdown, the government forecast in 2006 that a total of 6,226,000 cubic feet of L/ILRW will need to be managed.

ENRESA

In 1984, the Spanish government delegated overall responsibility for nuclear waste security, management and disposal to a new publicly owned organization, Empresa Nacional de Residuos Radiactivos S.A. (ENRESA).[4] Funded by a charge levied on taxpayers and waste producers, the entity was tasked with collection, transportation and treatment of radioactive waste; selection, design, construction, operation and long-term care of storage and disposal facilities; and supervision of nuclear facility decommissioning (ENRESA n.d., p. 59; Martess and Ferraro 2014, p. 62; "Sixth General Radioactive Waste Plan [6th GRWP]" [2006], p. 88).

Legislation

Spain does not have one piece of umbrella radioactive waste management legislation but rather four major regulatory protocols: regulations that govern nuclear safety and authorize nuclear/radiological installations; regulations concerning environmental impacts; regulations governing land uses and municipal functions; and regulations concerning the activities of ENRESA and the financing of radioactive waste management (ENRESA n.d., p. 60; Beceiro n.d.; Lamolla 2012, p. 7; Schneider 2006, p. 1).

The Ministry of Economy issues construction and operation licenses contingent upon validating reports from the Nuclear Safety Council (CSN) and Environmental Impact Statements from the Ministry of the Environment.[5] At the local level, various licenses must be obtained from the Autonomous Communities, including mining licenses, conventional waste licenses and land planning/usage licenses. A municipal urban planning license is also required for the construction of any nuclear facility ("Low and Intermediate Level Waste Management in Spain" n.d.). When a license to operate a facility is granted, a 10-year review providing a critical analysis of the site's long-term safety characteristics is required ("Low and Intermediate Level Waste Management in Spain" n.d.). However the Spanish Parliament has not seen fit to include any specific regulations governing the administrative aspects of licensing radioactive waste disposal facilities.[6] Rather, the process falls within the general ambit of industrial legislation (ENRESA n.d., p. 63). In 1996, the Senate created a working party to put in place specific nuclear waste regulations. Despite lengthy talks, no consensus was achieved and the effort was abandoned (Lang-Lenton, Castro and d'Abadal 2005).

The general radioactive waste plan

The Spanish government has put in place a series of General Radioactive Waste Plans (GRWPs) to properly administer its radioactive waste (Espartero n.d.). The Ministry of Economy has overall responsibility for drafting the plans and regulating the financial mechanisms to fund the radioactive waste management program (ENRESA n.d., pp. 59–60). When a GRWP has been approved by the federal Cabinet, it is sent to the Parliament for informational purposes ("Radioactive Waste Management Programmes" 2013, p. 4). The plan is updated by ENRESA annually depending on changing circumstances or improved technical or financial information (Espartero n.d.; ENRESA n.d., p. 64). The plan seeks to minimize waste generation; improve waste characterization, inventory and isolation techniques; enhance knowledge for the assessment of the long-term behavior of waste; and develop radioactive waste standards (Lang-Lenton and Neri 2007; ENRESA n.d., p. 3).

The sixth and most recent GRWP was approved by the Spanish Cabinet on 23 June 2006 for a 5-year period and has since been extended. It was the first plan to incorporate input from the Autonomous Communities and it established a planning process for a Centralised Temporary Storage facility for spent fuel and high level waste (Espejo and Abreu 2008, p. 1; Espartero n.d., pp. 15–18). The plan also extended the active radioactive waste management time frame out to 2070 (6th GRWP 2006, p. 9).

Funding

A fund finances the activities set out by the GRWP and the costs associated with radioactive waste management. There are four types of payments into the fund:

- a percentage of the electricity sales price, currently set at 1 percent of all electricity consumed nationwide;
- contributions by the nuclear power plant licensees;
- contributions by ENUSA;
- fees paid by other producers of radioactive waste (WNA updated 2014; Hearsey, Emmery, Kunsch, Bollingerfehr and Webster 2000, p. 2; Schneider 2006, p. 1).

The fees are set by the federal government. The revenue is collected by the National Energy Commission, which then passes it on to ENRESA tax-free. This method is considered highly effective since the ultimate end user, the consumer, pays for the benefit they derive (WNA updated 2014; Hearsey et al. 2000, p. 2). The fund is managed by ENRESA and supervised by a Tracking and Control Committee comprising high level members of various ministries chaired by the Ministry of Industry, Energy and Tourism (Schneider 2006; "Radioactive Waste Management Programmes" 2013, p. 10). The total cost of the national waste management program through 2070 has been estimated at €9,779.6 million (Hearsey et al. 2000, p. 2).

Spanish attitudes to nuclear activities

The Spanish government's commitment to nuclear power has at times been uncertain – moratoria on new plant construction were passed in 1983 and 1994 – but has recently "firmed up as the cost of subsidising renewables becomes unaffordable" (WNA updated 2014). In contrast, according to polling, a solid majority (roughly 60 percent) of Spaniards oppose nuclear power and almost three-quarters believe that nuclear power generation represents a serious risk. More than 80 percent of Spaniards feel generally uninformed about nuclear issues and, as a result, a significant proportion of Spaniards lack trust in the government overseeing the industry and believe that administrative practices are not transparent ("Public and Political Issues in Radwaste Management: The Spanish Approach" 1999; Losada 2013, p. 25). The issue of radioactive waste is closely linked to the ongoing debate about the role of nuclear energy (Lang-Lenton et al. 2005). For much of the Spanish populace, radioactive waste is regarded as a greater threat than the operation of nuclear power plants, and waste management proposals often elicit emotional responses (González, Armada and Molina n.d.).

The underlying reasons for these attitudes are complex, but two explanations appear to play at least an important contributory role: a growing sensitivity to protection of the environment and an ecological awareness that is becoming a major social and cultural trend and is generally extremely antinuclear in outlook; and a perception, promoted in large part by antinuclear groups, that the problems that led to the Chernobyl disaster in Ukraine are shared to a greater or lesser degree by the rest of the world's nuclear installations.[7] The first of these is particularly important in Spain because the ecological movement has deep roots in civil society.

The antinuclear movement was closely linked with the Spanish people's struggle for democracy against the fascist regime and still draws strength from that association, and the ecological movement grew out of the antinuclear movement. Established in 1979, the Coordinating Committee of Environmental Defence Organizations (CODA) functioned as the main umbrella organization for local grassroots groups over the course of the 1980s. Groups such as Greenpeace, Friends of the Earth and Ecologists in Action have been and continue to be active on nuclear issues. In general, they oppose spent fuel/high level waste disposal solutions while nuclear plants operate but are less committed to opposing L/ILRW disposal.[8] These groups have battled ENRESA over radioactive waste management from the organization's inception, and there have been cases where protest groups and the Spanish public have mobilized to prevent nuclear activities, for example, blocking construction of an underground research laboratory in 1987 and pressuring ENRESA to abandon a decade-long study of granite, salt and clay formations that had yielded an approximately 9,650 square mile inventory of potentially suitable land for spent nuclear fuel disposal in 1996 (ENRESA n.d., p. 65; Losada 2013, p. 19).

Like most other places, acceptance of nuclear energy is greatest amongst those who live near nuclear sites (Losada 2013, p. 25). One reason for this is the fact that where systematic information campaigns have been carried out, public perceptions of nuclear activities tend to be more positive. For example, surveys carried out by ENRESA show that 'nuclear communities' generally trust the organization and its workers on issues like safety. Similar findings have been observed by more independent researchers in other countries. Of course, the fact that these facilities are usually major local employers is also very important (ENRESA n.d., p. 64).

Disposing of radioactive waste: the El Cabril centralized low and intermediate level waste disposal facility

At the end of the 1950s the Franco regime closed the exhausted Mina Beta uranium mine on El Cabril Estate, located in the northwest corner of the province of Córdoba in the municipality of Hornachuelos (roughly 248 miles south of Madrid). In 1961, the Nuclear Energy Board (Junta de Energía Nuclear, JEN, which would become CIEMAT in 1986) began storing radioactive waste drums from research activities in drums in Mina Beta (Lang-Lenton et al. 2005; López, Navarro, Zuloago and Vargas 2009).[9] During the early years, the local municipality was largely unaware of the use the mine was being put to. Indeed, it was not until 1975 that JEN was granted a license to dispose of LLRW and short-lived intermediate level radioactive waste (Caravaca 2014). However, by the late 1970s it had also become clear that the mine was inadequate – both structurally and spatially – for anticipated future waste disposal needs, particularly with a new generation of power reactors expected to begin operation in the 1980s, so the federal government decided to construct a purpose-built surface facility (Bergström, Pers and Almén 2011, p. 25; "Radioactive Waste Management Programmes" 2013; "System at El Cabril Disposal Facility" n.d.; "Low and Intermediate Level Waste Management in Spain" n.d.).

At the beginning of the 1980s, three storage modules (metallic industrial sheds with concrete walls) were constructed, each with a 15,000-drum capacity. The waste was transferred to the modules, the mine was closed and planning began for a more comprehensive and permanent facility (IAEA 2003, p. 105). Site characterization work already underway was complemented by engineering, safety and environmental assessments commencing in 1986, the same year the fledgling ENRESA assumed responsibility for the site. In August 1989, following a public comment period, an Environmental Impact Statement together with a supporting report by the Nuclear Safety Council was sent to the Ministry of Industry and Energy; 2 months later the design for a 28-vault facility was approved. After receipt of a corroborating report by the Provincial Town Planning Commission, formal construction began in January 1990, and in October 1992 an operating permit was granted ("Radioactive Waste Management Programmes" 2013; Espartero; ENRESA 2012, p. 60).

In May 2003, ENRESA requested authority to build a very low level radioactive waste (VLLRW) installation. This was motivated by the expectation of a large amount of such waste resulting from power plant decommissioning activities and the accidental smelting of a cesium-137 source in a load of metallic scrap at a Cádiz steelyard in 1998 that created a large clean-up job and "a very appreciable volume of LILW/VLLW" (6th GRWP 2006, p. 25). The authorization was granted in February 2006, an operating permit was issued in July 2008 and waste began arriving 3 months later (López et al. 2009, pp. 4, 10). The VLLRW facility consists of four cells, each with a disposal capacity of between 1,059,000 and 1,236,000 cubic feet, designed to isolate the waste from the biosphere for 60 years, the period required for the activity from VLLRW to abate to background levels.

Originally consisting of 28 vaults on two platforms (a north platform of 16 vaults and a south platform of 12 vaults), vault 29 of the L/ILRW facility has been in operation since July 2008 (López et al. 2009, pp. 4, 10). ENRESA now wishes to utilize vaults 30 and 31, in part to accommodate the large amount of waste that will be generated by the decommissioning of the Vandellós I and Zorita nuclear plants (see Box 6.1) (Caravaca 2014). On 26 February 2013 work began on vault 30, which will take 18 months to complete and increase storage by 1,165,000 cubic feet ("El Cabril Received 1,681.78 Cubic Meters of Radioactive Waste in 2013" 2014).

In 2012, El Cabril received almost 102,400 cubic feet of waste: roughly 19,950 cubic feet of L/ILRW and 82,212 cubic feet of VLLRW (ENRESA 2013). The facility has a capacity of 3,531,000 cubic feet (100,000 cubic meters): the L/ILRW disposal vaults are at 70 percent capacity and the VLLRW cells are at 17 percent capacity. Problematically, in the coming years Spain is expected to generate far more waste than can be disposed of at El Cabril – 6,225,976 cubic feet during the remaining operational lives of the country's power reactors alone – and, as currently configured, the L/ILRW vaults are expected to be full by about 2020 (Zuloaga and Vargas n.d.; Espartero n.d.; Albert 2014a; "The Andalusian Parliament Approved Two Motions So That It Does Not Expand El Cabril" 2014). As a result, in 2014, the federal government indicated that El Cabril will need to be expanded again by the early 2020s (Alba 2014). The president of ENRESA, Gil Ortega, has explained that capacity will need to be virtually doubled by building another 28 vaults ("The Andalusian Parliament Approved Two Motions" 2014).

Site specifications

Set on a 2,782 acre site in the foothills of the Sierra Albarrana, El Cabril is a state-of-the-art waste management facility and the only disposal site in the country. Low population density, arid climate and low seismic risk were considered important long-term safety factors when ENRESA decided to expand the existing surface facility rather than attempting to find another site. However, the arid climate has obligated the company to put in place water conservation practices, and concerted efforts are also made to minimize disturbance of the indigenous flora and fauna (Bergström et al. 2011, p. 25; Nuñez-Villaveirán 2012). The complex is set out in two zones: a disposal zone of 29 concrete vaults designed so the waste can be retrieved if necessary, a rainwater collection pond and a factory dedicated to prefabricating concrete containers; and a zone containing the auxiliary buildings such as security, administration, workshops, storehouses and a treatment and conditioning building (López et al. 2009, p. 4). The treatment and conditioning building includes incineration, super-compaction, grout preparation/injection and characterization laboratories (Zuloago and Vargas n.d.; Zuloaga, Navarro and Vargas 2009). The nuclear power plants are responsible for treatment and conditioning of the waste they produce; ENRESA determines whether it meets acceptance criteria as approved by safety authorities. For institutional waste generators all required treatment and conditioning is carried out on site at El Cabril. Waste is generally handled remotely from a control room except certain categories of waste with low contact dose rates and incineration operations ("Radioactive Waste Management Programmes" 2013, p. 5). Annual operating costs have been estimated at €14.5 million (Bergmans 2010, p. 33).

Waste packages comprising drums (7.8 cubic feet) and metal boxes (46 cubic feet) are reconditioned in concrete to form 388 cubic feet disposal units comprising a first barrier. The drums and boxes are then placed inside 79×66×33-foot concrete vaults (each with a capacity of 320 containers), which are then backfilled with gravel and covered by slabs with impervious paint. After construction rainwater drainage systems are installed while each row of vaults is serviced by a metallic shelter on wheels (Zuloago and Vargas n.d.; Bergström et al. 2011, p. 27; "Radioactive Waste Management Programmes" 2013). El Cabril has been well run: apart from a leak in vault 16 in March 2003, there have been no safety incidents of note reported at the facility (Davilla n.d.). Once the facility reaches capacity, the L/ILRW vaults will be subject to a 300-year surveillance period until the activity of the waste has decayed to background levels (6th GRWP 2006, p. 37).[10]

Opposition to El Cabril

At the national level, some politicians and sections of the media have objected to the facility's basic existence ("Public and Political Issues in Radwaste Management" 1999, p. 85; González et al. n.d.). But the most important sources of opposition have been regional and local, in large part due to the narrow not-in-my-backyard (NIMBY) quality of antinuclear activism amongst the Spanish populace. Locals tend to mobilize only when they perceive their quality of life or economic welfare is directly threatened. As a result, environmental nongovernmental organizations (ENGOs) have struggled to elevate most protests to truly national campaigns (Jiménez 1999b, p. 18).

As discussed earlier, antinuclear sentiment was the original impetus for the creation of many Spanish ENGOs. Problematically for those wishing to promote environmental causes in the 1970s and early to mid-1980s, the new dominant political discourse – democracy – continued to emphasize modernity and growth to the detriment of the environment and the government actively opposed the demands of the environmental movement (Jiménez 1999a, pp. 153–154). However, by the late 1980s, as the country continued to liberalize, ENGOs had become more entrenched in society and consequently became more visible in the political realm (Jiménez 1999a, p. 155). Notably, environmental groups and local residents vigorously protested the construction of the Trillo and Vandellós 2 nuclear power plants. Although their efforts failed (both plants began operating in 1988), this failure served as the catalyst for the creation of the Associación de Municipios en Áreas con Centrales Nucleares (AMAC). A nonprofit organization comprised of 67 municipalities representing approximately 80,000 inhabitants living within 6 miles of nuclear facilities as of 2005, AMAC seeks greater transparency and public participation in nuclear decision-making through strategies such as lobbying (particularly of Parliament), participating in working groups with ENRESA and CSN, and seeking socioeconomic assistance for its constituents, particularly compensation. Over the course of its existence, AMAC has established Local Information Committees and has developed a network of relationships with key government ministries, ENRESA, CSN and the Spanish Electricity Industry Association. Importantly, AMAC is perceived by these stakeholders as their link to the local communities (Garcia 2005, p. 87; Lang-Lenton et al. 2005; Martess and Ferraro 2014, p. 63).

The Córdoban environmental movement has spent almost three decades advocating for the immediate closure of El Cabril. The first protest campaigns took place in 1985 (Albert 2014a). However, it was not until ENRESA announced its intention to upgrade the facility in the late 1980s that widespread regional and local opposition was galvanized. The Andalusian Parliament passed a resolution of opposition to the expansion in 1987 and there was significant discontent amongst neighboring communities at the perceived lack of transparency in the process (Lang-Lenton et al. 2005; González et al. n.d.). In 1988, a demonstration in Hornachuelos drew 2,000 protesters (González et al. n.d.). This and other protests were widely covered by the Spanish media. An 'Anti-Nuclear Cemetery' movement emerged out of the protests along with the Anti-Cabril Coordinating Committee, a coalition of ecological groups, far-left trade unions and political parties. These groups charged that the site was impeding the development of the region and the image of the local produce was being stigmatized because the region was associated with nuclear waste (Gil-Cerezo, González-Barrios and Domíngues-Vilches 2013, pp. 40–41; Jiménez 1999c, p. 11). Juan Escribano, a provincial spokesman for Ecologists in Action went further, arguing that the major problem with El Cabril was that the waste would pollute the site for centuries (Albert 2014a).

In December 1988, AEDENAT (Asociacíon Ecologista de Defensa de la Naturaleza) wrote to La Comisión Nacional de Energía (CNE) claiming that El Cabril was accepting waste from the nuclear power plants that it was not licensed to receive.[11] AEDENAT also petitioned the courts, and in July 1996 the Madrid High Court ordered that the facility be closed. Nuclear Safety Council chairman Juan Manuel Kindelan described the decision as "a very serious error." In contrast, the Andalusian government called for the judgment to be carried out "strictly and in all its terms" ("Spain: Court Orders Closure of Nuclear Dump" 1996). ENRESA continued operations at El Cabril while the government appealed to the Supreme Tribunal. The Tribunal denied the appeal in a 5 June 2002 judgment. However, the government maintained that legislative fixes had resolved the matter, and El Cabril remained open.

Box 6.1   Fire at Vandellós

While difficult to quantify in terms of attitudes to El Cabril, an accident at the Vandellós 1 nuclear plant in 1989 had a significant impact on the nuclear power debate. On 19 October, a hydrogen explosion started a fire that burned for 4.5 hours before being put out ("A Short History of Nuclear Power and Anti-Nuclear Movement in Spain" 1998).[12] The accident sparked fierce opposition to nuclear development throughout Spain, including protests outside the head office in Barcelona of the utility (Spanish–French consortium HIFRENSA) that operated Vandellós and was fresh in many minds when the moratorium on new nuclear plant construction was passed in 1994.[13] It also brought a number of simmering tensions to the surface, in particular the sense of alarm shared by mayors in neighboring towns about warning and evacuation procedures and concerns amongst firefighters and trade unions that their equipment and training procedures were inadequate ("Nuclear Reactor in Spain Catches Fire" 1989). Local opposition was led by residents of the village of l'Ametlla de Mar, 6 miles south of the site, and a committee was created to more effectively pressure the government. A general strike was called and a referendum held in which more than 90 percent of those voting demanded the reactor be permanently shut down. The national regulator responded by demanding safety improvements from the operator. On 30 May 1990, HIFRENSA decided to shutter the reactor for good, deeming the costs to meet the additional safety requirements prohibitive ("A Short History" 1998).

Widespread 'nuclear' protests continued throughout the 1990s, albeit less intensely than in 1989 (Jiménez 1999b, p. 5). Two factors help explain this persistence. First, ENRESA was encountering substantial opposition in its attempts to find suitable sites for a spent fuel repository.[14] Second, new restrictive environmental legislation was being promulgated by Parliament.

Attitudes to ENRESA's plans for future expansion at El Cabril in the surrounding communities vary. Córdoba representative Isabel Ambrosio argued against the expansion, maintaining it would be better to close the facility down once the vaults reach capacity (Albert 2014a). The Committee on the

Environment of the Andalusian Parliament has passed two motions opposing the expansion ("The Andalusian Parliament Approved Two Motions" 2014). The local ENGO Antinuclear Assembly Córdoba has called for a rally against the expansion, arguing the site should be dismantled, and several hundred residents have supported that position (Caravaca 2014). The Hornachuelos government declared in a press release that the site had been economically detrimental to the area even if it had contributed to the national good. The city council maintains that any expansion requires agreement between federal and regional governments before the municipality commits but there is no such agreement to date. And while there is opposition amongst Hornachuelos residents, the mayor of Hornachuelos, Carmen Murillo, has indicated his support is conditional on government compensation (Caravaca 2014).

ENRESA's response

The communications plan

Given this resistance, ENRESA crafted a Communications Plan that was designed to help inform key stakeholders of the organization's activities and increasing public acceptance of the facility's continued operation (González et al. n.d.). From the beginning, ENRESA has been sensitive to the need to communicate effectively with the Spanish public. The first communication plan in 1990 was crafted with the general aim of seeking public acceptance of El Cabril (González et al. n.d.; ENRESA n.d., p. 65). The second plan, released in 1994, focused heavily on the need for training and information and a communication strategy with the media (ENRESA n.d., p. 65). The fifth GRWP built on this, emphasizing that

> it should be pointed out that, in view of the obvious sensitivity of society to matters relating to radioactivity, based among other things on a lack of public understanding of the true nature of the technical solutions proposed, it will be necessary to carry out the widest possible information/educational campaigns, in order to facilitate better knowledge and understanding both of the problem to be solved and the technology to be used to achieve such a solution.
>
> (ENRESA n.d., p. 65)

The Communications Plan seeks to foster interaction with all facets of Spanish society including "universities, professional associations, electricity utilities, professionals from the field of nuclear medicine, consumer organisations, trade unions, political representatives," with the goal of reassuring the public that all key institutions are invested in the radioactive waste management process (6th GRWP 2006, pp. 89–90). ENRESA's strategic guidelines for public information and communication emphasize the need to provide transparent information to stakeholders, provide training to university students working in fields related to the organization's activities and work with local authorities to improve the infrastructure of those municipalities close to ENRESA sites (ENRESA n.d., p. 65).

ENRESA has instituted a number of strategies, drawing from surveys of local residents as well as more general lessons learned from stakeholder interaction, to enhance the acceptance of the site (Lang-Lenton et al. 2005). The main actions include:

- 'open days' to help demonstrate what the facility is doing;
- annual meetings with town councils in those areas it operates;
- operation of the El Cabril Information Centre, created in 1992 and staffed primarily by local residents, which provides information on all facets of the site, including exhibits that, through "a combination of models, audio visual systems and computer equipment, are aimed at eliciting participation by the visitors and allowing them to get a clear idea of the problems posed by radioactive wastes and the solutions currently applied." ENRESA also operates information centers in Madrid, Andújar, Córdoba and Vandellós;[15]
- focused interaction with the media, for example holding seminars for journalists and participating in radio and television debates;
- hosting exhibitions at museums;
- distribution of instructional materials and holding seminars to enhance stakeholder (business leaders, teachers and students in particular) knowledge of radioactivity and its applications as well as radioactive waste management (González et al. n.d.);
- financial sponsorship of organizations such as the Red Cross and the World Wildlife Fund;
- writing journal and magazine articles, books and brochures on ENRESA activities ("Public and Political Issues in Radwaste Management" 1999, pp. 84–85);
- conducting socioeconomic studies of neighboring communities to better tailor compensation programs ("Public and Political Issues in Radwaste Management" 1999, pp. 84–85).

According to ENRESA, the Communication Plan has assured many members of the public, and particularly those who have visited the site, that the staff there are diligent and professional and the facility is safe ("Public and Political Issues in Radwaste Management" 1999, p. 86; González et al. n.d.). These somewhat subjective conclusions are supported by a series of independent interviews undertaken by Gil-Cerezo, González-Barrios and Domíngues-Vilches with 20 local key stakeholders, including staff at the site. The authors concluded that local residents were not particularly worried about the safety of the site and had learned to live with the repository in their midst. Several nonsafety concerns were identified: more should be done to make the activities at the site more transparent, not enough compensation has been received and more needs to be done to ensure the regional development promoted by the Foundation is sustainable so the site is not a "millstone for future generations" (Gil-Cerezo et al. 2013, pp. 42–43).

At the national level, sustained cooperation with all levels of government has been critical to the licensing of continued and expanded operations at El Cabril (Molina 1996). ENRESA also believes its activities have granted the organization a healthy measure of respect from the media ("Public and Political Issues in Radwaste Management" 1999, p. 86). There are certainly indications that ENRESA's efforts have had a substantial impact on the media's perceptions. In 1999 the Andalusian media coverage of El Cabril was 37 percent neutral, 36 percent positive and 27 percent negative. By 2008 it was 50 percent neutral, 45 percent positive and 5 percent negative. Similarly, Spanish national media coverage in 1999 was 58 percent neutral, 26 percent positive and 16 percent negative. By 2008 it was 62 percent neutral, 33 percent positive and 4 percent negative (Molina 2010, p. 22).

However, Molina also notes that substantial hostility to El Cabril remains at the local level, particularly in Fuente Obejuna, Azuaga and Hornachuelos. There is evidence that as far as the citizens of Hornachuelos are concerned, the economic stimulus that the construction phase provided was short-lived and the population of the town has decreased from 17,000 to 14,000 (Davilla n.d.). Further construction would rectify this problem temporarily but not break the boom-and-bust cycle. The residents of Alanís and Las Navas are neutral on the issue. Only the citizens of Peñarroya truly embrace the site, primarily because they have historically provided the workers, but even they believe they should be better compensated (Molina 2010, p. 10).

Compensating local communities

By the late 1980s, the towns neighboring El Cabril – Fuente Obejuna, Hornachuelos, Peñarroya, Alanís and Las Navas – had identified employment, the agricultural sector, health services and urban infrastructure as the major problems facing the region (Molina 2010, p. 11). There was also a feeling that communication between the site operators and the community was less than ideal. For ENRESA, this was an opportunity to use its financial resources to ameliorate some major local socioeconomic challenges, improve its public engagement strategy and engender goodwill in the process. As a result, in December 1989 the Ministry of Industry and Energy agreed to compensate to affected communities ("Public and Political Issues in Radwaste Management" 1999, p. 85). Compensation has been proffered in a variety of ways.

Direct payments

Direct financial compensation commenced in 1992 and payments will continue throughout the life of the facility. However, the initial recipient list proved to be too narrow. Several neighboring municipalities that did not qualify for compensation threatened to blockade the trucks bringing waste to the site. While the municipalities' demands were opposed by towns already being compensated, negotiations with representatives from the host municipality of Hornachuelos resulted in a broader compensation package (Lang-Lenton et al. 2005). With the exception of a 10 percent special share for Hornachuelos, the annual payments are determined by a formula that takes into account inhabitants within a 10 mile radius and a percentage of territory within an 5 mile radius of the site. To ensure a reasonable distribution of funds, a single municipality may not receive more than a 50 percent share of the total compensation payout (Bergmans 2010, p. 27). In 2008, the last year for which public figures are available, €1.24 million was allocated to the four municipalities; the host town received €590,000 (Gil-Cerezo et al. 2013, p. 37; Bergmans 2010, p. 25).

The municipal authorities can decide how the monies should be spent and have been used to fund social development projects such as schools, nurseries, music academies and sporting facilities (Bergmans 2010, p. 25). They have also been utilized to provide basic services including lighting and asphalting roads, urban development projects, creating green zones and promoting rural tourism (Nuclear Energy Agency [NEA] 2010, p. 78). According to one report, €77 million has been spent in the region, including €5 million on improving local roads (Davilla n.d.).

Utilizing the local workforce

When El Cabril was modified in the late 1980s, all levels of government determined that ENRESA should prioritize using local resources wherever possible. To facilitate this goal, a commission was created. After a number of meetings the commission decided that studies needed to be undertaken to determine the characteristics of the workforce as well as the services that would be required. At the same time, the commission advised that a permanent Information Bureau be created in Hornachuelos to keep the community informed and to help collect data for the workforce study (Molina 1996, pp. 203–210; NEA 1995, p. 207).

In late 1988, an inventory of local businesses that could contribute to the construction work was carried out. At first blush results were not encouraging, with approximately 2 percent of companies qualified to contribute (Molina 1996, p. 208). Undeterred, ENRESA opened a dialogue with the local and regional governments, which led to an agreement to:

- incorporate as many local workers as possible, providing they had the requisite qualifications; in return the federal government agreed that the National Institute for Employment would provide training programs to outfit local workers with the required skills;
- give top priority to local businesses in the awarding of service contracts;
- upgrade critical infrastructure in the area (Molina 1996, pp. 208–209).

This approach was highly successful; indeed, an 'economic boom' was created in Hornachuelos (Nuñez-Villaveirán 2012). ENRESA employed 120 local residents on long-term contracts and more than 1,000 local workers (roughly 40 percent of the total workforce) on specific construction projects. Infrastructure development included improvements to the roads connecting Córdoba and Badajoz, repairing two roads leading to the facility, increasing the capacity of the cable telephone system and establishing a cell phone system to cover the area. Overall this amounted to an investment of €1.5 million by ENRESA (Molina 1996, pp. 203–210; NEA 2010, p. 81). These measures saw local participation increase from 2 percent to an estimated 25 percent (Molina 1996, pp. 203–210; NEA 1995, p. 209). Two-thirds of El Cabril's 127 full-time employees now live in the neighboring municipalities ("El Cabril Received 1,681.78 Cubic Meters of Radioactive Waste in 2013" 2014).

With more information and improved economic conditions in the region, many residents' opinions of ENRESA also improved. Indeed, in the next municipal election, the facility's presence was not even mentioned as a contentious issue in the political debates or by the media (Molina 1996, pp. 209–210).

ENRESA's Foundation

On 27 December 1990, ENRESA created a not-for-profit charitable foundation overseen by the Ministry of Health and Social Policy "to promote and develop social welfare in the municipalities within the area of influence of ENRESA facilities" (NEA 2010, p. 81).[16] Fifty percent of the foundation's outlays support projects in communities near ENRESA facilities with the rest disbursed nationwide (Bergmans 2010, p. 24). Of the four major recipients, Hornachuelos has received €21.3 million in total (€1.6 million in 2013), Fuente Obejuna more than €11 million (€867,000 in 2013), Las Navas roughly €9 million (almost €800,000 in 2013) and Alanís roughly €500,000 (more than €6,000 in 2013) (Alba 2014).

Agreements have been made with towns and some local bodies with supra-municipal functions. Specific projects have included construction of a Red Cross Medical Centre in Peñarroya and local schools in Hornachuelos; development of a national park and visitors' center in Sierra de Hornachuelos (which is geographically close to El Cabril); reconstruction of a historical building in Fuente Obejuna; provision of computer equipment to Hornachuelos and Fuente Obejuna schools; provision of social care to small communities in Fuente Obejuna; advice to local business entrepreneurs in Fuente Obejuna; sponsorship of various cultural activities; and endowment of university chairs in environmental studies at the Universities of Córdoba, Cataluña and Extremadura (NEA 2010, p. 82; Molina 2010, p. 19).

However, on 20 September 2013 the Spanish Cabinet liquidated the ENRESA Foundation as part of the restructure of the public business sector to make it more efficient in light of Spain's ongoing economic woes (Alba 2013). At the time, the federal government maintained that this meant that agreements between the Foundation and the neighboring municipalities were void (Alba 2014). Not surprisingly this was not well received by the towns that had been receiving Foundation money. Twenty-two mayors of neighboring towns demanded the compensation they believe they were promised. The mayor of Hornachuelos,

María del Carmen Murillo, maintains her town is owed €160,000 that has already been budgeted for public works such as the repair of a playground (Albert 2014b). The four principal neighboring mayors of Hornachuelos, Fuente Obejuna, Alanís and Las Navas claim they have not even been able to get the secretary of state to meet with them to discuss the issue (and, as a result, are demanding his resignation) and have threatened to halt operations at El Cabril ("The Mayors of the Environment Are Threatening to Block El Cabril" 2014).

The Foundation's activities have gone a long way toward ameliorating local concerns, so shutting it down runs the risk of undoing all of that goodwill as well as suggesting to potential host communities that the government may not be a trustworthy partner. There are already indications that the government is rethinking its decision to renege on the Foundation's existing commitments (Alba 2015).

Conclusion

ENRESA achieved its primary goals of keeping El Cabril open and expanding the facility, although not without significant resistance from environmental organizations and neighboring communities. However, the broader objective of building local and regional support for radioactive waste management remains a work in progress, as evidenced by the opposition in Hornachuelos and Andalusia to the federal government's stated desire to undertake another – major – expansion of the site. A number of lessons can be gleaned from the Spanish experience.

The government benefited greatly from the fact that it inherited a functioning disposal (brown field) site in a sparsely populated part of a province with a relatively low GDP per capita. El Cabril had been receiving radioactive waste since 1961 and although familiarity breeds contempt, it also breeds a measure of acceptance. While Córdobans had no say in the matter for more than two decades and many made (and continue to make) their displeasure known when given the opportunity, it is far more difficult to convince a community to host for the first time than to persuade it to allow a facility to continue operating, particularly when that facility has a good safety record. That said, Córdoba does not provide a 'natural' constituency for radioactive waste disposal; the province does not host any nuclear plants or similar facilities that are typically found in communities comfortable with industrial hazard, and this is one reason why there has been sustained opposition to El Cabril within the province and throughout the wider autonomous community.

The creation of a dedicated radioactive waste management organization – ENRESA – in 1984 provided a stable source of funding, a locus of expertise for project management and a single point of contact for the affected communities to convey their preferences and concerns. Under the rubric of the General Radioactive Waste Plans' high-level policy and technical direction, ENRESA took a number of steps to increase the transparency of its operations, improve both the quality and quantity of information available to the public in Córdoba and nationally as well as orient its messaging to target opinion leaders. The Communications Plan, the open days and the information centers all served this educational purpose.

ENRESA promoted local economic development by providing financial compensation to neighboring towns; the communities got to decide how best to use the money they received. Similarly, ENRESA prioritized employing the local workforce and utilizing local resources at El Cabril, particularly during construction phases and in staffing the information centers. Recognizing that most residents did not have the appropriate expertise, the Spanish government offered training programs to provide local workers with the requisite skill sets. ENRESA has also made significant financial contributions to improve the welfare of the surrounding communities. The company has invested in infrastructure projects (such as roads and telecommunications) and the ENRESA Foundation funded medical centers, schools, universities and historical/cultural projects, both in the region immediately surrounding El Cabril and across the country. The organization has also demonstrated ecological sensitivity by putting in place strategies to conserve water and protect the local flora and fauna.

All of these approaches have created goodwill and have helped to ameliorate concerns about the facility, although the damage that is being caused by the Cabinet's decision to liquidate the Foundation and terminate existing agreements with the municipalities should not be underestimated. Opponents from Hornachuelos, in particular, have been outspoken about the government reneging on its commitments, compounding a more profound frustration at being forced to shoulder the nation's L/ILRW burden effectively for the next 300 years. Not surprisingly, given El Cabril's early history, there are lingering concerns about the transparency of the government and ENRESA's decision-making and dissatisfaction with the amount of compensation being provided. The attitude of these communities might best be described as grudging acceptance. Even in Peñarroya, the most accepting of the neighboring towns, officials have complained about the level of financial compensation.

Opponents have employed standard tactics such as public protests and the court system (Ecologists in Action's suit contending that the site was illegal went all the way to the Supreme Court) and have claimed that the facility damages the environment and stigmatizes local produce – usually potent arguments in regions where agriculture is a key economic driver. Yet, in part because protests have tended to coalesce locally around specific events – the impending startup of Trillo 1 and Vandellós 2 in 1988, the fire at Vandellós 1 in 1989, a radioactive leak at Ascó 1 in 2007 – opposition to El Cabril has been largely confined to Córdoba and has not gained much traction nationally. In addition, AMAC played an effective role representing its constituents – the 'nuclear communities' – and serving as a trusted source of information.

ENRESA's reputation, which is in large part burnished by the continued safe operation of El Cabril and a demonstrated willingness to work with community groups, town councils and regional governments, appears to be having a positive effect on efforts to manage the country's most radioactive categories of waste. Significantly, in terms of demonstrating waste management technology, El Cabril relies primarily on engineered barriers to provide protection against radionuclide release, and that will prove valuable for ENRESA's reputation in other areas of radioactive waste management such as spent fuel storage and disposal. In mid-2006, the Spanish parliament approved ENRESA's plans to develop a centralized temporary storage facility (Almacén Temporal Centralizado) for spent fuel and high level waste. CSN approved a design similar to COVRA's HABOG facility in the Netherlands.[17] In December 2009, the government called for town councils to volunteer to host. To incentivize the process, a benefits package was offered that included monetary payments, employment and other social services. Fourteen towns volunteered, eight were deemed suitable candidates and of those, four were considered 'better' options. Interestingly, of the four finalists, the site that was selected in December 2011– Villar de Cañas in the province of Cuenca – came fourth in the rankings, prompting litigation from some of the more highly ranked municipalities (Beceiro n.d.).[18] One important factor in the selection of the site was its centrality to four of the country's nuclear power plants. However, opponents have mounted a campaign to prevent construction by claiming, amongst other things, that selection of the site is more about political patronage and support for the project within the governing party of the host Autonomous Community (the center-right People's Party in Castilla-La Mancha) than technical analysis of the site's geological suitability (WNA updated 2014; "The Project ATC Sinks" 2014; Losada 2013, pp. 17, 21–22).[19]

As for the future of El Cabril, unless it is enlarged, the facility is a short-term solution to Spain's L/ILRW disposal needs. Mission creep at a disposal site can be viewed positively (for example, as a way to get increased return on investment) or negatively (such as the siting authority exceeding the limits of what has been authorized by the host community). The steady increase in the waste categories received at Waste Control Specialists' disposal facility in Texas is representative of the former; the abrupt transition of Germany's Asse II facility from a pilot facility to a repository is representative of the latter. An informal social contract has developed since ENRESA took responsibility for El Cabril and, given that opposition groups have not proved strong or persuasive enough to prevent previous expansions, let alone close the facility, there is a good chance that the expansion will go ahead. If not, a new host will need to be found.

Notes

1 For a history of Spain under Franco see Payne 2011.
2 Spain has also produced a substantial amount of tailings from uranium mining and milling operations. While the level of radioactivity is very low, the volumes are very

high – almost 90 million tons in total (Sixth General Radioactive Waste Plan [6th GRWP] 2006, p. 7).

3 After 300 years the activity of these wastes will have decayed to natural background radiation levels (6th GRWP 2006, p. 37).

4 ENRESA's shareholders are CIEMAT (80%) and the Spanish State Industrial Holding, SEPI (20%). The organization reports to the Ministry of Industry via the Secretary of State for Energy and is a technical adviser to Parliament (Martess and Ferraro 2014, p. 62; Lang-Lenton and Neri 2007, p. 2).

5 The CSN was set up on 22 April 1980 to oversee nuclear safety and radiological protection issues and is responsible for the regulation and supervision of Spanish nuclear installations. It reports directly to the federal Parliament (Mellado 2007, p. 53; "Radioactive Waste Management Programmes" 2013, pp. 7, 9).

6 Spain's Parliament is a bicameral body comprising a Congress with 300–400 members. The Senate is the house of territorial representation and Spain's Autonomous Communities appoint one senator for every million inhabitants (Velasco 2007, p. 57).

7 The principle that an accident at any nuclear facility threatens the continued operation of nuclear facilities everywhere has been embraced by the global nuclear industry since at least 1989 (World Association of Nuclear Operators [WANO] n.d.).

8 These ENGOs receive some of their funding from the European Union, Spain's autonomous communities and Spain's International Agency for Developmental Aid (Jiménez 2007, p. 363; Lamolla 2012, pp. 6, 9; Lang-Lenton et al. 2005; "Public and Political Issues in Radwaste Management" 1999, pp. 83–84).

9 As discussed in chapter 1, definitions of low level waste in the 1950s were somewhat elastic. Some of the waste buried at El Cabril during the early years of operation, particularly in Mina Beta, was hotter than the waste that is accepted for disposal today.

10 The 300-year surveillance period was derived from the French standard (Ruíz López, Zuloaga and Alonso 1993, p. 132).

11 In 1998 several environmental groups, including CODA and AEDENAT, merged to form Ecologists in Action which is now a federation of over 300 environmental groups. It employs a decentralized model of decision-making and holds an annual convention to set strategy (Jiménez 2007, p. 363).

12 The Chernobyl disaster, which had a chilling effect on nuclear activities globally, had occurred only 4.5 years earlier (Koopmans and Duyvendak 1995, p. 237).

13 Plant workers leapt to HIFRENSA's defense, stating that the calls to close Vandellós were politically motivated ("Fire at Vandellos" 1989).

14 According to one report, large demonstrations occurred: 10,000 at Belalcazar in 1996; 15,000 at Villanueva in 1997; and 20,000 in Torrecampo in 1998 (LAKA Foundation n.d.).

15 The El Cabril Information Center has received more than 100,000 visitors since 1992. ENRESA has begun work on remodeling the visitor site to incorporate the latest technology ("System at El Cabril Disposal Facility" n.d.; González et al. n.d.; "El Cabril Received 1,681.78 Cubic Meters of Radioactive Waste in 2013" 2014; 6th GRWP 2006).

16 Alba described the Foundation's work as compensation for the 'inconvenience' of having the facility nearby (Alba 2014).

17 For more information on the innovative HABOG facility, see Kastelein 2005.

18 The final four, with point scores in parentheses, were Zarra (736); Asco (732); Yebra (714); and Villar de Cañas (692). A senior ENRESA official explained to one of the authors that throughout the process the organization was conscious that the 'nuclear' communities were ENRESA's best allies, so in principle Asco was the favored site and in retrospect publicly releasing the rankings was a mistake (ENRESA official, Madrid, personal communication, 12 December 2013).

19 AMAC has been heavily involved in the opposition movement.

References

Abreu, A., Espejo, J.M., Gonzalez, V., and Lazaro, C., "Spanish Fifth General Radioactive Waste Plan," *Waste Management 2000 Conference*, Tucson, Arizona (27 February–2 March 2000), www.wmsym.org/archives/2000/pdf/37/37–05.pdf

Alba, A., "The Government Expects to Recover the Lost Funds from the Enresa Foundation," *Cordopolis* (8 January 2015), http://cordopolis.es/2015/01/08/el-gobierno-confia-en-recuperar-los-fondos-perdidos-de-la-fundacion-enresa/

Alba, A., "The Government Suppresses the Enresa Foundation," *Cordopolis* (21 September 2013), http://cordopolis.es/2013/09/21/el-gobierno-suprime-la-fundacion-enresa/

Alba, A., "The People of Cabril Run Out of Money," *Cordopolis* (16 June 2014) http://cordopolis.es/2014/06/16/los-pueblos-del-cabril-se-quedan-sin-dinero/

Albert, M., "The Drum at El Cabril Is Uncovered," *El País* (2014a), http://ccaa.elpais.com/ccaa/2014/02/01/andalucia/1391272412_220000.html

Albert, M., "The Mayors of Nuclear Zones Ask to Settle Accounts with ENRESA," *Cordopolis* (2014b), http://cordopolis.es/2014/12/09/los-alcaldes-de-zonas-nucleares-piden-ajustar-cuentas-con-enresa/

"The Andalusian Parliament Approved Two Motions So That It Does Not Expand El Cabril," *Cordopolis* (2 April 2014), http://cordopolis.es/2014/04/02/el-parlamento-andaluz-aprueba-dos-mociones-para-que-no-se-amplie-el-cabril/

Beceiro, A.R., "ATC: The Centralized Interim Storage Facility for SNF and HLW," Madrid, on file with the authors.

Beceiro, A.R., "Spain Low and Intermediate Waste Management Programme: El Cabril Disposal Programme," Madrid (12 December 2013), on file with the authors.

Bergmans, A., "International Benchmarking of Community Benefits Related to Facilities for Radioactive Waste Management Report," Commissioned by EDRAM, NIROND 2010–01 E (January 2010), www.edram.info/uploads/media/2010–01_EDRAM_Com_Benefits_Final_ENG_.pdf

Bergström, U., Pers, K., and Almén, Y., *International Perspective on Repositories for Low Level Waste* (December 2011), www.skb.se/upload/publications/pdf/r-11–16.pdf

Caravaca, T., "El Cabril: The Resurrection of the Ghosts of the Nuclear Cemetery," *El Mundo* (2 August 2014), www.elmundo.es/andalucia/2014/02/08/52f667e8ca4741aa308b457d.html

Davilla, L., "El Cabril, Córdoba: Welcome to the Only Nuclear Cemetery in Spain" (n.d.), www.uniserral.com/51067_es/Bienvenidos-al-%C3%BAnico-cementerio-nuclear-de-Espa%C3%B1a/

"El Cabril Received 1,681.78 Cubic Meters of Radioactive Waste in 2013," *El País* (27 March 2014), http://ccaa.elpais.com/ccaa/2014/03/27/andalucia/1395938575_574712.html

Empresa Nacional de Residuos Radiactivos [ENRESA], *Nuclear Waste Management in Spain* (n.d.), http://newmdb.iaea.org/profiles.aspx?ByCountry=ES

ENRESA, "El Cabril Received 2,892.63 Cubic Meters of Radioactive Waste in 2012," Madrid (18 April 2013), www.sepi.es/default.aspx?cmd=0004&IdContent=21398&idLanguage=_EN&lang=

Espartero, A.G., "Radioactive and Nuclear Waste Management in Spain," Powerpoint Presentation, Workshop, Lisbon (October 2012), www.unece.org/fileadmin/DAM/energy/se/pdfs/UNFC/ws_IAEA_CYTED_UNECE_Oct12_Lisbon/20_Espartero.pdf

Espartero, A.G., "Spanish Management Issues in Radioactive and Nuclear Waste Materials," Powerpoint Presentation, Senior Researcher, Head of CIEMAT Quality

Management, CYTED Energy Area Technical Secretary of Spanish Alliance for Energy Research and Innovation (ALINNE), Radioactive and Nuclear Waste Management in Spain, Workshop, Lisbon (n.d.), www.unece.org/fileadmin/DAM/energy/se/pdfs/UNFC/ws_IAEA_CYTED_UNECE_Oct12_Lisbon/20_Espartero.pdf

Espejo, J.M., and Abreu, A., "The Spanish General Radioactive Waste Management Plan," *Waste Management 2008 Conference*, Phoenix, Arizona (24–28 February 2008), www.wmsym.org/archives/2008/pdfs/8475.pdf

"Fire at Vandellos," *World Information Service on Energy* (3 November 1989), www.wiseinternational.org/node/69

García, A., Universitat Autónoma de Barcelona, "A Relevant Spanish Actor: The Role Views and Singularity of AMAC," Radioactive Waste Management in Spain: Coordination and Projects, FSC Workshop Proceedings, L'Hospitalet de l'Infant, Spain (21–23 November 2005).

"Geological Disposal – Brief Overview of NGO Involvement in the Radioactive Waste Management Process in Eleven Overseas Countries," Nuclear Decommissioning Authority (July 2010), www.nda.gov.uk/publication/geological-disposal-brief-overview-of-ngo-involvement-in-radioactive-waste-management-process-in-eleven-overseas-countries-july-2010/

Gil-Cerezo, M.V., González-Barrios, A.J., and Domínigues-Vilches, E., "Socio-environmental Nuclear Conflicts: The Case of El Cabril," *International Journal of Nuclear Knowledge Management*, Vol. 6, No. 1 (2013).

González, V., Armada, J., and Molina, M., "Communications in the Field of Radioactive Waste Management in Spain," Session 49 – Public & Institutional Interactions (n.d.), Co-chairs: Jo-Ann Holst, S.M. Stoller Corporation, Ron Bhada, NMSU, Enresa Madrid, Spain.

Hearsey, C.J., Emmery, D.L., Kunsch, P., Bollingerfehr, W., and Webster, S., "The Financing of Radioactive Waste Storage and Disposal," in *Radioactive Waste Management Strategies and Issues*; Euradwaste 1999 International Conference; 5th, Radioactive Waste Management Strategies and Issues (2000).

International Atomic Energy Agency, *Radioactive Waste Management: Status and Trends* (2003), www-pub.iaea.org/MTCD/publications/PDF/rwmst3/IAEA-WMDB-ST-3-Part-5.pdf

International Atomic Energy Agency, *The Role of Research Reactors in Introducing Nuclear Power* (n.d.), www.iaea.org/sites/default/files/gc56inf-3-att5_en.pdf

International Atomic Energy Agency, *Country Profiles: Spain* (n.d.), http://newmdb.iaea.org/profiles.aspx?ByCountry=ES

International Atomic Energy Agency, *IAEA research Reactor Database* (n.d.), http://nucleus.iaea.org/RRDB/RR/ReactorSearch.aspx?rf=1

Jiménez, M., "Consolidation through Institutionalization? Dilemmas of the Spanish Environmental Movement in the 1990s," *Environmental Politics*, Vol. 8, No. 1 (1999a).

Jiménez, M., "The Environmental Movement in Spain: A Growing Force of Contention," *South European Society and Politics*, Vol. 12, No. 3 (September 2007).

Jiménez, M., "Environmental Protests in Comparative Perspective – Ten Years of Environmental Protests in Spain: Issues, Actors and Arenas," 27th ECPR Joint Sessions, Mannheim, Germany, Juan Institute, Madrid (1999b).

Jiménez, M., "Struggling for the Environment: A Profile of Recent Environmental Protests in Spain," Estudio/Working Paper 1999/143 (1999c).

Kastelein, J., HABOG: *One Building for High Level Waste and Spent Fuel in the Netherlands, The First Year of Experience*, RRFM 2005, Budapest (11–12 April 2005), www.euronuclear.org/meetings/rrfm2005/presentations/Kastelein.pdf

Koopmans, R., and Duyvendak, J. W., *The Political Construction of the Nuclear Energy Issue and Its Impact on the Mobilization of Anti-Nuclear Movements in Western Europe* (Berkeley: University of California Press, 1995).

LAKA Foundation, "Spain" (n.d.), www.laka.org/info/publicaties/afval/2-discussions-00/6-spain.htm

Lamolla, M.M., "Identifying Remaining Socio-Technical Challenges at the National Level: Spain," Working Paper in SOTEC (20 May 2012), http://newmdb.iaea.org/profiles.aspx?ByCountry=ES

Lang-Lenton, J., Castro, F., and d'Abadal, M., "Nuclear Waste Management in Spain: El Cabril and On Site Storage" (2005), www.cowam.com/?Nuclear-Waste-Management-in-Spain

Lang-Lenton, J., and Neri, E.G., "Current States of the Radioactive Waste Management Programme in Spain," ENRESA ICEMO7–7101 (2007).

López, I., Navarro, M., Zuloaga, P., and Vargas, E., "Safety Assessment of the New Very Low-Level Waste Disposal Installation at El Cabril, Spain," *Waste Management Conference*, Phoenix, Arizona (1–5 March 2009), www.wmsym.org/archives/2009/pdfs/9042.pdf

Losada, M, "Nuclear Waste Policy in Spain," 18th REFORM Group Meeting – Climate Policy Strategies and Energy Transition (August 2013), www.polsoz.fu-berlin.de/polwiss/forschung/systeme/ffu/veranstaltungen/termine/downloads/13_salzburg/Isidoro-Salzburg-2013.pdf

"Low and Intermediate Level Waste Management in Spain" (n.d.), http://newmdb.iaea.org/GetLibraryFile.aspx?RRoomID=423

Martess, M., and Ferraro, G., "Radioactive Waste Management Stakeholders Map in the European Union, Report May 2014," *JRC Science and Policy Reports* (2014).

"The Mayors of the Environment Are Threatening to Block El Cabril," *Cordopolis* (11 December 2014), http://cordopolis.es/2014/12/11/los-alcaldes-del-entorno-de-el-cabril-amagan-con

Mellado, I., "The Role of the Nuclear Safety Regulator," *OECD/NEA* (2007), Radioactive Waste Management in Spain: Co-ordination and Projects, FSC Workshop Proceedings, L'Hospitalet de l'Infant, Spain (21–23 November 2005).

Méndez, R., "Madrid Spain's Half-Forgotten Search for a Long-Term Nuclear Waste Solution," *El País* (14 September 2011), http://elpais.com/elpais/2011/09/14/inenglish/1315977644_850210.html

Molina, M., "LILW Management in Spain El Cabril Disposal Facility," Presentation to SKB, ENRESA (11 March 2010).

Molina, M., "The Role of Local Authorities in the Process of Siting the Spanish Repository for Low and Intermediate-Level Radioactive Waste," Nuclear Energy Agency, Paris, France (1996).

Nuclear Energy Agency, International Seminar, Rauma (Finland) (13–15 October 1995).

Nuclear Energy Agency, *Partnering for Long-Term Management of Radioactive Waste – Evolution and Current Practice in Thirteen Countries* (December 2010), www.keepeek.com/Digital-Asset-Management/oecd/nuclear-energy/partnering-for-long-term-management-of-radioactive-waste_9789264083707-en#page77

"Nuclear Reactor in Spain Catches Fire," *New York Times* (26 October 1989), www.nytimes.com/1989/10/26/world/nuclear-reactor-in-spain-catches-fire.html

Nuñez-Villaveirán, L., "El Cabril: Unique Spanish Nuclear Graveyard," *El Mundo* (23 January 2012), www.elmundo.es/blogs/elmundo/latrinchera/2012/01/23/el-cabril-unico-cementerio-nuclear.html

Payne, S.G., *The Franco Regime, 1936–1975* (Madison: University of Wisconsin Press, 2011).

"The Project ATC Sinks," *Platform against Nuclear Graveyard* (31 December 2014), http://cuencadicenoalcementerionuclear.blogspot.com/search?updated-min=2014-01-01T00:00:00-08:00&updated-max=2015-01-01T00:00:00-08:00&max-results=24

"Public and Political Issues in Radwaste Management: The Spanish Approach," European Nuclear Society (ENS), Berne (Switzerland), 1999, ENS PIME '99: 11. International Workshop on Nuclear Public Information in Practice, Avignon, France (7–10 February 1999).

"Radioactive Waste Management Programmes in OECD/NEA Member Countries: Spain" (2013), www.oeca-nea.org/rwm/profiles/spain-profile-web.pdf

Ruíz López, M.C., Zuloaga, P., and Alonso, J., "Design and Licensing of the El Cabril L/ILW Disposal Facility," *Waste Management 1993 Conference* (1993), www.wmsym.org/archives/1993/V1/28.pdf

Schneider, M. (assisted by Jacobs, D.), *Comparison among Different Decommissioning Funds Methodologies for Nuclear Installations, Final Country Report: Spain*, Paris (31 September 2006).

"A Short History of Nuclear Power and Anti-nuclear Movement in Spain," *Special: The Magazine of Hope* (October 16, 1998), www.wiseinternational.org/node/2128

"Sixth General Radioactive Waste Plan (6th GRWP)" (June 2006), http://newmdb.iaea.org/GetLibraryFile.aspx?RRoomID=471

"Spain: Court Orders Closure of Nuclear Dump," *World Information Service on Energy* (12 July 1996), www.wiseinternational.org/node/1593

"System at El Cabril Disposal Facility," *Environmental Policy at El Cabril Disposal Facility* (n.d.), http://pbadupws.nrc.gov/docs/ML0318/ML031890311.pdf

Velasco, R.G., "Parliamentarian, Industry, Trade and Tourism Commission," OECCD/NEA (2007), Radioactive Waste Management in Spain: Co-ordination and Projects, FSC Workshop Proceedings, L'Hospitalet de l'Infant, Spain (21–23 November 2005), doi:10.1787/9789264039421

World Association of Nuclear Operators, *Our Principles* (n.d.), www.wano.info/en-gb/aboutus/ourmission

World Nuclear Association, *Nuclear Power in Spain* (updated November 2014), www.world-nuclear.org/info/Country-Profiles/Countries-O-S/Spain/

Zuloago, P., Navarro, M., and Vargas, E., "Very Low Activity Waste Disposal Facility Recently Commissioned as an Extension of El Cabril LILW Disposal Facility in Spain," *Waste Management 2009 Conference*, Phoenix, Arizona (1–5 March 2009), www.wmsym.org/archives/2009/pdfs/9014.pdf

Zuloago, P., and Vargas, E., "New Developments in Low Level Radioactive Waste Management in Spain" (n.d.), www.euronuclear.org/events/topseal/transactions/Paper-Session-III-Zuloaga.pdf

7 "One of the most contentious and complex policy issues in the history of policy-making"

Low level radioactive waste disposal in South Korea

South Korea and nuclear power[1]

South Korea joined the International Atomic Energy Agency (IAEA) in 1957. The Framework Act No. 483 on Atomic Energy, the country's principal nuclear energy legislation, was passed in March of the following year (IAEA updated 2012). A small research reactor, the KRR-1 located in Seoul, went critical in 1962 and the regulation of radioactive sources began with the issuance of the first two licenses a year later. A second research reactor, KRR-2 also located in Seoul, went critical in 1972. In 1976, Colorado State University donated a critical assembly to Kyeong-Hee University (Ha, Lim, Oh and Wu 2011, p. 2).[2] The High-Flux Advanced Neutron Application Reactor (HANARO), located in Daecheon, went critical in 1995, replacing KRR-1 and KRR-2 that were both shutdown the same year ("High-Flux Advanced Neutron Application Reactor" 2010). A postirradiation examination facility, irradiated material examination facility, radioisotope production facility, fuel fabrication facility and other laboratories operate in conjunction with the reactors and critical assembly (Oak Ridge National Laboratory 2010, p. 11). While the infrastructure was and is used for basic science and to produce radioisotopes used in diagnostic medicine and in industries such as mining, its primary purpose has always been to develop the expertise required for an advanced indigenous nuclear industry, both in terms of power production and as a technology exporter. Being energy resource poor, and having experienced two "disastrous" oil crises during the 1970s, South Korea considers nuclear power its most reliable source of base load power (Ko and Kwon 2009, p. 3484).

By the end of 2006, just before Korea Hydro and Nuclear Power (KHNP) submitted its application to construct and operate a disposal facility, there were 3,073 licensed users of radioactive material across the country, all generating radioactive waste (Korean Nuclear International Cooperation Foundation [KONICOF] 2008). The largest producers are Korea's 23 operating nuclear reactors that provide almost one-third of the country's electricity. They are located at four sites: Kori (six reactors) in Gijang, Busan; Hanul (six reactors) in Uljin, North Gyeongsang Province; Wolsong (five reactors) in Gyeongju, North Gyeongsang Province; and Hanbit (six reactors) in Yeonggwang, South

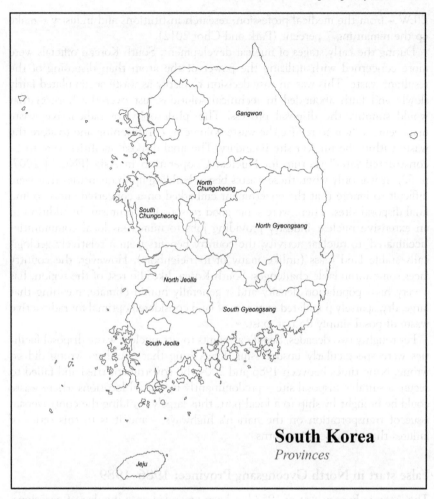

Figure 7.1 South Korea map

Jeolla Province.[3] Hanbit is the only plant on the west coast. The reactors generate roughly 2,300 drums of low and intermediate level waste (LILW) each year ("S. Korea's First Nuclear Waste Facility Gets Go-Ahead" 2014). As of 31 July 2014, 92,052 200-liter drums of LILW had been accumulated and stored on site at the plants; capacity is 115,669 200-liter drums, slightly smaller than a 55 gallon drum (Korea Hydro and Nuclear Power Co. Ltd. 2014). This amounts to about 79 percent of the country's low and intermediate level waste total. Of the four, Hanbit is the closest to reaching its limit at 92+ percent full, with Hanul at 84+ percent, Wolsong at 82+ percent and Kori at 68+ percent. The Korea Atomic Energy Research Institute (KAERI) and Korea Nuclear Fuel Co. (KNFC) produce about 14 percent of the national total, and other sources of

LILW – from the medical profession, research institutions and industry – make up the remaining 7 percent (Park and Choi 2012).

During the early stages of nuclear development, South Korean officials were more concerned with utilizing the power of the atom than disposing of the resultant waste. This was an easy decision to justify as waste accumulated fairly slowly and faith abounded in technical solutions just over the horizon that would simplify the disposal process. The 'philosophy' of radioactive waste management "was to reduce the waste volume by conditioning and to store the waste within the nuclear site boundary. The final disposal facilities were to be constructed later" (Forum for Nuclear Cooperation in Asia [FNCA] 2007, p. 50). It was only when these wastes began building up in quantities that were difficult to ignore that the government embarked on a concerted effort to find final disposal sites. There were some good reasons for optimism. In addition to an extensive nuclear industry providing jobs to numerous local communities 'acclimated' to nuclear activity, the country benefits from a relatively geologically stable land mass (unlike many of its neighbors). However, the country faces some formidable challenges: South Korea, like the rest of the region, has a very high population density and a generally humid climate, meaning that large, dry, sparsely populated expanses of land considered optimal for radioactive waste disposal simply do not exist.

For roughly two decades, Seoul's attempts to site nuclear waste disposal facilities were spectacularly unsuccessful. Everything that could go wrong did go wrong. Nine times between 1986 and 2004 the government tried and failed to secure a suitable disposal site – predominantly in coastal locations where waste could be brought by ship to a local port, thus largely avoiding the controversial issue of transportation on the nation's highways – and it is to this series of failures that the discussion turns.

False start in North Gyeongsang Province: 1986–1989

The Atomic Energy Act of 1958 has been amended on a number of occasions, but the most important amendment for the purposes of this study occurred on 12 May 1986, when Act No. 3850 gave KAERI responsibility for nuclear waste management and provided a legal basis for the establishment of a fund to finance its work (Organisation for Economic Co-operation and Development/Nuclear Energy Agency [OECD/NEA] 2009, p. 3). From the start, the plan was to provide a comprehensive solution to the country's nuclear waste problems, meaning that all categories of waste were to be buried in facilities in the same location.

KAERI tasked the Korea Power Engineering Corporation (KOPEC) with conducting a nationwide search that began in July 1987. A preliminary list of 89 candidate sites was narrowed down to 25; from those, the Ministry of Science and Technology (MOST) selected Uljin, Yeongdeok and Youngil in North Gyeongsang Province due in part to their proximity to the country's east coast nuclear plants. Earlier site investigations for North Gyeongsang's power plants provided KOPEC with a valuable source of geological data. In December 1988, government scientists travelled to the province to conduct survey work, having given little if any thought to how the host communities might react (Yoon, Ro and Park 1999, p. 50). Distraught local residents were quick to register their displeasure. In Yeongdeok, the locus of opposition was a community group numbering roughly 3,000 that held rallies at an elementary school and blocked highways (Yongsoo Hwang, personal communication, 18 September 2014; Choi 2005, p. 232). By the end of 1989, MOST had backed down in the face of strong public hostility at all sites. This successful social activism came at a politically charged time; South Korea's first free presidential election was held in December 1987.

False start offshore: Anmyeondo Island, 1990–1993

Still smarting from the failure in North Gyeongsang, the federal government and KAERI conducted a review and concluded that the prospect of hosting radioactive waste storage/disposal facilities did not provide sufficient incentive for communities to say yes. What was needed was a more attractive offer and it was determined that the inclusion of a 'nuclear research center' would provide this.

In 1990, MOST selected three potential sites: Anmyeondo Island, South Chungcheong Province; Buan-gun, North Jeolla Province; and Yeonggwang-gun, South Jeolla Province. Of those, Anmyeondo Island was considered the frontrunner and in confidential discussions between the president of KAERI and the South Chungcheong governor, KAERI offered to broaden the project's appeal by committing to the construction of a KAERI/Nuclear Environment Technology Center (NEMAC) branch office. NEMAC then held discussions with provincial officials on the purchase of land to establish the Yellow Sea Scientific Research Complex. The complex would provide low level radioactive waste (LLRW) disposal and spent fuel storage as well as spent fuel reprocessing research and development. Negotiations moved quickly, with KAERI committing to purchase 1,930 square miles of land with the disposal tunnels to be located in the seabed or on land depending on the results of the site investigation. In June, the two sides signed an agreement to this effect that was approved by the Atomic Energy Commission (AEC). However, riots broke out in October when the details leaked to the press, and in early November a committee was created to coordinate the efforts of the various protest groups.[4] Large and sometimes violent demonstrations ensued, combined with acts of civil disobedience ranging from the burning of effigies to parents keeping their children home from school to attacks on police stations and patrol cars being set alight. The furor forced MOST chief Dr. K. M. Chung to publicly announce on 9 November that the government would not force the facilities on the community without their consent, contradicting his own statement that Anmyeondo was to be the nation's radioactive waste disposal site made only 2 days earlier. It was not enough – Chung resigned on 10 November and the project was cancelled (Yongsoo Hwang, personal communication, 18 September 2014; Park, Pomper and Scheinman 2010, p. 2).

Figure 7.2 Anmyeondo Island protestors burn pro-nuclear effigies in 1990

Not surprisingly, by 1991 the issue of radioactive waste management had started to seep into the national consciousness and was becoming an election issue. As a result, there was a growing recognition within government circles that radioactive waste disposal was more than simply a technological challenge and some tentative steps were taken to address the social and economic aspects of hazardous facility siting.

In April, five universities (Seoul National, Choongnam National, Cheonbook National, Kyemyung and Kwandong) were contracted to develop cooperative siting proposals. In December the group, led by Seoul National's Institute of Social Studies, identified six potential host sites: Gosung-gun and Yangyang-gun in Gangwon Province; Uljin-gun and Yungil-gun in North Gyeongsang Province; Changheung-gun in South Jeolla Province; and Taean-gun in South Gyeongsang Province. In May, the Korea Institute of Geoscience and Mineral Resources (KIGAM) was tasked with determining the feasibility of siting storage/disposal facilities on small islands and in disused mines. Significantly, KIGAM reported back in December that such sites were not suitable for radioactive waste (Yongsoo Hwang, personal communication, 18 September 2014).

Box 7.1   Island disposal in Taiwan and the view from South Korea

Lanyu (Orchid) Island lies 30 miles east of the southernmost point of Taiwan. Most of the 4,000 residents of the 17 square mile island are Tao aboriginals. From 1982 to 1996, roughly 100,000 drums of predominantly

---

power reactor LLRW were shipped to the southern tip of the island and buried in trenches without residents' consent. When the Taiwan Power Company (Taipower) was building the facility, it held public meetings and posted signs in Chinese. Lanyu Nuclear Waste Manager Chih Gow-Tay later conceded:

> It is possible the local language doesn't have the words "waste materials" and the picture on the noticeboard looked like a can. They may also have used the word "can" to explain things to the residents. So they might have thought it was a cannery factory.
>
> (Willacy 2013)

The islanders have been protesting ever since, with particularly large demonstrations occurring in 2002 and 2012. Taipower was forced to renege on a promise to remove the waste in 2002 due to the inability to find another willing host community either inside or outside of Taiwan's borders (for example, Russia, China and North Korea) and is clearly going to miss its 2016 deadline as well. In the meantime, the company has been making payments, providing subsidies and offering benefits – including free electricity, scholarships for higher education and half-price transportation to the mainland – to the community and this has started to create a culture of dependency. According to Township Secretary Huang Cheng-de, "Taipower gives us quite a bit of money and our people are becoming pretty reliant." Making the situation worse, drums have been corroding (forcing the company to repackage a significant amount of the waste), a radiation leak outside the facility was detected in 2011 and there is evidence of rising cancer rates. The Fukushima accident exacerbated fears and invigorated calls for the waste to be removed ("Orchid Island Launches New Protests against Nuclear Waste" 2002; "Nuclear Disposal Site Still Unknown" 2008; Lok-sin 2012; "For Taiwan Aborigines, Nuclear Waste Is Blessing and Curse" 2012; Willacy 2013).

During the 1980s and 1990s, the South Korean government sent many residents from prospective host communities to the island to see a LLRW disposal facility in operation. However, these visits stopped in the 2000s, coincidently when volunteerism was embraced as an integral part of the siting process. No doubt the increasing unpopularity of the site played a large part in this decision. South Korean anti-nuclear groups did make reference to salt corrosion of the drums at Lanyu when Gyeongju was selected as the host for the republic's LILW, but differences between the designs of the two facilities – shallow trench system versus underground rock cavern – limited its resonance with the local community and the media.

In October, the national government made its first explicit acknowledgment of the public as a stakeholder, announcing a new policy of 'openness' and asking local communities to volunteer in return for regional development assistance. To help facilitate this process the Korea Nuclear Energy Foundation (KNEF) was created in March 1992 "to promote a proper understanding of the peaceful use of nuclear energy among the public." MOST chief J. Kim visited seven provinces to elicit support from local officials and the new policy appeared to have the desired effect: 44 communities submitted petitions to be considered as potential hosts. Seven were selected for further investigation, but the government decided to keep the exact locations secret, only revealing the provinces – North Gyeongsang, South Gyeongsang, South Jeolla, South Chungcheong and Gangwon. But the site in South Chungcheong was soon discovered to be Anmyeondo Island. Compounding the problem, the universities' study was released the day after Christmas, and also identified Anmyeondo Island as a candidate. The publicity triggered violent protests on the island and in North Gyeongsang Province. Any remaining goodwill was shattered in January 1993 when Mr. Y. N. Kim, a leader of the prodisposal groups on the island, informed the press that MOST and KAERI had secretly assisted the supporters' efforts. MOST chief J. Kim resigned shortly after this revelation (Cho and Whang 2009; KNEF n.d.).

False start in South and North Gyeongsang provinces: 1993–1994

In November 1993, local residents in Jangan-eup, Yangsan-gun, South Gyeongsang and Geeseong-myeon, Uljin-gun, North Gyeongsang petitioned MOST to be considered as disposal sites. In January 1994, the federal government announced the "Radioactive Waste Management Project Stimulation and Facility's Surrounding Region" law, which committed ₩50 billion in regional development funding to the selected host area, and an interministerial Radioactive Waste Management Project Stimulation Committee was established to provide institutional guidance.

A special siting committee was established in Jangan-eup in March 1994 and KAERI responded by opening an office to conduct outreach with the community.[5] However, this prompted a series of demonstrations that persuaded the national government to terminate all siting activities in May. In Geeseong-myeon, almost 60 percent of eligible voters petitioned MOST again in mid-May 1994. A week later, a local newspaper reported on the petition at about the same time that activities at Jangan-eup were being halted. This set off a series of protests by residents, people from neighboring communities and antinuclear activists that made national newspaper headlines for weeks, effectively killing the proposal (Yongsoo Hwang, personal communication, 18 September 2014; Cho and Whang 2009).

False start offshore: Gulup Island, 1994–1995

In response to these failures, the government created the Radioactive Waste Management Project Agency taskforce under the leadership of the Prime Minister. The taskforce revisited the six sites identified by the universities' study, Jangan-eup (based on the support that community had exhibited in its petition) as well as three small islands, despite KIGAM's December 1991 finding that islands were not suitable for radioactive waste disposal. On 22 December 1994, based on the taskforce's recommendation, the AEC selected Gulup Island – a 1.7-square-mile fishing community of less than a dozen households roughly 25 miles southwest of Incheon International Airport – as the nation's radioactive waste storage/disposal site. The government's intention was to relocate Gulup's residents in return for financial compensation and the locals expressed a willingness to go along, at least initially. Following consultation with the IAEA, the AEC selection became law in February 1995. However, during characterization work, KIGAM discovered an active fault line 1 mile away (Yongsoo Hwang, personal communication, 18 September 2014; Park et al. 2010, p. 2). At the same time, the Federation for Environmental Movement (KFEM) and smaller grassroots environmental and social groups began to stir up opposition on the island. Similarly, groups in Deokjeok Island and Incheon City, fearing that radioactive waste storage or disposal would adversely impact their fishing trade, tourist industry and traditional way of life, started agitating. In the spring of 1995, 300 Deokjeok Islanders protesting outside MOST's Seoul offices were faced down by riot police and while no serious clashes occurred, injuries were reported at other demonstrations in Seoul and Incheon. The government was then forced into an embarrassing retreat, as it became clear that in its haste to link a willing host with its foundering radioactive waste management plan, Gulup's acquiescence had convinced the government to commit completely to the island before determining whether the location was geologically safe. The government announced the decision to stop all further siting work on 16 December 1995.

New organizational approach, same result: 1996–2001

Gulup encapsulated every problem associated with the government's waste management strategy: lack of information about the proposed facilities; excessive secrecy in the decision-making process; public hearings that were more about style than substance; and "forceful countermeasures . . . against local residents' resistance" (Jang and Kang 2012, p. 5; Sayvetz 2012). Recognizing that the failure was at least partly organizational, in 1996 the government brought in a new ministry and divided responsibility for waste management: MOST/KAERI was charged with developing technology for the final disposal of spent fuel but was relieved of responsibility for finding a disposal site for LILW and an interim storage site for spent fuel; these tasks were assigned to the Ministry of

Commerce, Industry and Energy (MOCIE) and its subsidiary the Korea Electric Power Corporation (KEPCO). The AEC also decided to create a dedicated radioactive waste management organization – the Nuclear Environment Technology Institute (NETEC) – under KEPCO in June 1996.[6] NETEC wrote a report in 1997 that formed the basis for a new radioactive waste management policy that the AEC announced in September 1998, based on five fundamental principles: direct control by the government; safety as the top priority; emphasis on minimization of waste generation; adoption of a 'polluter pays' principle; and a commitment to transparency of the siting process. The centerpiece of the new strategy would be a national radioactive waste management complex constructed in two stages. Stage one would include a LILW repository with a 100,000-drum capacity accepting waste by 2008 and an interim spent fuel storage facility with a 2,000-metric-ton uranium (MTU) capacity built by 2016. Stage two would expand the capacity of the LILW repository to 800,000 drums and the spent fuel storage facility to 20,000 MTU. The AEC thought the most likely disposal medium/technology were rock cavern and/or near surface vault. Conceptual design studies and preliminary safety assessments had been completed for rock caverns in 1993 and NETEC would do the same for near surface vault in 1999 (FNCA 2007, pp. 50–51, 59). The complex would also house research and development facilities for volume reduction, safety assessment, storage and transportation, as well as spent fuel reprocessing. The National Assembly then chose to replace the AEC itself in December 1996 with an independent Nuclear Safety and Security Commission.

After 12 years of rejection, the government quite sensibly chose not to nominate more candidate sites in 1998 and 1999. This was a period described as "defensive and passive," with "not in my term" attitudes prevalent (Cho and Whang 2009). However, in September 1998, MOCIE did announce plans to build a disposal facility for all categories of waste by 2008 (Nuclear Threat Initiative [NTI] updated 2004). But it was not just its own radioactive waste that South Koreans had to worry about at this time. In September 1996, South Korean officials offered $1 million worth of disposal equipment to dissuade Russia from dumping radioactive waste into the ocean. Then in January 1997, Taipower signed a contract to ship up to 200,000 drums of LILW to North Korea at a price of $1,151 per drum. Under pressure from Seoul (where officials feared the North Koreans would dump the waste in abandoned mines near the Korean Demilitarized Zone [DMZ]) and Washington, DC, Taiwan insisted that several contract terms had not been fulfilled, so no waste was shipped and no payments were made to Pyongyang (NTI updated 2004). Interestingly, South Korean officials would voluntarily and enthusiastically revisit the subject of North Korea 3 years later. In October 2000, a proposal was floated to build a disposal facility north of the 38th parallel in return for energy aid. Officials thought it "would be a good example of mutual interests served between the two Koreas" (NTI updated 2004).

By 2000, the government had rethought its siting strategy again. In June the ₩50 billion regional development fund was increased to ₩300 billion with all local governments within a 3 mile radius of proposed facilities to be compensated "for the psychological burden on residents." At the same time, NETEC mailed letters of invitation to volunteer to 46 coastal local governments and followed up with local government briefings and a nationwide television/radio/newspaper information campaign. A tour of Japan's Rokkasho spent fuel reprocessing facility was also conducted. By June 2001, seven local governments had expressed interest: Yeonggwang-gun, Gangjin-gun, Jindo-gun and Wando-gun in South Jeolla Province; Gochang-gun in North Jeolla Province; Boryung-gun in South Chungcheong Province; and Uljin-gun in North Gyeongsang Province. Wando voluntarily dropped out and public opposition was widespread. In Jindo-gun, for example, protesters cited reports linking radioactivity with Down syndrome in babies and deformities in fish and animals as the sorts of risks posed by radioactive waste (Jang and Kang 2012, p. 10). Hundreds of protestors were injured by police during demonstrations, which "became a showcase for the environmentalists to question the legitimacy of the government's actions." The government responded by stating publicly that the police action was a legitimate response to maintain order and "protect local residents and government workers from the violent and irrational mobs that attacked the mayor" (Jang and Kang 2012, pp. 8–9). Any hope of exploring what those expressions of interest might mean was extinguished in 2001 by local government vetoes.

Some observers have noted that while the siting effort failed again, encouragingly there was more support, both publicly and at the government level, than in the past but upcoming local elections in 2002 might explain some local and national elected officials' reticence to invite siting authorities into their backyards at that time (Yongsoo Hwang, personal communication, 18 September 2014; Cho and Whang 2009; Lee 2011; World Nuclear Association [WNA] updated 2014; University of Illinois, Engineering Department n.d., p. 32).

The emergence of genuine volunteerism: 2002–2004

According to Cho and Whang, despite the years of frustration, by the beginning of the new millennium, there were reasons for cautious optimism: some communities had begun considering radioactive waste disposal as an economic revitalization opportunity and the press, which had been preoccupied with the controversial aspects of radioactive waste, began to take a more balanced approach in its reporting on the disposal search (Cho and Whang 2009).

In December 2002 KHNP – having been granted waste management responsibilities in April 2001 as a result of the partial deregulation of KEPCO and having expressed a preference for sites in communities that already hosted nuclear power plants[7] – identified four candidate sites: Geunnam-myeon, Uljin-gun, North Gyeongsang Province; Namjeong-myeon, Yungdeok-gun, North Gyeongsang Province; Hongneung-eup, Yeonggwang-gun, South Jeolla Province; and Haeri-myeon, Gochang-gun, North Jeolla Province. In February 2003, MOCIE (which, with the Ministries of Information and Communication and

Science and Technology, would shortly become the Ministry of Knowledge Economy) publicly announced the sites, stressing that only communities submitting formal applications would be considered. According to the *Chosun Ilbo*, the intention was to move ahead with detailed geological surveys, consult with local residents and reach a final decision on building two facilities – one in the east (North Gyeongsang) and one in the west (Jeollas) – by March 2004 (Eui-dal 2003). While wildly optimistic, the logic was sound. By proposing sites in distinct geographical regions, siting officials were trying to share the burden.

In April 2003, the pot was sweetened again with the inclusion of the Proton-Based Engineering Technology Development Project (proton accelerator) in the package of incentives, and on 26 June the government announced that it would accept petitions from local governments until 15 July. Officials in Gunsan-si in North Jeolla Province and Samcheok-si in Gangwon Province expressed interest but were denied by geology and public opinion. The day before the government's deadline ran out, the mayor of Buan-gun in North Jeolla Province submitted a petition to host the facilities on Wido Island (population 1,200), evidently without getting consent from the Municipal Assembly. The government also promised to provide $500 million in compensation 'for possible dangers,' two new golf practice ranges and an additional campus of the state-run Chŏnbuk National University (NTI updated 2004). The offer was approved by the Buan Congress 10 days later (Yongsoo Hwang, personal communication, 18 September 2014; Cho and Whang 2009). This led to sustained and violent opposition from environmental groups and local residents who felt that officials (the mayor in particular) were trying to get the facility sited surreptitiously ("Gyeongju Sets Nuclear Dump Project in Motion after 19-Year Delay" 2005). Opposition tactics included highway blockades, house-to-house petition drives and parents preventing their children from going to school. Tactics directed specifically at supporters included assaults (teachers were targeted and the Buan mayor was hospitalized after being attacked during a meeting with local residents who accused him of acting under instruction from the provincial governor), intimidating phone calls and letters, house break-ins, destruction of property and the burning of effigies (Kang 2004, slide 17; Yongsoo Hwang, personal communication, 18 September 2014; NTI updated 2004). One editorial declared that environmental groups scared female high school students by telling them that the disposal facility would cause them to give birth to deformed babies (Jeong-hoon 2010). Like the Deokjeok Islanders before them, about 100 Buan-gun residents travelled to Seoul to protest in front of the National Assembly building and succeeded in making national news (Jang and Kang 2012, p. 9).

On 17 September, in an attempt to sweeten the deal further, MOCIE Minister Yun Chin Shik announced that the government was considering the construction of a presidential villa on Wido Island to show support for the waste facility. However, a week later members of the National Assembly accused KHNP of concealing documents that revealed problems at the Wido site. According to lawmakers, KHNP requested, and the Korea Advanced Institute of Science and Technology (KAIST) and the Samil Accounting Corporation wrote, an economics and safety study that found it would cost an additional $564 million to construct the design proposed by the government and KHNP. KHNP officials responded that they did not make the report public because it contained so many negative points that the construction design was effectively not feasible. In an attempt to win back some public trust, the South Korean government hosted a symposium on the safety and development of nuclear waste facilities from 2 to 4 November. Local experts as well as experts from foreign countries attended, discussing the safety of nuclear waste facilities, the development of neighboring areas, the impact of waste facilities on the local economy and the health risks of radiation. The symposium also included a discussion session between nuclear experts and residents of Buan (NTI updated 2004). However, the damage had been done: the combination of government missteps and aggressive opposition tactics contributed greatly to the overwhelming rejection of the project in a local referendum. The government had no choice but to terminate all work, and the final indignity came on 12 December when Minister Shik announced his intention to resign (Yongsoo Hwang, personal communication, 18 September 2014; NTI updated 2004).

In February 2004, the Ministry of Knowledge Economy (MKE) announced a new site selection procedure – local residents would petition to host a disposal facility. The government also hoped to foster more productive dialogue with communities by creating formal discussion groups such as the Energy Round-Table Conference and the Energy Policy Civil-Governmental Forum (Ko 2004). Ultimately 10 communities petitioned, but none of their local governments submitted the requisite preliminary applications to move the process forward (Park et al. 2009, p. 478). In December 2004, this lack of progress led to the complete separation of the LILW from the spent fuel disposal efforts. The results were not long in coming.

Success in Gyeongju: 2005–present

On 11 March 2005, MKE established a Site Selection Committee to ensure "transparency and fairness" in the siting process. Twenty civilian experts from diverse fields – including science, technology, culture, society, media, law and civil society groups – were chosen to supervise the selection process. Subcommittees included site suitability, cooperation and public census (Park et al. 2009, p. 478; Cho and Whang 2009; Lee 2011). The federal government had also begun to appreciate the value of engaging experts beyond the narrow nuclear field, specialists in areas such as public relations, communication and sociology (Cho and Whang 2009). In addition, the government ran commercials on national television that featured bright yellow gloves, clothes, shoes and tools as examples of the sorts of lightly radioactive materials that would be buried in a LLRW facility (Jang and Kang 2012, p. 10).

On 31 March, the Special Act on Support for Areas Hosting Low and Intermediate Level Radioactive Waste Disposal Facilities was passed. For the first time, a package of benefits and protections for prospective host communities was backed by law. The package included special financial support (a 'special support fee' of ₩300 billion and a 'local support fee' of ₩637,500 per 200-liter waste drum); entry fees; relocation of the KHNP headquarters; a guarantee that site selection would be determined by resident voting in accordance with the Referendum Act; and a commitment that the selection plan, site survey results and selection process would be implemented openly and transparently with open forums for local residents (Park et al. 2009, p. 478; Lee 2011).

On 16 June, MKE announced the new selection procedures. A three-step process was required for local governments to be considered: local governors, with consent from their councils, applied to host; site suitability assessments were conducted; and for eligible sites, referenda were held. Then it was essentially a beauty contest – the site with the largest percentage of favorable responses won. Four local governments qualified: Gyeongju-si, Pohang-si and Yeongdeok-gun in North Gyeongsang Province on the southeast coast; and Gunsan-si in North Jeolla Province on the central west coast. With 11 reactors, it is no surprise that locations in North Gyeongsang Province kept coming up in site searches. The province is also home to the country's ruling, and pronu-clear, Saenuri Party and current Governor Kim Kwan-yong is a strong sup-porter of nuclear energy (Yongsoo Hwang, personal communication, 4 November 2014).

On 3 November 2005, based on 89.5 percent approval of the 70.8 percent of local residents who voted, the provincial city of Gyeongju was selected as the candidate national disposal site (Cho 2010). While the level of community support in Gyeongju as measured by the referendum was remarkable, the votes in the other three other candidates were only slightly less impressive: 84.4 percent approval in Gunsan with 70.2 percent voter turnout; 79.3 percent approval in Yeongdeok with 80.2 percent voter turnout; and 67.5 percent approval in Pohang with 47.7 percent voter turnout (Park et al. 2009, p. 478). KRMC Vice President Yong-Rae Lee later remarked that after the painful experiences of the last 20 years, "NIMBY [not in my backyard] became WIMBY [welcome in my backyard]" (Lee 2014). Importantly, South Korea had been providing progressively more autonomy to local governments at the expense of the provinces, leading to greater acceptance of the cities as the legitimate host communities whose consent was required before any site characterization work could go forward. And the selection of Gyeongju led to mixed reactions from the unsuccessful candidates as well as neighboring communities. While there was some anger that the region was about to become the nation's radioactive waste disposal home – Ulsan Metropolitan City, roughly 90 minutes south of Gyeongju, raised a constitutional appeal against the facility – the prevailing feeling in Gunsan, Yeongdeok and Pohang was disappointment that they had missed out on an opportunity to benefit from the economic development assis-tance that was being provided to Gyeongju; indeed, those lobbying hardest in favor of hosting the disposal facility labeled the opposition communists.

Located in Bonggil-ri, Yangbuk-myeon, Gyeongju-si, the Wolsong Low- and Intermediate-Level Radioactive Waste Disposal Center is bounded by a national park to the north and the Wolsong nuclear power plant to the south (Park et al. 2009, p. 479). The complex features two visitors' areas: a 'free visit area' right on the shore and a 'restricted visit area' further inland that includes the surface facilities (Lee 2014).

On 15 January 2007, KHNP submitted a license application to construct and operate the Wolsong Low-and Intermediate-Level Radioactive Waste Disposal Center to the Ministry of Education, Science and Technology (MEST). The main technical review consisted of three rounds of questions and answers between a multidisciplinary Korea Institute of Nuclear Safety (KINS) Review Team (KRT) and KHNP. External experts were also engaged, including an IAEA International Review Team peer review of the application program – it was felt that the agency's imprimatur would improve public confidence and acceptability ("IAEA Reviews Planned South Korean Waste Site" 2007). When it was satisfied with the completeness of the license application, the KRT drafted a Safety Evaluation Report (SER) and submitted it to the Special Committee on Nuclear Safety, an expert body within the Nuclear Safety and Security Commission (NSSC).[8] Once the KRT addressed the Special Committee's comments, a final SER was submitted to MEST. MEST then sent the SER to the NSSC for approval, which was duly given. Reflecting on the significance of the achievement at a ceremony for the beginning of construction, KHNP declared that licensing "proves natural environment conservation and sustainable nuclear power through safe disposal of radioactive waste, which serves as a precondition for nuclear power" (KHNP Press Release 2007). MEST issued the license in July 2008. Construction began the next month (Park et al. 2009, pp. 489–490).

Operations are expensive by international standards: each 200-liter waste drum will cost $1,200 to dispose at the facility. In addition, the government made a large financial and scientific infrastructure investment in the area: the ₩300 billion grant; the relocation of KHNP headquarters; the construction of a proton accelerator and related research and development in Hwachun-ri, Gyeongju-si; and a long-term commitment of federal support.[9] Significantly, a law was passed that guaranteed that Gyeongju would not be considered as a possible site for future spent fuel storage (Park et al. 2010, p. 3). However, the incentives package has generated its own controversy. The disposal center is in the village of Bonggil, which lies on the coast, but the city of Gyeongju is about 18 miles northwest. Gyeongju – a popular tourist destination that is home to Gyeongju University (and two Buddhist universities), Gyeongju Hospital and the proton accelerator – is making the not unreasonable argument that KHNP should be headquartered in this business district. Bonggil-ri is making the entirely reasonable counterargument that because it is bearing the burden of the disposal center, the village is entitled to reap some of the benefits, and since the proton accelerator is already in Gyeongju then the KHNP headquarters should be in Bonggil-ri (Yongsoo Hwang, personal communication, 17 October 2014). As of this writing, a decision has not been made on where Korea Hydro will be based.

Box 7.2   KORAD's low and intermediate level radioactive waste disposal center design

Overall Aerial View

Figure 7.3 Aerial view of the disposal facility

The roughly 0.8 square mile cave site contains a disposal facility with an initial capacity of 100,000 200-liter drums plus a 7,000-drum capacity examination compound. Disposal will occur 262–426 feet below ground in six 27.3×50-meter (89×164 foot) silos. Each silo will hold 16,700 drums. Sets of 16 drums will be encased in concrete boxes. Each silo will be capped with crushed rock and shotcrete; the construction and operations tunnels will be plugged with concrete and crushed rock (Park et al. 2009; KRWMC 2010; Lee 2011).

Construction began in 2007 and was completed in June 2014 (on schedule) at a cost of $1.53 billion. Construction of the second, near-surface phase of the repository, which will add a further 125,000 drums of space in a 764,000 square foot disposal facility, began in January 2012 and is expected to be complete by the end of 2019 ("First Phase of Korean Waste Facility Opens" 2014; Peachey 2014; KORAD Brochure 2014, p. 12). Total planned capacity is 800,000 drums.

To minimize waste volumes to the greatest extent possible before disposal, volume reduction processes, such as drying and compaction, are under-taken at the reactor sites before LLRW is packaged for disposal. In response to concerns about safety, KHNP committed to vitrify ILRW before burial to increase public acceptance.[10] Surface facilities at the center include waste reception and storage buildings as well as public access areas and a visitors center (the 'KORADIUM') (KORAD Brochure 2014, p. 38). The disposal center also uses a dedicated transport ship, the HJ *Cheongjeongnuri*, to bring waste from other power plants directly to Wolsong Harbor.

As required by law, the facility was designed to prevent failure due to natural phenomena, earthquakes in particular but also flooding, extreme winds, landslides and sedimentation. KHNP was expected to demonstrate that the facility would provide a standard of radiation protection for humans and the environment over a period of 1,000 years. "If the peak dose or peak risk do not occur during 1,000 years, the KHNP performs a safety assessment up to 1,000,000 years after facility closure." KHNP evaluated active and passive institutional control of the site for 100 years after the end of disposal operations. Various postclosure safety assessment scenarios were considered, including human intrusion caused by drilling into a disposal silo. It was estimated that the silos would completely degrade after 1,400 years due to corrosion of the steel reinforcement and the concomitant expansion of the corrosion products, causing the concrete to crack (Park et al. 2009, p. 485). All of KHNP's responsibilities were transferred to the Korea Radioactive Waste Management Corporation (KRMC) in January 2009 and KRMC was renamed the Korea Radioactive Waste Agency (KORAD) in July 2013. The facility will receive waste for the next 60 years before being closed and sealed.

In March 2008, the Radioactive Waste Management Act was passed. The Act facilitated the establishment of a radioactive waste management fund and the KRMC in January 2009. With a staff of almost 250, the KRMC was created to be the sole agency responsible for radioactive waste management and its broad responsibilities were sixfold:

1   transport and disposal of LILW;
2   safe construction and operation of the Wolsong disposal facility;
3   administration of the radioactive waste management fund;
4   derivation of a social consensus on interim management of spent fuel;
5   research and development on radioactive waste disposal and spent fuel management;
6   establishment of credibility with the Korean public (Park et al. 2009, p. 491; Lee 2011).

In December 2010, KRMC commenced limited operation of the facility, accepting the first waste shipment – 1,000 drums from the Uljin power plant – for temporary, outside storage while the disposal silos were completed. The event did not go completely smoothly. About 50 local politicians and civic activists delayed the delivery for 2 hours, protesting that the unfinished facility was unsafe (Tae-gyu 2010).

Full start-up was delayed by the NSSC because of public concerns about safety (Cho 2014a). There were two main drivers of this concern: the March 2011 accident in Fukushima, Japan, which increased sensitivity across the island about the extent to which South Korea relied on nuclear power; and a domestic scandal involving faked safety tests for critical nuclear plant equipment and employees at the state-financed design company taking bribes from testing company officials in return for accepting those substandard parts (Cho 2014b).[11] The combination of major accident and scandal has required a concerted effort to regain public trust. NSSC chairman Lee Un-chul believes that progress is being made: "If self-evaluated, our score is only in the fifties, compared with that in the thirties last year . . . we are making headway as we can correct even if the government if it does wrong" (Cho 2014b). With that in mind, the NSSC worked patiently to reassure the South Korean public that the facility would be safe. A slightly different motivation was ascribed to the commission by a senior government official who requested anonymity. The nine-member regulatory body is chaired by a nuclear engineer and made up of two mechanical engineers, a nuclear engineer, a microbiologist, the director of nuclear safety at KINS, a professor of public administration, a lawyer and the energy and climate chair at the KFEM. According to this official, a majority of members do not have strong opinions, so the antinuclear minority has a fair degree of influence; as a result, the slow-rolling reflected their predilections as much as careful regulation (senior South Korean official, personal communication, 12 November 2014).

On 11 December 2014, the NSSC announced that it had completed all safety inspections and the facility had been approved for full operation which commenced on 13 July 2015.

Conclusion

In 2012, Jiho Jang of Hankuk University and Minah Kang of the Ewha Womans University observed: "In many respects, finding a site for the radioactive waste disposal facility is one of the most contentious and complex policy issues in the history of Korean policy making" (Jang and Kang 2012, p. 5). For 20 years beginning in 1986, South Korea's search was an abject failure, a cautionary tale. Public opposition to authorities' selected sites was visceral and sometimes violent. Yet, in a remarkable turnaround, KHNP succeeded in finding a host site with strong public support in November 2005. It was a long, difficult road for South Korean siting authorities, a road that would begin and end in North Gyeongsang Province.

When the search commenced, the first site chosen was in North Gyeongsang Province. The logic of colocation was sound: choose a site close to several nuclear plants with surrounding communities that are largely supportive of nuclear activities. This is one very important reason why a disposal facility would eventually be embraced in the same area. But the approach, there in 1986 and in other parts of the country for years afterward, was all wrong. The central government selected sites then tried to convince the local communities to accept those choices. Public resistance finally convinced the government that the top-down approach of 'decide-announce-defend' was unworkable. The embarrassing failure at Gulup Island in 1995 served as the catalyst for the government to progressively rethink its strategy but as officials would learn, sometimes painfully, half-measures are often little better than no measures at all. A consent-based selection process would not be fully embraced until 2004. It took time for Korean officials to adjust to a bottom-up, consent-based approach to siting given the country democratized in the late 1980s; with little experience to draw on, an extended learning period should not be surprising. The presence of reactors does not always guarantee a welcome reception however. Yeonggwang is an interesting case – while it hosts Hanbit's nuclear plant, Yeonggwang is also home to the minority New Politics Alliance for Democracy (NPAD) party, which opposes nuclear power (Yongsoo Hwang, personal communication, 4 November 2014). Thus it is not a 'natural constituency' for nuclear activities in the way North Gyeongsang Province has been.

Along the same lines, it also took siting authorities time to determine exactly what sort of benefits a host community might want and calibrate its compensation package accordingly. The clearest example of this was the regional development fund: in 1994 the government offered ₩50 billion, but over the next few years it became clear that this was not even close to sufficient, so in 2000 the fund was increased to ₩300 billion.

The use of language was an important part of messaging for both sides. The government used the term 'radioactive waste' because of a belief that the public was reasonably familiar with its meaning and an expectation that a significant percentage would associate radiation with its health applications such as x-rays and cancer treatment. The government also hoped that describing the storage/disposal facilities as a "center for management of nuclear energy residual products" would "provide a more professional image." By contrast, opponents – particularly antinuclear and environmental groups – used pejorative terms like 'nuclear garbage' (making a subtle but important link with nuclear weapons) and 'dump' rather than 'waste' and 'facility' (Jang and Kang 2012, p. 6).

Both sides "selectively emphasized, and sometimes hid, critical information as well as exaggerated or distorted facts and information about safety issues." Initially, government officials dismissed opposition concerns, preferring to simply provide more public information about the safety of the proposed facility. When it became clear that this was not working, a more proactive approach was adopted that included field trips to nuclear waste facilities in other countries. There was also a concerted effort to shift the focus of the debate to the economic benefits that would accrue to the host community. At about the same time, opponents – particularly environmental groups – began to place more emphasis on procedural justice as there was much to criticize in the government's secretive decision-making. Opponents also used the Three Mile Island, Chernobyl and Fukushima accidents, as well as a sodium leak at the Monju fast breeder reactor and a criticality accident at Tokaimura in Japan, to indict the entire nuclear industry, willfully ignoring the differences between operations at nuclear reactors and radioactive waste storage/disposal (Jang and Kang 2012, pp. 7–8).[12]

Volunteerism is rarely completely spontaneous. Consequently, the government maintained unofficial contact with certain influential officials and residents in various towns that were considered geologically suitable. This is not unusual. However, for a government with a poor track record this was political dynamite, and when antinuclear groups found out, the communication was portrayed in the worst light possible. Anmyeondo Island was a particularly vivid example of this.

The government also made the classic mistake of prematurely committing to a site, writing the selection of Gulup Island into law in 1995. Unfortunately subsequent site characterization revealed an active fault line that made Gulup completely unsuitable. Such zeal results in a large loss of credibility when siting authorities guess wrong, as they did in this case.

So why specifically was there success in 2005? Three changes in the government's approach explain the reversal. First, to deal with concerns about safety, the waste streams were separated – LILW was deemed a tolerable risk once it became clear that there would not be any accompanying high level waste, even on an interim basis. It is important to remember that while LILW disposal was split off from spent fuel management in December 2004 through a process that had started to take shape in 1996, within 2.5 years the waste streams were brought back together organizationally with passage of the Radioactive Waste Management Act and the creation of the KRMC/KORAD. One of the benefits of this approach is that if KORAD does a good job managing the Wolsong disposal facility, the organization will build public trust and goodwill that can be leveraged to help site a spent fuel storage facility and eventually a final repository. The organization got off to a good start with the Wolsong facility being built on schedule and on budget. However, this also suggests that siting a spent fuel disposal facility will be extremely challenging in the short to medium term.

Second, the Special Act on Support for Areas Hosting Low and Intermediate Level Radioactive Waste Disposal Facilities was enacted to provide financial incentives in order to generate interest amongst prospective host communities. There was more to the deal than simply the direct and indirect financial benefits of the disposal facility; Gyeongju was also rewarded with the relocation of KHNP headquarters and the construction of a proton accelerator. In addition, Gyeongju received a commitment that it would not be considered as a potential spent fuel storage location.[13] This set a high benchmark, raising the question: What sort of package will the government need to offer a community to seriously consider hosting a facility to temporarily store or dispose of spent fuel and high level waste?

Third, a site selection committee was created to enhance transparency in decision-making and residential referenda were instituted to ensure stakeholder participation. Only by engaging with, rather than simply informing, local governments and the public could the siting authorities start to build trust with the stakeholders who would ultimately decide where the disposal facility would be built.

Lessons learned from the Wolsong experience are already being applied to the search for a spent nuclear fuel disposal site. In 2013, a 15-member Public Engagement

Commission made up of nuclear experts, academics, city council members and a representative from an environmental nongovernmental organization was established by the Ministry of Trade, Industry and Energy (MOTIE). Chaired by Seoul National University sociology professor Hong Doo-seung, the commission is scheduled to report back to MOTIE in 2015 and its recommendations will be incorporated into a federal disposal plan ("Dealing with Nuclear Waste" 2014; "As Nuclear Waste Piles Up, South Korea Faces Storage Crisis" 2014).

The South Korean example is enormously instructive as it demonstrates that trust can develop even after years of animosity between the government and its people. The challenge now is to build on that success. Safe operation over the life of the Gyeongju disposal facility will nurture that trust both in the province and throughout the country; conversely, poor operation will undermine goodwill, possibly prompting demands to close the facility, sending the government back to square one again or worse if an accident convinces the public that the responsible authorities cannot manage LILW disposal properly. Failure at Gyeongju will make attempts to site new LILW disposal facilities and provide a national solution to the country's increasingly urgent spent nuclear fuel disposal problem immeasurably harder.

Notes

1 A note on nomenclature: the Korean suffix -*do* equates with province, -*gun* with county, -*si* with city, -*eup* with town, -*myeon* with township and -*ri* with village.
2 A critical assembly contains fissile material and is operated at a low power level to investigate nuclear reactor cores.
3 In 2013, the Korean government renamed the Yonggwang plant Hanbit and the Uljin plant Hanul. According to a *World Nuclear News* report: "Fishermen near the Yonggwang plant catch yellow corvine fish and sell them under the name Yonggwang Gulbi, while the area around the Ulchin plant is known for its crabs. Residents near the plants signed petitions to have the facilities renamed claiming that problems at the plants led to a drop in their sales" ("Korean Nuclear Plants Renamed" 2013).
4 Public fears had already been stoked by a news report that staff at the Yeonggwang nuclear power plant had delivered a "brainless baby" on site (Park 2013, p. 5). While groundless, the propaganda effect of such scare tactics should not be underestimated.
5 Communities living near nuclear power plants in South Korea receive slightly lower electricity prices.
6 The government also created an Atomic Energy Research and Development Fund financed by a KEPCO contribution of ₩1.2 per kilowatt generated annually (NTI updated 2004).
7 The deregulation was 'partial' because while KEPCO was split into seven companies, they are all still strongly influenced by the government.
8 When the NSSC was established in October 2011, the former regulator KINS became a technical support organization.
9 Fifty-five local community projects totaling ₩3.2 trillion (almost $3 billion) were identified by KRMC (Lee 2011).
10 A pilot-scale vitrification facility was constructed in Daejeon in 1999.
11 Investigators discovered that the questionable components were installed in 14 of the country's 23 nuclear power plants. See Sang-Hun 2013.
12 In 1995, a sodium leak at the Monju fast breeder reactor cause a major fire that prompted authorities to shut the facility down for 15 years. The state-owned corporation that ran Monju did not report the accident immediately and tampered with

video footage in an attempt to conceal the seriousness of the damage. In 1999, three workers at the Tokaimura plant were heavily irradiated during the preparation of a batch of fuel for an experimental fast breeder reactor; two later died. More than 400 people received radiation doses of various levels. See Aldrich 2008 (p. 139) and WNA updated 2013.

13 This does not mean that Gyeongju cannot ask to be considered at some point if officials and the community so decide.

References

Aldrich, D., *Site Fights: Divisive Facilities and Civil Society in Japan and the West* (Ithaca, NY: Cornell University Press, 2008).

"As Nuclear Waste Piles Up, South Korea Faces Storage Crisis," *Reuters* (14 October 2014), www.japantimes.co.jp/news/2014/10/14/asia-pacific/nuclear-waste-piles-south-korea-faces-storage-crisis/#.VJifPsAeA

Cho, M., "S. Korea Approves Opening of Low-Radioactive Waste Storage Site," *Reuters* (11 December 2014a), http://news.asiaone.com/news/asia/s-korea-approves-opening-low-radioactive-waste-storage-site

Cho, M., "S. Korea to Store Low Radioactive Waste Next Month at the Earliest," *Reuters* (18 November 2014b), www.reuters.com/article/2014/11/18/us-southkorea-nuclear-idUSKCN0J20K120141118

Cho, S. K., "Stakeholder Engagement for Radioactive Waste Management Policy-Making in Korea," Presentation at the USKI/CSIS Workshop on Nuclear Fuel Cycles and Nuclear Security (10 December 2010), http://csis.org/files/attachments/101210_CHO%20Stakeholder%20Engagement%20for%20Korean%20RWM%20Policy.pdf

Cho, S. K., and Whang, J., "Status and Challenges of Nuclear Power Program and Reflections of Radioactive Waste Management Policy in Korea," Advanced Summer School of Radioactive Waste Disposal with Social-Scientific Literacy, University of California, Berkeley (6 August 2009), http://goneri.nuc.berkeley.edu/pages2009/slides/Whang.pdf

Choi, Y. N., "Nuclear Waste Management: Gaining Public Acceptance," *Journal of East Asian Affairs*, Vol. 19, No. 2 (Fall/Winter 2005).

"Dealing With Nuclear Waste," *Korea Herald* (18 December 2014).

Eui-dal, S., "Radioactive Waste Sites Proposed Again," *Chosun Ilbo* (4 February 2003), http://english.chosun.com/site/data/html_dir/2003/02/04/2003020461009.html

"First Phase of Korean Waste Facility Opens," *World Nuclear News* (12 December 2014), www.world-nuclear-news.org/WR-First-phase-of-Korean-waste-facility-opens-1212145.html

"For Taiwan Aborigines, Nuclear Waste Is Blessing and Curse," *Times Live* (16 September 2012), www.timeslive.co.za/scitech/2012/09/16/for-taiwan-aborigines-nuclear-waste-is-blessing-and-curse

Forum for Nuclear Cooperation in Asia (FNCA), *FNCA Consolidated Report on Radioactive Waste Management (Korea)* (updated March 2007), www.fnca.mext.go.jp/english/rwm/news_img/rwm_cr03_05.pdf

"Gyeongju Sets Nuclear Dump Project in Motion after 19-Year Delay," *Chosun Ilbo* (4 November 2005), http://english.chosun.com/site/data/html_dir/2005/11/04/2005110461001.html

Ha, J., Lim, I. C., Oh, S. Y., and Wu, S., "Research Reactor: A Powerhouse of Nuclear Technology in Korea," *IAEA Papers* (2011), www-pub.iaea.org/MTCD/Publications/PDF/P1575_CD_web/datasets/papers/F4%20Ha.pdf

"High-Flux Advanced Neutron Application Reactor," *Nuclear Threat Initiative* (2010), www.nti.org/facilities/9/

"IAEA Reviews Planned South Korean Waste Site," *World Nuclear News* (24 October 2007), www.world-nuclear-news.org/newsarticle.aspx?id=14278

International Atomic Energy Agency, Country Nuclear Power Profiles, *Republic of Korea* (updated 2012), www-pub.iaea.org/MTCD/Publications/PDF/CNPP2012_CD/countryprofiles/KoreaRepublicof/KoreaRepublicof.htm

Jang, J., and Kang, M., "Framing Analysis of Radioactive Waste Disposal Facility Placement in South Korea," *Western Political Science Association 2012 Meeting*, Portland, Oregon (23 March 2012), http://wpsa.research.pdx.edu/meet/2012/jangandkang.pdf

Jeong-hoon, L., "Memories of Buan," *Dong-A Ilbo* (11 January 2010), www.english.donga.com/srv/service.php3?biid=2010011177198

Kang, C. S., "Radioactive Waste Management in Korea and Public Acceptance," *14th Public Basin Nuclear Conference*, Honolulu, Hawaii (21–25 March 2004), www.aesj.or.jp/~sed/pbnc2004_1/pbnc2004/pbnc2004.3–2.pdf

Ko, K-J., "Eight Local Governments Petition for Radioactive Waste Management Facility," *Dong-A Ilbo* (31 May 2004), http://english.donga.com/srv/service.php3?bicode=020000&biid=2004060161748

Ko, W. I., and Kwon, E., "Implications of the New National Energy Basic Plan for Nuclear Waste Management in Korea," *Energy Policy*, Vol. 37, No. 9 (June 2009).

KORAD Brochure (October 2014), www.korad.or.kr/krmc2011/eng/pr/english_201410.pdf

Korea Hydro and Nuclear Power Co. Ltd., *Low and Intermediate Level Radioactive Wastes* (2014), https://cms.khnp.co.kr/eng/low-and-intermediate-level-radioactive-wastes/.

Korea Hydro and Nuclear Power Co. Ltd., Press Release, "Embarkment of Construction of the Wolsong Low and Intermediate Level Radioactive Waste Disposal Center on Nov. 9" (9 November 2007), https://cms.khnp.co.kr/eng/embarkment-of-construction-of-the-wolsong-low-and-intermediate-level-radioactive-waste-disposal-center-on-nov-9/

Korea Nuclear Energy Foundation, "The Purpose of KNEF" (n.d.), http://eng.knef.or.kr/profile/overview.asp

Korea Nuclear International Cooperation Foundation (KONICOF), "Nuclear Safety Regulation" (2008), http://eng.konicof.or.kr/03_atom/06_safety.php

Korea Radioactive Waste Management Corporation, *Radioactive Waste Management in Korea* (31 May 2010), http://pbadupws.nrc.gov/docs/ML1019/ML101950115.pdf

"Korean Nuclear Plants Renamed," *World Nuclear News* (21 May 2013), www.world-nuclear-news.org/C-Korean_nuclear_plants_renamed-2105134.html

Ku, H., "North Korea Suing Taipower," *Taipei Times* (2 March 2013), www.taipeitimes.com/News/front/archives/2013/03/02/2003556051

Lee, Y., "Experience of Siting Process for Radwaste Disposal Facility in Korea," Korea Radioactive Waste Management Corporation (15 February 2011), www.oecd-nea.org/ndd/pubsiting/documents/15February_Item2a_Y-RLee.pdf

Lok-Sin, L., "Tao Protest against Nuclear Facility," *Taipei Times* (21 February 2012), www.taipeitimes.com/News/front/archives/2012/02/21/2003525985

"Nuclear Disposal Site Still Unknown," *Taipei Times* (28 May 2008), www.taipeitimes.com/News/taiwan/archives/2008/05/28/2003413160

Nuclear Threat Initiative, *South Korea Nuclear Chronology* (last updated September 2004), www.nti.org/media/pdfs/south_korea_nuclear.pdf?_=1316466791

Oak Ridge National Laboratory, "Radioactive Waste Management in Rep. of Korea" (2010), http://curie.ornl.gov/system/files/documents/SEA/NEA_Korea_report_2010.pdf

OECD/NEA, *Nuclear Legislation in OECD and NEA Countries: Regulatory and Institutional Framework for Nuclear Activities – Republic of Korea* (2009), www.oecd-nea.org/law/legislation/korea.pdf

"Orchid Island Launches New Protests against Nuclear Waste," *Kyodo* (6 May 2002), www.thefreelibrary.com/Orchid+Island+launches+new+protests+against+nuclear+wa ste.-a085519940

Park, J. B., Jung, H., Lee, E.-Y., Kim, C.-L., Kim, G.-Y., Kim, K.-S., . . . Kim, K.-D., "Wolsong Low- and Intermediate-Level Radioactive Waste Disposal Center: Progress and Challenges," *Nuclear Engineering and Technology*, Vol. 41, No. 4 (May 2009), www. kns.org/jknsfile/v41/JK0410477.pdf

Park, S. W., Pomper, M. A., and Scheinman, L., "The Domestic and International Politics of Spent Nuclear Fuel in South Korea: Are We Approaching Meltdown?" *Korea Economic Institute*, Academic Paper Series, Vol. 5, No. 3 (March 2010), www.keia.org/ sites/default/files/publications/APS-ParkPomparScheinman.pdf

Park, S. Y., "Constrained Cooperation in South Korea's Nuclear Power Policy and Its Side Effects," Korea Advanced Institute of Science and Technology (September 2013), www.eai.or.kr/data/bbs/kor_report/epik2013_j2.pdf

Park, T., and Choi, J., "Radioactive Waste Disposal Research Division Korea Atomic Energy Research Institute (KAERI)," Hacettepe University, Ankara, Turkey (May 2012), www.nuke.hun.edu.tr/tr/webfiles/Activities/KEPCONF_DOOSAN/Workshop/ Presentations/1_1600_1630_9%20Radioactive%20Waste%20Management%20in%20 Korea-KAERI.pdf

Peachey, C., "Korean Repository Realised," *Nuclear Engineering International* (22 July 2014), www.neimagazine.com/features/featurekorean-repository-realised-4323899/

Sang-Hun, C., "Scandal in South Korea over Nuclear Revelations," *New York Times* (3 August 2013), www.nytimes.com/2013/08/04/world/asia/scandal-in-south-korea-over- nuclear-revelations.html

Sayvetz, L., "South Koreans Stop Plan for Nuclear Waste Dump on Gulup Island, 1994–95," *Global Nonviolent Action Database* (4 April 2012), http://nvdatabase.swarthmore.edu/ content/south-koreans-stop-plan-nuclear-waste-dump-gulup-island-1994–95

"S. Korea Faces Strong Opposition to Nuclear Power Despite Growing Need," *Yonhap News Agency* (15 June 2014), http://english.yonhapnews.co.kr/national/2014/06/15/5 6/0302000000AEN20140615001200320F.html

"S. Korea's First Nuclear Waste Facility Gets Go-Ahead," *Yonhap News Agency* (11 December 2014), http://english.yonhapnews.co.kr/business/2014/12/11/0/0501000000 AEN20141211010000320F.html

Tae-Gyu, K., "First Nuclear Waste Dump Goes Operational," *Korea Times* (24 December 2010), www.koreatimes.co.kr/www/news/biz/2013/08/123_78579.html

University of Illinois Engineering Department, "Radioactive Waste Management: an International Perspective" (n.d.), http://courses.engr.illinois.edu/npre442/International- part1-pdf.pdf

Willacy, M., "Standing on Shaky Ground," *ABC News (Australia)* (9 April 2013), www. abc.net.au/foreign/content/2013/s3733236.htm

World Nuclear Association, *Nuclear Power in South Korea* (updated August 2014), www. world-nuclear.org/info/Country-Profiles/Countries-O-S/South-Korea/

World Nuclear Association, *Tokaimura Criticality Accident 1999* (updated October 2013), http://world-nuclear.org/info/Safety-and-Security/Safety-of-Plants/Tokaimura- Criticality-Accident/

Yoon, J., Ro, S., and Park, H., "Korean Interim Storage Issues and R&D Activities on Spent Fuel Management," *IAEA*, Vienna (January 1999), www.iaea.org/inis/collection/ NCLCollectionStore/_Public/30/003/30003822.pdf

8 "Too fast, too comprehensive and too technocratic"

Low level radioactive waste disposal in Switzerland

Switzerland and nuclear power

Nuclear power provides 40 percent of Switzerland's electricity, but the Swiss have had a somewhat fraught relationship with nuclear energy. In 1984, a referendum on 'a future without further nuclear power stations' was defeated 55 to 45 percent. In September 1990, a referendum on the phasing out of nuclear power was defeated 53 to 47 percent but a referendum placing a 10-year construction moratorium on nuclear plants passed 55 to 45 percent. In May 2003, a referendum on 'electricity without atoms' was defeated 66 to 34 percent. More surprisingly, a referendum to extend the construction moratorium held at the same time was also defeated 58 to 42 percent. Finally, in May 2011, following the Fukushima accident, the government decided that the five operating reactors would not be replaced at the end of their operating lives (van Berg and Damveld 2000, p. 80).[1]

Unlike most other countries, the Swiss federal government has gone some way toward defining an 'affected community' by empowering people living more than 12 miles from a proposed nuclear facility – a fact maybe less remarkable when the Swiss confederation's long tradition of direct public involvement in the political decision-making process is taken into account. As a result, many have regularly made use of their right to participate in the consultation process for nuclear installation licensing. This, combined with a dense population, meant that a siting authority could expect significant 'local' interest when it came to choose a radioactive waste disposal site.[2]

The Atomic Law of 23 December 1959 gave licensing and supervisory authority over radioactive waste storage facilities to the federal government. A 6 October 1978 amendment to the Law declared that producers were responsible for safe radioactive waste disposal but the federal government retained the right, if necessary, to dispose of such waste at the producers' expense. Management of radioactive waste is regulated by the Radiation Protection Law of 22 March 1991 and the Radiation Protection Ordinance of 22 June 1994 (Expert Group for Disposal Concepts for Radioactive Waste [EKRA] 2000, p. 21). Swiss law requires that all radioactive waste be disposed of in repositories that do not depend on active institutional control to provide the necessary level of safety, a requirement that demands deep underground burial (Kowalski and Fritschi 1999, p. 115). For low and intermediate level waste (LILW), this is unusual because most countries prefer the less expensive, less geologically dependent and, as a result, less controversial options of shallow land disposal or aboveground vault disposal. This is a function of several factors, including population density, the importance of tourism to the Swiss economy and a determination by siting authorities that "even a small amount of geological barrier brings enormous safety advantages" (Dr. Charles McCombie and Linda McKinley, personal communication, 16 October 2014). This has also made the low level radioactive waste (LLRW) disposal facility siting process more complex, both technically and politically, than the other case studies examined in this book.

Switzerland has a long history in nuclear research, operating six research reactors and critical assemblies at various times. Three reactors have been decommissioned and three facilities currently operate: the AGN-211 P reactor in Basel went critical in August 1959; the CROCUS critical assembly in Lausanne began operation in July 1983; and the PROTEUS critical assembly in Villigen (Paul Scherrer Institute) began operation in January 1968 (International Atomic Energy Agency [IAEA] Research Reactors Database n.d.; Department of the Environment, Transport, Energy and Communications [DETEC] 2011, p. 7). In addition, two underground laboratories carry out disposal research – the Grimsel Test Site in Canton Berne investigates geology, geophysics, hydrogeology, rock mechanics and nuclide transport; and the Mont Terri Rock Laboratory in Canton Jura examines the hydrogeological, geochemical and rock mechanical properties of clay formations. Waste disposal is not allowed at either of the facilities ("30 Years of History at the Grimsel Test Site (GTS) n.d.; "Short Description of the Mont Terri Project" n.d.).

In 1958, the Swiss Association for Atomic Energy (SVA) was created to promote peaceful uses of nuclear energy. By the 1960s it had become clear that hydro could not keep up with energy demand. Coal and oil plants were protested by environmental groups so the government encouraged its utilities to go nuclear. However, the country's introduction to nuclear power generation was almost disastrous. Construction began on an experimental reactor in an underground rock cavern at Lucens in 1962 and operation commenced 4 years later. On 21 January 1969, the reactor suffered a loss of coolant accident. One fuel rod and its cladding melted, releasing radioactivity into the cavern. Four days after the accident, the residual radioactivity was vented through filters into the atmosphere. "There were no injuries, and there was no release of radioactivity beyond prescribed limits, but the reactor was severely damaged" (Bertini et al. 1980, pp. 121–123). The cavern was sealed, partially filled with concrete in 1992 and finally cleaned out in 2003 ("Switzerland's First Nuclear Plant Decommissioned" 2003).

The track record since then has been far better. Between 1969 and 1984, five power reactors were connected to the grid: Beznau 1 and 2 on an artificial island in the Aar River, Canton Aargau; Mühleberg 1, Canton Berne (an application to build Mühleberg 2 was suspended indefinitely in the wake of Fukushima[3]);

Gösgen, Canton Solothurn; and Leibstadt, Canton Aargau on the German border (WNA updated 2014). But support for nuclear power has been far from universal. For example, protestors occupied the site of the planned Kaiseraugst plant in Canton Aargau for 11 weeks in 1975 and the project was eventually cancelled by the Federal Assembly in 1988 (von Rohr 2008).[4]

In 1972, the nuclear utilities and the federal government founded Nagra (the National Cooperative for the Disposal of Radioactive Waste) to prepare for the disposal of all categories of radioactive waste. LLRW generated by the nuclear power plants is the utilities' financial responsibility until a disposal facility is sealed, at which point the state takes over (Organisation for Economic Co-operation and Development/Nuclear Energy Agency [OECD/NEA] 2003, p. 16). Medical, industrial and research waste is the federal government's responsibility. It has been estimated that 3,250,000 cubic feet of LILW will be generated during the 50-year operating life of the power plants.[5] Beyond temporary storage at each nuclear plant, the Swiss store LLRW at three interim sites:

• the Federal Interim Storage Facility (BZL) at the Paul Scherrer Institute, northwest of Zurich. BZL receives medical, industrial and research waste from around the country;
• ZWIBEZ at the Beznau nuclear plant. ZWIBEZ stores LLRW from the Beznau reactors, spent fuel and vitrified high level waste (Meyer 2006, slide 6);
• the Central Storage Facility (ZZL) in Würenlingen operated by Zwilag. ZZL stores LILW, spent fuel and vitrified high level waste. ZZL has facilities for waste sorting, decontamination and conditioning as well as a plasma furnace for incinerating LLRW – see below (Meyer 2006, slide 7).

Box 8.1   Zwilag's central storage facility

During the mid-1980s, the nuclear power plant operators and the federal government began to show interest in centralized interim waste storage. The municipality of Würenlingen, home to the Federal Institute for Reactor Research before it merged with the Swiss Institute for Nuclear Research in January 1988 to become the Paul Scherrer Institute, agreed to host a facility at a general meeting in 1989 by a vote of 214 to 174. Opponents agitated for a municipality-wide referendum that, when held, affirmed the previous decision by a similarly narrow vote of 707 to 662. In January 1990, the utilities formed a company – Zwilag Zwischenlager Würenlingen AG (Zwilag) – to operate the facility. Public input on matters not critical to safe construction and operation was elicited. Following a 7-year approval process that included numerous public objections from Swiss citizens and neighboring countries, the construction license was granted in August 1996. In order to reassure the host community, a compromise was reached guaranteeing that the facility would be operated for 25 years at which point the local community could request that it be removed within 10 years.

One of the most controversial aspects of the siting process for nuclear installations in Switzerland was the distribution of financial and infrastructure benefits. Resentment had built up amongst communities close to the facilities but not eligible for compensation like the 'host' community. As a result, a committee of 'wise men' recommended drawing concentric circles around the Zwilag facility out to roughly 12 miles with compensation decreasing the further out the community was located (Zwilag n.d.; McCombie and McKinley, personal communication, 16 October 2014).

Despite 40 years of concerted effort, the Swiss government and the nuclear utilities have yet to find a site to dispose of the country's radioactive waste. The following discussion examines why efforts thus far have failed, the lessons that have been learned and how these are being applied to the current search.

From 100 to 3: the site selection process[6]

Phase 1

Nagra's initial preference was for three repositories, each catering to a different category of waste with a surface facility for LLRW. However, the realization that Switzerland's population density made surface or near-surface disposal all but impossible, combined with an appreciation of the safety benefits afforded by geological media, resulted in the utilities and Nagra developing the country's first waste management concept in February 1978: deep geological disposal (Swiss Federal Office of Energy [SFOE] 2008b, pp. 12, 17). Given that the concepts being considered at the time for intermediate waste disposal were all horizontally accessed, it was expected that LLRW could be accommodated in an intermediate level radioactive waste (ILRW) repository at minimal expense. The same year, Nagra commenced proof-of-concept work – 'Project Gewähr' ('Project Guarantee'). In 1980, the Federal Nuclear Safety Inspectorate (HSK) and the Federal Nuclear Safety Commission (KSA) established guidelines for radioactive waste disposal: a repository design should enable the facility to be sealed at any time and remain passively safe, and any radionuclide release should not lead to individual exposure exceeding 0.1 millisievert per year (Junker, Flüeler, Stauffacher and Scholz 2008, p. 12). Five years later, the results of Project Gewähr were delivered to the Federal Council. The low and intermediate level waste findings were unconditional: "All aspects of the feasibility of disposing of L/ILW have been demonstrated" (EKRA 2000, pp. 7–8). In June 1988, the federal government approved the findings and Nagra started to narrow the list of possible repository sites (SFOE 2008b, p. 17).

The search had begun in 1978 with an inventory of potential host formations using geological maps and literature studies, resulting in a total of 100 sites by 1981. By scoring sites based on engineering (good-average-difficult-very difficult) and geological (good-average-satisfactory-unsatisfactory) criteria, the 100 were ranked. Supporting information – such as seismic activity, susceptibility to flooding and proximity to habitation – was considered but not incorporated into the scoring. After 3 years of study, the number of sites was reduced to 20.

Phase 2

In phase two, the 20 sites were subjected to detailed geological and hydrogeological study and supporting information discussed earlier was factored in. The same 4-point scoring system was used. Separately, repository construction methods were assessed using three criteria: technical feasibility, cost and time. Host rock-specific construction studies were also conducted. All of this work resulted in the elimination of nine sites – five because of geology, two because of construction difficulties, one because of spatial constraints and one because it was being considered for HLW disposal.

Phase 3

The next step was to determine the most realistic design, taking into account considerations such as entrance location and disposal of excavated material. Long-term safety, engineering feasibility and infrastructure requirements were also important factors. In all, eight criteria were used: landscape, settlements, traffic, water protection, military installations, proprietary considerations, disposal of excavated material, and the need for special local licenses (Vari, Reagan-Cirincione and Mumpower 1994, p. 209). However, there was little consideration of cost and no public acceptance weighting.

It was decided that three was a sufficient number of sites for field work. This was a compromise between studying a sufficient number of candidate formations to give a high probability of finding at least one suitable site and the high costs of programs involving geophysics that require drilling multiple boreholes. The three sites were to be spread across different potential host rock types: Bois de la Glaive in Canton Vaud; Oberbauenstock straddling Cantons Nidwalden and Uri; and Piz Pian Grand in Canton Graubünden. However, some peculiarities in the selection process would manifest later. Politically, all decisions were made by Nagra and the technical experts it hired; there was no attempt to elicit public input. The main technical drawback was that all three sites were located in "complex, high-topography, pre-Alpine regions (National Research Council of the National Academies 2003, p. 160).

The selection process was also contrived to ensure that one site was located in each of the three cultural/language regions of the country: Vaud (French); Nidwalden/Uri (German) and Graubünden (Italian). However, the cantons did not interpret this as an act of impartiality and opposition was considerable. In Vaud and Graubünden there was a feeling that because all of the power plants were located in the German-speaking part of the country, the repository should be put there also (McCombie and McKinley, personal communication, 16 October 2014).

Phase 4

On 30 September 1985, the Federal Council gave permission for field work to commence at the three sites. Only surface-based activities were allowed; test shafts were deferred until the surface tests results came in. The Federal Council also instructed Nagra, based on guidance from HSK, to submit an application to carry out exploratory work at at least one additional site for long-lived ILRW, with significantly different characteristics from the three selected sites. HSK wanted a site that was more easily explorable and with a greater depth of accessible host rock so longer-lived radionuclides could be included. Wellenberg in the municipality of Wolfenschiessen, Canton Nidwalden, was chosen. Ironically, Wellenberg did not actually fulfill all of HSK's requirements but surface exploration could be carried out (McCombie and McKinley, personal communication, 16 October 2014).

From 3 to 4: Wellenberg redux

Wellenberg had been identified in the original list of 100 potential host formations but passed over in favor of Oberbauenstock, 46 miles to the south, because construction of the Seelisberg Tunnel provided better geological data on the latter site. Wellenberg made the cut this time because the geometry of the rock formations would allow horizontal access to disposal caverns for short-lived wastes as well as shafts to dispose of longer-lived wastes. One small complicating factor was that a special cantonal mining concession was required to ensure the repository did not interfere with future mining projects. In January 1986, the canton government invited Nagra to conduct preliminary investigations. The initial reaction amongst Nidwalden's communities was fairly muted, particularly in comparison with some of the protests occurring in Vaud (where opposition delayed the commencement of characterization work until 1990) and Graubünden. The main concerns were the possible effect on tourism and obtaining assurances that the public would be involved in decision-making moving forward.

However, not everyone was comfortable with Wellenberg's sudden inclusion and the canton's invitation prompted the creation of MNA (the committee for the right of the people of Nidwalden to be heard on matters concerning nuclear facilities). Aktion kritisches Wolfenschiessen (AkW), a smaller

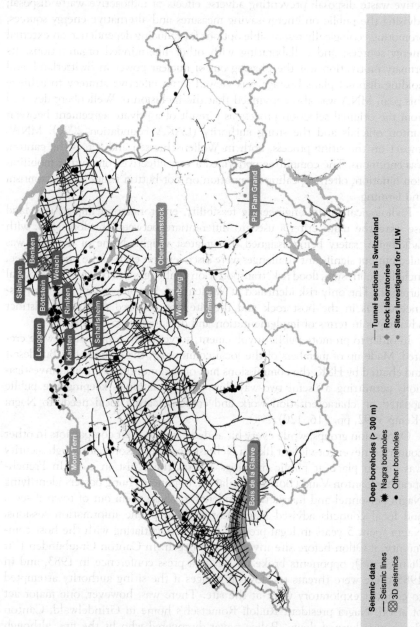

Figure 8.1 Sites of geological investigations in Switzerland

antinuclear organization formed a year later. MNA professed a commitment to securing cantonal voters' rights; providing comprehensive information on radioactive waste disposal; preventing adverse effects of radioactive waste disposal; advising the public on energy-saving measures and alternative energy sources; promoting ecologically responsible options for reducing dependence on external energy sources; and collaborating with other like-minded organizations. Its primary motivation was the phasing out of nuclear power in Switzerland, and holding disposal plans hostage was viewed as an effective strategy to achieve this goal. MNA was also convinced that the inclusion of Wellenberg deviated from the original selection process as a result of a private agreement between canton officials and the siting authority (LAKA Foundation 2000). MNA's impact on the siting process, both in Wolfenschiessen and across the canton, was enormous. The committee performed a very effective community mobilization function, often appealing to emotion on hot-button issues such as tourism and farming.

Radiological safety, engineering feasibility, environmental impact and land use were the main criteria used to differentiate between the four sites, with radiological safety being assigned the greatest weight. None of the sites was ruled out but significant challenges were discovered at each of the original three, including corrosion, flood risk, transportation challenges and potential 'geological surprises.' The only risk identified at Wellenberg, by comparison, was the presence of gas in the host rock and the site was believed to possess "distinct advantages in terms of implementation and demonstration of safety."

In order to promote public involvement, surveillance commissions were created. Made up of members of the local community, the canton, the Bundesrat and chaired by HSK, the commissions met once a month during field investigations permitting a useful two-way flow of information – keeping the public updated on characterization work and communicating local needs to Nagra (Kemp 1992, pp. 116, 120).

Opposition groups, while every bit as dedicated as their compatriots in other countries, never got violent like in Nebraska or South Korea, although security was put in place at public meetings several times just in case. In French-speaking Canton Vaud (Bois de la Glaive), opponents hung posters identifying Nagra personnel and instructing residents to chase them out of town if seen, and local councils advised Nagra not to hold public information sessions. Nagra spent 5 years in legal proceedings and negotiating with the host community of Ollon before site investigation began. In Canton Graubünden (Piz Pian Grand), opponents broke up a Nagra press conference in 1983, and in 1985 there were threats to blow up bridges if the siting authority attempted to conduct exploratory work at the site. There was, however, one major act of arson. Nagra president Rudolf Rometsch's home in Grindelwald, Canton Berne, was burned down. Police never discovered who lit the fire, although it was reported that steps had been taken to ensure that the house was empty when it occurred (McCombie and McKinley, personal communication, 16 October 2014).

From 4 to 1: Wellenberg's selection

In 1988, the federal government approved Nagra's application to conduct site investigation work at Wellenberg on condition that long-lived ILRW be excluded, thus reversing its 1985 guidance – which was of course the reason why Wellenberg was being considered. The ILRW rejection was prompted by the cantonal government. Thereafter, federal government permitting allowed for exploration via a 1.25-mile horizontal tunnel but did not authorize a deep shaft. In order to make up for the lack of data relative to the original three selections, Nagra drilled several deep boreholes at the site (Zurkinden, Kowalski, Steiner and Flüeler updated 2005; McCombie and McKinley, personal communication, 16 October 2014).

The federal government also made some effort to begin engaging the public in the process. In 1990, the Group to Resolve Conflict on Radioactive Waste Issues (KORA), consisting of government officials, industry representatives and nuclear energy opponents, was established. A series of meetings was held in 1992 but when the government decided to extend the Mühleberg power plant's license, opponents stopped participating activities and the group's work came to an end. The government also sponsored Waste Management Conference 1991, which brought together various groups to discuss disposal concepts, repository safety and waste inventories.

Nidwalden was having more success. In 1991, the canton created the 13-member Wellenberg Working Group (WWG). Consisting of a chairman, seven experts (including an engineer, geologist, physicist and medical doctor) and five nontechnical stakeholders (including a politician, host community representative and environmentalist), the group was tasked with advising the federal government on the license application. While the group's findings were described as generally "positive, although very critical of some aspects of the project," the WWG found the site selection process to be "transparent and acceptable" (Kowalski and Fritschi 1999, p. 116).

In 1993, Nagra recommended, and the Federal Council approved, the Wellenberg site for further investigation. Striking a slightly discordant note, the Federal Council proposed revising legislation to remove the formal cantonal role from the decision-making process. In June 1994, Wolfenschiessen voted to host the facility with a healthy 63 percent in favor.[7] The utilities created a construction and operation company – GNW (Genossenschaft für Nukleare Entsorgung Wellenberg) – and based its operations in Wolfenschiessen. The municipality council and Canton Nidwalden negotiated a compensation package consisting of a F2.5 million annual payment to Wolfenschiessen, F5 million to the canton and other local communities, the provision of free electricity (between F3.5 million and F4 million annually) and the establishment of a foundation in Wolfenschiessen to help the community when the compensation payments ended in 40 years. GNW also committed to give preference to Nidwalden businesses when issuing construction and related contracts and use local workers whenever possible. This was hardly unique: compensation for site-specific facilities that benefit society is common in Switzerland – for example, mountain communities that make their water rights available for electricity production receive compensation (Kowalski and Fritschi 1999, p. 117). Municipality voters approved the deal with GNW on 10 June by a vote of 322–189. The same month, GNW submitted a general license application to the federal government. The application stated that short-lived LILW as well as negligible levels of longer-lived radionuclides would be disposed of in the repository, prompting heated debate as to the distinction between short- and longer-lived waste (McCombie and McKinley, personal communication, 16 October 2014).

Much of the opposition came not from the host community but from a wider geographic region. In response to GNW's progress, MNA, environmental groups and several political parties set up an organization – 'Stop Wellenberg' – to coordinate their efforts.

Cantonal referendum take 1: June 1995

GNW was granted a special mining concession in January 1995 (Zurkinden et al. updated 2005). However, whether the canton had veto power over *all* underground activity was a matter of dispute. Did national competence on nuclear issues override cantonal rights? The courts said no, so a referendum was scheduled. On 25 June 1995, residents were asked to vote on the general repository license and the exploratory shaft/construction license. It is important to note that cantonal consent to the latter was required by law; cantonal consent to the former was consultative as the Federal Council was empowered to grant, with parliamentary ratification, the general license. In the lead up to the referendum, 25 public orientation events took place. Proponents focused mainly on the technical details of construction, geology and waste categories to make the case that the repository would be safe. Opponents appealed to voters on an emotional level by disputing the government's safety claims and 'evoking contamination scenarios' (Kowalski and Fritschi 1999, p. 118). Co-director of the Greenpeace Zurich office Ailia Ziegler declared: "This fight will continue to be on our agenda because there will never, ever be safe underground storage" (Prince 1995). MNA flew in a group of Native Americans to raise the profile of its protests (McCombie and McKinley, personal communication, 16 October 2014).

With 72 percent voter turnout (out of roughly 39,000 cantonal residents), Nidwaldeners rejected the applications by votes of 51.9 and 52.5 percent against respectively. Kowalski and Fritschi described the failed procedure simply as "wrong: too fast, too comprehensive and too technocratic" (1999, p. 122). The strongest support came from the municipalities of Wolfenschiessen and Emmetten in the northeast. The main reason for voting yes was a sense of responsibility; the repository needed to be built somewhere (Kowalski and Fritschi 1999, p. 118).

There was significant opposition in the alpine resort town of Engelberg about 9 miles south of Wolfenschiessen (Prince 1995). According to postreferendum analysis carried out at the federal and cantonal level, "the safety of the project was not contested at that stage, but the repository concept and the selection process needed substantial corrections" (Zurkinden et al. updated 2005). This was not entirely true – roughly 24 percent of respondents said they voted against the concession due to lack of safety – but it was clearly the most important factor. For a critical mass of voters, coupling the general license with the exploratory shaft license was interpreted as an attempt to obtain blanket approval for the project, a not unreasonable concern given that federal safety authorities did not even make a recommendation on the general license until almost a year after the referendum. This perception was reinforced by GNW's waste emplacement concept as envisioned at that time:

> It was planned to backfill the voids between the emplaced disposal contain-
> ers in the caverns successively, layer by layer. Retrieval of the waste after
> backfilling is possible in principle but would involve rather high expenditure
> and effort. . . . In the perception of the public, the mere fact that, during
> emplacement of the waste, empty space in the caverns would be backfilled
> immediately evoked a feeling of "loss of control." It was regarded as taking
> an irreversible decision at a much too early stage.
>
> (Fritschi, Kowalski and Zuidema 2000)

Opponents feared that if the licenses were granted and extensive investigations were conducted, Nagra would be so invested that it would be loathe to walk away from the site even if presented with evidence that it should. By taking a step-by-step approach – that is, only putting the exploratory shaft/construction license on the referendum and deferring a decision on the general license until the results of the investigative work became clear – those voters would likely have been more inclined to say 'yes' because they could exercise some control over the process if technical problems arose. This contention was supported by polling suggesting 77 percent of those who voted yes and 34 percent of those who voted no believed that a second vote on Wellenberg with an improved repository concept and more inclusive decision-making process should take place.

There was also a certain amount of discontent with how the compensation was to be distributed. Some felt that the payments should have been divided amongst the communities rather than disbursed to the general "treasury" of the canton (Kowalski and Fritschi 1999, p. 119). Others were upset that Wolfen-schiessen was guaranteed a generous compensation package while neighboring communities also sure to be affected would receive far less or nothing.

One of the criticisms leveled at Nagra was that it spent too much time building support in Wolfenschiessen and was blinded by the host community's enthusiasm. It was at a cantonal level that the referendum was defeated. Nagra's overconfidence also spilled over into the utilities' boardrooms and convinced the power companies to let Nagra do the 'campaigning.'

Siting officials interpreted the referendum as a vote against the siting *concept* and *process* rather than the site itself. Zurkinden et al. have provided some very interesting insights into government thinking at this juncture:

From the proponents' viewpoint . . . there was a dilemma: Should a site, likely to be geologically suitable, be abandoned for political reasons? . . . Can and should the federation override a canton using federal law? Could a repository be constructed against the will of the local/regional population even if this were legally possible? Or should the project be adapted and submitted to another cantonal vote?

(Zurkinden et al. updated 2005)

Indeed despite the no vote, GNW continued exploratory work at the site in 1996 and completed all geological investigation by 1997 ("History and Some Facts to Wellenberg: Project of a Swiss LLW Repository" 2002; Fritschi et al. 2000).

In July 1996, HSK and KSA completed a review of the Wellenberg site investigation, finding no technical faults with Nagra's work. Then in 1997, at Canton Nidwalden's request, the DETEC suspended GNW's general license application and announced that all aspects of Switzerland's waste management program would be reconsidered. However, the license suspension was viewed in Berne as more of an administrative measure; the previous year, DETEC had written to Canton Nidwalden expressing the hope that agreement could be reached on a modified process and second referendum.

In March 1997, the Wellenberg Steering Committee was created. Chaired by the director of the Federal Office of Energy (SFOE), the group consisted of representatives from Nidwalden, Obwalden, Wolfenschiessen and HSK. Environmental and opposition groups were also invited to participate but refused. Armin Braunwalder of the environmental organization Swiss Energy Foundation (SES) explained why:

A proponent of nuclear energy became chairman of the working group. And the goal of the working group was to turn back the results of the referendum. We, who won the referendum, did not feel like giving up our victory. Therefore, the environmental groups that acted as one group did not join the working group.

(LAKA Foundation 2000)

MNA did inform the steering committee that the focus on Wellenberg needed to stop and the site selection should begin again with a countrywide search.

The committee set up two working groups: a Technical Working Group (TAG), made up of steering group stakeholders as well as the Federal Geological Commission and GNW acting as technical adviser, tasked with reviewing the technical criteria for site selection and defining the minimum site requirements; and an Economic Working Group (AGV) tasked with examining how a repository would impact the regional economy (EKRA 2000, p. 8).

In July 1998, based on the input from TAG, the Wellenberg Steering Group determined that the site was still the best technical choice. AGV's finding that "the advantages of the construction and operation of the repository for the siting community outweigh the disadvantages considerably" reinforced the case for Wellenberg (Fritschi et al. 2000). The Nidwalden government was not opposed to the submission of a new license application but did insist that exclusionary criteria be incorporated into the selection process and monitoring, retrievability and liability questions be resolved.

EKRA and KFW

In November 1998, the 'Energy Dialogue on Waste Management Working Group,' an advisory body established by Federal Councilor/head of DETEC Moritz Leuenberger, chaired by Professor Hans Ruh of Zurich University and made up of representatives from the federal government, waste producers, environmental organizations, Nagra, GNW and opposition groups, concluded a frustrating 10 months of work by blandly recommending bridge-building between siting authorities/utilities and environmental organizations and that monitored, retrievable long-term storage be closely examined (OECD/NEA 2000, p. 91; "History and Some Facts to Wellenberg" 2002). Similarly, talks in early 1999 between Councilors Leuenberger and Pascal Couchepin (head of the Federal Department for Economic Affairs); Cantons Nidwalden, Aargau, Berne and Solothurn; and the utilities and environmental organizations failed to resolve questions over the operational life of the country's nuclear plants and waste management. As a result of these inconclusive efforts and the Wellenberg Steering Committee's finding, DETEC created the EKRA in June 1999. Chaired by University of Geneva geology professor Walter Wildi, the six other members held advanced degrees in geology, ethics, biophysics, hydrogeology and engineering. EKRA's mandate was to formulate basic principles for a variety of waste management options applicable to different waste categories. These were: long-term geological storage/disposal monitoring; geological disposal; interim storage ("generally restricted to a few decades"); and indefinite storage (where the "waste is accessible to authorised persons at all times"). The group determined that interim storage and indefinite storage failed to meet the criteria for long-term safety and settled on monitored long-term geological storage/disposal, which combined elements of disposal and reversibility, but conceded that questions remained about how to transition from long-term monitoring to repository closure.

By this stage, GNW had adopted a modified disposal concept emphasizing control and retrievability, based on retrievability studies conducted by Nagra from 1996 to 1997 (Kowalski and Fritschi 1999, p. 120). Key to the revised approach was the inclusion of a retrieval phase: before closure, the waste containers would be stacked but not backfilled for up to 100 years (Fritschi et al. 2000).

EKRA held seven meetings between June and December 1999 with participation from SFOE, HSK, Nagra, GNW, MNA, SES and Greenpeace. Stakeholders were also invited to offer comments on a preliminary draft of the group's report.

During one of these meetings, SES, Greenpeace Switzerland and MNA outlined why they were "disturbed" by the concept of final disposal:

> "Final" relates to the giving up of responsibility by those previously responsible under law and not to the transition of the waste to a permanently safe state . . . Even with a surface facility, maintenance should not be a long-term obligation. Monitored long-term storage should not be seen simply as a step to a repository, but calls for a new philosophy which would allow monitoring over hundreds or thousands of years and would require structures to be set up that would be functional over these time periods. The basic problem is that reversibility, as a key feature of monitored long-term storage, cannot be reconciled with final disposal.
>
> (EKRA 2000, p.38)

EKRA noted some "basic contradictions" in those requirements. In particular, "the guardianship concept is ruled out, while, at the same time, monitored long-term storage which will last for thousands of years is supported and disposal rejected" (EKRA 2000, pp. 37–38).

Taking a long-term view of the requirements of waste isolation – "The project structures have to be secured as far as possible against social crises. Economic depression, war, terrorism and epidemics are particularly threatening scenarios" – EKRA's final report was submitted to DETEC in January 2000. The overarching recommendation was monitored long-term geological storage; that is, "isolation of radioactive waste in deep geological layers with technical and natural barriers, and the option of retrievability" (EKRA 2000, p. 53; OECD/NEA 2010, p. 30). The group maintained that "no one should be discriminated against on the basis of his opinions or affiliation to a particular social group. This principle should also apply over time; no one should be discriminated against on the basis of belonging to a different generation," recommending a 100-year waste retrieval period to ensure this. The group determined that Wellenberg fulfilled the requirements for both geological disposal and monitored long-term geological storage. Two specific next steps were suggested: storage concepts should be validated by a pilot facility, and preparation for construction of the exploratory shaft should be undertaken. EKRA also recommended the siting authorities take a number of actions. Those applicable to LLRW were:

- encourage public debate;
- enshrine monitored long-term geological disposal in national legislation;
- ensure the waste management program is financially independent of the utilities;
- adopt a project timeline (EKRA 2000, pp. 27, 75).

While the Federal Council and the Canton Nidwalden executive decided to proceed along the lines recommended by EKRA, the canton adopted two additional conditions: a definition of exclusionary criteria for the exploratory shaft that, if present, would result in the abandonment of the project; and a definition of the waste categories to be buried, with an emphasis on the 'short-lived' character of the repository (Zurkinden et al. updated 2005).

A DETEC delegation met with Canton Nidwalden officials in March 2000 and an agreement was reached on how to proceed to construction of the exploratory shaft. Four months later the Nidwalden government called for monitored, long-term geological disposal to be enshrined in new legislation (HSK 2001).

In June, shortly before its public announcement, the Nidwalden government created the Cantonal Expert Group Wellenberg (KFW) with a mandate to assess the exclusionary criteria, the national waste inventory, the plan for construction of the exploratory shaft and the revised disposal concept (Flüeler 2002, slide 4). Chaired by former EKRA chairman Walter Wildi, KFW was made up of seven other scientific experts and a lawyer. KFW is a good example of how an independent, respected and trusted group established by an affected government can contribute constructively to the public debate through the provision of transparent and factual information. The advisory group conducted an open dialogue with safety authorities, GNW and the 'leading critical NGO' (MNA). One of the group's priorities was to identify project weaknesses, both scientific and organizational, early to avoid the imposition of quick fixes or very expensive corrective action at a later date. The group also embraced the broader objective of involving the public, through advisory committees, in the decision-making framework (Flüeler 2002, slides 10, 13, 14). KFW's final report, delivered in December 2000, recommended a clear separation of stakeholder roles, clarification of funding issues, transparency of all aspects of the project, controllability/retrievability and proceeding with the exploratory shaft.

In January 2001, GNW submitted an application for the exploratory shaft and in September the Nidwalden government gave its approval.[8] From 19 April to 25 May, all documentation was made available to the public. Throughout this process, opposition groups were satisfied with the role KFW played, listening to and reporting their concerns, but they still opposed the license because they felt "the site was not providing the necessary guarantees to continue the qualification process." Some had also come to distrust Nagra and, as a result, there was some suspicion that money being provided to the local community was "compensation for taking a risk" or, less generously, a bribe (Flüeler 2006, p. 159). In June 2001, the Nidwalden government created a working group to estimate the project's likely impact on the economy and tourist industry of the Nidwalden and Engelberg region (HSK 2001).

Cantonal referendum take 2: September 2002

In the lead up to the second Nidwalden vote, opponents made a variety of arguments: Nidwalden had already voted no in 1995; their concerns – particularly controllability and retrievability – were never taken seriously by siting authorities and therefore not addressed; it was not clear how much waste would be buried at the site (many had hoped that the 1990 referendum on the phasing out of nuclear power would provide a definite answer to this question but the proposition was defeated); Wellenberg didn't meet the criteria laid out when the fourth site was requested and was located in an earthquake and flood zone; construction and operation would reduce local property prices and have a detrimental impact on the landscape in the ecologically sensitive Engelberg Valley that was dependent on agriculture and tourism;[9] medical waste, one of the key reasons why the repository was needed, constituted only a tiny fraction of the overall waste total; the structural integrity of the waste containers; how could institutional control be maintained over centuries; waste would be trucked past Engelberg kindergartens, schools and homes; and the tunnel was not 'exploratory,' rather it was the first stage of a inexorable process that would culminate in the construction of a repository, particularly given that there was no money to investigate any alternative sites (MNA 2002).[10] The referendum on the exploratory tunnel was held on 22 September 2002. The result was an even more emphatic no: 58 percent to 42 percent. Wolfenschiessen was the only community to vote in favor, "illustrating the common 'donut' effect in which even if a local host community is prepared to accept the burdens of a wider public, communities close enough to feel affected but too far to derive direct benefits may still object to a repository" (National Research Council of the National Academies 2003, p. 169). There are several reasons why the referendum failed again:

- There was a lack of transparency and resultant lack of public understanding as to why Wellenberg – concerns remained that the siting process had been short-circuited.
- The institutional system did not change between 1995 and 2002.
- There was a lack of leadership, particularly at the national level.
- There was "a bit of complacency on Nagra's part in the lead up to the second vote. They felt they had done everything possible to address the things that had gone wrong in 1995 and that success was likely . . . emotional issues and voter fatigue were not fully considered" (McCombie and McKinley, personal communication, 16 October 2014).
- There was no tangible benefit to saying 'yes' therefore it was easier to say 'no'.
- There was difficulty of regaining trust after it had been lost in 1995.

Unlike 1995, this time Nidwalden concluded that Wellenberg was 'definitely out' of further consideration as a host site – after two referenda, Nidwaldeners had had enough. Nagra seemed to agree, indicating that the site would not be considered again in the future (Zurkinden et al. updated 2005; McCombie and McKinley, personal communication, 16 October 2014).

The referendum did spell the end for the utilities' construction and operating company. GNW had created an advisory group in 2000 made up of Nidwalden and Obwalden residents from a variety of walks of life in an attempt to better understand community concerns but its impact was marginal at best. GNW withdrew its general license application in 2002 and the company was dissolved in 2003.

The Nuclear Energy Act of 2003

Despite a second rebuke, there was a broad appreciation that waste disposal had to proceed and this prompted a decision to update the 1959 Atomic Law. Shortly after the result came in, the federal Energy Minister assured the public that the repository would not be forced upon an unwilling community. Interestingly, the end result was a law that in one important way gave potential host communities less control over the siting process.

Incorporating EKRA's repository recommendations, the *Nuclear Energy Act* passed on 21 March 2003 and the *Nuclear Energy Ordinance* passed on 10 December 2004. Both entered into force on 1 February 2005. Notably, the Act removed the cantonal veto and replaced it with an optional national referendum. The Federal Council was in favor of retaining the cantonal veto but was over-ruled by the Senate (McCombie and McKinley, personal communication, 16 October 2014). The Act described a public participation process in two phases: siting and construction. For siting, the concerns of the host canton as well as those of the cantons and countries whose borders lie in the immediate vicinity must be taken into account, "provided this does not place unreasonable limita-tions on the project." For construction, while consultation with the host canton is required and cantonal legislation "must be taken into account, insofar as this does not unduly compromise the project," cantonal licenses are not required for construction. If the canton rejects the application, but the Department still issues the license, the canton can file an appeal (Nuclear Energy Act 2003, Article 44 and Article 49).[11]

It has been noted that there was "surprisingly little public reaction" to the removal of the veto, as evidenced by responses received on the open consulta-tion process (McCombie and McKinley, personal communication, 16 October 2014). In Nidwalden, this may be partly explained by the fact that as far as residents were concerned, Wellenberg would no longer be considered as a reposi-tory site. Greenpeace, while registering its disagreement with the decision, chose not to push for a referendum.

The sectoral plan for deep geological repositories

The Nuclear Energy Ordinance required that the federal government specify the objectives and criteria for geological disposal in a 'sectoral plan' (Nuclear Energy Ordinance 2004, Article 5). SFOE took the lead in developing the plan, stressing that the disposal concept and the site selection procedure be step-by-step processes that allow reconsideration of decisions by future generations. According to the head of SFOE's radioactive waste management section, the office made policy adjustments

> based on the observation that safety ought to have priority, but that it is
> not sufficient on its own. The broad consultation and the early and con-
> tinued involvement of society are also necessary. Although a participatory

approach does not guarantee the success of a project, it can improve the quality of the project and promote its acceptance.

(OECD/NEA 2010, p. 29; Aebersold 2014)

At the end of each stage, a public hearing was conducted then approved by the Federal Council (OECD/NEA 2010, pp. 30–31). In March 2006, cantonal authorities received and commented on a first draft of the conceptual part of the plan. Federal authorities discussed a revised second draft with the cantons as well as German and Austrian officials. From June to November, consultative workshops for nongovernmental organizations (NGOs) and political parties were convened and public focus groups met between June and August. A third draft of the plan was completed in January 2007 and informational sessions were held in Germany and Austria. Following a final round of cantonal hearings in November and December, the 'conceptual' part of the plan was approved by the federal government on 2 April 2008 (DETEC 2008, p. 20).

Affected communities were defined as communes that lay completely or partly within the planning perimeter. In justified cases, other communes could also be included. Neighboring states (Germany and Austria) and regions (France and Italy) could also submit opinions. The plan still called for two repositories but left open the possibility that if a single site were to fulfill the requirements for both high level waste (HLW) and LILW, one site would suffice (DETEC 2008, pp. 5, 29). In fact, Walter Wildi had suggested including all of the LILW waste in an HLW repository planned for Opalinus clay north of Zurich more than a decade earlier. Nagra also became more convinced of the financial and political benefits of a combined repository when the results of exploratory drilling at the HLW site at Benken proved encouraging (McCombie and McKinley, personal communication, 16 October 2014).

In the first stage, waste producers would propose geologically suitable areas in a report to the federal government. A safety review would be conducted and cantonal commissions created to prepare the groundwork for regional participation. Working with the cantons in stage two, a spatial planning assessment would be conducted. Working with the siting regions, socioeconomic studies would be prepared and waste producers would draw up facility design proposals and select at least one site in each designated area/region with the goal of identifying at least two sites each for HLW and LILW. These sites would be incorporated into the sectoral plan on an interim basis, with the remaining sites kept on the books as reserve options. In the third stage, in-depth investigation of the potential sites would be conducted and the socioeconomic implications of construction and operation would be analyzed in greater depth. The siting regions would propose regional development programs and prepare background information for deciding compensation packages and monitoring socioeconomic and environmental impacts. Compensation packages would be negotiated and "made transparent." Once all of this was done, the waste producers would submit general license applications for two repositories (or one) and after a final 3-month consultation period the Federal Council would decide. If the site was deemed suitable, the parliament would ratify the decision. A national referendum was optional. However, if the federal government and the cantons could not come to agreement, a settlement procedure would be initiated. And if this was unsuccessful, the Federal Council would make the decision – a decision not challengeable in court (DETEC 2008, pp. 5–6, 34, 38, 43).

Following the granting of the general license, in-depth geological investigations would commence with the immediate goal of drilling of an exploratory shaft and construction of a rock laboratory at the planned disposal level. As discussed earlier, the design was required to incorporate long-term passive safety monitoring, repair and retrieval measures as well as enable the facility to be "closed within a few years."

DETEC created a National Waste Management Advisory Council to "bring an outside viewpoint into the process" and was responsible for ensuring public participation in the siting regions. A Technical Forum on Safety, made up of experts from the authorities (HSK and the federal office of topography Swisstopo), commissions (KSA and the Commission for Radioactive Waste Disposal) and the waste producers, was created to conduct outreach with the public, the communes, the siting regions, the cantons and affected neighboring countries on questions of science and geology (DETEC 2008, pp. 25, 82).

On 6 November 2008, SFOE announced Nagra's suggested siting locations for LILW disposal: Südranden, Zürich Nordost (Zürcher Weinland), Nördlich Lägern, Jura Ost (Bözberg), Jura-Südfuss and Wellenberg. Three of those sites – Zürich Nordost, Nördlich Lägern and Jura Ost – were also identified as potential sites for a HLW repository (SFOE 2015). SFOE's Walter Steinmann conceded that the choices were "unlikely to be very popular among the cantons and regions directly concerned . . . But voters will have the final say on the matter in a nationwide ballot" (Geiser 2008). Ignoring all of the work that had been done building controllability and retrievability into the disposal concept since 1995, SES was quick to register its opposition, complaining that "Nagra proposes long-term storage facilities which make it impossible for future generations to retrieve leaking containers if need be" and the removal of a cantonal veto was inimical to a genuinely cooperative process (Geiser 2008).

More difficult to justify was the reappearance of Wellenberg. As discussed previously, in the wake of the second failed Nidwalden referendum, Nagra had indicated that Wellenberg would no longer be considered as a possible disposal site. The public reaction was predictably harsh. The criticism persists today and Wellenberg is the only region that has not yet established a proper regional conference (McCombie and McKinley, personal communication, 16 October 2014).

In November 2011, the Federal Council agreed to incorporate Nagra's six siting regions into the sectoral plan (WNA 2012). Detailed studies of these sites have been completed and two sites have been selected for further investigation: Jura Ost for both LILW and HLW disposal and Zürich Nordost for HLW. SFOE currently predicts that the Federal Council will make a decision on the proposed sites by mid-2017 (SFOE 2015).

In mid-2012, SFOE briefed a detailed breakdown of the expected economic impacts of deep geological disposal of LILW, from construction of the rock laboratory to the sealing of the facility, to a series of cantonal workshops. Added value was estimated at F4.4 million in Wellenberg and F5.5 million in Jura-Südfuss.[12] Between 35 (Wellenberg) and 45 (Jura-Südfuss) full-time jobs would be created. While a repository would attract visitors, "a decline in the number of tourists seeking nature holidays has to be anticipated." As a result, annual tourism was expected to fall by F100,000 in Nördlich Lägern, F1.1 million in Jura Ost and F5.4 million in Wellenberg.[13] Direct sales of agricultural products could fall between F100,000 in Jura-Südfuss and Wellenberg and F600,000 in Südranden. Tax revenue was expected to decrease by F265,000 in Wellenberg and increase by F237,000 in Jura Sud.[14] Federal compensation would total F300 million for the LILW repository and F800 million for the combined repository. SFOE's conclusion was that "both the positive and the negative impacts are well below one percent of the present-day regional value chain, employment level and tax revenue" (SFOE 2012).

Conclusion

After two failed referenda on the Wellenberg site, SFOE took over responsibility for the management of Switzerland's radioactive waste from Nagra and is developing a sectoral plan for deep geological repositories. A number of important lessons emerge from the Swiss experience to this point.

Seemingly most counterintuitive, although there is broad societal agreement that Switzerland must provide a national solution to all of the radioactive that it generates, decision-makers have effectively bypassed any local opposition to a disposal facility by removing the cantonal veto and appealing to the country as a whole. Technically the siting authorities were only obligated to take into account the concerns of affected communities "provided this does not place unreasonable limitations on the project," although in practice the engagement process would never be so rigid. But the principle flies in the face of all the evidence suggesting that asserting federal preemption over local/regional opposition is a highly unproductive way to site such facilities. Cantonal veto still comes up regularly in parliament but there is never enough support for advocates to amend the Nuclear Energy Act. For example, Nidwalden introduced a cantonal veto initiative in September 2012. The National Council gave its approval a year later but the Council of States rejected the initiative 23–17 in December 2013. Canton Schaffhausen introduced the same initiative in January 2013 and it too was rejected by the Council of States (Ernst 2014). The public reaction was muted too; even Greenpeace chose not to fight for the veto.

As Thomas Flüeler has explained, the cantons represent the 'affected communities.' They are resourced with experts and have access to the safety data and it is their duty to ensure that participation "is more than just a buzzword or sophisticated public relations." They serve as "intermediaries between national deciders/experts and local affected/concerned laypersons and help transcend the traditional roles of experts vs. the public" (Flüeler 2013, p. 408). During site characterization, the surveillance commissions played a valuable role in keeping interested members of the public, both at the local and cantonal level, apprised of Nagra's work. From 2000, the most important conduit for the cantons was KFW. Created by cantonal officials and chaired by a respected University of Geneva geology professor who had already overseen the influential EKRA group's work, KFW was capable of engaging in complex technical as well as political, legal and socioeconomic discussions and trusted as an honest broker by both sides: it was viewed by the community as its most unbiased source of information and by the siting authorities as a key source of information about public concerns.

The requirement that all categories of waste be buried in deep repositories adds a layer of complexity to the site search and not just to the siting and design of the underground facilities. Siting authorities have stressed that the surface support structures for those repositories will be kept as small and nonintrusive as possible and be integrated into the surrounding landscape, such as in existing quarries. While separate sites are being pursued for HLW and LILW, authorities have not ruled out the possibility of a combined repository and, for a country that generates a relatively small amount of radioactive waste, this would be the safest and most cost-effective option just as it would for most countries. However, finding willing hosts for spent fuel and HLW has proved so difficult that other countries have settled for the more manageable task of storing and/or disposing of their LLRW first. And while anything is possible – it has been suggested that opposition in Switzerland tends to be directed at repositories in general rather than a particular type of waste – there is no conclusive evidence that Switzerland is any different at this point.

Wellenberg has been a source of controversy since its inclusion in 1985, despite consistently exhibiting suitable geology. After initially being passed over in the process due to its geological complexity, opponents made much of Nagra's late inclusion of the site by seemingly ignoring its own selection criteria. Cantonal voters rejected Nagra's Wellenberg proposals twice in 7 years. Then Wellenberg appeared once again in 2008 as one of six potential LILW disposal sites, despite indications from Nagra in 2002 that the site would not be considered again, an assurance from the Energy Minister that unwilling communities' wishes would be respected and a general feeling in Nidwalden that two cantonal no votes was a sufficient signal to siting authorities. Combined with the removal of the cantonal veto, the suspicion that Wellenberg was the preferred site and the authorities would persist until it was licensed appeared more and more plausible to numerous observers.

There has also been some confusion about what exactly was supposed to go into the repository. Wellenberg was originally included as the fourth site in order to accommodate long-lived ILRW. However, in 1988 Canton Nidwalden approved investigation work on the condition that long-lived ILRW be excluded.

Then in 1995, GNW's license application included short-lived LILW and negligible levels of longer-lived radionuclides. The difference between short-lived and long-lived ILRW, however, was lost on most members of the public. When combined with suspicions about the attachment to Wellenberg, the apparent lack of consistency fostered even more concern about exactly how candid the siting authorities were being.

While there have been some suggestions that compensation was a risk premium for accepting the facility, as there are in siting efforts everywhere, most of the controversy over compensation has been about fair distribution rather than perceived bribery. Siting authorities learned that cutting off all compensation at the border of a host community, particularly a small host community, can lead to resentment in neighboring communities. This realization led to the concept of a spatial distribution of compensation: that is, concentric circles around the facility, with compensation decreasing the further away from the site one lives. At Zwilag's central storage facility, for example, compensation extends out to 12 miles.

Siting authorities have developed innovative and socially sensitive waste management solutions in both the site characterization phase and the licensing phase. For example, the municipality of Benken agreed to accept an exploratory borehole for HLW disposal after negotiating specific benefits with Nagra that did not include direct financial compensation. In particular, the drill site would be left at the conclusion of work in a state easily convertible to a conventional household waste disposal facility that the community had told Nagra it needed. Similarly, at its ZZL facility, Zwilag guaranteed that it would operate for 25 years then close the facility and remove the waste if that was what the local community wanted. These are good ways to build trust – providing social services and giving the community a real say in its future – but Zwilag's guarantee does raise the question of where the waste will be moved to if the community wants the facility decommissioned.

Finally, Nagra's reputation has waxed and waned through the last four decades. During the 1970s, the organization was viewed as little more than an appendage of the utilities. By the mid-1980s, when Project Gewähr was completed, its image as a technical and scientific organization had improved greatly. But as potential repository sites were selected and licensing issues became more important, opposition to Nagra also grew and the organization's own conduct – overconfidence in 1995 and complacency in 2002 – contributed to the results of the Nidwalden referenda. The organization then recommended Zürcher Weinland for the HLW repository in June 2006 on the basis of findings at one borehole. Finally, in 2008 Wellenberg was nominated again as a potential low and intermediate level waste disposal site despite promises immediately following the 2002 referendum that it would no longer be considered. It was at this point, with public trust badly shaken, that SFOE stepped in to take the political lead, relegating Nagra to the role of a technical backup organization.[15] It remains to be seen whether the Federal Office of Energy will regain some of the credibility that Nagra lost and if it will be enough to assure prospective host community or communities.

Notes

1 In July 2008, SFOE sponsored a survey of Swiss citizens' attitudes to radioactive waste. Fifty-two percent of respondents indicated that they were opposed to nuclear energy but 37% of those said that they would change their opinion if there was a permanent and safe waste solution. Sizeable majorities of respondents understood that not all radioactive waste was the same and it came from different places. Yet 79% believed some radioactive waste was buried deep underground at special disposal facilities or sent to other countries for disposal, 42% believed some radioactive waste was dumped at sea, 34% knew that radioactive waste was not produced in similar quantities to other wastes and 81% thought all radioactive waste was very dangerous (SFOE 2008a).

2 'Disposal' was defined by the Federal Nuclear Safety Inspectorate HSK as "maintenance-free permanent isolation of radioactive waste from the biosphere without the intention of retrieval" (EKRA 2000, pp. 3, 36, 39, 66).

3 In a letter to the *Nidwaldner* a month before the 2002 Canton Nidwalden referendum to decide whether an exploratory tunnel would be drilled at Wellenberg, a Stans resident claimed that parts of the Mühleberg plant were no safer than the Chernobyl reactor that melted down (MNA 2002).

4 A proposed plant in Graben, Canton Berne, was also abandoned due to antinuclear opposition.

5 Of that total, 59,000 would be generated by the operation and dismantling of the country's five power plants and 33,000 would come from medicine, industry and research (Nagra n.d.d.). Of course, waste from the medical, industrial and research sectors will continue to accumulate.

6 It should be noted that the 'phases' presented here are of the authors' construction and may not align with siting phases as designated by the siting organization.

7 Because the repository entrance was to be located in a separate zoning area, a second authorization vote was required. This occurred in December 1994 with 70% of voters responding in the affirmative ("History and Some Facts to Wellenberg" 2002).

8 Validation work was conducted at the then-under-construction Lötschberg Tunnel about 80 miles southwest of Wolfenschiessen, which featured some similar rock formations to Wellenberg (HSK 2001).

9 It was claimed that a waterfall on the opposite side of the valley had been reduced to a trickle by construction of a tunnel and the repository was a much larger infrastructure project.

10 On public support for the project in the canton, Edith, Peter and Sascha Bieri of Stans commented: "We are amazed at how many 'experts' live in Canton Nidwalden, whether butcher, bricklayer, lawyer or nurse, each and every one seems to be a geologist."

11 Allowing for broad participation has always been a feature of the Swiss system. For example, when applying for drilling permits, even for the earliest nuclear projects, comments from Germany and Austria were accepted and responded to (McCombie and McKinley, personal communication, 16 October 2014).

12 Benefits vary across regions due to relative economic power and the degree of involvement of the construction industry.

13 The sharp decline in Wellenberg was attributed to the "high number of nature holiday visitors, who are likely to show very little tolerance for a deep geological repository."

14 The tax revenue loss in Wellenberg was attributed to negative impacts on agriculture and tourism.

15 At the end of 2002, Nagra submitted an Options Report on the feasibility of geological disposal of HLW to the federal government. The favored option – Opalinus clay in Zürcher Weinland – was approved by the Federal Council in June 2006 (OECD/NEA 2011, pp. 17–18).

References

Aebersold, M., "Living with Geological Risks: Sectoral Plan for Deep Geological Repositories," *EurGEOSurveys Workshop* (22 October 2014), www.swisstopo.admin.ch/internet/swisstopo/de/home/docu/Kolloquien/20141022.parsys.72367.downloadList.1890.DownloadFile.tmp/13geolrepositoriesaebersoldfoe.pdf

Bertini, H. W. et al., *Descriptions of Selected Accidents That Have Occurred at Nuclear Reactor Facilities*, Oak Ridge National Library (April 1980).

Department of the Environment, Transport, Energy and Communications (DETEC), *Implementation of the Obligations of the Joint Convention on the Safety of Spent Fuel Management and on the Safety of Radioactive Waste Management*, Fourth National Report of Switzerland in Accordance with Article 32 of the Convention (October 2011), http://static.ensi.ch/1318509060/cns-2011-national-report-switzerland.pdf

Department of the Environment, Transport, Energy and Communications (DETEC), *Sectoral Plan for Deep Geological Repositories: Conceptual Part* (2 April 2008).

Ernst, T., Nagra, "Switzerland Update," *EDRAM Spring Meeting*, Yokohama, Japan (19 May 2014), www.edram.info/fileadmin/edram/pdf/Item-06_Update-Switzerland.pdf

European Commission Press Release, "Eurobarometer Survey on Radioactive Waste: Europeans Ask for the Implementation of Nuclear Waste Disposal Facilities and for the Development of a More Common European Approach," Brussels, Belgium (3 July 2008), http://europa.eu/rapid/press-release_IP-08-1100_en.htm?locale=en

Expert Group on Disposal Concepts for Radioactive Waste (EKRA), *Disposal Concepts for Radioactive Waste: Final Report*, on behalf of Department of the Environment, Transport, Energy and Communications (DETEC), Berne, Switzerland (31 January 2000).

Flüeler, T., *Decision Making for Complex Socio-Technical Systems: Robustness from Lessons Learned in Long-Term Radioactive Waste Governance* (Dordrecht: Springer, 2006).

Flüeler, T., "Extended Reviewing on the Role of Potential Siting Cantons in the Ongoing Swiss Site Selection Procedure ('Sectoral Plan')" in OECD/NEA, *The Safety Case for Deep Geological Disposal of Radioactive Waste: 2013 State of the Art*, Symposium Proceedings, Paris, France (7–9 October 2013), www.oecd-nea.org/rwm/docs/2013/rwm-r2013-9.pdf

Flüeler, T., "KFW Cantonal Expert Group Wellenberg: An Advisory Body to Support Regional Decision Makers in LLW Siting," Third COWAM Seminar in Fürigen, Switzerland (12–15 September 2002), www.cowam.com/IMG/pdf/present_KFW.pdf

Fritschi, M., Kowalski, E., and Zuidema, P., "Developments in the Swiss Radioactive Waste Disposal Programme," *Waste Management 2000 Conference*, Tucson, Arizona (27 February–2 March 2000), www.wmsym.org/archives/2000/pdf/48/48-1.pdf

Geiser, U., "Nuclear Storage Debate Heats Up," *SWI* (6 November 2008), www.swissinfo.ch/eng/nuclear-storage-debate-heats-up/7025514

"History and Some Facts to Wellenberg: Project of a Swiss LLW Repository," Third COWAM Seminar in Fürigen, Switzerland (12–15 September 2002), www.cowam.com/IMG/pdf/FactsWLB-20729.pdf

HSK [Federal Nuclear Safety Inspectorate], "Geological Repositories for Radioactive Waste" (2001), www.cowam.com/IMG/pdf/JaBe-Chap-10_E.pdf

IAEA Research Reactors Database, "Switzerland (n.d.)," http://nucleus.iaea.org/RRDB/RR/ReactorSearch.aspx?filter=0

Junker, B., Flüeler, T., Stauffacher, M., and Scholz, R., *Description of the Safety Case for Long-Term Disposal of Radioactive Waste – The Iterative Safety Analysis Approach as Utilized in Switzerland*, NSSI Working Paper 46 (July 2008), www.uns.ethz.ch/pub/wp/WP_46.pdf

Kemp, R., *The Politics of Radioactive Waste Disposal* (Manchester: Manchester University Press, 1992).

Kowalski, E., and Fritschi, M., "Has Wellenberg Shown the Way, or Is It Merely Postponing the Inevitable?," in *Retrievability of High Level Waste and Spent Nuclear Fuel*, Proceedings of an International Seminar Organized by the Swedish National Council for Nuclear Waste in Co-operation with the International Atomic Energy Agency, Saltsjöbaden, Sweden, IAEA-TECDOC-1187 (24–27 October 1999), www-pub.iaea.org/MTCD/publications/PDF/te_1187_prn.pdf

LAKA Foundation, "Switzerland" (2000), www.laka.org/info/publicaties/afval/2-discussions-00/8-switzerland.htm

Meyer, P., "Switzerland: Regulatory Control of Radioactive Waste Management," *NERS-Meeting 2006*, Bled, Slovenia (8–9 June 2006), http://ners.co/9th/RWMSW.pdf

MNA, "Leserinnen – and Letters to the Editor in the Newspaper *Nidwaldner*" (3–30 August 2002), www.mna.ch/StopWellenberg/html/lbaugust.htm

Nagra, "Developments of Nagra 1972 to 1980" (n.d.a.), www.nagra.ch/en/developmentsofnagra1972to1980.htm

Nagra, "Developments of Nagra 1991 to 2000" (n.d.b.), www.nagra.ch/en/developmentsfrom1991to2000.htm

Nagra, "History and Focus of Activities of Nagra: Developments Since 2001" (n.d.c.), www.nagra.ch/en/developmentssince2001.htm

Nagra, "Opalinus Clay Project: Demonstration of Feasibility of Disposal ("Entsorgungsnachweis") for Spent Fuel, Vitrified High-Level Waste and Long-Lived Intermediate-Level Waste – Summary Overview" (December 2002), www.nagra.ch/disply.cfm/id/100188

Nagra, "Volumes (as of end 2013)" (n.d.d.), www.nagra.ch/en/volumesen.htm

National Research Council of the National Academies, *One Step at a Time: The Staged Development of Geologic Repositories for High-Level Radioactive Waste*, Committee on Principles and Operational Strategies for Staged Repository Systems, Board on Radioactive Waste Management, Division on Earth and Life Studies (Washington, DC: National Academies Press, 2003).

Nuclear Energy Act, Article 44 (21 March 2003), www.admin.ch/ch/e/rs/732_1/a44.html

Nuclear Energy Act, Article 49 (21 March 2003), www.admin.ch/ch/e/rs/732_1/a49.html

Nuclear Energy Ordinance, Article 5 (10 December 2004), www.admin.ch/opc/en/classified-compilation/20042217/index.html

OECD/NEA, *The Control of Safety of Radioactive Waste Management and Decommissioning in Switzerland ('Country Report')* (2011), www.oecd-nea.org/rwm/profiles/Switzerland_report_web.pdf

OECD/NEA, *Nuclear Legislation in OECD and NEA Countries – Switzerland* (2003), www.oecd-nea.org/law/legislationswitzerland.pdf

OECD/NEA, *Reversibility and Retrievability in Planning for Geological Disposal of Radioactive Waste: Proceedings of the 'R&R' International Conference and Dialogue*, Reims, France (14–17 December 2010), www.oecd-nea.org/rwm/docs/2012/6993-proceedings-rr-reims.pdf

OECD/NEA, *Stakeholder Confidence and Radioactive Waste Disposal: Inauguration, First Workshop and Meeting of the NEA Forum on Stakeholder Confidence in the Area of Radioactive Waste Management*, Paris, France (28–31 August 2000), www.oecd-nea.org/rwm/reports/2000/nea2829.pdf

Prince, C., "A Swiss Mountain May Soon Be Alive with Nuclear Waste," *Christian Science Monitor* (3 October 1995), www.csmonitor.com/1995/1003/03061.html

"The Public Prosecutor Gives Reason to Whistleblower Marcos Buser," *SWI* (15 June 2014), www.swissinfo.ch/fre/le-ministére-public-donne-raison-an-lanceur-d-alerte-marcos-buser/38791438

"Short Description of the Mont Terri Project," *Swisstopo* (n.d.), www.swisstopo.admin.ch/internet/swisstopo/en/home/topics/geology/MTProject/MTPshortly.html

Swiss Federal Office of Energy (SFOE), *Current Situation in Respect of the Search for Sites* (10 February 2015), www.bfe.admin.ch/radioaktiveabfaelle/05182/index.html?lang=en

Swiss Federal Office of Energy (SFOE), *Economic Impacts of a Deep Geological Repository on the Siting Region* (2 July 2012), www.bfe.admin.ch/energie/00588/00589/00644/index.html?lang=en&msg-id=45225

Swiss Federal Office of Energy (SFOE), DETEC, *Attitudes to Radioactive Waste in Switzerland* (September 2008a), www.news.admin.ch/NSBSubscriber/message/attachments/15395.pdf

Swiss Federal Office of Energy (SFOE), DETEC, *Sectoral Plan for Deep Geological Repositories: Conceptual Part* (2 April 2008b), www.bfe.admin.ch/radioaktiveabfaelle/01375/04389/index.html?lang=en

"Switzerland's First Nuclear Plant Decommissioned," *SWI* (17 September 2003), www.swissinfo.ch/eng/switzerland-s-first-nuclear-plant-decommissioned/3518582

"30 Years of History at the Grimsel Test Site (GTS)," *Grimsel Test Site* (n.d.), www.grimsel.com/gts-information/about-the-gts/30-years-of-history-at-the-gts

van Berg, R., and Damveld, H., *Discussions on Nuclear Waste – A Survey on Public Participation, Decision-Making and Discussions in Eight Countries: Belgium, Canada, France, Germany, Spain, Sweden, Switzerland, United Kingdom*, Dutch Commission for the Disposal of Radioactive Waste (CORA) (January 2000).

Vari, A., Reagan-Cirincione, P., and Mumpower, J., *LLRW Disposal Facility Siting: Successes and Failures in Six Countries* (Boston, MA: Kluwer Academic, 1994).

von Rohr, M., "Switzerland: Putting Nuclear to the Vote," *Spiegel* (11 July 2008), www.spiegel.de/international/europe/switzerland-putting-nuclear-to-the-vote-a-565156.htm

World Nuclear Association, *Nuclear Power in Switzerland* (updated May 2014), www.world-nuclear.org/info/Country-Profiles/Countries-O-S/Switzerland

World Nuclear Association, *Swiss Radwaste Consultation Opens* (19 June 2012), www.world-nuclear-news.org/WR-Swiss_radwaste_consultation_opens-1906127.html

Zurkinden, A., Kowalski, E., Steiner, P., and Flüeler, T., "Wellenberg," *Community Waste Management (COWAM)* (last updated February 2005), www.cowam.com/?Wellenberg

Zwilag, "History" (n.d.), www.zwilag.ch/en/history-_content--1-1068.html

Conclusion

The generation of radioactive waste is a by-product of many of the essential services that sustain modern society, from the production of electricity and life-saving medical procedures to exploration in the mining industry and basic scientific research. Low level radioactive waste (LLRW) disposal facilities have been, and continue to be, licensed with strong community support in various parts of the world but siting is difficult: the stars need to align for things to go right and any number of factors can cause things to go wrong. There is no road map that can guarantee success – siting strategies, as shown by the case studies examined here, are dependent on unique cultural dynamics and a complex interplay of local, regional and national politics (as well as international politics in some cases) that are often highly fluid. That being said, a number of distinct themes emerge from the case studies: a set of common challenges faced by all siting authorities and a longer list of approaches to siting that have had varying degrees of success. The findings and recommendations that follow can be considered a general good-practice guide that should inform a specific siting strategy adopted by decision-makers.

Common challenges

There is a common perception that radioactive waste is fundamentally different to, and more dangerous than, other forms of hazardous waste. As discussed in chapter 3, in 1988 a group of Nebraska senators argued that a LLRW disposal facility was a public good essentially no different from a school, road or car wash and, as such, should simply built when needed. To require a community referendum before doing so was considered bad public policy. However, a majority of Boyd County residents, as well as the governor's office after 1990, felt very differently and the issue of community consent over what they considered to be a dangerous facility that posed a serious health risk was central to their fight against US Ecology and the rest of the compact members.[1]

This belief in the inherent difference or uniqueness of radiation has become so engrained in the public consciousness that there is a stigma associated with any activity that involves 'insidious' radioactivity that makes siting waste disposal facilities extremely challenging.[2] Despite the fact that we are "immersed in a sea of radiation," most people's instinctive reaction is fear; these fears can range from the realistic, such as increased risk of cancer, to the irrational, such as 'brainless babies' being born at nuclear power plants (Gerrard 1995, p. 100; Park 2013, p. 5). Yet LLRW decays over time (it becomes safer as it becomes less radioactive) and the disposal facilities will eventually become ordinary landfills. Compare this with inorganic waste such as lead and arsenic, which remains toxic and carcinogenic forever and is regularly buried in landfills with far less controversy (e-mail communication with Voss, January 2015). This stigma underpins almost everything the antinuclear movement does and it was particularly prevalent in Nebraska, South Korea and Australia. Rational discussion of the risks, which are very real but often misunderstood or exaggerated, between scientific experts and members of the public can break down some of the barriers, but distrust of government officials and industry representatives, stoked by the antinuclear movement, can undermine even the most basic efforts at information exchange.

Public distrust is exacerbated by the legacy of past disposal practices. As discussed in chapter 1, the history of radioactive waste disposal has been far from perfect. Many of those decisions were based on the best information available at the time. But the somewhat lax approach to ocean disposal and the poor safety record of first-generation land disposal technology, combined with a widespread 'decide-announce-defend' approach to siting adopted by governments that minimized or ignored public opinion, continues to play a role in siting debates, particularly when some of those disposal sites are still being remediated. While modern disposal designs like those used in Texas, Spain and South Korea are vastly superior to their rudimentary ancestors, it is the mistakes of the past that continue to make news and loom large in the public consciousness.

For antinuclear organizations and many environmental organizations, opposing radioactive waste disposal solutions is a tactic that supports the broader objective of undermining the nuclear industry, and their effectiveness is in large part dependent on the groups' support bases. Where antinuclear sentiment is widespread, opposition groups garner strong regional and national support; this has been evidenced in Australia and in much of South Korea's siting history. In contrast, protests in Spain tended to coalesce locally around specific events and, as a result, opponents struggled to gain national traction on El Cabril. Opposition in Switzerland has also been local and regional rather than national, although concerns about the integrity of Nagra's siting process played more of a role in Nidwalden's rejection of the Wellenberg site in 1995 and 2002 than antinuclear sentiment. In West Texas, where industrial hazard is an accepted part of daily life, antinuclear groups have found very little sympathy for their warnings.

An organized and energized opposition can be highly effective at stopping a disposal program. Opponents in Nebraska exhibited, and in Australia they continue to exhibit, both of these traits. And if the government officials who are ultimately responsible for oversight are also actively opposed, it is almost impossible to make progress. As Gerrard has noted: "adamant, sustained citizen opposition, when backed by local government, almost always wins" (1995, p. 97). This observation can be extended to state/regional government.

Nebraska under Governor Nelson is the clearest example but similar resistance is also evident in Australia and for extended periods in Texas and South Korea. This is not to suggest that such opposition is immutable – Texas and South Korea both experienced roughly two decades of sustained opposition over wide geographic areas before willing host communities were found – but pushing against a closed door in one location is not likely to win the battle of hearts and minds and is generally counterproductive.

All of these factors tend to lead to a reflexive not-in-my-backyard (NIMBY) response to waste disposal facility proposals. As the siting failures in Nebraska, Texas, Australia and South Korea have shown, in addition to the local and regional opposition to El Cabril in Spain, NIMBY arguments are a powerful motivator. In addition to a general aversion to nuclear facilities, opposition can be piqued by several specific concerns. In the United States, there was a wide-spread fear amongst prospective host communities that the regional facilities they were being asked to accept would eventually become national disposal sites.[3] This antipathy at being forced to take any sort of waste not generated 'locally' was also evident in Australia and Switzerland. Additionally, despite a very good safety record, transportation and the perceived risk of accidents near population centers served as lightning rods for opposition; one of the reasons so many of the candidate sites in South Korea were in coastal locations accessible by local ports was to avoid transportation on the nation's highways.

Factors and strategies that contribute to successful siting outcomes

Despite these considerable challenges, Texas and South Korea have successfully sited disposal facilities with overwhelming local support, and Empresa Nacional de Residuos Radiactivos S.A. (ENRESA) has made a convincing public case not only for continued operation of El Cabril but also for expansion of the facility. The remainder of the conclusion describes the factors and strategies that can have a positive impact on siting efforts.

Brown field sites and natural constituencies for radioactive waste disposal

Communities that already host radioactive or industrial waste storage and/or disposal operations and communities that live near nuclear power plants tend to be supportive of nuclear activities, which is why colocation is a favored strategy for hazardous facilities in general and nuclear facilities in particular. Texas's Waste Control Specialists (WCS) benefited from locating its LLRW disposal facility at a brown field site in a burgeoning 'nuclear corridor.' South Korea clearly benefited from colocation: the disposal center was situated right next to the Wolsong nuclear plant. Similarly, two decades of waste disposal helped ENRESA make the case that it could continue to safely manage operations at El Cabril once public opinion began to play a role in government decision-making in Spain. In contrast, siting authorities in Nebraska, Australia and Switzerland had neither of these advantages. Risk perception is the key and is best exemplified by Andrews Industrial Forum President Lloyd Eisenrich's observation about West Texas: "You've got a county with over ten thousand holes poked in the ground and H$_2$S gas out there that could wipe out this whole community with one leak and the wind blowing in the right direction. They understand hazard" (Homans 2012).

Advantages can also accrue to the selection of sites on public land. While government-owned land certainly does not guarantee the availability of real estate, as evidenced by US Ecology's unsuccessful efforts to site a disposal facility in Ward Valley, California (discussed in chapter 2), it does avoid many of the challenges associated with acquiring private property and negates any temptation for a government to invoke the highly provocative strategy of enforcing eminent domain.

The role of geology

Perfect geology or meteorology for LLRW disposal is exceedingly rare and in any event is not required for a facility to be built safely. Suitable geology, on the other hand, is reasonably common and engineered barriers (discussed later) provide multiple layers of redundancy to ensure safety under a variety of conditions but this is not always understood by the public or government officials. That being said, and while not an option for many countries, there are clear advantages to choosing a prospective site in an arid, sparsely populated location (such as Córdoba, Spain, and Andrews County, Texas) because, unlike a high rainfall area such as Boyd County, Nebraska, they intuitively make sense to nonexperts given moving water is the most likely cause of radionuclide leakage. By contrast, sites requiring complex modeling can be difficult to explain to neighboring communities, particularly if those communities are unfamiliar with nuclear operations as they were in northern Nebraska. Yet such advantageous geography is far from a guarantee, as events in Australia have clearly demonstrated.

The role of engineered barriers

The use of engineered barriers in a disposal facility has proven an easy target for opponents to mischaracterize and for the general public to misunderstand. While engineered barriers are considered best practice for a defense-in-depth approach, opponents regularly portray them as evidence that a site is unsuitable; this can be very difficult to rebut, particularly when the affected communities are unaware that engineered barriers are essential to all disposal facilities, regardless of design. The only way to mitigate this is for governments and siting authorities to conduct coordinated and ongoing public outreach explaining what is required for safe disposal, preferably as soon as a decision is made that a disposal facility needs to be built. When engineered barriers are accepted as an integral part of the disposal design, as they have been in Texas, South Korea and Spain (as well as Switzerland, despite the inability of authorities to find a willing host), it becomes easier for potential host communities to accept that a site does not require ideal geology for a safe disposal facility to be built, and emphasizing the search for a 'suitable' (geologically, politically, etc.) site can help to prevent the perfect being the enemy of the good.

Innovative design and siting strategies

Innovative and community-friendly approaches to facility design and siting can be important in terms of building public knowledge and trust. The examples that follow are not taken from strictly LLRW but could easily be applied to LLRW operations. The spent nuclear fuel (SNF) and high level waste (HLW) storage facility HABOG in the Netherlands is painted bright orange and every time it needs to be repainted, it will receive a lighter coat reflecting the steady cooling of the stored waste until, in roughly 100 years, it will be painted white.[4] Taking a different approach, Zwilag guaranteed that the radioactive waste storage facility in Würenlingen, Switzerland, would be operated for 25 years, at which point the local community could request that it be removed within 10 years.

A dedicated waste management organization

The existence of a dedicated waste management organization has proven to be an important factor because it provides a stable source of funding, a locus of expertise, a single point of contact for affected communities and a source of organizational continuity that does not exist when government officials subject to the whims of bureaucratic politics and the electoral cycle have responsibility for day-to-day operations. The record is mixed, however, on whether that organization is likely to be more successful at siting a disposal facility if it is private, public or a combination of the two. In Texas, state agencies tried and failed for two decades to find an acceptable site before the legislature authorized private companies to dispose of LLRW in 2003; from that point, it took less than 10 years for WCS to build local support, license and construct a facility and receive the first waste shipment at its Andrews site. In contrast, US Ecology led the site search in Nebraska but, as has been discussed, senior state officials were vehemently opposed to hosting a disposal facility, so the company's efforts were doomed by forces largely beyond its control from 1991. Spain's ENRESA, a government-created, publicly owned company, had a different task: build local and regional support for continued waste disposal operations at El Cabril as well as for expansion of operations, which it has done successfully. Australia has chosen not to set up a dedicated organization and is still looking for a national host community while responsibility remains fragmented between state and federal governments.

The creation of a dedicated organization is not enough, however; it needs to be technically competent and trusted by stakeholders. And, in order to do this, the organization's reputation is its most precious commodity. ENRESA and WCS had good safety records at El Cabril (operational since 1961) and Andrews (15 years of waste disposal operations prior to the LLRW facility being licensed in 2009), respectively. US Ecology's record was mixed in Nebraska. Leaks and other problems at the company's older disposal facilities at Beatty, Maxey Flats and Sheffield were continually highlighted by opponents. In Switzerland, the government and the waste producers created Nagra to prepare for the disposal of all categories of radioactive waste but the organization's political missteps created a serious public trust deficit, which is why the Swiss Federal Office of Energy (SFOE) took over from Nagra and the latter was relegated to the role of a technical backup organization in 2008.[5] More successfully, the Swiss utilities created Zwilag to provide an interim centralized storage solution for all categories of waste in Würenlingen.

A good reputation can also build support for expanded operations (El Cabril in Spain) or new missions entirely (WCS and SNF storage in Texas, discussed in more detail later). Increased opposition due to fears of 'mission creep' is certainly possible – it was precisely this outcome that motivated some of the most visceral opposition in Nebraska, Texas and many other US states – but continued safe operations usually build more trust, not less.

A clear and generally accepted definition of host community and consent

Generally accepted definitions of what constituted 'host community' and what was required for that community to give 'consent' existed in Texas and South Korea. In South Korea, referenda in four locations were sufficient for Gyeongju to be chosen. The legitimacy of the votes in November 2005 was enhanced by the fact that the country had been moving progressively toward more autonomy for local governments at the expense of the provinces.[6] The process was less formal but no less legitimate in Andrews County: radioactive waste disposal in general and WCS's plans in particular were supported by local officials, the broader business community (especially the Andrews Industrial Foundation), as well as a majority of residents, and they were not opposed by surrounding counties in Texas or New Mexico.

The same was true of Switzerland: even though Nidwalden voted no to a disposal facility in two referenda, it was generally accepted that the canton was the host community and had it voted yes, this would have constituted sufficient consent for the site to be approved. In Spain, while the municipality of Hornachuelos is the geographic host in the narrowest sense and the beneficiary of the largest share of compensation, the expansion of the compensation package to include residents within a 10 mile radius of the site (incorporating four municipalities) indicates that the concept of 'host community' is broader than first envisioned. Subsequent successful negotiations with these surrounding communities over compensation suggest that consent has in fact been achieved, even if it is grudging in some cases. By contrast, both definitions were contested in Nebraska and they remain in dispute in Australia.

Transparent decision-making

Transparency is crucial to building public trust. In Nebraska, when the compact commission was selecting a disposal site developer, it required that the companies place copies of their bids in public reading rooms in each state, that company representatives appear before public technical advisory panels in each state and that company representatives participate in a 3-week tour of the region including appearances at public meetings (Vari, Reagan-Cirincione and Mumpower 1994, p. 112). This was an unusual (at least in the US context) but constructive example of transparent decision-making. However, as was demonstrated in the case of South Korea, the provision of more and more information is not always the answer. The siting process needs to be clear and consistent, with a fixed definition of both general siting criteria and the specific waste categories that the facility will be licensed to receive.

This is best illustrated by examples of opaque or ambiguous decision-making. The perception that Nagra was not being candid about the criteria being used to find a suitable site (evidenced by the late inclusion of Wellenberg) and the sorts of waste that would eventually be buried there (including 'negligible levels' of long-lived intermediate level radioactive waste after it had been decided that long-lived intermediate waste would not be sent to the repository) generated public confusion and distrust in Switzerland.

The Swiss case study is also instructive in that the process that led to the selection of Bois de la Glaive, Oberbauenstock and Piz Pian Grand was conducted exclusively by Nagra and the technical experts it hired. There was no attempt to elicit public input. This fed into an increasingly accepted narrative that Nagra was not being completely transparent and suspicion that political criteria were playing a decisive role in site selection. Accusations of decision-making by executive fiat and secret deals with governors and mayors were also the main reasons why government efforts to find a disposal site for the country's radioactive waste failed in South Korea until 2005.

In this context, several unsuccessful siting efforts should not necessarily be seen as failures and can actually reinforce the integrity of both the process and the responsible authority by demonstrating that sites will be rejected even though resources have been spent characterizing them if they are found to be unsuitable. However, premature commitment to a site that proves deficient (for example, Gulup Island in South Korea) or a perceived commitment to a specific location regardless of the host community's wishes (for example, Nagra and Wellenberg in Switzerland and Muckaty Station in Australia) can badly damage the credibility of the siting authority.

The role of incentives/compensation

Even the most enthusiastic communities will not host disposal facilities for free. Incentives and compensation play a critical role in tipping the cost/benefit matrix in favor of the latter. Financial assistance can be indirect in the form of providing tax revenue to local, state/regional and federal governments and offering tax breaks to local businesses, but most analyses focus on direct financial assistance, which can certainly play an important role in host community decision-making but can also be difficult to quantify. However, large monetary payouts also run the risk of being viewed as bribes. This is why financial incentives are most effective when they are part of broader benefits packages. And the most comprehensive of these packages include the provision of social services. Often referred to as 'sustainable development' or more simply the 'good neighbor policy,' examples can be drawn from all of the case studies but were particularly common in Switzerland, Spain, Texas and South Korea. Investments in local infrastructure such as schools, hospitals and fire stations are typical, but projects such as water conservation and protection of local flora and fauna have also been funded. The popularity of these programs can be measured by the harsh reaction of 22 neighboring communities to the Spanish Cabinet's decision to liquidate the ENRESA Foundation in September 2013.

Disposal operations can also contribute to local/regional welfare in other important ways such as in the case of Switzerland the nuclear utilities providing free electricity to Wolfenschiessen and the site operator guaranteeing property prices should disposal operations negatively impact the local real estate market. Employing the local workforce and using local resources is also a productive strategy although it may not be simple. ENRESA found that most local workers did not have the requisite skills to work at El Cabril, so the Spanish government stepped up to offer training programs to ensure local employment. In Texas, 'local' is a relative term, as roughly half of the workforce at WCS's Andrews site lives in New Mexico.

The precise makeup and monetary value of these benefits may not be immediately obvious, in large part because the affected communities often do not know what they need and/or want at the outset and how those needs/wants can best be met. The details are negotiated over time. Sometimes substantially more direct financial assistance may be required than initially offered, as was the case in South Korea with the regional development fund being increased from ₩50 billion to ₩300 billion. In other cases, financial payouts are less important than the provision of ongoing social services. In Spain, some Hornachuelos officials viewed El Cabril as a double-edged sword because the facility simply created boom-and-bust cycles that only boomed during construction periods.

The distribution of compensation is equally important. As discussed in chapter 8, the only community to vote in favor of drilling an exploratory tunnel in the cantonal referendum of 2002 in Switzerland was Wolfenschiessen, the closest community to the proposed construction site, "illustrating the common 'donut' effect in which even if a local host community is prepared to accept the burdens of a wider public, communities close enough to feel affected but too far to derive direct benefits may still object" to a disposal facility (National Research Council of the National Academies 2003, p. 169). In these cases, one approach is to apply a spatial distribution of compensation, that is, drawing concentric circles around the facility with compensation decreasing the further away from the site one lives.

While no amount of compensation can convince a community implacably opposed to radioactive waste disposal to suddenly embrace the construction of a facility, a carefully calibrated incentives and compensation package can create a genuine constituency for disposal operations. Once a constituency exists, it is vital that the incentives and compensation be provided throughout the life of the disposal project. This should include the site selection and characterization phases so communities willing to consider hosting duties receive benefits for participating in the search whether or not they are ultimately selected.

The role of experts

Ideally, experts from government and the waste management industry would be viewed as apolitical by prospective host communities, but this is not always the case. Clearly the public is more likely to accept siting recommendations and outcomes if the experts involved in the site searches are not perceived as suffering from 'agency capture.' As a result, affected communities need independent sources of information from individuals and organizations that they trust. The Nebraska local monitoring committees (LMCs), for example, relied heavily on contracting geologists to provide a second opinion on the work being done by US Ecology and its subcontractors. Of course, the Boyd and Nuckolls LMCs were also looking for their consultants to deliver findings that contradicted US Ecology's conclusions. In Switzerland, the Cantonal Expert Group Wellenberg (KFW) played a similarly important role. Created by the Nidwalden government to help the canton make an informed decision on the Wellenberg site, KFW was made up of scientific experts and a lawyer. KFW conducted an open dialogue with siting authorities as well as the leading critical nongovernmental organization (NGO) and involved the public, through advisory committees, in the institutional and political decision-making framework. In both cases, these groups served an enormously important role as a conduit between the potential host communities and the government/siting authority.

The role of citizens' groups

In a number of cases, citizens' groups formed spontaneously or were created by government or the company doing the siting work, sometimes in cooperation with civic organizations. In some cases these groups also included government/ siting authority representation. In Nebraska, the governor and the legislature created LMCs to represent the citizens of the proposed site. The LMCs were given access to all monitoring data and were authorized to contract technical experts to advise them during the site characterization process. US Ecology and the League of Women Voters also established a productive but short-lived Citizens Advisory Committee to involve the public in the site selection process as well as facility design questions.

In Spain, the Associación de Municipios en Áreas con Centrales Nucleares (AMAC) included 67 municipalities and represented roughly 80,000 people living within 6 miles of nuclear facilities. In part a product of the environmental movement's antinuclear campaign, AMAC's objective is increasing transparency and public participation in nuclear decision-making. Critically, AMAC is viewed by the relevant government ministries, ENRESA, the Nuclear Safety Council (CSN) and the Spanish Electricity Industry Association as the most appropriate conduit to local communities.

In South Korea, the Ministry of Knowledge Economy established a Site Selection Committee in March 2005 to ensure "transparency and fairness" in the siting process. Twenty civilian experts from diverse fields – including science, technology, culture, society, media, law and civil society groups – were chosen to supervise the selection process.

Four groups emerged in Switzerland. Surveillance commissions were created at the four potential host sites. Consisting of representatives of the local community, canton and Bundesrat and chaired by the Federal Nuclear Safety Inspectorate, the commissions kept the public informed on characterization work and communicated local concerns to Nagra. MNA (the committee for the right of the people of Nidwalden to be heard on matters concerning nuclear facilities) was formed as a result of Nidwalden's invitation to Nagra to conduct preliminary investigations at Wellenberg. As distinct from most of the groups discussed here, MNA was explicitly antinuclear in its outlook, and its mobilization tactics, focusing on emotional issues like the impact a disposal facility might have on tourism and farming, were effective. In 1991, Canton Nidwalden created a 13-member Wellenberg Working Group (WWG) consisting of technical experts and nontechnical stakeholders including a politician, a host community representative and an environmentalist. The WWG advised the federal government on the license application. Most ambitiously, an Energy Dialogue on Waste Management Working Group made up of representatives from the federal government, Nagra, waste producers, environmental organizations and opposition groups was created. Perhaps not surprisingly given its membership, after 10 months of work the group could only reach consensus on anodyne language regarding the need for further research and bridge-building between siting authorities and environmental organizations.

The value of these groups is rooted in their legitimacy: they were and are seen as legitimate representatives of the local communities' interests by both those communities and the siting authorities. As a result, the communities' concerns, as transmitted by the groups, are listened to and addressed by decision-makers or ignored at their peril. However, the Energy Dialogue demonstrated that there are limits to the effectiveness of these groups when too many voices are accommodated, and the Boyd County LMC demonstrated how these groups can operate as highly effective loci of opposition when membership is dominated by organizations and individuals trying to prevent the facility from being built.

Communication

With the stigma that surrounds radioactive waste, messaging is critical. It is important to avoid absolutes, such as "no possibility" of groundwater contamination, and overstatements, such as LLRW is "just not that hazardous" (Robbins 1999; "Radioactive Waste Dump Proposal Hits Dell City" 1983, p. 6). These statements are simply not true (the latter in part because it applies to LLRW in the United States, which can be highly radioactive in certain circumstances, as explained in the introduction) and usually lead to public overreactions the moment the disposal facility does not operate exactly as promised. Language is something that anti-nuclear groups in particular have used to great effect. Terms like 'cemetery,' 'nuclear garbage,' and 'dump' are used regularly; indeed, the latter term is common parlance just about everywhere. As a result, overemphasizing 'neutral language' runs the risk of being interpreted as insincerity. When Texcor's president Charles Salsman was selling naturally occurring radioactive material (NORM) disposal to Spofford, some residents noted suspiciously that Salsman always used the words 'waste facility' rather than 'dump' (Siegel 1991).

The 'who' can also make a big difference. Experts that are seen as independent from the siting process such as medical doctors and university scientists are often trusted by the general public more than government officials and industry spokesmen, and these professionals sometimes played an active role in the debate, particularly in the United States.

Public education

Because radiation is not well understood by the general public, it is incumbent upon siting authorities to provide enough information for potentially affected communities to make up their own minds about the risks posed by disposal facilities. There are a variety of ways this can be achieved. For example, public meetings and workshops have been used extensively to share information with interested residents. Governments have hosted field trips to disposal operations elsewhere to show residents from prospective host communities operating LLRW disposal facilities (for example, the South Korean government's field trips to Lanyu Island in Taiwan during the 1980s and 1990s). Siting authorities have also built visitors' centers (e.g., Korea Hydro and Nuclear Power's [KHNP's] two visitors' centers at the Wolsong Disposal Center) and information centers (for example, ENRESA's information centers at El Cabril, Madrid, Andújar, Córdoba and Vandellós). And, as discussed earlier, citizens' groups play a very important in enabling members of the public to educate themselves.

A matter of trust

Public involvement in the decision-making process fulfills certain key functions:

> Participation is a fundamental element in realizing democratic ideals; involvement in decision making increases support for the eventual decision; participation can reduce tensions and control conflict; and the public may provide perspectives dealing with crucial issues overlooked by the technical specialists.
>
> (Bord 1988, pp. 200, 203)

The aim should be to integrate the general public into the process as legitimate partners. Ultimately, community support for disposal operations can only be generated through trust. Stakeholders must believe the siting authority is competent, the siting process is fair, the disposal facility will be safe and its operation will not have an adverse affect on their livelihood. In Andrews County, there was a high level of trust in WCS operations from the outset, based in large part on general familiarity with hazardous technology. In Spain, ENRESA worked diligently with neighboring communities to build trust. Safe operations and transparent decision-making combined with financial and social welfare assistance facilitated community consent to several expansions of the facility in order to meet the country's growing LLRW and ILRW disposal needs.

The South Korean case study demonstrated that trust can develop even after years of mutual distrust and animosity between the government and its populace. In Switzerland, trust in Nagra, which was severely impacted with the 2002 referendum defeat, reached its nadir in 2008; SFOE is now tasked with rebuilding public confidence. In Nebraska, a substantial section of Boyd County believed that the Central Compact (with the passive complicity of Governor Orr) was riding roughshod over its interests and did not believe that US Ecology could construct a safe disposal facility. An important corollary to this is that the company's decisions to redraw the site boundaries and scale back the facility design led to less rather than more trust in the project.

In Australia, the rushed processes and top-down approaches implemented by the federal government served to marginalize key stakeholders. Indigenous populaces in particular, given a long history of broken promises, do not have much faith in the government's promises anyway. As a result, there was little buy-in to the decision-making methodology, and without that trust, the government has found it hard to make any headway.

Environmental justice

LLRW disposal facilities occupy a relatively limited geographic area so, while the benefits accrue to society broadly defined (whether it be a state, several states, a region or a country), the size of the community that will be directly affected by disposal operations is always going to be small. As a result, questions of equity are often raised when siting decisions are made, and these can be particularly divisive when lower socioeconomic and indigenous groups make up large percentages of those potential host communities. The perception that these disadvantaged groups are being selected because they are 'desperate' and do not have the economic and political resources to resist like more affluent communities can be difficult to rebut. The catch is that many of the most suitable sites – in terms of geology and population density – are located in just these areas and the optics of site selection that focuses predominantly on these communities can imply intent where there is none.

In Australia, many of the attempts to site LLRW facilities have been on aboriginal land, prompting charges that these communities were being targeted by siting authorities (McGurty 1997, pp. 301–323). Similarly, charges of environmental and economic racism were levelled at state siting authorities in Texas by local residents, Mexican Congressmen and opposition groups. For example, the Sierra Blanca Legal Defense Fund noted in 1999 that none of the licensing documents had been translated into Spanish despite the fact that it is the first language for many of potentially affected parties in far West Texas (Sierra Blanca Legal Defense Fund 1999). In Nebraska, opponents argued that the three candidate sites were chosen because they were "rural and sparsely populated, have low incomes, are mostly above middle age, politically conservative, free-market oriented, have a high school education or less and [are] staunchly patriotic" (Bartimus 1989).

Environmental justice is the fair treatment and meaningful involvement of all people regardless of race, color, national origin or income. Fair treatment in the context of this book means that no group of people should bear a disproportionate share of the negative environmental consequences resulting from the construction and operation of a LLRW disposal facility. Meaningful involvement means that people have an opportunity to participate in decisions about activities that may affect their environment and/or health, the public's contribution will be considered and can influence decision-making, and decision-makers seek out and facilitate the involvement of those potentially affected (United States Environmental Protection Agency [EPA] updated 2012).

Sidney Wolf has explained:

> Protection of the public is not achieved by the mere existence of strict standards for hazardous waste facilities – although these are a necessary element in any effort to achieve this end. In order to protect the public it is essential to afford citizens the means and a forum to protect themselves. This can be accomplished by full and consequential participation in the regulatory process.
>
> (Wolf 1980, p. 481)

To achieve this, a procedural justice approach offers some distinct benefits. Procedural justice is not concerned with outcomes per se, individual rights and responsibilities or finding a way to satisfy everyone; there will always be opposition, particularly on an issue as controversial as radioactive waste disposal. Rather the focus is on whether the process itself is fair to all affected stakeholders. For many stakeholders, outcomes can be accepted if they are generated as part of a perceived fair process that takes their concerns into consideration. In pluralistic societies like the ones examined here, a "fair process seems like the most appropriate way to satisfy the demands of justice, especially on contentious issues such as LLW disposal" and its impact on the most vulnerable members of society (English 1992, p. 151).

Toward holistic radioactive waste management?

Attempts to combine LLRW and SNF/HLW disposal have either been rejected or have failed. An example of the former: in the United States, Congress originally intended to consolidate all categories of commercial waste into one piece of disposal legislation but stripped out the SNF/HLW sections when it became clear that they would derail the bill. An example of the latter: South Korea's efforts to find a location for all categories of waste simultaneously were unsuccessful until 2005, less than a year after the government separated LLRW and ILRW from the SNF disposal efforts. This is a function of risk perception; SNF and HLW are much more radioactive than LLRW over vastly longer periods of time and require much more extensive shielding from the biosphere. When exposed to a rational dialogue, people understand this. And most people are more comfortable with LLRW disposal than HLW disposal.

Once a LLRW disposal facility has been operating for a period of time, a track record of safety can help to build public confidence in other sorts of radioactive waste storage and disposal. In Texas, WCS appears to have made significant progress toward exactly this outcome. The governor and the host community are supportive of the company's plans to provide an interim storage option for SNF. Similarly, ENRESA has pursued a very deliberate step-by-step strategy in Spain of demonstrating safe operations at El Cabril as a way to build public confidence in the organization's ability to construct and operate an interim SNF storage facility and eventually develop a deep geological repository for SNF/ HLW. And although a law presently guarantees that Gyeongju will not be considered as a site for future SNF storage, the Wolsong Disposal Center could serve a similar confidence-building function for South Korea.

Given that LLRW continues to be produced in large volumes and these wastes need to be shielded for extended periods of time, building new disposal facilities and expanding existing facilities will be required indefinitely. The difficulties involved in siting these facilities are often portrayed as intractable – zero-sum games between multiple stakeholders with incompatible objectives and goals. But, as the preceding analysis has demonstrated, this is not true. While the challenges should not be understated, it is possible to license and construct disposal facilities with strong political and community support. Although there is no one pathway to success, decision-makers who heed the lessons described in this book will greatly enhance the likelihood of achieving their goals of successfully siting LLRW disposal facilities and identifying broader nuclear waste management solutions.

Notes

1   For more on health concerns and radioactive waste disposal facility siting see Gerrard 1995, p. 129–30; Susskind 1990, p. 309; Bingham 1985; McGuire 1985; Sassaman 1992; Shanabrook 1987.
2   Insidious is a word often associated with radiation by opponents as it cannot be seen, smelled or tasted. See Weart 1988, p. 54.
3   At the beginning of March 2015, EnergySolutions, operator of the Barnwell LLRW disposal facility in South Carolina, launched a media campaign to reopen the site to the nation – since 2008 Barnwell has received waste only from the three Atlantic Compact member states (South Carolina, Connecticut and New Jersey). EnergySolutions' aim is to optimize operations at the two disposal facilities it operates by directing hotter and more lucrative Class B and C waste to Barnwell and the least radioactive waste category to its Class A facility in Utah. According to newspaper reports, there is significant political opposition to the company's bid to compete nationally with WCS (Fretwell 2015; O'Briant 2015; Roldan 2015).
4   Orange was chosen for the initial color because it is the national color of the Netherlands and symbolically it is halfway between red (danger) and green (safety) ("HABOG – Nuclear Waste Management in an Artistic Way" 2010).
5   While referring to spent fuel and high level waste, the Blue Ribbon Commission on America's Nuclear Future found that the "overall record of DOE [the Department of Energy] and of the federal government as a whole, however, has not inspired widespread confidence or trust in our nation's nuclear waste management program." For this and other reasons, the commission concluded that a "new, single-purpose organization is needed to provide the stability, focus, and credibility that are essential to get the waste program back on track" (Blue Ribbon Commission on America's Nuclear Future, Report to the Secretary of Energy 2012, p. x).
6   Waste Control Specialists is taking the same approach to community consent for its spent nuclear fuel storage plans; that is, ensure Andrews County officials and residents support the plan first then engage with neighboring counties in Texas and New Mexico.

References

Bartimus, T., "Plan for Nuclear Dump Stirs Rancor in Rural Nebraska," Los Angeles Times (26 March 1989), http://articles.latimes.com/1989–03–26/news/mn-778_1_nuclear-waste-dump

Bingham, G., "Prospects for Negotiations of Hazardous Waste Siting Disputes," Environmental Law Reporter, 15 ELR 10249, Issue 1 (January 1985).

Blue Ribbon Commission on America's Nuclear Future, Report to the Secretary of Energy, Washington, DC (January 2012), http://cybercemetery.unt.edu/archive/brc/20120620220235/ http://brc.gov/sites/default/files/documents/brc_finalreport_jan2012.pdf

Bord, R., "The Low-Level Radioactive Waste Crisis: Is More Citizen Participation the Answer?," in M. E. Burns (ed.), Low-Level Radioactive Waste Regulation: Science, Politics and Fear (Chelsea, MI: Lewis, 1988).

English, M., Siting Low-Level Radioactive Waste Disposal Facilities: The Public Policy Dilemma (New York: Quorum Books, 1992), http://trove.nla.gov.au/version/42542117

Fretwell, S., "Utah Company Launches Media Blitz to Reopen SC Atomic Waste Landfill," State (13 March 2015), www.thestate.com/news/local/article14662532.html

Gerrard, M. B., Whose Backyard, Whose Risk (Cambridge, MA: MIT Press, 1995).

"HABOG – Nuclear Waste Management in an Artistic Way," Travelogue of an Armchair Traveller (December 2010), http://armchairtravelogue.blogspot.com/2010/12/habog-nuclear-waste-management-in.html

Homans, C., The Operator," *New Republic* (20 April 2012), www.newrepublic.com/article/politics/magazine/102778/harold-simmons-campaign-donor-2012-gop#

McGuire, J., *The Dilemma of Public Participation in Facility Siting Decisions and the Mediation Alternative*, 9 Seton Hall Legis. J. 467 (1985).

McGurty, E., "From NIMBY to Civil Rights: The Origins of the Environmental Justice Movement," *Environmental History*, Vol. 2, No. 3 (1997): 301–323.

National Research Council of the National Academies, *One Step at a Time: The Staged Development of Geologic Repositories for High-Level Radioactive Waste*, Committee on Principles and Operational Strategies for Staged Repository Systems, Board on Radioactive Waste Management, Division on Earth and Life Studies (Washington, DC: National Academy Press, 2003).

O'Briant, T., "Ex-governor Fought Chem-Nuclear Dump, Wants It to Stay Closed," *Times and Democrat* (22 March 2015), http://thetandd.com/business/ex-governor-fought-chem-nuclear-dump-wants-it-to-stay/article_dbdbbcd5-2885-5059-b1e0-dc521f802ea2.html

Park, S. Y., "Constrained Cooperation in South Korea's Nuclear Power Policy and Its Side Effects," *Korea Advanced Institute of Science and Technology* (September 2013), www.eai.or.kr/data/bbs/kor_report/epik2013_j2.pdf

"Radioactive Waste Dump Proposal Hit Dell City," *Galveston Daily News* (12 November 1983), www.newspapers.com/newspage/14548726/

Robbins, M. A., "Opinion Sought on Waste Disposal," *Lubbock Avalanche-Journal* (16 March 1999b), http://lubbockonline.com/stories/031699/sta_031699094.shtml

Roldan, C., "Charleston Republican Files Bill Restricting Use of Nuclear Waste Dump," *Post and Courier* (27 March 2015), www.postandcourier.com/article/20150327/PC1603/150329364/charleston-republican-files-bill-restricting-use-of-nuclear-waste-dump

Sassaman, J. C., Jr., *Siting Without Fighting: the Role of Mediation in Enhancing Public Participation in Siting Radioactive Waste Facilities*, 2 Alb. L.J. Sci. and Tech. 207 (1992).

Shanabrook, K., *Low-Level Radioactive Waste Disposal Facility Sitings: Negotiating a Role for the Public*, 3 J. Dispute Resol. 219 (1987).

Siegel, B., "A Perfect Place for a Waste Dump," *Los Angeles Times* (22 December 1991), http://articles.latimes.com/1991-12-22/magazine/tm-1262_1_waste-dump-county-seat-grand-champion

Sierra Blanca Legal Defense Fund, "Environmental Justice Case Study: The Struggle for Sierra Blanca, Texas against a Low-Level Nuclear Waste Site" (1999), www.umich.edu/~snre492/blanca.html

Susskind, L., "A Negotiation Credo for Controversial Siting Disputes," Negotiation J (October 1990).

United States Environmental Protection Agency, *Environmental Justice* (updated 24 May 2012), www.epa.gov/environmentaljustice/basics/index.html

Vari, A., Reagan-Cirincione, P., and Mumpower, J. *LLRW Disposal Facility Siting: Successes and Failures in Six Countries* (Boston, MA: Kluwer Academic, 1994).

Weart, S., *Nuclear Fear: A History of Images* (Cambridge, MA: Harvard University Press, 1988).

Wolf, S., "Public Opposition to Hazardous Waste Sites: The Self-Defeating Approach to National Hazardous Waste Control Under Subtitle C of the Resource Conservation and Recovery Act of 1976," *Boston College Environmental Affairs Law Review*, Vol. 8, No. 3 (1980), http://lawdigitalcommons.bc.edu/cgi/viewcontent.cgi?article=1786&context=ealr

Bibliography

Abbott, H., and Davies, E., "Management and Retrieval of Historical Nuclear Waste Previously Prepared and Concrete for Sea Disposal," *Waste Management 2002 Conference*, Tucson, Arizona (24–28 February 2002), www.wmsym.org/archives/2002/Proceedings/43/291.pdf

The Aboriginal Land Rights Act 1976 (NT), www.austlii.edu.au/au/legis/cth/consol_act/alrta1976444/

Abreu, A., Espejo, J.M., Gonzalez, V., and Lazaro, C., "Spanish Fifth General Radioactive Waste Plan," *Waste Management 2000 Conference*, Tucson, Arizona (27 February–2 March 2000), www.wmsym.org/archives/2000/pdf/37/37–05.pdf

Acton, J., and Hibbs, M., "Why Fukushima Was Preventable," *Nuclear Policy*, Carnegie Endowment for International Peace, Washington, DC (March 2012), http://carnegieendowment.org/files/fukushima.pdf

"An Act to Withdraw from the Texas Low-level Radioactive Waste Disposal Compact," Public Laws of Maine, 2nd Regular Session of the 120th, Ch. 629, H.P.1666 – L.D.2171 (5 April 2002), www.mainelegislature.org/ros/LOM/lom120th/4pub601–650/pub601–650–28.htm

Advisory Council on Historic Preservation, Executive Order No. 13007: Indian Sacred Sites (24 May 1996), www.achp.gov/EO13007.html

Advisory Report on the Bill, Parliament of Australia [National Radioactive Waste Bill 2010], (Chapter 1) (n.d.), www.aph.gov.au/About_Parliament/Parliamentary_Departments/Parliamentary_Library/pubs/BN/2011–2012/RadioActiveWaste

Aebersold, M., "Living with Geological Risks: Sectoral Plan for Deep Geological Repositories," *EurGEOSurveys Workshop* (22 October 2014), www.swisstopo.admin.ch/internet/swisstopo/de/home/docu/Kolloquien/20141022.parsys.72367.downloadList.1890.DownloadFile.tmp/13geolrepositoriesaebersoldfoe.pdf

Akerman, P., "Northern Territory Muckaty Waste Dump Plan Abandoned," *Australian* (9 June 2014), www.theaustralian.com.au/news/nation/northern-territory-muckaty-waste-dump-plan-abandoned/story-e6frg6nf-1226959705496?nk=dc2e9b1ed0711b6123e6c33fdde05a39

Alba, A., "The Government Expects to Recover the Lost Funds from the Enresa Foundation," *Cordopolis* (8 January 2015), http://cordopolis.es/2015/01/08/el-gobierno-confia-en-recuperar-los-fondos-perdidos-de-la-fundacion-enresa/

Alba, A., "The Government Suppresses the Enresa Foundation," *Cordopolis* (21 September 2013), http://cordopolis.es/2013/09/21/el-gobierno-suprime-la-fundacion-enresa/

Alba, A., "The People of Cabril Run Out of Money," *Cordopolis* (16 June 2014) http://cordopolis.es/2014/06/16/los-pueblos-del-cabril-se-quedan-sin-dinero/

Albert, M., "The Drum at El Cabril Is Uncovered," *El País* (2014a), http://ccaa.elpais.com/ccaa/2014/02/01/andalucia/1391272412_220000.html

Albert, M., "The Mayors of Nuclear Zones Ask to Settle Accounts with ENRESA," *Cordopolis* (2014b), http://cordopolis.es/2014/12/09/los-alcaldes-de-zonas-nucleares-piden-ajustar-cuentas-con-enresa/

Aldrich, D., *Site Fights: Divisive Facilities and Civil Society in Japan and the West* (Ithaca, NY: Cornell University Press, 2008).

Allardice, C., and Trapnell, E., *The Atomic Energy Commission* (New York: Praeger, 1974).

"Alternative Location Sought on Muckaty Station for Nuclear Waste Dump," *SBS News Online* (26 August 2013), www.sbs.com.au/news/article/2012/11/08/alternative-location-sought-muckaty-station-nuclear-waste-dump

American Geological Institute, *Texas Compact Legislative Background* (23 October 1998), www.agiweb.org/legis105/lownuke.html

"The Andalusian Parliament Approved Two Motions So That It Does Not Expand El Cabril," *Cordopolis* (2 April 2014), http://cordopolis.es/2014/04/02/el-parlamento-andaluz-aprueba-dos-mociones-para-que-no-se-amplie-el-cabril/

"Andrews Residents Leary [sic] of Possible Radioactive Waste Facility," *Lubbock Avalanche-Journal* (18 January 1999), http://lubbockonline.com/stories/011899/LD0638.shtml

Appalachian States Low-Level Radioactive Waste Compact, reprinted in NRC, *Nuclear Regulatory Legislation*, NUREG-0980, Vol. 1, No. 10 (2012).

Arms Control Association, *Nuclear Testing Tally* (updated February 2013), www.armscontrol.org/factsheets/nucleartesttally

"As Nuclear Waste Piles Up, South Korea Faces Storage Crisis," *Reuters* (14 October 2014), www.japantimes.co.jp/news/2014/10/14/asia-pacific/nuclear-waste-piles-south-korea-faces-storage-crisis/#.VJifPsAeA

Aston, H., "Radioactive Waste Haunts Hunters Hill Residents," *Sydney Morning Herald* (30 October 2011), www.smh.com.au/environment/radioactive-waste-haunts-hunters-hill-residents-20111029–1mpb6.html

Australian Conservation Foundation Submission Inquiry of the Senate Standing Committee on Legal and Constitutional Affairs into the National Radioactive Waste Management Bill 2010, www.acfonline.org.au/sites/default/files/resources/ACF_National_Radioactive_Waste_Management_Bill_2010_Senate_Inquiry_Sub.pdf

Australian Heritage Places Inventory, *About the Australian Heritage Places Inventory* (n.d.), www.heritage.gov.au/ahpi/about.html

Australian Nuclear Science and Technology Organisation, *Decommissioning Earlier Reactors* (n.d.), www.ansto.gov.au/AboutANSTO/OPAL/Decommissioningearlierreactors/

Australian Nuclear Science and Technology Organisation, *Management of Radioactive Waste in Australia* (January 2011), www.ansto.gov.au/cs/groups/corporate/documents/webcontent/mdaw/mday/~edisp/acstest_040440.pdf

Australian Nuclear Science and Technology Organisation, *Managing Radioactive Waste* (n.d.), www.ansto.gov.au/NuclearFacts/ManagingRadioActiveWaste/index.htm

Australian Radiation Protection and Nuclear Safety Act (1998), www.austlii.edu.au/au/legis/cth/consol_act/arpansa1998487/

Baltimore, C., Henderson, P., and Brooks, K., "Perry Sought to Sideline Nuclear Waste Site Critic," *Reuters* (1 September 2011), www.reuters.com/article/2011/09/01/us-usa-campaign-perry-dump-idUSTRE78053Z20110901

Barer, D., "Radioactive Waste Site Fees Push Texas Users Out-of-State," *Statesman* (29 November 2012), www.statesman.com/news/news/radioactive-waste-site-fees-push-texas-users-out-o/nTJpP/

Barrett, R., "Ethics Board Says Official Had No Conflict in Waste Panel Vote," *News and Observer (Raleigh)* (14 August 1990), reprinted in *Summary of Significant Findings Regarding the Process of Site Selection for the North Carolina Low-Level Radioactive Waste Facility,* prepared by James, McElroy & Diehl, P.A. (19 February 1992), http://infohouse.p2ric. org/ref/28/27585.pdf

Bartimus, T., "Plan for Nuclear Dump Stirs Rancor in Rural Nebraska," *Los Angeles Times* (26 March 1989), http://articles.latimes.com/1989–03–26/news/mn-778_1_nuclear-waste-dump

Beceiro, A.R., "ATC: The Centralized Interim Storage Facility for SNF and HLW," Madrid, on file with the authors.

Beceiro, A.R., "Spain Low and Intermediate Waste Management Programme: El Cabril Disposal Programme," Madrid (12 December 2013), on file with the authors.

Beck, M., "Radioactive Dump – With 10 Days' Notice, Court Told," *Sydney Morning Herald* (28 March 2012), www.smh.com.au/environment/radioactive-dump–with-10-days-notice-court-told-20120328–1vxdz.html

Bedinger, M.S., *Geohydrologic Aspects for Siting and Design of Low-Level Radioactive-Waste Disposal,* U.S. Geological Survey Circular 1034 (1989), http://pubs.usgs.gov/circ/1989/1034/report.pdf

Beliles, D., "Nuclear Waste Isn't Going Away," *Grand Island Independent* (13 October 1990).

Bennett, D., "The Constitutional Decisions of Justice Selway: (I) Nuclear Waste Dumps and Fire Brigades; (II) Low Flying Planes and (III) What Is State Insurance?" *2007 Adelaide Law Review,* www.austlii.edu.au/au/journals/AdelLawRw/2007/4.pdf

Bergmans, A., "International Benchmarking of Community Benefits Related to Facilities for Radioactive Waste Management Report," Commissioned by EDRAM, NIROND 2010–01 E (January 2010), www.edram.info/uploads/media/2010–01_EDRAM_Com_Benefits_Final_ENG_.pdf

Bergström, U., Pers, K., and Almén, Y., *International Perspective on Repositories for Low Level Waste* (December 2011), www.skb.se/upload/publications/pdf/r-11–16.pdf

Berlin, R., and Stanton, C., *Radioactive Waste Management* (New York: John Wiley & Sons, 1989).

Bertini, H.W. et al., *Descriptions of Selected Accidents That Have Occurred at Nuclear Reactor Facilities,* Oak Ridge National Library (April 1980).

Betancourt, A., "Border Skirmish," *Bulletin of the Atomic Scientists,* Vol. 54, No. 3 (1998): 14–16.

Beyea, J., "Special Issue on the Risks of Exposure to Low-Level Radiation," *Bulletin of the Atomic Scientists,* Vol. 68, No. 3 (2012): 10–12.

Bingham, G., "Prospects for Negotiations of Hazardous Waste Siting Disputes," *Environmental Law Reporter,* 15 ELR 10249, Issue 1 (January 1985).

Bisconti, A., " 'Not' in My Back Yard! Is Really 'Yes' in My Back Yard," *Natural Gas and Electricity* (January 2010), www.nei.org/resourcesandstats/documentlibrary/newplants/reports/article-not-in-my-back-yard-is-really-yes-in-my-back-yard-ann-bisconti-january-2010

Blake, M., "The GOP's Nuke Dump Donor," *Salon* (5 April 2012), www.salon.com/2012/04/05/the_gops_nuke_dump_donor/

Blakeslee, N., "The West Texas Waste Wars," *Texas Observer* (28 March 1997), www.texasradiation.org/andrews/wastewar.html

Blaney, B., "Loving County Wants to Store Spent Nuclear Fuel," *Washington Times* (15 March 2014), www.washingtontimes.com/news/2014/mar/15/loving-county-wants-to-store-spent-nuclear-fuel/

Blaney, B., "Texas Company Could Bury First Nuclear Waste in April," *Lubbock Avalanche-Journal* (19 March 2012), http://lubbockonline.com/texas/2012-03-19/texas-company-could-bury-first-nuclear-waste-april#.Uzmsz6hdW7w

Blaney, B., "Texas House OK's Taking in More Radioactive Waste," *Businessweek* (17 May 2011), www.businessweek.com/ap/financialnews/D9N9GCT81.htm

Blaney, B., "Texas Site Begins Taking Federal Nuclear Waste," *ABC News* (7 June 2013), http://abcnews.go.com/US/wireStory/texas-site-begins-taking-federal-nuclear-waste-19343196#.UbJBx-dgS8A

Blue Ribbon Commission on America's Nuclear Future, *Report to the Secretary of Energy*, Washington, DC (January 2012), http://cybercemetery.unt.edu/archive/brc/20120620220235/http://brc.gov/sites/default/files/documents/brc_finalreport_jan2012.pdf

Bodansky, D., *Nuclear Energy: Principles, Practices, and Prospects* (New York: Springer, 2004).

Bonacci, M., "Federal Court Goes to Muckaty," *Green Left Weekly* (14 June 2014), www.greenleft.org.au/node/56628

Bonfield, T., "Fernald: History Repeats Itself," *Cincinnati Enquirer* (11 February 1996), www.enquirer.com/fernald/stories/021196c_fernald.html

Bord, R., "The Low-Level Radioactive Waste Crisis: Is More Citizen Participation the Answer?," in M. E. Burns (ed.), *Low-Level Radioactive Waste Regulation: Science, Politics and Fear* (Chelsea, MI: Lewis, 1988).

"Boundary Shift Due on Texas Dump Sites," *Victoria Advocate* (1 December 1984).

Boyd County, Nebraska. "About Boyd County" (n.d.), www.boydcounty.ne.gov/webpages/about/about.html

"Boyd County Residents Expect Violence," *McCook Daily Gazette* (29 July 1992).

Bradbury, R., "Nuclear Dump Panel 'In the Dark' on Compact," *Rapid City Journal* (10 June 1983), http://bhodian.com/nuclearwaste.html

Bradley, D., *Behind the Nuclear Curtain: Radioactive Waste Management in the Former Soviet Union*, ed. D. R. Payson (Columbus, OH: Battelle Press, 1997).

Brain, C., "Federal Minister Visits Muckaty Station," *ABS News Online* (1 August 2013), www.abc.net.au/news/2013-08-01/muckaty-resources-minister/4857690

Branson, M., "Should Maine Ship Its Low-Level Radioactive Waste to Texas? A Critical Look at the Texas Low-Level Radioactive Waste Disposal Compact," *Maine Law Review*, Vol. 49, No. 2 (1997).

Bremen, S., and Visocki, K., "In Search of Equity: Development of a Regional System for Managing Low-Level Radioactive Waste in the United States," for publication in the *Forum for Applied Research and Public Policy*, University of Tennessee (30 January 1992), http://secompact.org/speechestestimony/

Breslow, B., "Yucca Mountain – Lessons to Be Learned and a Strategy for the Future," *Blue Ribbon Commission on America's Nuclear Future – Disposal Subcommittee* (7 July 2010), http://brc.gov/Disposal_SC/docs/Bruce%20Breslow-NV%20Agency%20for%20NP-Final.pdf

Brokaw, C., "South Dakotans Vote Down Radioactive Waste Plan," *Associated Press* (12 November 1985), www.apnewsarchive.com/1985/South-Dakotans-Vote-Down-Radioactive-Waste-Plan/id-886c48abc491fd60654b3d3ebd84c53f

Brokaw, C., "What Do They Want in Edgemont? Low-Level Nuclear Waste," *Spokane Chronicle* (13 January 1984), http://news.google.com/newspapers?nid=1345&dat=19840113&id=av1LAAAAIBAJ&sjid=f_kDAAAAIBAJ&pg=6979,2290451

Brulle, J., and Pellow, D., "Environmental Justice: Human Health and Environmental Inequalities," *Annual Review of Public Health*, Vol. 27 (2006): 103–124.

Bukro, C., "Nuclear-Waste Plant Moves in without Whisper," *Chicago Tribune* (26 January 1987), http://articles.chicagotribune.com/1987-01-26/news/8701070195_1_radioactive-waste-low-level-nuclear-power-plants

Bullard, R., *Dumping in Dixie: Race, Class and Environmental Quality* (Boulder, CO: Westview Press, 2000).

Burns, M. E., "Living in the Past, Facing the Future," in Michael E. Burns (ed.), *Low-Level Radioactive Waste Regulation: Science, Politics and Fear* (Chelsea, MI: Lewis, 1998).

Burns, M. E., *Low-Level Radioactive Waste Regulation: Science, Politics and Fear* (Chelsea, MI: Lewis, 1998).

Burns, M. E., and Briner, W. H., "Setting the Stage," in Michael E. Burns (ed.), *Low-Level Radioactive Waste Regulation: Science, Politics and Fear* (Chelsea, MI: Lewis, 1998).

Burrough, B., *The Big Rich: The Rise and Fall of the Greatest Texas Oil Fortunes* (New York: Penguin, 2009).

"Butte Community Survey" (n.d.) in Nebraska State Historical Society, Government Records, RG/41, Series 8, Central Interstate Low-Level Radioactive Waste Compact (LLRW-NE), Misc. Files, Committee/State/Legislature, 1987–2005, Box 1 of 2.

Butterfield, F., "Idaho Firm on Barring Atomic Waste," *New York Times* (23 October 1988), www.nytimes.com/1988/10/23/us/idaho-firm-on-barring-atomic-waste.html

Calmet, D., "Ocean Disposal of Radioactive Waste: Status Report," *IAEA Bulletin*, Vol. 31, No. 4 (1989): 47–49, www.iaea.org/Publications/Magazines/Bulletin/Bull314/31404684750.pdf

Campbell, B., "Andrews' Nuclear Reactor Progresses, Albeit Slowly," *Midland Reporter-Telegram* (1 May 2010), www.mrt.com/news/top_stories/article_0e94744d-c92c-51bb-acf5-f5e6afc038b2.html

Campbell, R., "Waste Control Specialists to Begin Storing Waste from Tennessee Company," *Midland Reporter-Telegram* (3 June 2009), www.mrt.com/news/top_stories/article_eec0090f-ed79-5e9e-bf68-146729883828.html

Camper, L., "Low-Level Radioactive Waste Management in the United States: Where Have We Been: Where Are We Going," *Waste Management 2010 Conference*, Phoenix, Arizona (7–11 March 2010), www.wmsym.org/archives/2010/pdfs/10417.pdf

Caravaca, T., "El Cabril: The Resurrection of the Ghosts of the Nuclear Cemetery," *El Mundo* (2 August 2014), www.elmundo.es/andalucia/2014/02/08/52f667e8ca4741aa308b457d.html

Cart, J., "There's Smoke on Tobacco Road: N.C. State Tries to Cool Valvano Controversy," *Los Angeles Times* (31 August 1989), http://articles.latimes.com/1989-08-31/sports/sp-1885_1_jim-valvano

Carter, L., *Nuclear Imperatives and Public Trust: Dealing with Radioactive Waste* (Washington, DC: Resources for the Future, 1987).

Cary, A., "DOE Says Just 1, Not 6, Hanford Single-Shell Tanks Leaking," *Tri-City Herald* (6 November 2013a), www.tri-cityherald.com/2013/11/06/2661413/doe-says-just-1-not-6-handford.html

Cary, A., "Hanford Radioactive Leak May Have Been Transfer System," *Tri-City Herald* (22 August 2013b), www.tri-cityherald.com/2013/08/22/2534379/hanford-tank-farm-evacuated-for.html

Casey, S., *The Devil's Teeth* (New York: Henry Holt, 2005).

Cates, K., "Colorado, D.C. Fire Shots at Envirocare," *Deseret News* (27 June 1997a) www.deseretnews.com/article/568872/Colorado-DC-fire-shots-at-Envirocare.html?pg=all

Cates, K., "Envirocare Official Says Suit Is Merely Harassment," *Deseret News* (14 March 1997b), www.deseretnews.com/article/548718/Envirocare-official-says-suit-is-merely-harassment-html?pg=all

Cawley, C., Sabbe, M., Bisese, P., et al., *An Approach to the Licensing of a Mixed Waste Unit* (n.d.), in Nebraska State Historical Society, Government Records, RG/41, Series 1, Central Interstate Low-Level Radioactive Waste Compact (LLRW-NE), Research Files, Misc. Reports, 1989–2003, Box 5 of 5.

"Central Compact Issues Export Authorizations over Nebraska's Objection," LLW Notes, LLW Forum (July 1997), in Nebraska State Historical Society, Government Records, RG/41, Series 1, Central Interstate Low-Level Radioactive Waste Compact (LLRW-NE), Research Files, Articles and Books, 1961–2006, Box 2 of 5.

Central Interstate Low-Level Radioactive Waste Commission, *Actions in Which the Commission Is or Was a Party* (1999), www.cillrwcc.org/Legal_Action/SumLit_A.html

Central Interstate Low-Level Radioactive Waste Commission, *Annual Report 2004–2005* (n.d.), www.cillrwcc.org/2004–2005%20Annual%20Report.pdf

Central Interstate Low-Level Radioactive Waste Commission, *Resolutions of the Central Interstate LLRW Commission* (14–15 July 2005), www.cillrwcc.org/2005–07–14–15_Resolutions.pdf

Central Interstate Low-Level Radioactive Waste Commission, *Rules* (amended 12 June 2013), www.cillrwcc.org/CIC%20Rules%202013-June.pdf

Central Interstate Low-Level Radioactive Waste Compact, Pub. L. No. 99–240, 99 Stat. 1864 (15 January 1986), www.cillrwcc.org/PL99–240-CICsection.pdf

Central Midwest Interstate Low-Level Radioactive Waste Compact, reprinted in NRC, *Nuclear Regulatory Legislation*, NUREG-0980, Vol. 1, No. 10 (2012).

Chandrasoma, S., Texas Commission on Environmental Quality, "Low-Level Radioactive Waste Disposal Rate Setting Activities," *Texas Radiation Regulatory Conference*, Austin, Texas (3 September 2010), www.google.com/url?sa=t&rct=j&q=&esrc=s&source=web&cd=5&ved=0CEIQFjAE&url=http%3A%2F%2Fwww.dshs.state.tx.us%2FWorkArea%2Flinkit.aspx%3FLinkIdentifier%3Did%26ItemID%3D8589936815&ei=eTM3Uv7EBOXk4APa7IAg&usg=AFQjCNGgATq2eB6nTnBXo55eKIktAVICtw

"Chief of Waste Panel Is Charged with Theft," *New York Times* (24 April 1991), www.nytimes.com/1991/04/24/us/chief-of-waste-panel-is-charged-with-theft.html

Cho, M., "S. Korea Approves Opening of Low-Radioactive Waste Storage Site," *Reuters* (11 December 2014a), http://news.asiaone.com/news/asia/s-korea-approves-opening-low-radioactive-waste-storage-site

Cho, M., "S. Korea to Store Low Radioactive Waste Next Month at the Earliest," *Reuters* (18 November 2014b), www.reuters.com/article/2014/11/18/us-southkorea-nuclear-idUSKCN0J20K120141118

Cho, S.K., "Stakeholder Engagement for Radioactive Waste Management Policy-Making in Korea," Presentation at the USKI/CSIS Workshop on Nuclear Fuel Cycles and Nuclear Security (10 December 2010), http://csis.org/files/attachments/101210_CHO%20Stakeholder%20Engagement%20for%20Korean%20RWM%20Policy.pdf

Cho, S.K., and Whang, J., "Status and Challenges of Nuclear Power Program and Reflections of Radioactive Waste Management Policy in Korea," Advanced Summer School of Radioactive Waste Disposal with Social-Scientific Literacy, University of California, Berkeley (6 August 2009), http://goneri.nuc.berkeley.edu/pages2009/slides/Whang.pdf

Choi, Y.N., "Nuclear Waste Management: Gaining Public Acceptance," *Journal of East Asian Affairs*, Vol. 19, No. 2 (Fall/Winter 2005).

City of Andrews, " 'Father' of Andrews: R.M. 'Bob' Means" (2011), www.cityofandrews.org/history/father_of_andrews.html

"City Wants Radioactive Dump," *Boca Raton News* (27 February 1983), http://news.google.com/newspapers?nid=1291&dat=19830227&id=U-o0AAAAIBAJ&sjid=T40D AAAAIBAJ&pg=6746%2c7254700

Clifford, F., "Caught in Fallout of Waste War," *Los Angeles Times* (14 January 1994), http://articles.latimes.com/1994-01-14/news/mn-11695_1_ward-valley

Clifford, F., "Ruling Apparently Kills Ward Valley Nuclear Dump Plan," *Los Angeles Times* (3 April 1999), http://articles.latimes.com/1999/apr/03/news/mn-23861

Coates, J., "Still a Hot Time in the Old Town, but in Roentgens," *Chicago Tribune* (8 June 1990).

"Co-chairmen of Anti-nuclear Waste Dump Group Resign," *McCook Daily Gazette* (18 August 1992).

Cole, F., "Indigenous Community Pleads with Minister on NT Nuclear Dump," *Crikey* (9 February 2012), www.crikey.com.au/2012/02/09/indigenous-community-pleads-with-minister-on-nt-nuclear-dump/

Colombo, P., and Kendig, M.W., *Analysis and Evaluation of A Radioactive Waste Package Retrieved from the Farallon Islands 900-Meter Disposal Site*, EPA-520/1-90-014 (September 1990), www.epa.gov/nscep/index.html

"Colorado Should Become a Better Neighbor to Utah," *Deseret News* (5 January 1989), www.deseretnews.com/article/29519/COLORADO-SHOULD-BECOME-A-BETTER-NEIGHBOR-TO-UTAH.html?pg=all

"Committee Member Quits in Boyd County," *Lincoln Journal* (14 August 1991), in Nebraska State Historical Society, Government Records, RG1-Gov. Nelson (SG44).

Committee on Judiciary, *LB 761* (23 October 1989), pp. 33, 35, in Nebraska State Historical Society, Government Records, RG/41, Series 1, Central Interstate Low-Level Radioactive Waste Compact (LLRW-NE), Research Files, Misc. Reports, 1989–2003, Box 5 of 5.

Committee on Natural Resources, *LR 202 Transcript* (13 December 1997), in Nebraska State Historical Society, Government Records, RG/41, Series 8, Central Interstate Low-Level Radioactive Waste Compact (LLRW-NE), Misc. Files, Committee/State/Legislature, 1987–2005, Box 1 of 2.

Committee on Radioactive Waste Management, *Sea Disposal: A Report by NNC Limited*, CoRWM Document No. 624 (August 2004).

Commonwealth of Kentucky, Department of Environmental Protection, *Maxey Flats Project* (n.d.), http://waste.ky.gov/SFB/Pages/MaxeyFlatsProject.aspx

Commonwealth of Pennsylvania, Legislative Reference Bureau, *Appalachian States Low-Level Radioactive Waste Compact*, SB 417, Act 1985–120 (22 December 1985), www.palrb.us/pamphletlaws/19001999/1985/0/act/0120.pdf

Commonwealth Radioactive Waste Management Act 2005 (Cth), www.comlaw.gov.au/Details/C2006C00710

Concerned Citizens of Nebraska v. United States Nuclear Regulatory Commission, 970 F.2d 421 (8th Cir. 1992), http://openjurist.org/970/f2d/421/concerned-citizens-of-nebraska-v-united-states-nuclear-regulatory-commission

Congressional Record: Proceedings and Debates of the 105th Congress, 2nd Session, Vol. 144, Part 8 (2–15 June 1998).

Convention on the Prevention of Marine Pollution by Dumping Wastes and Other Matter (29 December 1972), www.gc.noaa.gov/documents/gcil_lc.pdf

Coordinated Research and Environmental Surveillance Programme Related to Sea Disposal of Radioactive Waste, *CRESP Final Report, 1981–1995* (Paris: OECD, 1996), www.oecd-nea.org/rwm/reports/1996/CRESP-1981–1995.pdf

Corpstein, P., "Major Considerations for Development of a License Application for a New Low-Level Radioactive Waste Disposal Facility in Illinois," *Waste Management 1992 Conference*, Tucson, Arizona (23–27 February 1992), www.wmsym.org/archives/1992/V2/134.pdf

Costanzo, J., "Envirocare Chief Pleads Guilty to Tax Charge," *Deseret News* (2 August 1998), www.deseretnews.com/article/644509/Envirocare-chief-pleads-guilty-to-tax-charge.html?pg=all

County of Andrews, "Andrews County History" (n.d.), www.co.andrews.tx.us/about.php

Cragin, S., *Nuclear Nebraska: The Remarkable Story of the Little County That Couldn't Be Bought* (New York: AMACOM, 2007).

Crump, A.E., "Prepared Testimony: The History of the Central Interstate Low-Level Radioactive Waste Compact Commission," *Natural Resources Committee* (20 March 1997), in Nebraska State Historical Society, Government Records, RG/41, Series 8, Central Interstate Low-Level Radioactive Waste Compact (LLRW-NE), Misc. Files, Committee/State/Legislature, 1987–2005, Box 1 of 2.

Curd, P.J., "The Development of the Sellafield Repository Project Communications Program," *Waste Management 1993 Conference*, Tucson, Arizona (28 February–4 March 1993).

"Date Set for Court Fight over Muckaty Nuclear Waste Dump," *ABC News Online* (26 August 2013), www.abc.net.au/news/2013–08–26/court-date-set-for-nuclear-waste-dump-fight/4912730

Davidson, H., "Muckaty Landowners Say Nuclear Dump Fight Is 'Back to Square One,'" *Guardian* (13 November 2014), www.theguardian.com/australia-news/2014/nov/13/muckaty-landowners-say-nuclear-dump-fight-is-back-to-square-one

Davilla, L., "El Cabril, Córdoba: Welcome to the Only Nuclear Cemetery in Spain" (n.d.), www.uniserral.com/51067_es/Bienvenidos-al-%C3%BAnico-cementerio-nuclear-de-Espa%C3%B1a/

Davis, L., "Fallout: Newly Released Documents Indicate the Navy Dumped Far More Nuclear Waste Than It's Ever Acknowledged in a Major Commercial Fishery Just 30 Miles West of San Francisco. Why Won't the Government Even Study the Farallon Islands Nuclear Waste Site?" *SF Weekly* (9 May 2001), www.sfweekly.com/2001–05–09/news/fallout/

"Dealing with Asse: Where Should Germany Store Its Nuclear Waste?" *Der Spiegel* (8 September 2008), www.spiegel.de/international/germany/dealing-with-asse-where-should-germany-store-its-nuclear-waste-a-577018.html

"Dealing With Nuclear Waste," *Korea Herald* (18 December 2014).

De la Garza, P., "A Nuclear Waste Dump Becomes a Border Issue," *Chicago Tribune* (19 October 1998), http://articles.chicagotribune.com/1998–10–19/news/9810190189_1_sierra-blanca-border-issue-gas-station

DeOld, J., Neal, J., Sabbe, M., and Bagchi, M., "Low-Level Radioactive Waste Disposal: Status of the Central Interstate Compact Nebraska Project," *Waste Management 1994 Symposium*, Tucson, Arizona (27 February–3 March 1994), www.wmsym.org/archives/1994/V2/103.pdf

Department of Industry, *Amounts of Radioactive Waste in Australia: About the Amounts of Australia's Radioactive Waste* (n.d.), www.industry.gov.au/resource/RadioactiveWaste/RadiationandRadioactiveWaste/Pages/Amounts.aspx

Department of Industry, *Managing Australia's Nuclear Waste, Australian Government* (n.d.), www.managingnuclearwaste.gov.au

Department of Industry, *Potential Sites under the 2005 Act* (n.d.), www.industry.gov.au/resource/RadioactiveWaste/RadioactivewastemanagementinAustralia/CommonwealthRadioactiveWasteManagementAct2005/Pages/Potentialsitesunderthe2005Act.aspx

Department of Prime Minister and Cabinet, *Uranium Mining, Process and Nuclear Energy Review* (2006), www.ansto.gov.au/__data/assets/pdf_file/0005/38975/Umpner_report_2006.pdf

Department of Resources, Energy and Tourism, "Proposed Commonwealth Radioactive Waste Management Facility Northern Territory: Synthesis Report" (13 March 2009), www.industry.gov.au/resource/Documents/radioactive_waste/radioactive-waste-management/08–0589–01–2145479A%20(Synthesis).pdf

Department of the Environment, Transport, Energy and Communications (DETEC), *Implementation of the Obligations of the Joint Convention on the Safety of Spent Fuel Management and on the Safety of Radioactive Waste Management*, Fourth National Report of Switzerland in Accordance with Article 32 of the Convention (October 2011), http://static.ensi.ch/1318509060/cns-2011-national-report-switzerland.pdf

Department of the Environment, Transport, Energy and Communications (DETEC), *Sectoral Plan for Deep Geological Repositories: Conceptual Part* (2 April 2008).

Department of the Navy, History and Heritage Command, *Operations Crossroads: Fact Sheet* (undated), www.history.navy.mil/faqs/faq76–1.htm

De Rouffignac, A., "Attorney General Takes Action in Radioactive Waste Dispute," *Houston Business Journal* (1998a), www.bizjournals.com/houston/stories/1998/04/06/story8.html

De Rouffignac, A., "Firm Files Lawsuit in Dispute over Radioactive Waste Site," *Houston Business Journal* (1997), www.bizjournals.com/houston/stories/1997/06/09/story4.html

De Rouffignac, A., "Houston Firm Loses Legal Round in Federal Waste Disposal Fight," *Houston Business Journal* (1998b), www.bizjournals.com/houston/stories/1998/05/25/story7.html

De Rouffignac, A., "Nuclear Plants Contract with WCS to Store Waste at West Texas Site," *Houston Business Journal* (7 March 1999), www.bizjournals.comhouston/stories/1999/03/08/story6.html

De Rouffignac, A., "Small Firm Sees Bonanza in DOE Waste," *Houston Business Journal* (1996a), www.bizjournals.com/houston/stories/1996/09/09/story1.html

De Rouffignac, A., "Utah Firm Joins Rush to Dump Radioactive Waste in West Texas," *Houston Business Journal* (1996b), www.bizjournals.com/houston/stories/1996/10/07/story2.html

Dininny, S., "Hanford Initiative Spurs Legal Rematch," *Seattle Times* (13 December 2004), http://seattletimes.com/html/localnews/2002117556_hanfordside13m.html

Directions in Low-Level Radioactive Waste Management: A Brief History of Commercial Low-Level Radioactive Waste Disposal, prepared at the Idaho National Engineering Laboratory by the National Low-Level Waste Management Program for the Department of Energy, DOE/LLW-103 (10 January 1990), www.osti.gov/scitech/servlets/purl/6161759

"Disposing NY Sewage in Region to End," *Lubbock Avalanche-Journal* (20 June 2001), http://lubbockonline.com/stories/062001/sta_062001108.shtml

"Dissenting Views of Hon. John Bryant (H.R. 558)," *House Report 104–148 – Texas Low-Level Radioactive Waste Disposal Compact Consent Act* (20 June 1995).

Di Tullio, L., and Resnikoff, M., Radioactive Waste Management Associates, *Review of Safety Analysis Report, Part 1 – Geology and Hydrology, Proposed Low-Level Waste Facility, Butte, Nebraska* (29 June 1992), in Nebraska State Historical Society, Government Records, RG/41, Series 1, Central Interstate Low-Level Radioactive Waste Compact (LLRW-NE), Research Files, Misc. Reports, 1989–2003, Box 5 of 5.

Draft of Governor List's Executive Order Relating to Transport of Commercial Low-Level Radioactive Waste (10 July 1979), GOV-0820, File #33, Governor Robert List Records, Nevada State Archives.

"Dump Battle Can Move to Federal Court," *Lubbock Avalanche-Journal* (3 June 1998), http://lubbockonline.com/stories/060398/053–0714.001.shtml

Duncan, D., and Eadie, G., *Surveys of the Uranium Mill Tailings Pile and Surrounding Areas: Salt Lake City, Utah*, EPA-520/6–74–006 (Las Vegas: EPA, 1974).

Dunlap, R., Kraft, M.E., and Rosa, E.A., *Public Reactions to Nuclear Waste* (Durham, NC: Duke University Press, 1993).

Dupuis, M.C., "Current Status of the French Radioactive Waste Disposal Programme," European Nuclear Society (2006), www.euronuclear.org/events/topseal/transactions/Paper-Session-I-Dupuis.pdf

Eakins, W., Junge, W.R., and Hynes, J.L., *Candidate Area Evaluation Report: Low-Level Radioactive Waste Disposal, Colorado*, Open File 86–7, Colorado Geological Survey, Department of Natural Resources, State of Colorado (1986), http://geosurvey.state.co.us/pubs/online/Documents/1986%20OF%2086–07.pdf

Edwards, R., "Cumbrian Nuclear Dump 'Virtually Certain' to Be Eroded by Rising Sea Levels," *Guardian* (20 April 2014), www.theguardian.com/environment/2014/apr/20/choice-cumbria-nuclear-dump-mistake-environment-agency

"El Cabril Received 1,681.78 Cubic Meters of Radioactive Waste in 2013," *El País* (27 March 2014), http://ccaa.elpais.com/ccaa/2014/03/27/andalucia/1395938575_574712.html

Empresa Nacional de Residuos Radiactivos [ENRESA], *Nuclear Waste Management in Spain* (n.d.), http://newmdb.iaea.org/profiles.aspx?ByCountry=ES

Emshwiller, J., and Searcey, D., "Nuclear Waste Sits on Ocean Floor: U.S. Has Few Answers on How to Handle Atomic Waste It Dumped in the Sea," *Wall Street Journal* (31 December 2013).

EnergySolutions, *Bulk Waste Disposal and Treatment Facilities: Waste Acceptance Criteria*, Revision 6 (March 2006), www.doeal.gov/SWEIS/OtherDocuments/534%20EnergySolutions_of_Utah_WAC_R6.pdf

English, M., *Siting Low-Level Radioactive Waste Disposal Facilities: The Public Policy Dilemma* (New York: Quorum Books, 1992), http://trove.nla.gov.au/version/42542117

ENRESA, "El Cabril Received 2,892.63 Cubic Meters of Radioactive Waste in 2012," Madrid (18 April 2013), www.sepi.es/default.aspx?cmd=0004&IdContent=21398&idLanguage=_EN&lang=

Entergy Arkansas, Inc. v. Nebraska, 46 F. Supp. 2d 977 (D. Neb. 1999), http://law.justia.com/cases/federal/district-courts/FSupp2/46/977/2488216/

Entergy Arkansas, Inc. v. Nebraska, 226 F. Supp. 2d 1047 (D. Neb. 2002), http://law.justia.com/cases/federal/district-courts/FSupp2/226/1047/2323080/

"Envirocare, NFS Settle Conspiracy Suit," *Deseret News* (25 August 1999), www.deseretnews.com/article/714480/Envirocare-NFS-settle-conspiracy-suit.html?pg=all

Ernst, T., Nagra, "Switzerland Update," *EDRAM Spring Meeting*, Yokohama, Japan (19 May 2014), www.edram.info/fileadmin/edram/pdf/Item-06_Update-Switzerland.pdf

Espartero, A.G., "Radioactive and Nuclear Waste Management in Spain," Powerpoint Presentation, Workshop, Lisbon (October 2012), www.unece.org/fileadmin/DAM/energy/se/pdfs/UNFC/ws_IAEA_CYTED_UNECE_Oct12_Lisbon/20_Espartero.pdf

Espartero, A.G., "Spanish Management Issues in Radioactive and Nuclear Waste Materials," Powerpoint Presentation, Senior Researcher, Head of CIEMAT Quality Management, CYTED Energy Area Technical Secretary of Spanish Alliance for Energy Research and Innovation (ALINNE), Radioactive and Nuclear Waste Management in Spain, Workshop, Lisbon (n.d.), www.unece.org/fileadmin/DAM/energy/se/pdfs/UNFC/ws_IAEA_CYTED_UNECE_Oct12_Lisbon/20_Espartero.pdf

Espejo, J.M., and Abreu, A., "The Spanish General Radioactive Waste Management Plan," *Waste Management 2008 Conference*, Phoenix, Arizona (24–28 February 2008), www.wmsym.org/archives/2008/pdfs/8475.pdf

Eui-dal, S., "Radioactive Waste Sites Proposed Again," *Chosun Ilbo* (4 February 2003), http://english.chosun.com/site/data/html_dir/2003/02/04/2003020461009.html

European Commission Press Release, "Eurobarometer Survey on Radioactive Waste: Europeans Ask for the Implementation of Nuclear Waste Disposal Facilities and for the Development of a More Common European Approach," Brussels, Belgium (3 July 2008), http://europa.eu/rapid/press-release_IP-08-1100_en.htm?locale=en

Expert Group on Disposal Concepts for Radioactive Waste (EKRA), *Disposal Concepts for Radioactive Waste: Final Report*, on behalf of Department of the Environment, Transport, Energy and Communications (DETEC), Berne, Switzerland (31 January 2000).

Expert Report of Arden D. Davis (South Dakota: No. 4663) (30 January 2002), in Nebraska State Historical Society, Government Records, RG/41, Series 1, Central Interstate Low-Level Radioactive Waste Compact (LLRW-NE), Research Files, Misc. Reports, 1989–2003, Box 5 of 5.

Expert Report of Dr. John Osnes (January 2002) in Nebraska State Historical Society, Government Records, RG/41, Series 1, Central Interstate Low-Level Radioactive Waste Compact (LLRW-NE), Research Files, Misc. Reports, 1989–2003, Box 5 of 5.

Falk, J., Green, J., and Mudd, G., "Australia, Uranium and Nuclear Power," *International Journal of Environmental Studies*, Vol. 63, No. 6 (December 2006).

Federal Office for Radiation Protection (Germany), "From Salt Dome to Nuclear Repository: The Eventful History of the Asse II Mine" (16 October 2012), www.endlager-asse.de/EN/2_WhatIs/History/_node.html

Federal Parliament of Australia, *Radioactive Waste*, www.aph.gov.au/About_Parliament/Parliamentary_Departments/Parliamentary_Library/Publications_Archive/online/RadioactiveWaste

Federal Parliament of Australia, *Radioactive Waste and Spent Nuclear Fuel Management in Australia* (updated 21 July 2011), www.aph.gov.au/About_Parliament/Parliamentary_Departments/Parliamentary_Library/pubs/BN/2011–2012/RadioActiveWaste#_Toc299022834

"Fire at Vandellos," *World Information Service on Energy* (3 November 1989), www.wiseinternational.org/node/69

"First Phase of Korean Waste Facility Opens," *World Nuclear News* (12 December 2014), www.world-nuclear-news.org/WR-First-phase-of-Korean-waste-facility-opens-1212145.html

"Flamanville Costs Up €2 Billion," *World Nuclear News* (4 December 2012), www.world-nuclear-news.org/NN-Flamanville_costs_up_2_billion_Euros-0412127.html

Flores, R., "Envirocare Dumps Barstow Waste Site Plan," *Pecos Enterprise* (30 January 2001), www.pecos.net/news/arch2001/013001p.htm

Flüeler, T., *Decision Making for Complex Socio-Technical Systems: Robustness from Lessons Learned in Long-Term Radioactive Waste Governance* (Dordrecht: Springer, 2006).

Flüeler, T., "Extended Reviewing on the Role of Potential Siting Cantons in the Ongoing Swiss Site Selection Procedure ('Sectoral Plan')" in OECD/NEA, *The Safety Case for Deep Geological Disposal of Radioactive Waste: 2013 State of the Art*, Symposium Proceedings, Paris, France (7–9 October 2013), www.oecd-nea.org/rwm/docs/2013/rwm-r2013-9.pdf

Flüeler, T., "KFW Cantonal Expert Group Wellenberg: An Advisory Body to Support Regional Decision Makers in LLW Siting," Third COWAM Seminar in Fürigen, Switzerland (12–15 September 2002), www.cowam.com/IMG/pdf/present_KFW.pdf

"For Taiwan Aborigines, Nuclear Waste Is Blessing and Curse," *Times Live* (16 September 2012), www.timeslive.co.za/scitech/2012/09/16/for-taiwan-aborigines-nuclear-waste-is-blessing-and-curse

Forcella, D., Gingerich, R., and Holeman, G., "LLRW Disposal Facility Siting Approaches: Connecticut's Innovative Volunteer Approach," *Waste Management 1994 Conference*, Tucson, Arizona (27 February–3 March 1994), www.wmsym.org/archives/1994/V2/100.pdf

"Former Compact Director Given Four Years," *McCook Daily Gazette* (24 January 1992).

Forum for Nuclear Cooperation in Asia (FNCA), *FNCA Consolidated Report on Radioactive Waste Management* (Australia) (n.d.), www.fnca.mext.go.jp/english/rwm/news_img/rwm_cr03_01.pdf

Forum for Nuclear Cooperation in Asia (FNCA), *FNCA Consolidated Report on Radioactive Waste Management (Korea)* (updated March 2007), www.fnca.mext.go.jp/english/rwm/news_img/rwm_cr03_05.pdf

Freeman, E., *Strategic Management: A Stakeholder Approach* (Boston, MA: Pitman, 1984).

Fretwell, S., "Utah Company Launches Media Blitz to Reopen SC Atomic Waste Landfill," *State* (13 March 2015), www.thestate.com/news/local/article14662532.html

Freudenburg, W., and Grevers, J., *Nebraska Statewide Attitudes toward Nuclear Waste Facilities: A Preliminary Analysis*, Social Science Research Associates (1990), in Nebraska State Historical Society, Government Records, RG/41, Series 1, Central Interstate Low-Level Radioactive Waste Compact (LLRW-NE), Research Files, Misc. Reports, 1989–2003, Box 5 of 5.

Fritschi, M., Kowalski, E., and Zuidema, P., "Developments in the Swiss Radioactive Waste Disposal Programme," *Waste Management 2000 Conference*, Tucson, Arizona (27 February–2 March 2000), www.wmsym.org/archives/2000/pdf/48/48-1.pdf

Fröhlingsdorf, M., Ludwig, U., and Weinzierl, A., "Abyss of Uncertainty: Germany's Homemade Nuclear Waste Disaster," *Der Spiegel* (21 February 2013), www.spiegel.de/international/germany/germany-weighs-options-for-handling-nuclear-waste-in-asse-mine-a-884523.html

García, A., Universitat Autónoma de Barcelona, "A Relevant Spanish Actor: The Role Views and Singularity of AMAC," Radioactive Waste Management in Spain: Coordination and Projects, FSC Workshop Proceedings, L'Hospitalet de l'Infant, Spain (21–23 November 2005).

Garwin, R., and Charpak, G., *Megawatts and Megatons: A Turning Point in the Nuclear Age?* (New York: Alfred A. Knopf, 2001).

Geiser, U., "Nuclear Storage Debate Heats Up," *SWI* (6 November 2008), www.swissinfo.ch/eng/nuclear-storage-debate-heats-up/7025514

General Accounting Office, *Hazards of Past Low-Level Radioactive Waste Ocean Dumping Have Been Overemphasized*, EMD-82-9 (21 October 1981), www.gao.gov/assets/140/135757.pdf

General Accounting Office, *Low-Level Radioactive Waste: Disposal Availability Adequate in the Short Term, but Oversight Needed to Identify Any Future Shortfalls*, GAO-04-604 (June 2004), www.gao.gov/new.items/d04604.pdf

General Accounting Office, *Low-Level Radioactive Waste: Future Waste Volumes and Disposal Options Are Uncertain – Statement of (Ms.) Robin Nazzaro, Director, Natural Resources and Environment before the Senate Committee on Energy and Natural Resources*, GAO-04-1097T (30 September 2004), www.gao.gov/assets/120/111273.html

General Accounting Office, *Low-Level Radioactive Waste: States Are Not Developing Disposal Facilities*, GAO-RCED-99-238 (September 1999), www.gao.gov/assets/160/156717.pdf

General Accounting Office, *Nuclear Waste: Agreement Among Agencies Responsible for the West Valley Site Is Critically Needed*, GAO-01-314 (May 2001), www.gao.gov/new.items/d01314.pdf

General Accounting Office, *Nuclear Waste: Extensive Process to Site Low-Level Waste Disposal Facility in Nebraska*, GAO/RCED-91-149 (July 1991), www.gao.gov/assets/220/214543.pdf

General Accounting Office, *Nuclear Waste: Slow Progress Developing Low-Level Radioactive Waste Disposal Facilities*, GAO/RCED-92-61 (January 1992), www.gao.gov/assets/160/151432.pdf

General Accounting Office, *Radioactive Waste: Answers to Questions Related to the Proposed Ward Valley Low-Level Radioactive Waste Disposal Facility*, GAO/RCED-98-40R (22 May 1998), www.gao.gov/assets/90/87895.pdf

General Accounting Office, *Radioactive Waste: Interior's Review of the Proposed Ward Valley Waste Site*, Testimony of Gary Jones Before the Committee on Energy and Natural Resources, U.S. Senate, GAO/T-RCED-97-212 (22 July 1997), www.gao.gov/assets/110/106999.pdf

General Accounting Office, *Radioactive Waste: Status of Commercial Low-Level Waste Facilities*, GAO/RCED-95-67 (May 1995), www.gpo.gov/fdsys/pkg/GAOREPORTS-RCED-95-67/pdf/GAOREPORTS-RCED-95-67.pdf

"Geological Disposal – Brief Overview of NGO Involvement in the Radioactive Waste Management Process in Eleven Overseas Countries," Nuclear Decommissioning Authority (July 2010), www.nda.gov.uk/publication/geological-disposal-brief-overview-of-ngo-involvement-in-radioactive-waste-management-process-in-eleven-overseas-countries-july-2010/

Gerrard, M. B., *Whose Backyard, Whose Risk* (Cambridge, MA: MIT Press, 1995).

Gershey, E., Klein, R., Party, E., and Wilkerson, A., *Low-Level Radioactive Waste: From Cradle to Grave* (New York: Van Nostrand Reinhold, 1990).

Gil-Cerezo, M. V., González-Barrios, A. J., and Domínigues-Vilches, E., "Socio-environmental Nuclear Conflicts: The Case of El Cabril," *International Journal of Nuclear Knowledge Management*, Vol. 6, No. 1 (2013).

Gillam, J., "Capitol Political Bombshell Fused by Nuclear Dump," *Los Angeles Times* (20 May 1985), http://articles.latimes.com/1985-05-20/news/mn-16536_1_nuclear-waste

Glicksman, R., "Interstate Compacts for Low-Level Radioactive Waste Disposal: A Mechanism for Excluding Out-of-State Waste," in Michael E. Burns (ed.), *Low-Level Radioactive Waste Regulation: Science, Politics and Fear* (Chelsea, MI: Lewis, 1988).

GlobalSecurity.org, *Weapons of Mass Destruction (WMD): Krasnoyarsk/Zheleznogorsk Mining and Chemical Combine* (updated 8 February 2011), www.globalsecurity.org/wmd/world/russia/krasnoyarsk-26_nuc.htm

Golden, T., "Dump Bid Assailed along Rio Grande," *New York Times* (29 March 1992), www.nytimes.com/1992/03/29/world/dump-bid-assailed-along-rio-grande.html

Gonzalez, S., "More Talks Held on Possible Nuclear Site in Howard County," *NewsWest 9* (8 April 2013), www.newswest9.com/story/21913262/more-talks-on-possible-nuclear-site-in-howard-county

González, V., Armada, J., and Molina, M., "Communications in the Field of Radioactive Waste Management in Spain," Session 49 – Public & Institutional Interactions (n.d.), Co-chairs: Jo-Ann Holst, S.M. Stoller Corporation, Ron Bhada, NMSU, Enresa Madrid, Spain.

Goozner, M., "Judge Blocks Use of Nuclear Waste Compactor," *Chicago Tribune* (4 June 1987), http://articles.chicagotribune.com/1987–06–04/business/8702110132_1_nuclear-power-plants-waste-processing-plant-chem-nuclear-systems

Government Printing Office, H.R. 629, Report No. 105–181, 105th Congress, 1st Session (6 February 1997), www.gpo.gov/fdsys/pkg/BILLS-105hr629rh/BILLS-105hr629rh.pdf

Government Printing Office, Texas Low-Level Radioactive Waste Disposal Compact Consent Act, Pub. L. No. 105–236 (20 September 1998), www.gpo.gov/fdsys/pkg/PLAW-105publ236/pdf/PLAW-105publ236.pdf

Governor's Office News Release (23 April 1991), in Nebraska State Historical Society, Government Records, RG1-Gov. Nelson (SG44).

Green, J., *Proposed Radioactive Waste Dump at Muckaty, NT*, Briefing Paper (February 2011).

Greenwood, T., "Nuclear Waste Management in the United States," in E. William Colglazier (ed.), *The Politics of Nuclear Waste* (New York: Pergamon Press, 1982).

Grissom, B., "Sierra Blancans Again Debate Possible Sludge Dump," *El Paso Times* (15 July 2007), www.elpasotimes.com/news/ci_6379497%22

"Gyeongju Sets Nuclear Dump Project in Motion after 19-Year Delay," *Chosun Ilbo* (4 November 2005), http://english.chosun.com/site/data/html_dir/2005/11/04/2005110461001.html

Ha, J., Lim, I.C., Oh, S.Y., and Wu, S., "Research Reactor: A Powerhouse of Nuclear Technology in Korea," *IAEA Papers* (2011), www-pub.iaea.org/MTCD/Publications/PDF/P1575_CD_web/datasets/papers/F4%20Ha.pdf

"HABOG – Nuclear Waste Management in an Artistic Way," *Travelogue of an Armchair Traveller* (December 2010), http://armchairtravelogue.blogspot.com/2010/12/habog-nuclear-waste-management-in.html

H.AMDT.419, 105th Congress (1997–1998) (7 October 1997).

Haddow, E., "Depressed Colorado Town Recruits Low-Level Radioactive Dump," *Lawrence Journal-World* (27 February 1983), http://news.google.com/newspapers?nid=2199&dat=19830227&id=idBeAAAAIBAJ&sjid=g-gFAAAAIBAJ&pg=6838,4833551

Hagen, A., and Ruegger, B., "Deep-Sea Disposal: Scientific Bases to Control Pollution," *IAEA Bulletin*, Vol. 28, No. 1 (1986): 29–32, www.iaea.org/Publications/Magazines/Bulletin/Bull281/28104682932.pdf

Hamblin, J.D., *Poison in the Well: Radioactive Waste in the Oceans at the Dawn of the Nuclear Age* (New Brunswick, NJ: Rutgers University Press, 2009).

Harf, J., "Recommendations for Siting, Development, and Operation of a Regional Low-Level Radioactive Waste Disposal Facility in Ohio," *Waste Management 1994 Conference*, Tucson, Arizona (27 February–3 March 1994), www.wmsym.org/archives/1994/V2/102.pdf

Hastings, D., "Firm's History of Safety Violations Fuels Fears in Ward Valley," *Los Angeles Times* (28 April 1996), http://articles.latimes.com/1996–04–28/local/me-63660_1_ward-valley

"Has US Ecology Cleaned Up Its Act?" *Businessweek* (7 November 1993), www.business-week.com/stories/1993–11–07/has-us-ecology-cleaned-up-its-act

Hayden, F.G., and Bolduc, S.R., "Political and Economic Analysis of Low-Level Radio-active Waste," *University of Nebraska – Lincoln Economics Department Faculty*

Publications, Paper 17 (1 June 1997), http://digitalcommons.unl.edu/cgi/viewcontent.cgi?article=1016&context=econfacpub

Hazardous Materials Management – Chemical, Toxic and Low-Level Radioactive Wastes: An Overview of the State of Nevada Program, Memorandum from Donald Bayer, Senior Research Analyst, Radioactive Waste Program (25 September 1985).

H.B. 449: Relating to Disposal Sites of the Texas Low-Level Radioactive Waste Disposal Authority, Texas Legislature Online (14 June 1985), www.lrl.state.tx.us/LASDOCS/69R/HB449/HB449_69R.pdf#page=60

H.B. 674: Relating to the Texas Low-Level Radioactive Waste Disposal Authority, the Disposal of Low-Level Radioactive Waste, and the Site for That Disposal (8 March 1999), www.capitol.state.tx.us/BillLookup/History.aspx?LegSess=76R&Bill=HB674

H.B. 1171: Relating to Regulation of Radioactive Materials and Other Sources of Radiation (22 May 1999), www.capitol.state.tx.us/BillLookup/History.aspx?LegSess=76R&Bill=HB1171

H.B. 1533: Relating to the Creation, Administration, Powers, Duties, Operations, and Financing of the Texas Low-Level Radioactive Waste Disposal Authority (14 May 1981), www.lrl.state.tx.us/legis/billSearch/text.cfm?legSession=67-0&billtypeDetail=HB&billNumberDetail=1533&billSuffixDetail=&startRow=1&IDlist=&unClicklist=&number=50

H.B. 1567: Relating to the Disposal of Low-Level Radioactive Waste; Authorizing the Exercise of the Power of Eminent Domain (1 September 2003), www.lrl.state.tx.us/legis/billSearch/text.cfm?legSession=78-0&billtypeDetail=HB&billNumberDetail=1567&billSuffixDetail=&startRow=1&IDlist=&unClicklist=&number=50

H.B. 1910: Relating to the Disposal or Assured Isolation of Low-Level Radioactive Waste (13 May 1999), www.capitol.state.tx.us/BillLookup/History.aspx?LegSess=76R&Bill=HB1910

H.B. 2589: Relating to the Assured Isolation of Low-Level Radioactive Waste (13 March 2003), www.legis.state.tx.us/BillLookup/History.aspx?LegSess=78R&Bill=HB2589

H.B. 2905: Relating to the Regulation and Management of Low-Level Radioactive Waste (3 April 2001), www.lrl.state.tx.us/legis/billSearch/text.cfm?legSession=78-0&billtypeDetail=HB&billNumberDetail=1567&billSuffixDetail=&startRow=1&IDlist=&unClicklist=&number=50

H.B. 2954: Relating to the Application of the Sunset Review Process to Certain State Agencies (30 May 1999), www.lrl.state.tx.us/legis/billSearch/text.cfm?legSession=67-0&billtypeDetail=HB&billNumberDetail=1177&billSuffixDetail=&startRow=1&IDlist=&unClicklist=&number=50

H.B. 3320: Relating to the Selection of the Disposal Site Designated by the Texas Low-Level Radioactive Waste Disposal Authority (16 March 1999), www.capitol.state.tx.us/BillLookup/History.aspx?LegSess=76R&Bill=HB3320

Hearsey, C. J., Emmery, D. L., Kunsch, P., Bollingerfehr, W., and Webster, S., "The Financing of Radioactive Waste Storage and Disposal," in *Radioactive Waste Management Strategies and Issues*; Euradwaste 1999 International Conference; 5th, Radioactive Waste Management Strategies and Issues (2000).

Highfield, R., "Windscale Fire: 'We Were Too Busy to Panic,' " *Telegraph* (9 October 2007), www.telegraph.co.uk/science/science-news/3309842/Windscale-fire-We-were-too-busy-to-panic.html

"High-Flux Advanced Neutron Application Reactor," *Nuclear Threat Initiative* (2010), www.nti.org/facilities/9/

"History and Some Facts to Wellenberg: Project of a Swiss LLW Repository," Third COWAM Seminar in Fürigen, Switzerland (12–15 September 2002), www.cowam. com/IMG/pdf/FactsWLB-20729.pdf

Holland, I., "Consultation, Constraints and Norms: The Case of Nuclear Waste," *Australian Journal of Public Administration*, Vol. 61, No. 1 (2002a).

Holland, I., "Waste Not Want Not: Australia and the Politics of High Level Waste," *Australian Journal of Political Science*, Vol. 37, No. 2 (2002b).

Homans, C., The Operator," *New Republic* (20 April 2012), www.newrepublic.com/article/ politics/magazine/102778/harold-simmons-campaign-donor-2012-gop#

House Committee on Environmental Affairs, *Committee Report: SB1177*, 67th Regular Session, Legislative Reference Library of Texas (12 May 1981), www.lrl.state.tx.us/

House Group Bill Analysis, *S.B. 1177 by Brooks (C.S.S.B. 1177 by Bock)* (14 May 1981), www.lrl.state.tx.us/scanned/hroBillAnalyses/67–0/SB1177.pdf

House of Lords, Select Committee on Science and Technology Third Report, *Management of Nuclear Waste* (10 March 1999), www.parliament.the-stationery-office.co.uk/ pa/ld199899/ldselect/ldsctech/41/4103.htm

House Report 105–630 to the Texas Low-Level Radioactive Waste Disposal Compact Consent Act (n.d.), http://thomas.loc.gov/cgi-bin/bdquery/z?d105:HR00629:@@@K

House Research Organization Bill Analysis, H.B. 85, by Gallego (10 April 2001), www. hro.house.state.tx.us/pdf/ba77r/hb0085.pdf#navpanes=0

House Research Organization Bill Analysis, H.B. 1567 by West, Chisum, W. Smith (CSHB by West) (22 April 2003), www.lrl.state.tx.us/scanned/hroBillAnalyses/78–0/ HB1567.PDF

House Research Organization Bill Analysis, H.B. 1910 by Chisum (29 April 1999), www. lrl.state.tx.us/scanned/hroBillAnalyses/76–0/HB1910.pdf

House Research Organization Bill Analysis, S.B. 1697 by Bivins (Walker) (23 May 2015), www.lrl.state.tx.us/scanned/hroBillAnalyses/74–0/SB1697.pdf

How Sites in South Australia Were Chosen: Site Selection Study and Community Consultation, The Facts, Not Fiction (July 2001), www.aph.gov.au/About_Parliament/Parliamentary_ Departments/Parliamentary_Library/pubs/BN/2011–2012/RadioActiveWaste

H.R. 558: Texas Low-Level Radioactive Waste Disposal Compact Consent Act (18 January 1995).

H.R. 629: Texas Low-Level Radioactive Waste Disposal Compact Consent Act (6 February 1997), www.congress.gov/bill/105th-congress/house-bill/629/text?q=%7B%22searc h%22%3A%5B%22cite%3A%28hr629%29%22%5D%7D&resultIndex=2

H.R. 1681: Relating to the Lease and Sale of Certain Land by the Texas Low-Level Radioactive Waste Disposal Authority (17 May 1995), www.lrl.state.tx.us/legis/billSearch/text. cfm?legSession=67-0&billtypeDetail=HB&billNumberDetail=1177&billSuffixDetail= &startRow=1&IDlist=&unClicklist=&number=50

HSK [Federal Nuclear Safety Inspectorate], "Geological Repositories for Radioactive Waste" (2001), www.cowam.com/IMG/pdf/JaBe-Chap-10_E.pdf

Hubler, S., "Only California Is on Track for Nuclear Dump," *Los Angeles Times* (20 May 1991), http://articles.latimes.com/1991–05–20/news/mn-1454_1_nuclear-waste

"The Human Toll of Coal vs. Nuclear," *Washington Post* (2 April 2011), www.washingtonpost. com/national/the-human-toll-of-coal-vs-nuclear/2011/04/02/AFOVHsRC_graphic. html

"Huskers' Probe Turns up New Violations," *Tulsa World* (14 June 1991), www.tulsaworld. com/archives/huskers-probe-turns-up-new-violations/article_c3f6df2e-922f-5c7d-8541- c704be0f9964.html

IAEA Research Reactors Database, "Switzerland," http://nucleus.iaea.org/RRDB/RR/ReactorSearch.aspx?filter=0

"IAEA Reviews Planned South Korean Waste Site," *World Nuclear News* (24 October 2007), www.world-nuclear-news.org/newsarticle.aspx?id=14278

Illinois Emergency Management Agency, *Site History and Environmental Monitoring Report for Sheffield Low-Level Radioactive Waste Disposal Site* (October 2009), www.state.il.us/iema/environmental/pdfs/SheffieldReport.pdf

Imrie, B., "Igloo Area Men Protest Proposed Nuclear Dump," *Rapid City Journal* (29 April 1983), http://bhodian.com/nuclearwaste.html

Inspector's Report, *Cumbria County Council, Appeal by United Kingdom Nirex Limited*, File No. APP1H09001M9412470 19 (21 November 1996), www.westcumbriamrws.org.uk/documents/Inspectors_Report.doc

Interim Council, Ponca Tribe of Nebraska, Resolution 5–93 (4 January 1993), in Nebraska State Historical Society, Government Records, RG1-Gov. Nelson (SG44).

International Atomic Energy Agency, *Classification of Radioactive Waste*, General Safety Guide No. GSG-1 (November 2009), www-pub.iaea.org/MTCD/publications/PDF/Pub1419_web.pdf

International Atomic Energy Agency, "Country Nuclear Power Profiles," *Republic of Korea* (updated 2012), www-pub.iaea.org/MTCD/Publications/PDF/CNPP2012_CD/countryprofiles/KoreaRepublicof/KoreaRepublicof.htm

International Atomic Energy Agency, *Estimation of Global Inventories of Radioactive Waste and Other Radioactive Materials*, IAEA-TECDOC-1591 (June 2008), www-pub.iaea.org/MTCD/publications/PDF/te_1591_web.pdf

International Atomic Energy Agency, *Inventory of Radioactive Waste Disposals at Sea*, IAEA TECDOC-1105 (August 1999), www-pub.iaea.org/MTCD/publications/PDF/te_1105_prn.pdf

International Atomic Energy Agency, *Managing Radioactive Waste* (n.d.), www.iaea.org/Publications/Factsheets/English/manradwa.html

International Atomic Energy Agency, *Managing Radioactive Wastes Factsheet* (n.d.), www.iaea.org/Publications/Factsheets/English/manradwa.html#note_b

International Atomic Energy Agency, *Radioactive Waste Management: Status and Trends* (2003), www-pub.iaea.org/MTCD/publications/PDF/rwmst3/IAEA-WMDB-ST-3-Part-5.pdf

International Atomic Energy Agency, "Radiological Assessment: Waste Disposal in the Arctic Seas," *IAEA Bulletin*, Vol. 39, No. 1 (1997): 21–28, www.iaea.org/Publications/Magazines/Bulletin/Bull391/specialreport.html

International Atomic Energy Agency, *The Role of Research Reactors in Introducing Nuclear Power* (n.d.), www.iaea.org/sites/default/files/gc56inf-3-att5_en.pdf

International Atomic Energy Agency, *Status and Trends in Spent Fuel Reprocessing*, IAEA-TECDOC-1467 (September 2005), www-pub.iaea.org/MTCD/publications/PDF/te_1467_web.pdf

International Atomic Energy Agency, *Worldwide Marine Radioactivity Studies (WOMARS): Radionuclide Levels in Oceans and Seas*, IAEA-TECDOC-1429 (January 2005), www-pub.iaea.org/MTCD/publications/PDF/TE_1429_web.pdf

International Maritime Organization, *London Convention Protocol* (2013), www.imo.org/OurWork/Environment/SpecialProgrammesAndInitiatives/Pages/London-Convention-and-Protocol.aspx

"Iredell, Rowan Residents Blast Waste Officials," *Dispatch (Lexington)* (1 June 1990), http://news.google.com/newspapers?nid=1734&dat=19900601&id=VeYbAAAAIBAJ&sjid=aFIEAAAAIBAJ&pg=5930,4707323

Irvine, M. "Suffering Endures for 'Radium Girls' Who Painted Watches in the '20s," *Associated Press* (4 October 1998), www.hartford-hwp.com/archives/40/046.html

Israelsen, B., "Utah Officials See Red over Plans to Expand Colorado N-waste Site," *Deseret News* (27 October 1993), www.deseretnews.com/article/317366/UTAH-OFFI-CIALS-SEE-RED-OVER-PLANS-TO-EXPAND-COLORADO-N-WASTE-SITE.html?pg=all

Ivins, M., " 'Environmental Racism' in West Texas," *Abilene Reporter-News* (1 November 1997), www.texnews.com/opinion97/molly110197.html

Jacob, G., *Site Unseen: The Politics of Siting a Nuclear Waste Repository* (Pittsburgh, PA: Pittsburgh University Press, 1990).

Jacobi, L., "Texas Approach to the Management of Low Level Radioactive Waste After 1992," *Waste Management 1992 Conference*, Tucson, Arizona (22–26 February 1992), www.wmsym.org/archives/1992/V1/52.pdf

James, M., and Rann, A., "Radioactive Waste and Spent Nuclear Fuel Management in Australia," Parliamentary Library, Department of Parliamentary Services, Parliament of Australia (n.d.), www.aph.gov.au/About_Parliament/Parliamentary_Departments/Parliamentary_Library/pubs/BN/2011–2012/RadioActiveWaste

Jang, J., and Kang, M., "Framing Analysis of Radioactive Waste Disposal Facility Placement in South Korea," *Western Political Science Association 2012 Meeting*, Portland, Oregon (23 March 2012), http://wpsa.research.pdx.edu/meet/2012/jangandkang.pdf

Jeong-hoon, L., "Memories of Buan," *Dong-A Ilbo* (11 January 2010), www.english.donga.com/srv/service.php3?biid=2010011177198

Jiménez, M., "Consolidation through Institutionalization? Dilemmas of the Spanish Environmental Movement in the 1990s," *Environmental Politics*, Vol. 8, No. 1 (1999a).

Jiménez, M., "The Environmental Movement in Spain: A Growing Force of Contention," *South European Society and Politics*, Vol. 12, No. 3 (September 2007).

Jiménez, M., "Environmental Protests in Comparative Perspective – Ten Years of Environmental Protests in Spain: Issues, Actors and Arenas," 27th ECPR Joint Sessions, Mannheim, Germany, Juan Institute, Madrid (1999b).

Jiménez, M., "Struggling for the Environment: A Profile of Recent Environmental Protests in Spain," Estudio/Working Paper 1999/143 (1999c).

Johnson, R., "Take the V out of TV, Please," *Sports Illustrated* (18 June 1990), http://sportsillustrated.cnn.com/vault/article/magazine/MAG1136788/1/index.htm

Joint Convention on the Safety of Spent Fuel Management and on the Safety of Radioactive Waste Management (2001), www.iaea.org/Publications/Documents/Infcircs/1997/infcirc546.pdf

Jones, D., "Nuclear-Waste Firm Has Checkered Past," *Hartford Courant* (7 July 1991), http://articles.courant.com/1991–07–07/news/0000214343_1_radioactive-waste-disposal-site-radioactive-waste-low-level-radioactive-waste

Jones, D. G., Roberts, P. D., Limburg, J., Karl, H., Chin, J. L., Shanks, W. C., . . . Howard, D., *Measurement of Seafloor Radioactivity at the Farallon Islands Radioactive Waste Dump Site, California*, United States Department of the Interior/United States Geological Survey, Open-File Report 01–62 (2001), http://pubs.usgs.gov/of/2001/of01-062/OFR_01_062.pdf

"Judge Dismisses $1 Billion Waste Lawsuit," *Lubbock Avalanche-Journal* (2 September 1998), http://lubbockonline.com/stories/090298/0902980016.shtml

Junker, B., Flüeler, T., Stauffacher, M., and Scholz, R., *Description of the Safety Case for Long-Term Disposal of Radioactive Waste – The Iterative Safety Analysis Approach as Utilized in Switzerland*, NSSI Working Paper 46 (July 2008), www.uns.ethz.ch/pub/wp/WP_46.pdf

Junkert, R., Dressen, A. L., Siefken, D. L., Serie, P. J., and Jennrich, E. A., "Licensing the California Low-Level Waste Disposal Facility – Charting a New Course," *Waste Management 1991 Conference*, Tucson, Arizona (24–28 February 1991), www.wmsym.org/archives/1991/V2/40.pdf

Kane, L., "Childress County Ruled Out as Nuclear Waste Dump," *Lubbock Avalanche-Journal* (27 August 1999), http://lubbockonline.com/stories/082799/sta_0827990072.shtml

Kane, L., "Waste Case Must Stay in Andrews," *Lubbock Avalanche-Journal* (2000a), http://lubbockonline.com/stories/012000/sta_012000063.shtml

Kane, L., "Waste Firms Settle Differences," *Lubbock Avalanche-Journal* (2000b), http://lubbockonline.com/stories/112800/upd_075-5309.shtml

Kang, C. S., "Radioactive Waste Management in Korea and Public Acceptance," *14th Public Basin Nuclear Conference*, Honolulu, Hawaii (21–25 March 2004), www.aesj.or.jp/~sed/pbnc2004_1/pbnc2004/pbnc2004.3-2.pdf

Karl, H. A., Schwab, W. C., Drake, D. E., and Chin, J. L., *Detection of Barrels That Contain Low-Level Radioactive Waste in Farallon Island Radioactive Waste Dumpsite Using Side-Scan Sonar and Underwater-Optical Systems – Preliminary Interpretation of Barrel Distribution*, United States Department of the Interior/United States Geological Survey, Open-File Report 92–178 (January 1992), http://pubs.usgs.gov/of/1992/0178/report.pdf

Karner, D., and Mullen, J., "Financial Risk Management Issues for Low-Level Radioactive Waste Disposal Facilities," *Waste Management 1991 Conference*, Tucson, Arizona (24–28 February 1991), www.wmsym.org/archives/1991/V2/74.pdf

Karwath, R., "Deal Ok'd to Build Nuclear Waste Dump In Illinois," *Chicago Tribune* (26 July 1989), http://articles.chicagotribune.com/1989–07–26/news/8902200414_1_low-level-nuclear-waste-nuclear-plants-chem-nuclear-systems

Kasperson, R., "The Social Amplification of Risk and Low-Level Radiation," *Bulletin of the Atomic Scientists*, Vol. 68, No. 3 (2012): 59–66.

Kastelein, J., *HABOG: One Building for High Level Waste and Spent Fuel in the Netherlands, The First Year of Experience*, RRFM 2005, Budapest (11–12 April 2005), www.euronuclear.org/meetings/rrfm2005/presentations/Kastelein.pdf

Kaufman, H., and Moorer, L., "The Nuke Dump NIMBY Game: Why Nebraska Was Targeted," *Public Utilities Fortnightly*, Vol. 128, No. 2 (15 July 1991), in Nebraska State Historical Society, Government Records, RG141, Series 1, Central Interstate Low-Level Radioactive Waste Compact (LLRW-Nebraska), Research Files, Articles and Books, 1961–2006, Box 2 of 5.

Kemp, R., *The Politics of Radioactive Waste Disposal* (Manchester: Manchester University Press, 1992).

Kerr, G. W., "The Evolvement of Federal/State Relationships in the Regulation of Low-Level Radioactive Wastes," *Waste Management 1982 Conference*, Tucson, Arizona (28 February–4 March 1982), http://wmsym.org/archives/1982/V1/8.pdf

Kerr, K., and McDonald, C., *Final Report on the Citizens Advisory Committee on Low-Level Radioactive Waste*, League of Women Voters of Nebraska (May 1989).

Kerr, T., and Neal, J., *What Makes an Effective Citizens Advisory Group? An Analysis of the Effectiveness of Local Citizens Advisory Groups in Siting Low-Level Radioactive Waste Disposal Facilities in the United States*, Afton Associates (5 September 1995), in Nebraska State Historical Society, Government Records, RG/141, Series 1, Central Interstate Low-Level Radioactive Waste Compact (LLRW-NE), Research Files, Reports/Printed Publications, 1992–2006, Box 4 of 5.

Key Issues and Problems Requiring Resolution Prior to Siting and Operating Nuclear and Hazardous Waste Facilities in the State of Nebraska, 1990 Annual Report of the Nuckolls

County, Nebraska Nuclear and Hazardous Waste Monitoring Committee, in Nebraska State Historical Society, Government Records, RG/41, Series 1, Central Interstate Low-Level Radioactive Waste Compact (LLRW-NE), Research Files, Misc. Reports, 1989–2003, Box 5 of 5.

Kirby, A., "Nuclear Dumping Leak Sparks Concern," *BBC News* (17 January 2002), http://news.bbc.co.uk/2/hi/science/nature/1766365.stm

Knight, D., "Nuclear Waste Dump Planned on U.S.–Mexican border," *Albion Monitor* (1 July 1998), www.monitor.net/monitor/9807a/copyright/texmexdump.html

Knipe, C., *UK Nirex – 1995/96 Public Inquiry into the Proposed Construction of a "Rock Characterisation Facility" (Underground Rock Laboratory) at Longlands Farm Near Sellafield, Cumbria* (n.d.), www.jpb.co.uk/nirexinquiry/nirex.htm

Ko, K-J., "Eight Local Governments Petition for Radioactive Waste Management Facility," *Dong-A Ilbo* (31 May 2004), http://english.donga.com/srv/service.php3?bicode=0 20000&biid=2004060161748

Ko, W.I., and Kwon, E., "Implications of the New National Energy Basic Plan for Nuclear Waste Management in Korea," *Energy Policy*, Vol. 37, No. 9 (June 2009).

Kohout, M.D., *Sierra Blanca, TX,* Texas State Historical Association (n.d.), www.tshaonline. org/handbook/online/articles/hls47

Koopmans, R., and Duyvendak, J.W., *The Political Construction of the Nuclear Energy Issue and Its Impact on the Mobilization of Anti-Nuclear Movements in Western Europe* (Berkeley: University of California Press, 1995).

KORAD Brochure (October 2014), www.korad.or.kr/krmc2011/eng/pr/english_201410.pdf

Korea Hydro and Nuclear Power Co. Ltd., *Low and Intermediate Level Radioactive Wastes* (2014), https://cms.khnp.co.kr/eng/low-and-intermediate-level-radioactive-wastes/.

Korea Hydro and Nuclear Power Co. Ltd., Press Release, "Embarkment of Construction of the Wolsong Low and Intermediate Level Radioactive Waste Disposal Center on Nov. 9" (9 November 2007), https://cms.khnp.co.kr/eng/embarkment-of-construction-of-the-wolsong-low-and-intermediate-level-radioactive-waste-disposal-center-on-nov-9/

"Korean Nuclear Plants Renamed," *World Nuclear News* (21 May 2013), www.world-nuclear-news.org/C-Korean_nuclear_plants_renamed-2105134.html

Korea Nuclear Energy Foundation, "The Purpose of KNEF" (n.d.), http://eng.knef.or.kr/ profile/overview.asp

Korea Nuclear International Cooperation Foundation (KONICOF), "Nuclear Safety Regulation" (2008), http://eng.konicof.or.kr/03_atom/06_safety.php

Korea Radioactive Waste Management Corporation, *Radioactive Waste Management in Korea* (31 May 2010), http://pbadupws.nrc.gov/docs/ML1019/ML101950115.pdf

Kowalski, E., and Fritschi, M., "Has Wellenberg Shown the Way, or Is It Merely Postponing the Inevitable?," in *Retrievability of High Level Waste and Spent Nuclear Fuel*, Proceedings of an International Seminar Organized by the Swedish National Council for Nuclear Waste in Co-operation with the International Atomic Energy Agency, Saltsjöbaden, Sweden, IAEA-TECDOC-1187 (24–27 October 1999), www-pub.iaea. org/MTCD/publications/PDF/te_1187_prn.pdf

Kraft, M.E., Rosa, E.A., and Dunlap, R.E., "Public Opinion and Nuclear Waste Policymaking," in R.E. Dunlap, M.E. Kraft, and E.A. Rosa (eds.), *Public Reactions to Nuclear Waste: Citizen's Views of Repository Siting* (Durham, NC: Duke University Press, 1993).

Ku, H., "North Korea Suing Taipower," *Taipei Times* (2 March 2013), www.taipeitimes. com/News/front/archives/2013/03/02/2003556051

Kuhrt, N., "Nuclear Waste Barrels Litter English Channel," *Spiegel Online* (12 April 2013), www.spiegel.de/international/europe/legacy-danger-old-nuclear-waste-found-in-english-channel-a-893991.html

Kurzeme, M., "The Pangea Concept for an International Radioactive Waste Repository" (n.d.), www.iaea.org/inis/collection/NCLCollectionStore/_Public/31/033/31033869.pdf

LAKA Foundation, "Spain" (n.d.), www.laka.org/info/publicaties/afval/2-discussions-00/6-spain.htm

LAKA Foundation, "Switzerland" (2000), www.laka.org/info/publicaties/afval/2-discussions-00/8-switzerland.htm

Lamolla, M.M., "Identifying Remaining Socio-Technical Challenges at the National Level: Spain," Working Paper in SOTEC (20 May 2012), http://newmdb.iaea.org/profiles.aspx?ByCountry=ES

Landa, J., "Eagle Ford Shale Oil Company Seeks Permit to Dispose Oil & Gas Waste Underground in Maverick County," *Eagle Pass Business Journal* (7 January 2013), www.epbusinessjournal.com/2013/01/eagle-ford-shale-oil-company-seeks-permit-to-dispose-oil-gas-waste-underground-in-maverick-county/

Lang-Lenton, J., and Neri, E.G., "Current States of the Radioactive Waste Management Programme in Spain," ENRESA ICEMO7–7101 (2007).

Lang-Lenton, J., Castro, F., and d'Abadal, M., "Nuclear Waste Management in Spain: El Cabril and On Site Storage" (2005), www.cowam.com/?Nuclear-Waste-Management-in-Spain

Laukaitis, A., "Call Finally Ends Nuke Waste Dispute," *Lincoln Star Journal* (1 August 2005), http://journalstar.com/news/local/call-finally-ends-nuke-waste-dispute/article_d45d3c67-cf09-5053-98df-8ab5a7f8eeb6.html

League of Women Voters in Utah, *Political Decisions and Nuclear Waste in Utah* (January 2005), www.lwvutah.org/Studies/Political%20Decisions%20and%20Nuclear%20Waste%20Storage%20in%20Utah.pdf

Lee, J., "Federal Court Case Opens on Muckaty Station Nuclear Waste Dump," *Sydney Morning Herald* (3 June 2014), www.smh.com.au/federal-politics/political-news/federal-court-case-opens-on-muckaty-station-nuclear-waste-dump-20140602-39es9.html#ixzz3A3sNvAbq

Lee, Y., "Experience of Siting Process for Radwaste Disposal Facility in Korea," Korea Radioactive Waste Management Corporation (15 February 2011), www.oecd-nea.org/ndd/pubsiting/documents/15February_Item2a_Y-RLee.pdf

Legislative Commission of the Legislative Counsel Bureau, *Transportation and Disposal of Radioactive Material*, Bulletin No. 81–6 (October 1980), www.leg.state.nv.us/Division/Research/Publications/InterimReports/1981/Bulletin81–06.pdf

Legislative Journal of the State of Nebraska, Vol. 1, 90th Legislature, 2nd Session (convened 6 January 1988, adjourned 8 April 1988), Lincoln, Nebraska, www.nebraskalegislature.gov/FloorDocs/90/PDF/Journal/r2journal.pdf

LeMone, D., Xie, H., Keller, G.R., and Dodge, R., "Remote Sensing Analysis of the Fort Hancock Low-Level Radioactive Waste Disposal Site: Hudspeth County, Texas," *Waste Management 2001 Conference*, Tucson, Arizona (25 February–1 March 2001), www.wmsym.org/archives/2001/21C/21C-21.pdf

Letter from Alan Woods (offering 235 acres in Blue Hill) (30 December 1987), in Nebraska State Historical Society, Government Records, RG001, Government, SG43, Orr, Kay, S1 Correspondence, Public Opinion, LLRW, Box 42.

Letter from Beatty Pierce to Kay Orr (3 May 1990), in Nebraska State Historical Society, Government Records, RG001, Government, SG43, Orr, Kay, S1, Correspondence, Public Opinion, LLRW, Box 42.

Letter from Dan Meyer to Governor Orr (offering 160 acres in Wisner) (14 January 1988), in Nebraska State Historical Society, Government Records, RG001, Government, SG43, Orr, Kay, S1 Correspondence, Public Opinion, LLRW, Box 42.

Letter from Eugene Crump to Governor Nelson (12 September 1997), in Nebraska State Historical Society, Government Records, RG1-Gov. Nelson (SG44).

Letter from Eugene Crump to Loren Sieh (2 December 1992), in Nebraska State Historical Society, Government Records, RG1-Gov. Nelson (SG44).

Letter from Governor Kay Orr to David Beliles (17 October 1990), in Nebraska State Historical Society, Government Records, RG001, Government, SG43, Orr, Kay, S1, Correspondence, Public Opinion, LLRW, Box 42.

Letter from Governor Kay Orr to Jane Vogt (22 October 1990), in Nebraska State Historical Society, Government Records, RG001, Government, SG43, Orr, Kay, S1, Correspondence, Public Opinion, LLRW, Box 42.

Letter from Governor Nelson to Loren Sieh (13 November 1992), in Nebraska State Historical Society, Government Records, RG1-Gov. Nelson (SG44).

Letter from Governor Nelson to the Central Interstate Compact Commissioners (23 December 1992), in Nebraska State Historical Society, Government Records, RG1-Gov. Nelson (SG44).

Letter from Governor Nelson to the Secretary of the Commission, Docketing and Service Branch, Nuclear Regulatory Commission (28 November 1994), in Nebraska State Historical Society, Government Records, RG1-Gov. Nelson (SG44).

Letter from Harold Reiser to Governor Nelson (12 December 1994), in Nebraska State Historical Society, Government Records, RG1-Gov. Nelson (SG44).

Letter from Jerry Heermann et al. to Carl Schuman (Boyd Attorney) and Governor Kay Orr re: Potential Criminal Violations of Nebraska Public Meetings Law (23 February 1990), in Nebraska State Historical Society, Government Records, RG001, Government, SG43, Orr, Kay, S1, Correspondence, Public Opinion, LLRW, Box 42.

Letter from Khosrow Semnani to Governor Nelson (12 May 1995), in Nebraska State Historical Society, Government Records, RG1-Gov. Nelson (SG44).

Letter from Loren Sieh to Governor Nelson (11 December 1992), in Nebraska State Historical Society, Government Records, RG1-Gov. Nelson (SG44).

Letter from Norma Boettcher to Governor Kay Orr (2 April 1990), in Nebraska State Historical Society, Government Records, RG001, Government, SG43, Orr, Kay, S1, Correspondence, Public Opinion, LLRW, Box 42.

Letter from Nuckolls County Nuclear and Hazardous Waste Monitoring Committee Chairman Mick Karmazin to John DeOld (21 June 1990), in Nebraska State Historical Society, Government Records, RG001, Government, SG43, Orr, Kay, S1, Correspondence, Public Opinion, LLRW, Box 42.

Letter from Phyllis Weakly (Co-chair, Save Boyd County) to the Central Interstate Compact Commissioners (25 June 1997), in Nebraska State Historical Society, Government Records, RG/41, Series 8, Central Interstate Low-Level Radioactive Waste Compact (LLRW-NE), Misc. Files, Committee/State/Legislature, 1987–2005, Box 1 of 2.

Letter from Richard Paton (US Ecology) to Vera May Lutz (Nebraska League of Women Voters) (3 March 1988), in Nebraska State Historical Society, Government Records, RG001, Government, SG43, Orr, Kay, S1, Correspondence, Public Opinion, LLRW, Box 42.

Letter from Rose Selle to Governor Orr (15 May 1990), in Nebraska State Historical Society, Government Records, RG001, Government, SG43, Orr, Kay, S1 Correspondence, Public Opinion, LLRW, Box 42.

Letter from South Carolina Water Resources Commission Executive Director Alfred Vang to North Carolina Low-Level Radioactive Waste Management Authority Executive Director John MacMillan (6 November 1991), reprinted in *Summary of Significant Findings Regarding the Process of Site Selection for the North Carolina Low-Level Radioactive Waste Facility*, prepared by James, McElroy & Diehl, P.A. (19 February 1992).

Letter from Steve Moeller to Harold Reiser (18 August 1997), in Nebraska State Historical Society, Government Records, RG1-Gov. Nelson (SG44).

Letter of Invitation from Governor Nelson to Charles Zidko (31 July 1997), in Nebraska State Historical Society, Government Records, RG1-Gov. Nelson (SG44).

Letter of Invitation from Governor Nelson to Loren Sieh (31 July 1997), in Nebraska State Historical Society, Government Records, RG1-Gov. Nelson (SG44).

Letter to Governor Kay Orr from Ivy Nielsen (14 January 1988), in Nebraska State Historical Society, Government Records, RG001, Government, SG43, Orr, Kay, S1, Correspondence, Public Opinion, LLRW, Box 42.

Levesque, W.R., "USS *Calhoun County* Sailors Dumped Thousands of Tons of Radioactive Waste into Ocean," *Tampa Bay Times* (20 December 2013), www.tampabay.com/news/military/veterans/the-atomic-sailors/2157927

Levett, A., "Santa Went Ballistic over Nuclear Dump," *Hartlepool Mail* (17 December 2013), www.hartlepoolmail.co.uk/news/nostalgia/santa-went-ballistic-over-nuclear-dump-1-6306213

Lloyd, B., *The National Radioactive Waste Facility*, Research Papers of the Parliamentary Library Service, no. 1 (2006), Northern Territory Library.

Lok-Sin, L., "Tao Protest against Nuclear Facility," *Taipei Times* (21 February 2012), www.taipeitimes.com/News/front/archives/2012/02/21/2003525985

Lomenick, T.F., *The Siting Record: An Account of the Programs of Federal Agencies and Events That Have Led to the Selection of a Potential Site for a Geologic Repository for High-Level Radioactive Waste*, Oak Ridge National Laboratory, ORNL/TM-12940 (March 1996).

López, I., Navarro, M., Zuloaga, P., and Vargas, E., "Safety Assessment of the New Very Low-Level Waste Disposal Installation at El Cabril, Spain," *Waste Management Conference*, Phoenix, Arizona (1–5 March 2009), www.wmsym.org/archives/2009/pdfs/9042.pdf

Lorna Fejo, Dick Foster and Ronald Brown v. The Northern Land Council, The Minister for Resources and Energy and Minister for Tourism Named in the Schedule, Third Further Amended Application, No. VID 433 of 2010, Federal Court of Australia (10 June 2014).

Losada, M, "Nuclear Waste Policy in Spain," 18th REFORM Group Meeting – Climate Policy Strategies and Energy Transition (August 2013), www.polsoz.fu-berlin.de/polwiss/forschung/systeme/ffu/veranstaltungen/termine/downloads/13_salzburg/Isidoro-Salzburg-2013.pdf

"Low and Intermediate Level Waste Management in Spain" (n.d.), http://newmdb.iaea.org/GetLibraryFile.aspx?RRoomID=423

"Low-Level Radioactive Waste Disposal Company Shows Interest in Locating Here in West End," *San Miguel Basin Forum* (29 April 1982).

Low-Level Radioactive Waste Forum, Discussion of Issues Statement, "Management of Commercial Low-Level Radioactive Waste" (adopted 22 September 2005; amended

18 September 2006), www.llwforum.org/pdfs/ForumPolicyAmended10–18–06FINALFORPUBLICATION.pdf

Low-Level Radioactive Waste Policy Act of 1985, Amended, Pub. L. No. 99–240, 99 Stat. 1864 (15 January 1986), www.gtcceis.anl.gov/documents/docs/LLRWPAA.pdf

Low Level Waste Repository Ltd., "History" (n.d.), http://llwrsite.com/our-company/history/

Ludlam, Scott, "This Land Is Not Nowhere, These People Are Not No-one." *Human Rights in Australia* (13 August 2012), http://rightnow.org.au/writing-cat/article/this-land-is-not-nowhere-these-people-are-not-no-one/

Lyman, R., "For Some, Texas Town Is Too Popular as Waste Disposal Site," *New York Times* (2 September 1998), www.nytimes.com/1998/09/02/us/for-some-texas-town-is-too-popular-as-waste-disposal-site.html

Maine.gov, Division of Environmental Health, "Radioactive Waste Section" (updated 2011), www.maine.gov/dhhs/mecdc/environmental-health/rad/hp-waste.htm

Maine Legislature, "An Act to Withdraw from the Texas Low-level Radioactive Waste Disposal Compact," Chapter 629, H.P. 1666-L.D. 2171 (effective 5 April 2002), www.mainelegislature.org/ros/LOM/lom120th/4pub601–650/pub601–650–28.htm

Malewitz, J., "Nuclear Waste Storage on Texas Lawmakers' Agenda," *Texas Tribune* (12 February 2014a), www.texastribune.org/2014/02/12/strauss-puts-nuclear-waste-texas-lawmakers-agenda/

Malewitz, J., "Texas' Nuclear Waste Dump Gets Wriggle Room," *Texas Tribune* (20 August 2014b), www.texastribune.org/2014/08/20/texas-nuclear-waste-dump-poised-get-wiggle-room/

Mark Lane Jangala & Ors v. Commonwealth of Australia & Ors, Amended Defence of Second and Fourth Respondents, No. VID 433 of 2010, The Federal Court of Australia Victorian District Registry (19 April 2012).

Mark Lane Jangala & Ors v. Commonwealth of Australia & Ors, Amended Defence of Second and Fourth Respondents, No. VID 433 of 2010, The Federal Court of Australia Victorian District Registry (24 September 2013).

Mark Lane Jangala & Ors v. Commonwealth of Australia & Ors, Further Amended Defence of Second and Fourth Respondents, No. VID 433 of 2010, The Federal Court of Australia Victorian District Registry (26 February 2014).

Mark Lane Jangala & Ors v. Commonwealth of Australia & Ors, Further Amended Statement of Claim, No. VID433 of 2010, Federal Court of Australia (23 April 2012).

Mark Lane Jangala v. The Commonwealth of Australia, The Northern Land Council & The Minister for Resources, Energy & Tourism, Statement of Claim, No. VID 433 of 2010, The Federal Court of Australia Victorian District Registry (16 August 2010).

Markandya, A., and Wilkinson, P., "Electricity Generation and Health," *Lancet*, Vol. 370, No. 9591 (2007): 979–990.

Marks, P., "State Finding Few Takers for Its Low-Level Nuclear Waste," *Hartford Courant* (24 May 1992), http://articles.courant.com/1992–05–24/news/0000201589_1_radioactive-waste-low-level-waste-disposal-low-level-nuclear-waste

Martess, M., and Ferraro, G., "Radioactive Waste Management Stakeholders Map in the European Union, Report May 2014," *JRC Science and Policy Reports* (2014).

Mashhood, F., "District Judge Grants Hearing in Fight against West Texas Radioactive Waste Dump," *Austin American-Statesman* (8 May 2012), www.statesman.com/news/texas/district-judge-grants-hearing-in-fight-against-west-2346916.html

Mathews, L., "A Low-Level Radioactive Waste Disposal Site in Texas – Will It Become a Reality?" *Waste Management 1997 Conference*, Tucson, Arizona (22–26 February 1992), www.wmsym.org/archives/1997/sess_8/08–03.htm

Mathews, L., and Bowmer, W., "The Texas Situation," *Waste Management 1986 Conference*, Tucson, Arizona (22–26 February 1992), www.wmsym.org/archives/1986/V3/11.pdf

Mayer, C., "Neighbors Become Enemies over Toxic Dump," *Philadelphia Inquirer* (26 November 1992), http://articles.philly.com/1992-11-26/news/26009053_1_radioactive-waste-butte-boyd-county

"The Mayors of the Environment Are Threatening to Block El Cabril," *Cordopolis* (11 December 2014), http://cordopolis.es/2014/12/11/los-alcaldes-del-entorno-de-el-cabril-amagan-con

Mazuan, G. T., and Walker, J. S, *Controlling the Atom: The Beginnings of Nuclear Regulation, 1946–1962* (Berkeley: University of California Press, 1984).

McCardle, J., "No Retreat for Veteran EPA Whistleblower in Era of 'Harsher and Vicious' Retaliation," *New York Times* (6 January 2011), www.nytimes.com/gwire/2011/01/06/06greenwire-no-retreat-for-veteran-epa-whistleblower-in-er-76194.html

McCarthy, M., "Nuclear Waste Plans 'Progressing,' " *ABC News* (8 October 2013), www.abc.net.au/news/2013-10-07/nuclear-dump/5002944

McCutcheon, C., "N-Dumps Trigger Opposite Reactions," *Albuquerque Journal* (24 February 1991).

McGuire, J., *The Dilemma of Public Participation in Facility Siting Decisions and the Mediation Alternative*, 9 Seton Hall Legis. J. 467 (1985).

McGurty, E., "From NIMBY to Civil Rights: The Origins of the Environmental Justice Movement," *Environmental History*, Vol. 2, No. 3 (1997): 301–323.

McKie, R., "Windscale Radiation 'Doubly Dangerous,' " *Guardian* (7 October 2007), www.theguardian.com/science/2007/oct/07/nuclearpower

Mellado, I., "The Role of the Nuclear Safety Regulator," *OECD/NEA* (2007), Radioactive Waste Management in Spain: Co-ordination and Projects, FSC Workshop Proceedings, L'Hospitalet de l'Infant, Spain (21–23 November 2005).

Memorandum to Governor-Elect Ben Nelson from Central Interstate Low-Level Radioactive Waste Compact Commission re: Community Consent, Cline, Williams, Wright, Johnson and Oldfather – Counsel (7 December 1990), in Nebraska State Historical Society, Government Records, RG1-Gov. Nelson (SG44).

Méndez, R., "Madrid Spain's Half-Forgotten Search for a Long-Term Nuclear Waste Solution," *El País* (14 September 2011), http://elpais.com/elpais/2011/09/14/inenglish/1315977644_850210.html

Meyer, P., "Switzerland: Regulatory Control of Radioactive Waste Management," *NERS-Meeting 2006*, Bled, Slovenia (8–9 June 2006), http://ners.co/9th/RWMSW.pdf

Miller, C., "Looking to the STARS to Reduce Class B/C Waste," *Radwaste Solutions* (November/December 2003).

Miller, S., "N.C. State Rethinks Its Affairs with Valvano," *Daily Press (Newport News)* (22 November 1989), http://articles.dailypress.com/1989-11-22/sports/8911210486_1_jim-valvano-wolfpack-academic-improprieties

Mitchell, R. K., Agle, B. R., and Wood, D. J., "Toward a Theory of Stakeholder Identification and Salience: Defining the Principle of Who and What Really Counts," *Academy of Management Review*, Vol. 22, No. 4 (1997): 853–888.

Mittelstadt, M., "Wellstone Will Seek to Amend Texas Low-Level Radioactive Compact," *Abilene Reporter-News* (23 October 1997), www.texnews.com/texas97/waste102397.html

MNA, "Leserinnen – and Letters to the Editor in the Newspaper *Nidwaldner*" (3–30 August 2002), www.mna.ch/StopWellenberg/html/lbaugust.htm

"The Modern Texas Economy," in *Texas Politics*, University of Texas at Austin (2009), http://texaspolitics.laits.utexas.edu/9_3_0.html

Mohai, P., and Bryant, B., "Environmental Justice: Weighing Race and Class as Factors in the Distribution of Environmental Hazards," *University of Colorado Law Review*, Vol. 63, No. 4 (1992): 921–932.

Molina, M., "LILW Management in Spain El Cabril Disposal Facility," Presentation to SKB, ENRESA (11 March 2010).

Molina, M., "The Role of Local Authorities in the Process of Siting the Spanish Repository for Low and Intermediate-Level Radioactive Waste," Nuclear Energy Agency, 75 – Paris, France (1996).

Montes, E., "Texas Opposition Mounting to Further Shipments of New York Sludge," *Abilene Reporter-News* (18 May 1997), www.texnews.com/texas97/sludge051897.html

Mount, P., "Texcor Talks to Witnesses," *Del Rio News Herald* (15 August 1992), www.newspapers.com/newspage/6340541/

"Muckaty Station: Northern Land Council Withdraws Nomination of Site of First Nuclear Waste Dump," *ABC News* (19 June 2014), www.abc.net.au/news/2014–06–19/northern-land-council-withdraws-muckaty-creek-nomination/5535318

Mullner, R., *Deadly Glow: The Radium Dial Worker Tragedy* (Washington, DC: American Public Health Association, 1999).

Murphy, T., "GOP Candidate Asks Residents to Mail Him Their Pee," *Mother Jones* (20 August 2014), www.motherjones.com/politics/2014/08/art-robinson-nuclear-waste-pete-defazio

Mutchler, T., "Contender for Nuclear Safety Job Resigned Under Fire in Illinois," *Associated Press* (10 December 1993), www.apnewsarchive.com/1993/Contender-for-Nuclear-Safety-Job-Resigned-Under-Fire-in-Illinois/id-ddf57e241a9f39aedce6f69a20bc02cc

Myerson, A., "Buying an Uneasy Home for New York City Waste," *New York Times* (16 July 1995), www.nytimes.com/1995/07/16/nyregion/buying-an-uneasy-home-for-new-york-city-waste.html

Nagra, "Developments of Nagra 1972 to 1980" (n.d.a.), www.nagra.ch/en/developmentsofnagra1972to1980.htm

Nagra, "Developments of Nagra 1991 to 2000" (n.d.b.), www.nagra.ch/en/developments-from1991to2000.htm

Nagra, "History and Focus of Activities of Nagra: Developments Since 2001" (n.d.c.), www.nagra.ch/en/developmentssince2001.htm

Nagra, "Opalinus Clay Project: Demonstration of Feasibility of Disposal ("Entsorgungsnachweis") for Spent Fuel, Vitrified High-Level Waste and Long-Lived Intermediate-Level Waste – Summary Overview" (December 2002), www.nagra.ch/disply.cfm/id/100188

Nagra, "Volumes (as of end 2013)" (n.d.d.), www.nagra.ch/en/volumesen.htm

Nagtzaam, G. "Pass the Parcel: Australia and the Vexing Issue of a Federal Nuclear Waste Repository' *Alternative Law Journal*, http://search.informit.com.au/browsePublication; py=2014;vol=39;res=IELHSS;issn=1037-969X;iss=4" Vol. 39, No. 4, (Dec 2014), pp. 246-248.

Nagtzaam, G., and Newman, A. "Merely Unpicking the Gordian Knot: The Ongoing Quest to Build a Federal Low level radioactive waste disposal Facility in Australia," *Australasian Journal of Natural Resource Law and Policy*, Winter, 2015 (forthcoming).

National Academy of Sciences, National Research Council, *Radioactive Waste Disposal into Atlantic and Gulf Coastal Waters*, Publication 655, Washington, DC (1959), https://ia600407.us.archive.org/33/items/radioactivewaste00nati/radioactivewaste00nati.pdf

National Radioactive Waste Management Act 2012 (Cth), www.comlaw.gov.au/Details/C2012A00029

National Radioactive Waste Repository, Site Selection Study (Australia), Phase 1 (August 1993).

National Radioactive Waste Repository, Site Selection Study, Phase 2, Australian Government Publishing Service Canberra (November 1995), www.industry.gov.au/resource/Documents/radioactive_waste/report_on_public_comment_phase_2.pdf

National Research Council of the National Academies, *One Step at a Time: The Staged Development of Geologic Repositories for High-Level Radioactive Waste*, Committee on Principles and Operational Strategies for Staged Repository Systems, Board on Radioactive Waste Management, Division on Earth and Life Studies (Washington, DC: National Academies Press, 2003).

"Naturally-Occurring Radiation: Overview," Environmental Protection Agency (updated 29 June 2015), www.epa.gov/radiation/natural-radiation-overview.html

"Naturally-Occurring Radioactive Materials," World Nuclear Association (updated May 2015), www.world-nuclear.org/info/Safety-and-Security/Radiation-and-Health/Naturally-Occurring-Radioactive-Materials-NORM/

Nebraska Department of Environmental Quality, *Before the Nebraska Department of Environmental Quality and the Nebraska Department of Health and Human Services Regulation and Licensure, in the Matter of the Application by US Ecology, Inc. for a License to Construct, Operate, and Close a Commercial Low-Level Radioactive Waste Disposal Facility, Denial of Application for a License* (18 December 1998a), www.deq.state.ne.us/Priority.nsf/pages/denial

Nebraska Department of Environmental Quality, *Proposed License Decision* (revised 30 December 1998b), www.deq.state.ne.us/Priority.nsf/23e5e39594c064ee852564ae004fa010/6df9ad234fe147458625665d0059d07d?OpenDocument

"Nebraska Governor Curbs Campaign after Threat," *New York Times* (10 October 1990), www.nytimes.com/1990/10/10/us/nebraska-governor-curbs-campaign-after-threat.html

"Nebraska Is Wary on Proposed Site for Nuclear Waste," *Seattle Times* (25 November 1990), http://community.seattletimes.nwsource.com/archive/?date=19901125&slug=1106030

Nebraska Legislative Bill 761, "An Act to Amend the Low-Level Waste Disposal Act," (approved by the Governor May 25, 1989).

Nebraska Legislature, *Floor Debate Transcript for the 90th Legislature*, http://nebraskalegislature.gov/transcripts/browse_past.php?leg=90

Nebraska Legislature, Legislative Research Division, *A Review: Ninety-Sixth Legislature, First Session, 1999* (August 1999), http://nebraskalegislature.gov/pdf/reports/research/review99.pdf

Nebraska Revised Statute 81–1579 (n.d.), http://nebraskalegislature.gov/laws/statutes.php?statute=81–1579

Nebraska Unicameral Legislature, Seq. No. 420, Final Reading, LB 530 Dierks (6 May 1999), in Nebraska State Historical Society, Government Records, RG/41, Series 8, Central Interstate Low-Level Radioactive Waste Compact (LLRW-NE), Misc. Files, Committee/State/Legislature, 1987–2005, Box 1 of 2.

Nebraska v. Central Interstate Low-Level Radioactive Waste Commission, 834 F. Supp. 1205 (D. Neb. 1993), http://elr.info/sites/default/files/litigation/24.20434.htm

"Nebraska Wants Nuclear Waste Dump to Be in Kansas," *CJ Online* (21 September 1998), in Nebraska State Historical Society, Government Records, RG1-Gov. Nelson (SG44).

Nelson Campaign, "The Issues" (print), in Nebraska State Historical Society, Government Records, RG/41, Series 1, Central Interstate Low-Level Radioactive Waste Compact (LLRW-NE), Research Files, Articles and Books, 1961–2006, Box 2 of 5.

Nevada Assembly Bill 444 (1961), www.leg.state.nv.us/Division/Research/Library/LegHistory/LHs/pre1965/AB444,1961.pdf

"Nevadans Warned of Exposure to Items Taken from Nuclear Dump," *Eugene Register-Guard* (16 March 1976).

Newberry, W. F., "Idaho National Engineering Laboratory," *Comparative Approaches to Siting Low-Level Radioactive Waste Disposal Facilities*, DOE-LLW-199 (July 1994), www.osti.gov/scitech/servlets/purl/114010

Newberry, W. F., "The Rise and Fall and Rise and Fall of American Public Policy on Disposal of Low-Level Radioactive Waste," *South Carolina Environmental Law Journal* (Winter 1993).

Newman, A., " 'An Area Previously Determined to Be the Best Adapted for Such Purposes': Nevada, Nuclear Waste and Assembly Joint Resolution 15 of 1975," *Journal of Policy History*, Vol. 24, No. 3 (2012): 432–465.

Newton, C., "Chisum Debates Low Level Nuclear Dump for Andrews County," *Lubbock Avalanche-Journal* (21 March 1999), http://lubbockonline.com/stories/032199/reg_LD0787.001.shtml

New York State Department of Environmental Conservation, Division of Solid & Hazardous Material, *2000 New York State Low-Level Radioactive Waste Transportation Report* (October 2001), www.dec.ny.gov/docs/materials_minerals_pdf/llwrpt00.pdf

New York v. United States, 488 U.S. 1041 (1992), www.law.cornell.edu/supct/html/91–543.ZS.html

Nicholson, L., "Western Australia in Nation's Nuclear Waste Dump Sights," *Sydney Morning Herald* (12 November 2013), www.smh.com.au/federal-politics/western-australia-in-nations-nuclear-waste-dump-sights-20131112–2xdzn.html

Nikipelov, B. V., Suslov, A. P., and Tsarenko, A. F., "Radioactive Waste Management in the USSR: Experience and Perspective," *Waste Management 1997 Conference*, Tucson, Arizona (23–27 February 1997), www.wmsym.org/archives/1990/V1/7.pdf

Nixon, P., "NORM Waste Dump Shakes Brackettville," *Del Rio News Herald* (15 April 1990), www.newspapers.com/newspage/9726310/

North Carolina Radiation Protection Act 1975, § 104E-25 (c), (d), www.ncga.state.nc.us/EnactedLegislation/Statutes/HTML/ByChapter/Chapter_104E.html

Northern Land Council, "NLC Settles on Muckaty" (19 June 2014), www.nlc.org.au/media-releases/article/nlc-settles-on-muckaty

Northwest Interstate Compact on Low-Level Radioactive Waste Management, reprinted in NRC, *Nuclear Regulatory Legislation*, NUREG-0980, Vol. 1, No. 10 (2012).

"No Threat From Radioactive Waste Dumping at Culmore," *Derry Daily* (4 January 2014), www.derrydaily.net/2014/01/04/no-threat-from-radioactive-waste-dumping-at-culmore/

"Nuclear Bill Gets Derailed," *Brownsville Herald* (24 May 1995).

Nuclear Decommissioning Authority, "LLW Repository Near Drigg" (2013), www.nda.gov.uk/ukinventory/sites/LLW_Repository_near_Drigg/

Nuclear Decommissioning Authority, "Radioactive Waste Inventory" (reported 1 April 2013), www.nda.gov.uk/ukinventory/

Nuclear Decommissioning Authority, *Sellafield Geological and Hydrogeological Investigations: A Synthesis of Data Used to Assess the Hydraulic Character of the Sherwood Sandstone Group at Sellafield*, Report No. S (n.d.), www.nda.gov.uk/documents/biblio/detail.cfm?fuseaction=search.view_doc&doc_id=2500

"Nuclear Disposal Site Still Unknown," *Taipei Times* (28 May 2008), www.taipeitimes.com/News/taiwan/archives/2008/05/28/2003413160

"Nuclear Dump Still in Limbo," *Lawrence Journal-World* (27 June 1994).

Nuclear Energy Act, Article 49 (21 March 2003), www.admin.ch/ch/e/rs/732_1/a49.html

Nuclear Energy Agency, International Seminar, Rauma (Finland) (13–15 October 1995).

Nuclear Energy Agency, *Partnering for Long-Term Management of Radioactive Waste – Evolution and Current Practice in Thirteen Countries* (December 2010), www.keepeek. com/Digital-Asset-Management/oecd/nuclear-energy/partnering-for-long-term-management-of-radioactive-waste_9789264083707-en#page77

Nuclear Energy Agency, *Radioactive Waste Management Programmes in OECD/NEA Member Countries, France Profile 2014* (March 2014), www.oecd-nea.org/rwm/profiles/France_profile_web.pdf

Nuclear Energy Ordinance, Article 5 (10 December 2004), www.admin.ch/opc/en/classified-compilation/20042217/index.html

"Nuclear Reactor in Spain Catches Fire," *New York Times* (26 October 1989), www.nytimes.com/1989/10/26/world/nuclear-reactor-in-spain-catches-fire.html

Nuclear Threat Initiative, *South Korea Nuclear Chronology* (last updated September 2004), www.nti.org/media/pdfs/south_korea_nuclear.pdf?_=1316466791

"Nuclear Waste Barrels Remain Strewn across Floor of English Channel," *RT.com* (12 April 2013), http://rt.com/news/nuclear-waste-english-channel-785/

Nuclear Waste Transport, Storage, Disposal (Prohibition) Act 2004 (NT), http://notes.nt.gov.au/dcm/legislat/legislat.nsf/linkreference/NUCLEAR%20WASTE%20TRANSPORT,%20STORAGE%20AND%20DISPOSAL%20%28PROHIBITION%29%20ACT%202004

Nuñez-Villaveirán, L., "El Cabril: Unique Spanish Nuclear Graveyard," *El Mundo* (23 January 2012), www.elmundo.es/blogs/elmundo/latrinchera/2012/01/23/el-cabril-unico-cementerio-nuclear.html

O'Briant, T., "Ex-governor Fought Chem-Nuclear Dump, Wants It to Stay Closed," *Times and Democrat* (22 March 2015), http://thetandd.com/business/ex-governor-fought-chem-nuclear-dump-wants-it-to-stay/article_dbdbbcd5-2885-5059-b1e0-dc521f802ea2.html

O'Hanlon, K., "Epilogue: Nuke Dump Battle Peaked 10 Years Ago This Month," *Lincoln Journal Star* (4 July 2011), http://journalstar.com/special-section/epilogue/epilogue-nuke-dump-battle-peaked-years-ago-this-month/article_8fe7f462-7662-5c03-8d03-7f4cc4729a0f.html

O'Hanlon, K., "Nebraska to Pay for Blocking Nuclear Waste Dump," *Topeka Capital Journal* (10 August 2004), www.cjonline.com/stories/081004/bus_nebraskawaste.shtml

O'Toole, T., "A Dump Closing Threatens to Halt Cancer Research," *Washington Post* (24 October 1979).

Oak Ridge National Laboratory, "Radioactive Waste Management in Rep. of Korea" (2010), http://curie.ornl.gov/system/files/documents/SEA/NEA_Korea_report_2010.pdf

OECD/NEA, *The Control of Safety of Radioactive Waste Management and Decommissioning in Switzerland ('Country Report')* (2011), www.oecd-nea.org/rwm/profiles/Switzerland_report_web.pdf

OECD/NEA, *Nuclear Legislation in OECD and NEA Countries: Regulatory and Institutional Framework for Nuclear Activities – Republic of Korea* (2009), www.oecd-nea.org/law/legislation/korea.pdf

OECD/NEA, *Nuclear Legislation in OECD and NEA Countries – Switzerland* (2003), www.oecd-nea.org/law/legislationswitzerland.pdf

OECD/NEA, *Reversibility and Retrievability in Planning for Geological Disposal of Radioactive Waste: Proceedings of the 'R&R' International Conference and Dialogue*, Reims, France (14–17 December 2010), www.oecd-nea.org/rwm/docs/2012/6993-proceedings-rr-reims.pdf

OECD/NEA, *Stakeholder Confidence and Radioactive Waste Disposal: Inauguration, First Workshop and Meeting of the NEA Forum on Stakeholder Confidence in the Area of*

Radioactive Waste Management, Paris, France (28–31 August 2000), www.oecd-nea.org/rwm/reports/2000/nea2829.pdf

Office of House Bill Analysis, C.S.S.B. 1541 by Duncan (17 May 2001), in S.B. 1541 Relating to the Permanent Management of Low-Level Radioactive Waste (20 May 2001).

Office of Technology Assessment, *Nuclear Wastes in the Arctic: An Analysis of Arctic and Other Regional Impacts from Soviet Nuclear Contamination*, OTA-ENV-632 (September 1995), http://ota.fas.org/reports/9504.pdf

Office of the Attorney General – State of Texas (John Cornyn), Opinion No. JC-0052 (18 May 1999), www.texasattorneygeneral.gov/opinions/opinions/49cornyn/op/1999/htm/jc0052.htm

Office of the Governor, Letter to the Honorable David Dewhurst and the Honorable Joe Straus, Austin (28 March 2014), http://media.cmgdigital.com/shared/news/documents/2014/03/31/SKMBT_36314033117180.pdf

Options Meeting (Dec. 13 notes) between Tom Burke, Michael Harsh, Greg Hayden and Kate Allen at Kennedy, Holland (n.d.) in Nebraska State Historical Society, Government Records, RG/41, Series 8, Central Interstate Low-Level Radioactive Waste Compact (LLRW-NE), Misc. Files, Committee/State/Legislature, 1987–2005, Box 1 of 2.

"Orchid Island Launches New Protests against Nuclear Waste," *Kyodo* (6 May 2002), www.thefreelibrary.com/Orchid+Island+launches+new+protests+against+nuclear+waste.-a085519940

Panter, R., Science, Technology & Environment Group, Parliamentary Research Service, Issues Paper No. 6, *Radioactive Waste Disposal in Australia* (28 April 1992).

Park, J.B., Jung, H., Lee, E.-Y., Kim, C.-L., Kim, G.-Y., Kim, K.-S., . . . Kim, K.-D., "Wolsong Low- and Intermediate-Level Radioactive Waste Disposal Center: Progress and Challenges," *Nuclear Engineering and Technology*, Vol. 41, No. 4 (May 2009), www.kns.org/jknsfile/v41/JK0410477.pdf

Park, S.W., Pomper, M.A., and Scheinman, L., "The Domestic and International Politics of Spent Nuclear Fuel in South Korea: Are We Approaching Meltdown?" *Korea Economic Institute*, Academic Paper Series, Vol. 5, No. 3 (March 2010), www.keia.org/sites/default/files/publications/APS-ParkPomparScheinman.pdf

Park, S.Y., "Constrained Cooperation in South Korea's Nuclear Power Policy and Its Side Effects," Korea Advanced Institute of Science and Technology (September 2013), www.eai.or.kr/data/bbs/kor_report/epik2013_j2.pdf

Park, T., and Choi, J., "Radioactive Waste Disposal Research Division Korea Atomic Energy Research Institute (KAERI)," Hacettepe University, Ankara, Turkey (May 2012), www.nuke.hun.edu.tr/tr/webfiles/Activities/KEPCONF_DOOSAN/Workshop/Presentations/1_1600_1630_9%20Radioactive%20Waste%20Management%20in%20Korea-KAERI.pdf

Parker, P., "Senate OKs Andrews Waste Site," *Lubbock Avalanche-Journal* (22 May 1999), http://lubbockonline.com/stories/052299/reg_052299125.shtml

Pasternak, A., "The California and Southwestern Compact Low-Level Waste Disposal Program: Waste Generators' Perspective, 1983–1999," *Waste Management 1999 Conference* (28 February–4 March 1999), www.wmsym.org/archives/1999/16/16–1.pdf

Payne, S.G., *The Franco Regime, 1936–1975* (Madison: University of Wisconsin Press, 2011).

Peachey, C., "Korean Repository Realised," *Nuclear Engineering International* (22 July 2014), www.neimagazine.com/features/featurekorean-repository-realised-4323899/

Pearson, R., "Rock Tells Thompson to Oust State's Nuclear Safety Director," *Chicago Tribune* (1 November 1989), http://articles.chicagotribune.com/1989–11–01/news/8901270317_1_nuclear-safety-director-james-thompson-site

Pennsylvania Bureau of Radiation Protection, *2010 Annual Low-Level Radioactive Waste Program Report to the Pennsylvania General Assembly and the Appalachian Compact Commission* (n.d.), www.elibrary.dep.state.pa.us/dsweb/Get/Document-87697/2930-BK-DEP4322%202010.pdf

Permanent Management of Low-Level Radioactive Waste, Committee Substitute for S.B. No. 1541 by Duncan (20 April 2001), –www.capitol.state.tx.us/BillLookup/Text.aspx?LegSess=77R&Bill=SB1541

Petrella, M.E., "Wasting Away Again: Facing the Low-Level Radioactive Waste Debacle in the United States," *Fordham Environmental Law Review*, Vol. 5, No. 1 (2011).

Pfeiffer, B., "Burial Plan Brings Cash, Fear to Poor Desert Town," *Bangor Daily News* (31 January–1 February 1998).

Pflieger, M., "State's Disposal Firm Had Run-In over Bias Chem-Nuclear Sites Questioned in N.C.," *Morning Call (Lehigh Valley)* (9 April 1992), http://articles.mcall.com/1992–04–09/news/2863029_1_radioactive-waste-disposal-site-chem-nuclear-systems-dump

Phoenix, E., "NI State Papers: Files Reveal Secret Dumping of Radioactive Waste," *BBC News* (28 December 2013), www.bbc.co.uk/news/uk-northern-ireland-25470028

Piot, D.K., "States Seek Control of Atomic Waste Sites," *Christian Science Monitor* (5 August 1980), www.csmonitor.com/1980/0805/080541.html

Piro, N., "Rural Queensland Fears Radioactive Dump," *Green Left Weekly* (25 September 1991), www.greenleft.org.au/node/574

"Plan for Nuclear Dump Divides Dakota Town," *New York Times* (4 November 1984), www.nytimes.com/1984/11/04/us/plan-for-nuclear-dump-divides-dakota-town.html

Polk, L., "Harold Simmons Is Dallas' Most Evil Genius," *D Magazine* (2010a), www.dmagazine.com/publications/d-magazine/2010/february/harold-simmons-is-dallas-most-evil-genius?single=1

Polk, L., "How Does Your Water Glow?" *In These Times* (2010b), http://inthesetimes.com/article/6075/how_does_your_water_glow/

"Position Paper on the Implications of Deep Sea Disposal of Radioactive Waste," RSC 10/4/3-E, OSPAR Convention for the Protection of the Marine Environment of the North-East Atlantic, Meeting of the Radioactive Substances Committee, Stockholm (20–23 April 2010), www.swr.de/report/-/id=8816210/property=download/nid=233454/1l17ugb/ospar-position-paper.pdf

Press Statement of Lowell Fisher (20 October 1990), in Nebraska State Historical Society, Government Records, RG001, Government, SG43, Orr, Kay, S1 Correspondence, Public Opinion, LLRW, Box 42.

Prince, C., "A Swiss Mountain May Soon Be Alive with Nuclear Waste," *Christian Science Monitor* (3 October 1995), www.csmonitor.com/1995/1003/03061.html

Princeton University, *Open Source Radiation Safety Training, Module 2: Background Radiation & Other Sources of Exposure* (updated 30 March 2011), http://web.princeton.edu/sites/ehs/osradtraining/backgroundradiation/background.htm

"The Project ATC Sinks," *Platform against Nuclear Graveyard* (31 December 2014), http://cuencadicenoalcementerionuclear.blogspot.com/search?updated-min=2014-01-01T00:00:00-08:00&updated-max=2015-01-01T00:00:00-08:00&max-results=24

"Public and Political Issues in Radwaste Management: The Spanish Approach," European Nuclear Society (ENS), Berne (Switzerland), 1999, ENS PIME '99: 11. International

Workshop on Nuclear Public Information in Practice, Avignon, France (7–10 February 1999).

"The Public Prosecutor Gives Reason to Whistleblower Marcos Buser," *SWI* (15 June 2014), www.swissinfo.ch/fre/le-ministére-public-donne-raison-an-lanceur-d-alerte-marcos-buser/38791438

Quirk, T., "How Texas Lost the World's Largest Super Collider," *Texas Monthly* (21 October 2013), www.texasmonthly.com/story/how-texas-lost-worlds-largest-super-collider

Rabe, B., *Beyond NIMBY: Hazardous Waste Siting in Canada and the United States* (Washington, DC: Brookings Institution, 1994).

Rabin, J., "L.A., San Diego Split on Ward Valley Dump," *Los Angeles Times* (24 April 1996), http://articles.latimes.com/1996-04-24/news/mn-62166_1_ward-valley

"Rad Fear Creates City of 'Lepers' in Brazil," *Sunday World-Herald* (3 January 1998), as found in the Letter to Governor Kay Orr from Ivy Nielsen (14 January 1988), in Nebraska State Historical Society, Government Records, RG001, Government, SG43, Orr, Kay, S1, Correspondence, Public Opinion, LLRW, Box 42.

Radian Corp., *Preliminary Assessment Report: Farallon Islands FUDS*, submitted to U.S. Army Corps of Engineers (June 1996), www.corpsfuds.net/reports/OTHER/J09CA-7067finalPAJune96.pdf

"Radioactive Leakage: Berlin Takes Steps to Address Nuclear Waste Scandal," *Der Spiegel* (4 September 2008), www.spiegel.de/international/germany/radioactive-leakage-berlin-takes-steps-to-address-nuclear-waste-scandal-a-576362.html

"Radioactive Waste Dump Proposal Hit Dell City," *Galveston Daily News* (12 November 1983), www.newspapers.com/newspage/14548726/

"Radioactive Waste Management Programmes in OECD/NEA Member Countries: Spain" (2013), www.oeca-nea.org/rwm/profiles/spain-profile-web.pdf

"A Radioactive Waste Repository for Australia, Commonwealth Australia, Site Selection Study – Phase 3," (1997), www.industry.gov.au/resource/Documents/radioactive_waste/public_discussion_paper_phase_3.pdf

"Radioactive Waste Store Feasibility Study – Stage Two," URS, prepared for the Environmental Protection Authority (3 November 2005), www.epa.sa.gov.au/xstd_files/Radiation/Report/radioactive_stage2.pdf

Raupach, M.R., Marland, G., Ciais, P., Le Quéré, C., Canadell, J.G., Klepper, G., and Field, C.B., "Global and Regional Drivers of Accelerating CO_2 Emissions," *Proceedings of the National Academy of Sciences*, Vol. 104, No. 24 (2007): 10288–10293.

RCRA Permit Application for a Hazardous Waste Storage, Treatment and Disposal Facility: Andrews County, Texas, Section VI. Geology Report, prepared for Waste Control Specialists, Inc. by Terra Dynamics Incorporated, Project No. 92–152 (March 1993), http://pbadupws.nrc.gov/docs/ML0419/ML041910484.pdf

Rechtschaffen, C., Guana, E., and O'Neill, C., *Environmental Justice: Law, Policy and Regulation*, 2nd ed. (Durham, NC: Carolina Academic Press, 2009).

Rees, J., *Hostages of Each Other: The Transformation of Nuclear Safety Since Three Mile Island* (Chicago: University of Chicago Press, 1994).

Reiman, J., and Nelson, P., "Report Notes for LLRW Forum" (received 5 June 1996), in Nebraska State Historical Society, Government Records, RG/41, Series 8, Central Interstate Low-Level Radioactive Waste Compact (LLRW-NE), Misc. Files, Committee/State/Legislature, 1987–2005, Box 1 of 2.

Reynolds, W., *Australia's Bid for the Atomic Bomb* (Melbourne: Melbourne University Press, 2000).

"Revocation Hearing Set for Beatty Dump Site," *Nevada State Journal* (14 November 1979) in Governor Robert List Records, Nevada State Archives.

RG/41, Series 1, Central Interstate Low-Level Radioactive Waste Compact (LLRW-NE) (n.d.), Research Files, Misc. Reports, 1989–2003, Box 5 of 5.

Rhodes, R., *Dark Sun: The Making of the Hydrogen Bomb* (New York: Simon and Schuster, 1995).

Riley, P., *Nuclear Waste: Law, Policy and Pragmatism* (Aldershot: Ashgate, 2004).

Ringenberg, J., and Jacobson, C., "Lessons Learned during Review of the First Above-Grade Concrete Facility for LLRW Disposal," *Waste Management 1991 Symposium*, Tucson, Arizona (24–28 February 1991), www.wmsym.org/archives/1991/V2/39.pdf

Robbins, M.A., "House Debates Nuclear Waste Dump Bill," *Lubbock Avalanche-Journal* (7 May 1999a), http://lubbockonline.com/stories/050799/sta_050799053.shtml

Robbins, M.A., "Opinion Sought on Waste Disposal," *Lubbock Avalanche-Journal* (16 March 1999b), http://lubbockonline.com/stories/031699/sta_031699094.shtml

Robbins, W., "Politics Overtake Selecting Nuclear Dump Sites," *New York Times* (30 September 1990), www.nytimes.com/1990/09/30/us/politics-overtake-selecting-nuclear-dump-sites.html

Robbins, M.A., "Radioactive Waste Disposal Discussed," *Lubbock Avalanche-Journal* (4 May 2000), http://lubbockonline.com/stories/050400/sta_050400069.shtml

Robbins, M.A., "Texas Legislature Set to Battle Radioactive Waste Site Issue," *Lubbock Avalanche-Journal* (1999c), http://lubbockonline.com/stories/020799/AST-3177.shtml

Robinson, D., "Semnani Living American Dream," *Deseret News* (11 November 2002), www.deseretnews.com/article/440014760/Semnani-living-American-dream.html?pg=all

Rocky Mountain Low-Level Radioactive Waste Compact, Pub. L. No. 99–240, 99 Stat. 1903 (15 January 1986), www.rmllwb.us/documents/rocky-mtn-compact-statute.pdf

Rogers, E., "Run to the Border: Nuclear and Toxic Industries Find Opposition Where They Least Expected It," *UT Watch*, Vol. 1, No. 44 (December 1994), www.utwatch.org/archives/subtex/toxic_issue4.html

Roldan, C., "Charleston Republican Files Bill Restricting Use of Nuclear Waste Dump," *Post and Courier* (27 March 2015), www.postandcourier.com/article/20150327/PC1603/150329364/charleston-republican-files-bill-restricting-use-of-nuclear-waste-dump

Romano, S., and Nagel, J., "White House Involvement in Ward Valley Land Transfer Delays," *Waste Management 1999 Conference* (28 February–4 March 1999), www.wmsym.org/archives/1999/16/16–4.pdf

Ruíz López, M.C., Zuloaga, P., and Alonso, J., "Design and Licensing of the El Cabril L/ILW Disposal Facility," *Waste Management 1993 Conference* (1993), www.wmsym.org/archives/1993/V1/28.pdf

Runyon, L.C., "Low-Level Radioactive Waste Legislative Activity Update," National Conference of State Legislators – Environment, Energy and Transportation Program (July 1999), www.texasradiation.org/andrews/LegisActupdate.html

Russell, D., "Dumping the Dump: Nebraskans Use Ballot to Fight Nuclear Industry," *In These Times* (31 August 1988), www.unz.org/Pub/InTheseTimes-1988aug31–00006

S. 270, Texas Low-Level Radioactive Waste Disposal Compact Consent Act (5 February 1997).

S. 419, Texas Low-Level Radioactive Waste Disposal Compact Consent Act (15 February 1995), http://thomas.loc.gov/cgi-bin/bdquery/D?d104:30:./temp/~bdLq8V::|/home/LegislativeData.php?n=BSS;c=104

Salisbury, D., "Storing Nuclear Waste/The Deaf Smith Site: Prospect of Nuclear Waste Dump Draws Scowls from Farmers in Texas Panhandle," *Christian Science Monitor* (25 June 1985), www.csmonitor.com/1985/0625/arad2.html

Salisbury, D., "This Town Wanted a Nuclear Dump," *Christian Science Monitor* (18 March 1983), www.csmonitor.com/1983/0318/031864.html

Sandström, B., "Radiation as a Weapon: A View from Open Source Studies," NKS-B NordThreat Seminar (30–31 October 2008), www.nks.org/download/seminar/2008_b_nordthreat/NKS_B_NordThreat_1–2.pdf

Sanger, D., "Nuclear Material Dumped Off Japan," *New York Times* (19 October 1993), www.nytimes.com/1993/10/19/world/nuclear-material-dumped-off-japan.html

Sanger, D., "With Expectations Low, Yeltsin Arrives in Japan," *New York Times* (12 October 1993b), www.nytimes.com/1993/10/12/world/with-expectations-low-yeltsin-arrives-in-japan.html

Sang-Hun, C., "Scandal in South Korea over Nuclear Revelations," *New York Times* (3 August 2013), www.nytimes.com/2013/08/04/world/asia/scandal-in-south-korea-over-nuclear-revelations.html

Sassaman, J. C., Jr., *Siting Without Fighting: the Role of Mediation in Enhancing Public Participation in Siting Radioactive Waste Facilities*, 2 Alb. L.J. Sci. and Tech. 207 (1992).

Sayvetz, L., "South Koreans Stop Plan for Nuclear Waste Dump on Gulup Island, 1994–95," *Global Nonviolent Action Database* (4 April 2012), http://nvdatabase.swarthmore.edu/content/south-koreans-stop-plan-nuclear-waste-dump-gulup-island-1994–95

S.B. 62: Relating to the Reporting of Waste Volumes and the Study, Selection, Acquisition, and Operation of Disposal Sites by the Texas Low-Level Radioactive Waste Disposal Authority (3 August 1987), www.lrl.state.tx.us/LASDOCS/70CS2/SB62/SB62_70CS2.pdf

S.B. 347: Relating to Funding for the Operations of the Texas Low-Level Radioactive Waste Disposal Compact Commission and to the Disposal of Certain Low-Level Radioactive Waste (14 June 2013), http://openstates.org/tx/bills/83/SB347/

S.B. 791: Relating to the Regulation of Low-Level Radioactive Waste Disposal Facilities and Radioactive Substances (20 May 2013), http://openstates.org/tx/bills/83/SB791/

S.B. 1177: Relating to the Creation, Administration, Powers, Duties, Operations, and Financing of the Texas Low-Level Radioactive Waste Disposal Authority, Providing for Civil Penalties; Making an Appropriation (1 June 1981), www.lrl.state.tx.us/legis/billSearch/text.cfm?legSession=67-0&billtypeDetail=HB&billNumberDetail=1177&billSuffixDetail=&startRow=1&IDlist=&unClicklist=&number=50

S.B. 1206: Relating to the Texas Low-Level Radioactive Waste Disposal Compact (9 June 1993), www.capitol.state.tx.us/BillLookup/History.aspx?LegSess=73R&Bill=SB1206

S.B. 1418: Relating to the Texas Low-Level Radioactive Waste Disposal Authority and the Transportation of Radioactive Materials and Waste (23 April 1993), www.capitol.state.tx.us/BillLookup/Text.aspx?LegSess=73R&Bill=SB1418

S.B. 1697: Relating to the Storage, Processing and Disposal of Radioactive Waste, Low-Level Waste and Mixed Waste (23 May 1995), www.lrl.state.tx.us/legis/billSearch/text.cfm?legSession=67-0&billtypeDetail=HB&billNumberDetail=1177&billSuffixDetail=&startRow=1&IDlist=&unClicklist=&number=50

Schmidt, J. L., "Developer Picks Northern Nebraska for Nuclear Waste Dump," *Associated Press* (29 December 1989), www.apnewsarchive.com/1989/Developer-Picks-Northern-Nebraska-For-Nuclear-Waste-Dump/id-3b87fba16f6ff42ff734e98e3c52885b

Schmidt, J. L., "Hunger Strike, Politics, Nuclear Waste Cloud Scenic Hillsides," *Associated Press* (22 October 1990), www.apnewsarchive.com/1990/Hunger-Strike-Politics-Nuclear-Waste-Cloud-Scenic-Hillsides/id-c964d4a5fbca969d75a6a68189f92adb

"Schmit Attacks Waste Site Publicity Funds," *Omaha World-Herald* (5 July 1990).

Schneider, K., "Idaho Governor Blocks Shipments of Atom Waste to U.S. Dump Site," *New York Times* (8 February 1991), www.nytimes.com/1991/02/08/us/idaho-governor-blocks-shipments-of-atom-waste-to-us-dump-site.html

Schneider, K., "Idaho Shuts Border to Nuclear Waste from Colorado Weapons Plant," *New York Times* (1 September 1989), www.nytimes.com/1989/09/01/us/idaho-shuts-border-to-nuclear-waste-from-colorado-weapons-plant.html

Schneider, M. (assisted by Jacobs, D.), *Comparison among Different Decommissioning Funds Methodologies for Nuclear Installations, Final Country Report: Spain*, Paris (31 September 2006).

Schwartz, M., "Clearing out Asse 2," *Nuclear Engineering International* (24 August 2010), www.neimagazine.com/features/featureclearing-out-asse-2

Scott, D.C., "US Waste-Dump Proposals Bring Protests from Mexico," *Christian Science Monitor* (6 April 1992), www.csmonitor.com/1992/0406/06013.html

Selvaratnam, N., "Government Searching for Nuclear Waste Site as Time Runs Out," *SBS News* (30 September 2014), www.sbs.com.au/news/article/2014/09/30/government-searching-nuclear-waste-site-time-runs-out

Senate Interim Committee on Natural Resources, Interim Report to the 77th Legislature, *Storage and Disposal Options for Low-Level Radioactive Waste* (November 2000), www.senate.state.tx.us/75r/senate/commit/archive/c580/pdf/LLRWreport.pdf

Senate Research Center, Bill Analysis: C.S.H.B. 1171 by Chisum (Brown), Natural Resources, Committee Report [Substituted] (14 May 1999), www.capitol.state.tx.us/BillLookup/Text.aspx?LegSess=76R&Bill=HB1171

Senator Judith Zaffirini, *Summary of Legislation Passed, 1987–2011* (n.d.), http://107.20.245.137/zaffirini/wp-content/uploads/2012/09/Senator-Judith-Zaffirini-Summary-of-Legislation-Passed-1987–201116.pdf

Senator Nick Minchin, Media Release, "Two Radioactive Repository Sites Withdrawn Following Community Consultation" (18 November 1999), http://parlinfo.aph.gov.au/parlInfo/search/display/display.w3p;query=%28Id:media/pressrel/aoi06%29;rec=0

Senator Warwick Parer, Media Release, "SA Region Selected for National Radioactive Waste Repository Site, DPIE 98/276P (18 February 1998).

Shanabrook, K., *Low-Level Radioactive Waste Disposal Facility Sitings: Negotiating a Role for the Public*, 3 J. Dispute Resol. 219 (1987).

Shannon, K., "South Texans Battle over Proposed Hazardous Dumps," *Kerrville Daily Times* (12 April 1992).

Sheehy, S., *Texas Big Rich: Exploits, Eccentricities, and Fabulous Wealth Won and Lost* (New York: William Morrow, 1990).

Sherman, D., *Not Here, Not There, Not Anywhere: Politics, Social Movements, and the Disposal of Low-Level Radioactive Waste* (Washington, DC: Resources for the Future, 2011).

Shevory, K., "Waste Operator Donates to Senator," *Amarillo Globe News* (2 April 2001), http://amarillo.com/stories/2001/04/02/tex_waste.shtml

"Shocked by State Radioactive Dump, Proponent Changes Mind," *Nevada State Journal* (1 April 1976).

"Short Description of the Mont Terri Project," *Swisstopo* (n.d.), www.swisstopo.admin.ch/internet/swisstopo/en/home/topics/geology/MTProject/MTPshortly.html

"A Short History of Nuclear Power and Anti-nuclear Movement in Spain," #499–500 *Special: The Magazine of Hope* (October 16, 1998), www.wiseinternational.org/node/2128

Siegel, B., "A Perfect Place for a Waste Dump," *Los Angeles Times* (22 December 1991), http://articles.latimes.com/1991-12-22/magazine/tm-1262_1_waste-dump-county-seat-grand-champion

Sierra Blanca Legal Defense Fund, "Environmental Justice Case Study: The Struggle for Sierra Blanca, Texas against a Low-Level Nuclear Waste Site" (1999), www.umich.edu/~snre492/blanca.html

Sierra Blanca Legal Defense Fund, Press Release (30 September 1997), in Nebraska State Historical Society, Government Records, RG141, Series 1, Central Interstate Low-Level Radioactive Waste Compact (LLRW-Nebraska), Research Files, Articles and Books, 1961–2006, Box 2 of 5.

"$600 Million Suit Targets Envirocare," *Deseret News* (11 March 1997), www.deseretnews.com/article/548113/600-million-suit-targets-Envirocare.html?pg=all

"Sixth General Radioactive Waste Plan (6th GRWP)" (June 2006), http://newmdb.iaea.org/GetLibraryFile.aspx?RRoomID=471

Sjöblom, K.-L., and Linsley, G., "Sea Disposal of Radioactive Wastes: The London Convention 1972," *IAEA Bulletin*, Vol. 36, No. 2 (1994): 12–16, www.iaea.org/Publications/Magazines/Bulletin/Bull362/36205981216.pdf

"S. Korea Faces Strong Opposition to Nuclear Power Despite Growing Need," *Yonhap News Agency* (15 June 2014), http://english.yonhapnews.co.kr/national/2014/06/15/56/0302000000AEN20140615001200320F.html

"S. Korea's First Nuclear Waste Facility Gets Go-Ahead," *Yonhap News Agency* (11 December 2014), http://english.yonhapnews.co.kr/business/2014/12/11/0/0501000000AEN20141211010000320F.html

Slovic, P., "The Perception Gap: Radiation and Risk," *Bulletin of the Atomic Scientists*, Vol. 68, No. 3 (2012): 67–75.

Smith, D., "Victory: No Dump in Spofford," *Del Rio News Herald* (1 July 1993), www.newspapers.com/newspage/7652208/

Smyrl, V., "Texas Low-Level Radioactive Waste Disposal Authority," *Texas State Historical Society* (n.d.), www.tshaonline.org/handbook/online/articles/metur

Sobelev, I. A., Ojovan, M. I., and Karlina, O. K., "Management of Spent Radiation Sources at Regional Facilities 'RADON' in Russian Federation," *Waste Management 2001 Conference*, Tucson, Arizona (25 February–1 March 2001), www.wmsym.org/archives/2001/39/39–7.pdf

Solomon, B., *Review of Colorado Department of Health Hearing Exhibits Related to a Proposed Low-Level Radioactive Waste Disposal Facility, Montrose County, Colorado*, Utah Division of Environmental Level Health, Bureau of Radiation Control, Job No. (R-6) 89–03 (1 March 1989), reprinted in *Technical Report for 1989–1990: Applied Geology Program*, compiled by Bill D. Black, Utah Geological and Mineral Survey, Utah Department of Natural Resources (May 1990), http://ugspub.nr.utah.gov/publications/reports_of_investigations/RI-220.pdf

South Australia v Honourable Peter Slipper MP (2004), ALR, 473.

South Dakota Legislature Release, "South Dakota Senate Offers Support to Nebraska in Rejecting Waste Site" (28 January 1993), in Nebraska State Historical Society, Government Records, RG1-Gov. Nelson (SG44).

Southeast Compact Commission, "Southeast Compact Commission Takes Legal Action in U.S. Supreme Court Against North Carolina," News Release (10 July 2000).

Southeast Interstate Low-Level Radioactive Waste Management Compact, reprinted in NRC, *Nuclear Regulatory Legislation*, NUREG-0980, Vol. 1, No. 10 (2012).

Southwestern Low-Level Radioactive Waste Disposal Compact Consent Act, reprinted in NRC, *Nuclear Regulatory Legislation*, NUREG-0980, Vol. 1, No. 10 (2012).

"Spain: Court Orders Closure of Nuclear Dump," *World Information Service on Energy* (12 July 1996), www.wiseinternational.org/node/1593

Spangler, J., "Owner of Envirocare Files Defamation Lawsuit," *Deseret News* (15 April 2000), www.deseretnews.com/article/812945/Owner-of-Envirocare-files-defamation-lawsuit.html?pg=all

Spent Fuel Test-Climax: An Evaluation of the Technical Feasibility of Geologic Storage of Spent Nuclear Fuel in Granite, Final Report (UCRL-53702), compiled by W. C. Patrick, Lawrence Livermore National Laboratory (30 March 1986).

Spire, R., and Willard, L., *Identification and Election Relative to Low-Level Radioactive Waste Facility Site*, Department of Justice, State of Nebraska (23 February 1988), www.ago.ne.gov/resources/dyn/files/632471zbe/ae23f/_fn/88012_2–24–88.pdf

"A Spread of One's Own," *Economist* (19 November 1998), www.economist.com/node/176738

"State Board Rejects McMullen for Waste Disposal Site," *Victoria Advocate* (23 February 1985).

State of Nebraska, Department of Health and Human Services, Division of Public Health, Office of Radiological Health, *Statutes Relating to Radiation Control Act* (2008), http://dhhs.ne.gov/publichealth/Documents/RADACT.pdf

State of Washington, Department of Ecology, *Nuclear Waste – Frequently Asked Questions: Leaking Underground Tanks at Hanford* (n.d.), www.ecy.wa.gov/programs/nwp/sections/tankwaste/closure/pages/tank_leak_FAQ.html

State of Washington, Office of the Secretary of State, *Initiatives to the People: Initiative Measure No. 383* (n.d.), www.sos.wa.gov/elections/initiatives/statistics_initiatives.aspx

Statement of Dierks, Committee on Natural Resources, LB 606 (rough draft) (17 February 1999), in Nebraska State Historical Society, Government Records, RG/41, Series 8, Central Interstate Low-Level Radioactive Waste Compact (LLRW-NE), Misc. Files, Committee/State/Legislature, 1987–2005, Box 1 of 2.

Statement of Eric C. Peus, Waste Control Specialists LLC in "Disposal of Low-Level Radioactive Waste," Hearing before the Committee on Environment and Public Works, U.S. Senate Hearing 106–959 (25 July 2000), www.gpo.gov/fdsys/pkg/CHRG-106shrg71521/html/CHRG-106shrg71521.htm

Statement of Senator Chris Beutler in Committee on Natural Resources, LR 202 (transcript) (13 December 1997).

"States Join Nuclear Waste Suit against Nebraska," *Amarillo Globe News* (14 January 1999), http://amarillo.com/stories/1999/01/14/wtf_LO0732.002.shtml

States of Guernsey, "Radiation Levels in the Hurd Deep Are Regularly Monitored" (26 April 2013), www.gov.gg/article/107407/Radiation-levels-in-the-Hurd-Deep-are-regularly-monitored

"Studsvik Signs Teaming Agreement with Waste Control Specialists LLC (WCS)," Studsvik Press Release (7 September 2007), http://investors.studsvik.com/files/press/studsvik/1152103en1.pdf

"Suburban Profile: Muckaty Station NT, 0862," *Tomorrow Finance* (n.d.), www.tomorrowfinance.com.au/PropertyReports/NT/City+subs/Muckaty+Station-0862

Summary of Significant Findings Regarding the Process of Site Selection for the North Carolina Low-Level Radioactive Waste Facility, prepared by James, McElroy & Diehl, P.A. (19 February 1992), http://infohouse.p2ric.org/ref/28/27585.pdf

Susskind, L., "A Negotiation Credo for Controversial Siting Disputes," Negotiation J (October 1990).

Swanson, S., and Pearson, R., "Caution Flag up in Nuclear Dump Search," *Chicago Tribune* (18 October 1989), http://articles.chicagotribune.com/1989–10–18/news/8901230252_1_radioactive-waste-nuclear-safety-siting-process

Swartsell, N., "Harold Simmons' Waste Company Pays County, State," *Texas Tribune* (12 September 2012a), www.texastribune.org/2012/09/12/wcs-pays-andrews-county-and-texas/

Swartsell, N., "Texas Sierra Club Fight over Radioactive Waste Heats Up," *Texas Tribune* (21 October 2012b), www.texastribune.org/2012/10/21/texas-sierra-club-fights-wcs-radioactive-waste-sit/

Sweeney, D. "Plan to Use Aboriginal Land as a Nuclear Waste Dump Is Flawed and Misguided." *The Guardian*, (31 July 2013), www.theguardian.com/commentisfree/2013/jul/31/muckaty-aboriginal-land-nuclear-waste

Swiss Federal Office of Energy (SFOE), *Current Situation in Respect of the Search for Sites* (10 February 2015), www.bfe.admin.ch/radioaktiveabfaelle/05182/index.html?lang=en

Swiss Federal Office of Energy (SFOE), DETEC, *Attitudes to Radioactive Waste in Switzerland* (September 2008), www.news.admin.ch/NSBSubscriber/message/attachments/15395.pdf

Swiss Federal Office of Energy (SFOE), DETEC, *Sectoral Plan for Deep Geological Repositories: Conceptual Part* (2 April 2008), www.bfe.admin.ch/radioaktiveabfaelle/01375/04389/index.html?lang=en

Swiss Federal Office of Energy (SFOE), *Economic Impacts of a Deep Geological Repository on the Siting Region* (2 July 2012), www.bfe.admin.ch/energie/00588/00589/00644/index.html?lang=en&msg-id=45225

"Switzerland's First Nuclear Plant Decommissioned," *SWI* (17 September 2003), www.swissinfo.ch/eng/switzerland-s-first-nuclear-plant-decommissioned/3518582

"System at El Cabril Disposal Facility," *Environmental Policy at El Cabril Disposal Facility* (n.d.), http://pbadupws.nrc.gov/docs/ML0318/ML031890311.pdf

Tae-Gyu, K., "First Nuclear Waste Dump Goes Operational," *Korea Times* (24 December 2010), www.koreatimes.co.kr/www/news/biz/2013/08/123_78579.html

"Targeting 'Cerrell' Communities," *Energy Justice Network* (n.d.), www.ejnet.org/ej/cerrell.pdf

Taylor, G., "Australia: Host for a Nuclear Waste Storage Site?," *International Journal of Environmental Studies*, Vol. 63, No. 6 (December 2006).

Testimony of Governor Robert List before the United States House Interior Subcommittee on Energy and Environment (19 July 1979), GOV-0820, File #33, Governor Robert List Records, Nevada State Archives.

Testimony of Lowell Fisher before the Committee on Natural Resources (18 December 1989), in Nebraska State Historical Society, Government Records, RG001, Government, SG43, Orr, Kay, S1 Correspondence, Public Opinion, LLRW, Box 42.

Testimony of Lynn Moorer, Committee on Judiciary, LB 761 (23 October 1989).

Testimony of Ray Peery in Nebraska LB 426, Senator Sandra Scofield (Principal Introducer), Introducer's Statement of Intent, Ninetieth Legislature, First Session (19 February 1987), in Nebraska State Historical Society, Government Records, RG/41, Series 8, Central Interstate Low-Level Radioactive Waste Compact (LLRW-NE), Misc. Files, Committee/State/Legislature, 1987–2005, Box 1 of 2.

Testimony of Tom Grube, Nemaha County LMC, Committee on Judiciary, LB 761 (23 October 1989), and Save Boyd County Association (25 June 1997), in Nebraska State Historical Society, Government Records, RG/41, Series 8, Central Interstate Low-Level Radioactive Waste Compact (LLRW-NE), Misc. Files, Committee/State/Legislature, 1987–2005, Box 1 of 2.

Testimony of University of Nebraska Law Professor Norm Thorson, Committee on Judiciary, LB 761 (23 October 1989), in Nebraska State Historical Society, Government Records, RG/41, Series 1, Central Interstate Low-Level Radioactive Waste Compact (LLRW-NE), Research Files, Misc. Reports, 1989–2003, Box 5 of 5.

"Texas Agency Denies Permit for Waste Site," *New York Times* (23 October 1998), www.nytimes.com/1998/10/23/us/texas-agency-denies-permit-for-waste-site.html

Texas Commission on Environmental Quality, *Radioactive Material License*, Amendment 00 (10 September 2009), www.tceq.state.tx.us/assets/public/permitting/rad/wcs/20090910%20License%20R04100%20issued%20CCO.pdf

Texas Commission on Environmental Quality, *Radioactive Material License*, Section 9, "General Requirements" (18 September 2012), www.wcstexas.com/PDF_downloads/WCS%20LLW-Disposal%20License%20R04100%20Amend%2018.pdf

Texas Compact Low-Level Radioactive Waste Generation Trends and Management Alternatives Study: Technical Report, RAE-42774–019–5407–2, prepared by Rogers & Associates Engineering Branch, URS Corporation (August 2000), www.tceq.state.tx.us/assets/public/permitting/llrw/entire.pdf

Texas Department of Agriculture, "Texas Ag Stats" (n.d.), www.texasagriculture.gov/About/TexasAgStats.aspx

Texas Disposal Systems, "About Us" (2011), www.texasdisposal.com/our-history

Texas House Study Group, *Bill Analysis, CSHB 1533 by Bock* (11 May 1981), www.lrl.state.tx.us/scanned/hroBillAnalyses/67–0/HB1533.pdf

Texas Low Level Radioactive Waste Disposal Compact Commission, *Agreement for Importation of Nonparty Low-level Radioactive Waste for Disposal in the Texas Low-Level Radioactive Waste Disposal Compact Facility* (1 July 2012), www.tllrwdcc.org/wp-content/uploads/2012/08/Studsvik-Signed-Agreement-TLLRWDCC-2–0009–00.pdf

Texas-Maine-Vermont Compact, *Congressional Record*, Vol. 144, No. 42 (3 April 1998), www.gpo.gov/fdsys/pkg/CREC-1998–04–03/html/CREC-1998–04–03-pt1-PgS3233–2.htm

Texas-Maine-Vermont Compact, Statement of Senator Paul Wellstone, *Congressional Record*, Vol. 144, No. 77 (15 June 1998), www.gpo.gov/fdsys/pkg/CREC-1998–06–15/html/CREC-1998–06–15-pt1-PgS6349.htm

"Texas Regulators Vote against Sierra Blanca Nuke Waste Dump," *Livestock Weekly* (29 October 1998), www.livestockweekly.com/papers/98/10/29/whlnukedump.asp

Texas State Historical Association, "Ranching" (n.d.), www.tshaonline.org/handbook/online/articles/azr02

"30 Years of History at the Grimsel Test Site (GTS)," *Grimsel Test Site* (n.d.), www.grimsel.com/gts-information/about-the-gts/30-years-of-history-at-the-gts

"Time Is Running Out to Find a Nuclear Waste Site in Australia," *ABC News* (9 October 2014), www.abc.net.au/radionational/programs/bushtelegraph/nuclear-waste/5798278

Trip Report and Meeting Notes, Boyd County Local Monitoring Committee (19 August 1996), in Nebraska State Historical Society, Government Records, RG/41, Series 8, Central Interstate Low-Level Radioactive Waste Compact (LLRW-NE), Misc. Files, Committee/State/Legislature, 1987–2005, Box 1 of 2.

Tyler, P., "The U.S., Too, Has Dumped Waste at Sea," *New York Times* (4 May 1992), www.nytimes.com/1992/05/04/world/the-us-too-has-dumped-waste-at-sea.html

United Kingdom Nirex Limited, *Options for Radioactive Waste Management That Have Been Considered by Nirex*, Nirex Report No. N/049 (May 2002).

United Kingdom Nirex Limited, *Review of 1987–1991 Site Selection for an ILW/LLW Repository*, Technical Note No. 477002 (June 2005).

United Nations General Assembly, *United Nations Declaration on the Rights of Indigenous Peoples: Resolution Adopted by the General Assembly* (2 October 2007), A/RES/61/295, www.un.org/esa/socdev/unpfii/documents/DRIPS_en.pdf

United States Census Bureau, "Boyd County 1990," www.census.gov/population/cencounts/ne190090.txt

United States Census Bureau, *State-County QuickFacts: Howard County* (2013 Estimate), http://quickfacts.census.gov/qfd/states/48/48227.html

United States Census Bureau, *State-County QuickFacts: Loving County* (2013 Estimate), http://quickfacts.census.gov/qfd/states/48/48301.html

United States Congress, Office of Technology Assessment, *Partnerships under Pressure: Managing Commercial Low-Level Radioactive Waste*, OTA-O-426 (Washington, DC: U.S. Government Printing Office, November 1989), www.fas.org/ota/reports/8923.pdf

United States Department of Commerce, National Oceanic and Atmospheric Administration, *Natural Disaster Survey Report, Hurricane Hugo: September 10–22, 1989* (May 1990), www.nws.noaa.gov/om/assessments/pdfs/hugo1.pdf

United States Department of Ecology, *Low-Level Radioactive Waste Disposal: Information for Nebraskans* (n.d.), in Nebraska State Historical Society, Government Records, RG/41, Series 1, Central Interstate Low-Level Radioactive Waste Compact (LLRW-NE), Research Files, Articles and Books, 1961–2006, Box 2 of 5.

United States Department of Energy, *Atomic Energy Act* (July 2001), Rev. 2, http://hss.doe.gov/sesa/environment/training/envlawsregs256/aeamanual.pdf

United States Department of Energy, Hanford, *Tank Farms* (updated 24 April 2013), www.hanford.gov/page.cfm/TankFarms

United States Department of Energy, *Manifest Information Management Systems* (n.d.), http://mims.doe.gov/GeneratorData.aspx

United States Department of Energy, Office of Environmental Management, *Hanford Site* (n.d.), http://energy.gov/em/hanford-site

United States Department of Energy, Office of Environmental Management, *Low-Level Radioactive Waste (LLRW)* (n.d.), www.gtcceis.anl.gov/guide/llw/index.cfm

United States Department of Energy, Office of Environmental Management, *Report to Congress: 1995 Annual Report on Low-Level Radioactive Waste Management Progress*, DOE/EM-0292 (June 1996), www.nirs.org/radwaste/llw/annual95.pdf

United States Department of Energy, Office of Legacy Management, *Edgemont, South Dakota, Disposal Site: Fact Sheet* (4 April 2009), www.lm.doe.gov/Edgemont/edgemont-factsheet.pdf

United States Department of Energy, Office of Legacy Management, *Programmatic Framework: UMTRCA Title I Disposal and Processing Sites* (n.d.), http://energy.gov/lm/sites/lm-sites/programmatic-framework

United States Department of Energy, *Waste Isolation Pilot Project, "Why WIPP?"* (n.d.), www.wipp.energy.gov/fctshts/Why_WIPP.pdf

United States Environmental Protection Agency, *Environmental Justice* (updated 24 May 2012), www.epa.gov/environmentaljustice/basics/index.html

United States Environmental Protection Agency, *Executive Order 12898: Federal Actions to Address Environmental Justice in Minority Populations and Low-Income Populations* (11 February 1994), www.epa.gov/region2/ej/exec_order_12898.pdf

United States Environmental Protection Agency, *Fernald Preserve* (June 2010), www.epa.gov/reg5sfun/redevelop/pdfs/Fernald_Preserve.pdf

United States Environmental Protection Agency, *Former Nebraska Ordnance Plant* (13 March 2009), www.epa.gov/region7/cleanup/npl_files/ne6211890011.pdf

United States Environmental Protection Agency, *Operation Report: A Survey of the Farallon Islands 500-Fathom Radioactive Waste Disposal Site*, Office of Radiation Programs and Office of Water Program Operations, ORP-75–1 (December 1975), www.epa.gov/nscep/index.html

United States Environmental Protection Agency, *Radiation: Non-Ionizing and Ionizing* (updated 17 May 2013), www.epa.gov/radiation/understand/radiation.html

United States Environmental Protection Agency, *Region 2: Western New York Nuclear Service Center* (updated 21 March 2011), www.epa.gov/region2/waste/fswester.htm

United States Environmental Protection Agency, *Region 4: Superfund – Maxey Flats Nuclear Disposal* (updated 3 January 2012), www.epa.gov/region4/superfund/sites/npl/kentucky/maxfltky.html

United States Environmental Protection Agency, Office of Radiation Programs, *Fact Sheet on Ocean Dumping of Radioactive Waste Materials*, prepared for the House of Representatives Subcommittee on Oceanography of the Committee on Merchant Marine and Fisheries (20 November 1980).

United States Environmental Protection Agency, Office of Radiation Programs, *Radiological Quality of the Environment in the United States, 1977*, EPA 520/1–77–009, Washington, DC (September 1977).

United States General Accounting Office Letter to the Honorable J. James Exon, "Nebraska Low-Level Waste," GAO/RCED-93-47R (14 October 1992), www.gao.gov/assets/90/82665.pdf

United States Geological Survey, *A Marine GIS Library for Massachusetts Bay: Focusing on Disposal Sites, Contaminated Sediments, and Sea Floor Mapping*, Open-File Report 99–439 (October 1999), http://pubs.usgs.gov/of/1999/of99–439/mbaygis/chapt2a.htm

United States Nuclear Regulatory Commission, Advisory Committee on Nuclear Waste White Paper, *History and Framework of Commercial Low-Level Radioactive Waste Management in the United States*, NUREG-1853, Washington, DC (January 2007), www.nrc.gov/reading-rm/doc-collections/nuregs/staff/sr1853/sr1853.pdf

United States Nuclear Regulatory Commission, *Decommissioned Nuclear Power Plants* (updated 10 July 2013), www.nrc.gov/reading-rm/doc-collections/fact-sheets/decommissioning.html

United States Nuclear Regulatory Commission, *Fact Sheet on Plutonium* (updated 4 February 2011), www.nrc.gov/reading-rm/doc-collections/fact-sheets/plutonium.html

United States Nuclear Regulatory Commission, *Glossary: REM (Roentgen Equivalent Man)* (updated 10 December 2012), www.nrc.gov/reading-rm/basic-ref/glossary/rem-roentgen-equivalent-man.html

United States Nuclear Regulatory Commission, *High-Level Waste* (n.d.), www.nrc.gov/waste/high-level-waste.html

United States Nuclear Regulatory Commission, Information Notice 91–65, *Emergency Access to Low-Level Radioactive Waste Disposal Facilities* (16 October 1991), www.nrc.gov/reading-rm/doc-collections/gen-comm/info-notices/1991/in91065.html

United States Nuclear Regulatory Commission, *Licensing Requirements for Land Disposal of Radioactive Waste*, 10 CFR § 61.56 (1982), www.nrc.gov/reading-rm/doc-collections/cfr/part061/part061–0056.html

United States Nuclear Regulatory Commission, *Locations of Power Reactor Sites Undergoing Decommissioning* (updated 17 September 2013), www.nrc.gov/info-finder/decommissioning/power-reactor/

United States Nuclear Regulatory Commission, *Low-Level Waste* (n.d.), www.nrc.gov/waste/low-level-waste.html

United States Nuclear Regulatory Commission, *National Materials Program* (4 June 2009), http://nrc-stp.ornl.gov/materials/nmpbkgrd090604.pdf

United States Nuclear Regulatory Commission, *NRC News*, No. 97–026 (14 February 1997), www.nrc.gov/reading-rm/doc-collections/news/1997/97–026.html

United States Nuclear Regulatory Commission, *NRC Regulations*, 10 CFR §61.55, Waste classification (updated July 2014), www.nrc.gov/reading-rm/doc-collections/cfr/part061/part061–0055.html

United States Nuclear Regulatory Commission, *Operating Nuclear Power Reactors (by Location or Name)* (updated 9 September 2013), www.nrc.gov/info-finder/reactor/

United States Nuclear Regulatory Commission, *Radiation Basics: Neutrons* (updated 17 October 2014), www.nrc.gov/about-nrc/radiation/health-effects/radiation-basics.html#neutron

United States Nuclear Regulatory Commission, *Radiation Exposure and Cancer* (updated 17 October 2014), www.nrc.gov/about-nrc/radiation/health-effecs/rad-exposure-cancer.html

United States Nuclear Regulatory Commission, *Review Process for Low-Level Radioactive Waste Disposal License Application under Low-Level Radioactive Waste Amendments Act*, NUREG-1274 (reprinted April 1991), http://pbadupws.nrc.gov/docs/ML1321/ML13217A156.pdf

United States Nuclear Regulatory Commission, Office of the General Counsel, *Nuclear Regulatory Legislation – 5. Low Level Radioactive Waste*, "Central Interstate Low-Level Radioactive Waste Compact," NUREG -0980, Vol. 1, No. 9 (January 2011), www.nrc.gov/reading-rm/doc-collections/nuregs/staff/sr0980/v1/sr0980v1.pdf

United States Senate Committee on Energy and Natural Resources, *Ward Valley Land Transfer Act*, Report 104–247, 104th Congress, 2nd Session (28 March 1996), www.gpo.gov/fdsys/pkg/CRPT-104srpt247/html/CRPT-104srpt247.htm

University of Illinois Engineering Department, "Radioactive Waste Management: an International Perspective" (n.d.), http://courses.engr.illinois.edu/npre442/International-part1-pdf.pdf

University of Texas of the Permian Basin, "HT³R" (2014), www.utpb.edu/research-grants/ht3r/

US Ecology, Inc. v. Boyd County Board of Equalization, Boyd County, Nebraska, No. A-97–802 (decided 5 May 1998), http://caselaw.findlaw.com/ne-court-of-appeals/1261651.html

"US Nuclear Fuel Cycle," *World Nuclear Association* (updated April 2014), www.world-nuclear.org/info/Country-Profiles/Countries-T-Z/USA – Nuclear-Fuel-Cycle/

"Valhi, Inc. Announces Low-Level Radioactive Waste Disposal License Decision," *iStock-Analyst.com* (12 August 2008), www.istockanalyst.com/article/viewiStockNews/articleid/2506754

van Berg, R., and Damveld, H., *Discussions on Nuclear Waste – A Survey on Public Participation, Decision-Making and Discussions in Eight Countries: Belgium, Canada, France, Germany, Spain, Sweden, Switzerland, United Kingdom*, Dutch Commission for the Disposal of Radioactive Waste (CORA) (January 2000).

Van Vliet, J., "Construction, Startup and Operation of a New LLRW Disposal Facility in Andrews County, Texas," *Waste Management 2012 Conference*, Phoenix, Arizona (26 February–1 March 2012), www.wmsym.org/archives/2012/papers/12151.pdf

Vari, A., Reagan-Cirincione, P., and Mumpower, J., *LLRW Disposal Facility Siting: Successes and Failures in Six Countries* (Boston, MA: Kluwer Academic, 1994).

Velasco, R.G., "Parliamentarian, Industry, Trade and Tourism Commission," OECCD/NEA (2007), Radioactive Waste Management in Spain: Co-ordination and Projects,

FSC Workshop Proceedings, L'Hospitalet de l'Infant, Spain (21–23 November 2005), doi:10.1787/9789264039421

von Rohr, M., "Switzerland: Putting Nuclear to the Vote," *Spiegel* (11 July 2008), www.spiegel.de/international/europe/switzerland-putting-nuclear-to-the-vote-a-565156.htm

"Vt. Begins Shipping Radioactive Waste to Texas," *Associated Press* (27 September 2012), http://fuelfix.com/blog/2012/09/27/vt-begins-shipping-radioactive-waste-to-texas/

Wald, M., "Texas Company, Alone in U.S., Cashes in on Nuclear Waste," *New York Times* (20 January 2014), www.nytimes.com/2014/01/21/business/energy-environment/texas-company-alone-in-us-cashes-in-on-nuclear-waste.html

Walden, B., *Recovery of Low-Level Radioactive Waste Packages from Deep-Ocean Disposal Sites*, EPA 520/1–90–027 (September 1990), www.epa.gov/nscep/index.html

Walker, C., and MacMillan, J., "Siting the North Carolina Low-Level Radioactive Waste Facility," *Waste Management 1994 Conference*, Tucson, Arizona (27 February–3 March 1994), www.wmsym.org/archives/1994/V2/96.pdf

Walker, G., *Environmental Justice: Concepts, Evidence and Politics* (London: Routledge, 2012).

Walker, J.S., *The Road to Yucca Mountain: The Development of Radioactive Waste Policy in the United States* (Berkeley: University of California Press, 2009).

Walker, T., "Eddy-Lea Energy Alliance Envisions Southeastern New Mexico Home for Spent Nuclear Fuel," *Carlsbad Current-Argus* (4 October 2012), www.currentargus.com/ci_21697228/eddy-lea-energy-alliance-envisions-southeastern-new-mexico

Walton, D., "Opening the History Books on Kay Orr's Legacy," *Lincoln Journal Star* (10 February 2013), http://journalstar.com/news/state-and-regional/statehouse/opening-the-history-books-on-kay-orr-s-legacy/article_0feb29de-0d35-5495-93a5-14a7a2f6ce2f.html

Washington State Bldg. and Constr. Trades Council v. Spellman, 684 F.2d 627 (9th Cir. 1982), http://openjurist.org/684/f2d/627/washington-state-building-and-construction-trades-council-v-c-spellman-united-states

Washington State Department Ecology Nuclear Waste Program, *Interim Remedial Action Plan, Commercial Low-Level Radioactive Waste Disposal Site, Richland, Washington* (April 2010), www.ecy.wa.gov/programs/nwp/llrw/llrw_iap.pdf

Washington State Legislature, Chapter 43.145 RCW, *Northwest Interstate Compact on Low-Level Radioactive Waste Management*, Article VI, http://apps.leg.wa.gov/rcw/default.aspx?cite=43.145&full=true

Waste Control Specialists, "Press Release: WCS Commences Low-Level Radioactive Waste Disposal Operations: Texas Compact Operator Safely Disposes of First Shipment of Low-Level Radioactive Waste" (27 April 2012), www.wcstexas.com/PDF_downloads/WCS%20Press%Release%20First%20LLRW%20Disposed.pdf

Waste Control Specialists, "Providing a Solution for Every Disposal Need" (n.d.), www.texassolution.com/documents/wcsoverview.pdf

Waste Control Specialists LLC v. Envirocare, Khosrow B. Semnani, Charles A Judd, Frank C. Thorley, George W. Hellstrom, Billy W. Clayton and Nancy M. Molleda, No. 14,580, Plaintiff's Original Petition in the District Court of Andrews County, Texas (2 May 1997), http://pbadupws.nrc.gov/docs/ML0301/ML030130112.pdf

Weart, S., *Nuclear Fear: A History of Images* (Cambridge, MA: Harvard University Press, 1988).

Weingart, J., *Waste Is a Terrible Thing to Mind: Risk, Radiation, and Distrust of Government* (Princeton, NJ: Center for Analysis of Public Issues, 2001).

Wellstone Amendment No. 2277, 1 April 1998, H.R. 629RH, *Texas Low-Level Radioactive Waste Disposal Compact Consent Act* (15 July 1997), http://thomas.loc.gov/cgi-bin/query/D?c105:6:./temp/~c105g293KK

Western Australia Parliamentary Debates, House of Assembly (7 September 1999).

"What This Town Needs Is . . . Nuclear Waste?," *Businessweek* (18 August 1991), www.businessweek.com/stories/1991–08–18/what-this-town-needs-is-dot-dot-dot-nuclear-waste

Whinnet, E., "Nuke Waste Worry – Where Will We Bury It?" *Herald Sun* (18 August 2014).

Whitman, M., and Slosky, L., "A Regional Low-Level Waste Management System: The Siting Process," *Waste Management 1983 Conference*, Tucson, Arizona (27 February–3 March 1983), www.wmsym.org/archives/1983/V1/19.pdf

Wilder, F., "Good to Glow," *Texas Observer* (4 April 2008), www.texasobserver.org/2729-good-to-glow-despite-its-own-scientists-objections-state-regulators-are-greenlighting-a-massive-nuclear-waste-dump-in-west-texas/

Wilder, F., "TCEQ Rolls Over for Harold Simmons," *Texas Observer* (10 September 2010), www.texasobserver.org/tceq-rolls-over-for-harold-simmons/

Wilder, F., "Waste Texas," *Texas Observer* (6 March 2009), www.texasobserver.org/2978-waste-texas-why-andrews-county-is-so-eager-to-get-dumped-on/

Willacy, M., "Standing on Shaky Ground," *ABC News (Australia)* (9 April 2013), www.abc.net.au/foreign/content/2013/s3733236.htm

Wingfield, B., "Nuclear Trashmen Gain from Record U.S. Reactor Shutdowns," *Bloomberg* (4 September 2013), www.bloomberg.com/news/2013–09–04/nuclear-trashmen-gain-from-record-u-s-reactor-shutdowns.html

Winkley, N., "Area Minister Studies Igloo Nuclear Site Plan," *Rapid City Journal* (16 April 1983), http://bhodian.com/nuclearwaste.html

Wise, J., "Andrews Cleans Up on Vacuum Cleaners," *Lubbock Avalanche-Journal* (1997), http://lubbockonline.com/news/040697/andrews.htm

Wise, J., "Andrews Company Lands Federal Nuclear Waste Disposal Contracts," *Lubbock Avalanche-Journal* (1999a), http://lubbockonline.com/stories/070199/loc_070199100.shtml

Wise, J., "Andrews Still Courting Waste Facility," *Lubbock Avalanche-Journal* (1999b), http://lubbockonline.com/stories/061299/loc_0612990089.shtml

Wise, J., "Borden Commissioners Ask to Be Dropped from Waste List," *Lubbock Avalanche-Journal* (1999c), http://lubbockonline.com/stories/101299/loc_101299074.shtml

Wise, J., "Ex-radioactive Waste Regulator Joins Envirocare," *Lubbock Avalanche-Journal* (1999d), http://lubbockonline.com/stories/020399/053–1524.shtml

Wise, J., "Nuclear Waste Company Considering Area Sites," *Lubbock Avalanche-Journal* (1999e), http://lubbockonline.com/stories/072899/loc_072899037.shtml

Wise, J., "Officials Survey Andrews County for Nuke Dump Site," *Lubbock Avalanche-Journal* (1998a), http://lubbockonline.com/stories/111998/053–1269.shtml

Wise, J., "Radioactive Waste Site Questioned," *Lubbock Avalanche-Journal* (1999f), http://lubbockonline.com/stories/031999/reg_031999103.shtml

Wise, J., "Waste Control Removes Hance from Lineup," *Lubbock Avalanche-Journal* (1999g), http://lubbockonline.com/stories/102999/loc_1029990121.shtml

Wise, J., "Waste Control Ups Ante by Seeking $1 Billion from Envirocare," *Lubbock Avalanche-Journal* (1998b), http://lubbockonline.com/stories/032798/053–0659.shtml

Wishart, M., "Muckaty Traditional Owners Fighting Ferguson's Dump," *Chain Reaction* (17 June 2013).

Wolf, S., "Public Opposition to Hazardous Waste Sites: The Self-Defeating Approach to National Hazardous Waste Control Under Subtitle C of the Resource Conservation and Recovery Act of 1976," *Boston College Environmental Affairs Law Review*, Vol. 8, No. 3 (1980), http://lawdigitalcommons.bc.edu/cgi/viewcontent.cgi?article=1786&context=ealr

Womeldorf, D., Junkert, R., and Huck, R., Jr., "California's Review of US Ecology's Low-Level Radioactive Waste License Application," *Waste Management 1990 Conference*, Tucson, Arizona (25 February–1 March 1990), www.wmsym.org/archives/1990/V2/26.pdf

Wood, D., "Australia Has Nowhere to Put French Nuclear Waste," *Vice News* (14 July 2014), https://news.vice.com/article/australia-has-nowhere-to-put-its-shipment-of-french-nuclear-waste

Woolfenden, J., "Arizona's Need for a Low-Level Radioactive Waste Disposal Site," *Waste Management 1999 Conference*, Tucson, Arizona (28 February–4 March 1999), www.wmsym.org/archives/1999/16/16–2.pdf

World Association of Nuclear Operators, *Our Principles* (n.d.), www.wano.info/en-gb/aboutus/ourmission

World Nuclear Association, *Nuclear Power in South Korea* (updated August 2014), www.world-nuclear.org/info/Country-Profiles/Countries-O-S/South-Korea/

World Nuclear Association, *Nuclear Power in Spain* (updated November 2014), www.world-nuclear.org/info/Country-Profiles/Countries-O-S/Spain/

World Nuclear Association, *Nuclear Power in Switzerland* (updated May 2014), www.world-nuclear.org/info/Country-Profiles/Countries-O-S/Switzerland

World Nuclear Association, *Nuclear Power in the World Today* (updated April 2014), www.world-nuclear.org/info/inf01.html

World Nuclear Association, *Radioactive Waste Management* (updated July 2015), www.world-nuclear.org/info/Nuclear-Fuel-Cycle/Nuclear-Wastes/Radioactive-Waste-Management/

World Nuclear Association, *Radioactive Waste Repository and Store for Australia* (updated June 2014), www.world-nuclear.org/info/Country-Profiles/Countries-A-F/Appendices/Radioactive-waste-repository–store-for-Australia/

World Nuclear Association, *Swiss Radwaste Consultation Opens* (19 June 2012), www.world-nuclear-news.org/WR-Swiss_radwaste_consultation_opens-1906127.html

World Nuclear Association, *Tokaimura Criticality Accident 1999* (updated October 2013), http://world-nuclear.org/info/Safety-and-Security/Safety-of-Plants/Tokaimura-Criticality-Accident/

Worthington, R., "Nebraska County Split over Nuclear Dump," *Chicago Tribune* (22 October 1990).

Wright, J., "High-Temperature Teaching and Test Reactor (HT^3R): Program Objectives," Presentation to the NRC, Rockville, MD (11 May 2006), http://pbadupws.nrc.gov/docs/ML0613/ML061320066.pdf

Yergin, D., *The Prize: The Epic Quest for Oil, Money & Power* (New York: Free Press, 1991).

Yoon, J., Ro, S., and Park, H., "Korean Interim Storage Issues and R&D Activities on Spent Fuel Management," *IAEA*, Vienna (January 1999), www.iaea.org/inis/collection/NCLCollectionStore/_Public/30/003/30003822.pdf

Zaitseva, L., and Hand, K. "Nuclear Smuggling Chains: Suppliers, Intermediaries, and End-Users," *American Behavioral Scientist*, Vol. 46, No. 6 (2003): 822–844, http://cisac.fsi.stanford.edu/sites/default/files/abs_zaitseva.pdf

Zuloago, P., and Vargas, E., "New Developments in Low Level Radioactive Waste Management in Spain" (n.d.), www.euronuclear.org/events/topseal/transactions/Paper-Session-III-Zuloaga.pdf

Zuloago, P., Navarro, M., and Vargas, E., "Very Low Activity Waste Disposal Facility Recently Commissioned as an Extension of El Cabril LILW Disposal Facility in Spain," *Waste Management 2009 Conference*, Phoenix, Arizona (1–5 March 2009), www.wmsym.org/archives/2009/pdfs/9014.pdf

Zurkinden, A., Kowalski, E., Steiner, P., and Flüeler, T., "Wellenberg," *Community Waste Management (COWAM)* (last updated February 2005), www.cowam.com/?Wellenberg

Zwilag, "History" (n.d.), www.zwilag.ch/en/history-_content--1-1068.html

Index

For Product Safety Concerns and Information please contact our
EU representative GPSR@taylorandfrancis.com Taylor & Francis
Verlag GmbH, Kaufingerstraße 24, 80331 München, Germany